Broken Contract?

TRANSFORMING AMERICAN POLITICS
Lawrence C. Dodd, Series Editor

Dramatic changes in political institutions and behavior over the past three decades have underscored the dynamic nature of American politics, confronting
political scientists with a new and pressing intellectual agenda. The pioneering
work of early postwar scholars, while laying a firm empirical foundation for contemporary scholarship, failed to consider how American politics might change or
recognize the forces that would make fundamental change inevitable. In reassessing
the static interpretations fostered by these classic studies, political scientists are
now examining the underlying dynamics that generate transformational change.

Transforming American Politics brings together texts and monographs that
address four closely related aspects of change. A first concern is documenting and
explaining recent changes in American politics—in institutions, processes, behavior, and policymaking. A second is reinterpreting classic studies and theories to
provide a more accurate perspective on postwar politics. The series looks at historical change to identify recurring patterns of political transformation within
and across the distinctive eras of American politics. Last and perhaps most
important, the series presents new theories and interpretations that explain the
dynamic processes at work and thus clarify the direction of contemporary politics. All of the books focus on the central theme of transformation—transformation in both the conduct of American politics and in the way we study and understand its many aspects.

FORTHCOMING TITLES

Midterm: The Elections of 1994 in Context, edited by Philip A. Klinkner

The Divided Democrats: Ideological Unity, Party Reform, and Presidential Elections, William G. Mayer

Revolving Gridlock, David Brady and Craig Volden

The Irony of Reform: Roots of American Disenchantment, G. Calvin Mackenzie

Governing Partners: State-Local Relations in the United States, Russell L. Hanson

Seeing Red: How the Cold War Shaped American Politics, John Kenneth White

Congress and the Administrative State, Second Edition, Lawrence C. Dodd and Richard L. Schott

New Media in American Politics, Richard Davis and Diana Owen

Extraordinary Politics: Dissent and Collective Action in the American System, Charles C. Euchner

The Tragic Presidency, Robert L. Lineberry

Broken Contract?

CHANGING RELATIONSHIPS BETWEEN AMERICANS AND THEIR GOVERNMENT

EDITED BY

Stephen C. Craig

University of Florida

WestviewPress

A Division of HarperCollins*Publishers*

Transforming American Politics

Copyright © 1996 by Westview Press, Inc., A Division of HarperCollins Publishers, Inc.

Published in 1996 in the United States of America by Westview Press, 5500 Central Avenue, Boulder
Colorado 80301-2877, and in the United Kingdom by Westview Press, 12 Hid's Copse Road, Cumnor
Hill, Oxford OX2 9JJ.

Library of Congress Cataloging-in-Publication Data
Broken contract? : changing relationships between Americans and their
    government / edited by Stephen C. Craig.
        p.   cm.—(Transforming American politics)
    Includes bibliographical references and index.
    ISBN 0-8133-2262-6.—ISBN 0-8133-2263-4 (pbk.)
      1. Political participation—United States.   2. Political culture—
    United States.   3. Legitimacy of governments—United States.
    4. United States—Politics and government—1989–   5. Political
    leadership—United States—Public opinion.   6. Public opinion—
    United States.   I. Craig, Stephen C.   II. Series.
    JK1764.B76   1995
    306.2'0973'09049—dc20   95-18230
                                                                                    CIP

The paper used in this publication meets the requirements of the American National Standard for
Permanence of Paper for Printed Library Materials Z39.48-1984.

10   9   8   7   6   5   4   3   2   1

Contents

1

Change and the
American Electorate

STEPHEN C. CRAIG

On January 20, 1993, with Bill Clinton sworn in as our forty-second president
and the Democrats assuming control of both elected branches of government, it
seemed possible to believe that the era of gridlock was over and that maybe—just
maybe—Washington's political class would respond to the message of urgency
and concern sent by voters when they cast their ballots two-and-a-half months
earlier. According to *Newsweek* columnist Joe Klein, 1992 had been a year in
which "civilians dragged the politicians, [campaign professionals] and press kick-
ing and screaming into the election *they* wanted. It was a year [when] the mys-
tique of pollsters, strategists and mediamasters was put in proper perspective. It
was, at long last, the Year of the Voter." An electorate that was typically "apathetic,
malleable" and bored with politics became suddenly "obsessed" with the process,
seeing the presidential contest in particular as a "turning point" for the nation and
following campaign events with a heightened sense of purpose. "Everywhere you
went," said Klein (1992, p. 14), "on supermarket checkout lines, in coffee shops
and saloons, around kitchen tables . . . the talk was of Ross and George and Bill."
And when it was over, there was a cautious optimism that things would be different.

That, however, was then and this is now. On January 4, 1995, Newt Gingrich
took the oath as Speaker of the House of Representatives, Republicans ascended
to the majority in both houses of Congress for the first time in more than forty
years, and the world of Washington politics—along with the politics of many
states (where the GOP enjoyed dramatic gains in 1994 gubernatorial and legislative races)—was turned upside down once again. Clinton and the Democrats had
not necessarily failed, at least by traditional standards, but they fell far short of
implementing the agenda of social and institutional "change" that was critical to
their success in the previous election. As it happens, voters were not of a mood to
be patient: Given the choice between politics as usual and a bold (albeit uncertain) new beginning, they resoundingly opted for the latter.

1

Only with the passage of time will we truly be able to understand the meaning of that choice. Perhaps, as many on the political right fervently hope, it marked an end to the already tottering New Deal coalition and a triumph for the conservative ideal of limited government. Or perhaps it was primarily an indictment of the Democratic majority for its inability to address the fears and concerns of citizens (especially middle-class citizens) around the country—in which case, Republicans must act quickly and effectively or else face a similar judgment in the not-too-distant future (Broder 1995). A third possible scenario is that voters today have little confidence in either party, and so Republican failure may set the stage for a third-party challenge stronger than any since the 1850s. Whatever the eventual outcome, there can be no doubt that the elections of 1992 and 1994 left the relationship between the American public and its leaders in a state of flux. Although the nature of that relationship remains unclear, it almost certainly will be quite different than in the past.

For now, though, all eyes are focused on Capitol Hill—and, more specifically, on efforts by GOP congressional leaders to fulfill the Contract with America put forth during the 1994 campaign by Gingrich and his allies (see Chapter 13). This contract identifies ten areas of policy action (including balanced-budget and term-limits amendments, middle-class and capital-gains tax cuts, increased attention to national defense, Social Security protection, welfare reform, anticrime measures, and several others) on which Republican candidates for the House pledged a floor vote within the first 100 days of the 104th Congress. Not everyone believes that the contract represents a step forward, especially in terms of its economic implications. Robert Samuelson, for example, complained that "as a governing blueprint, it fails because it panders to popular inconsistency. Americans are [both] hopelessly dependent on Big Government and rabidly contemptuous of it. Rhetorically, liberals and conservatives appeal to one impulse or the other by making promises they cannot fulfill. Liberals are too scared of a public that scorns government to raise taxes; and conservatives are too scared of a public dependent on government to cut spending. The result is much noisy fiddling around the edges" (Samuelson 1994, p. 45). There are, according to Samuelson, only two possibilities: "Either Republicans keep their promises and disappoint; or they break their promises and disappoint"—and public cynicism will continue unabated in each instance (p. 45).

Still, whatever limitations the Contract with America might have as a "governing blueprint," the 1994 election results would seem to suggest that it made for very effective campaign symbolism. Caution is advised before accepting this conclusion at face value, however. One postelection poll found that only 25 percent of the public viewed the contract as "a serious promise for which the new Republican Congress should be held responsible," 24 percent thought it was "just a campaign promise," and 47 percent claimed never to have heard of it (Fineman 1995, p. 28; also see Times Mirror 1994d). In the same survey, roughly three-quarters of all citizens said they "would be upset" if:

- tax cuts lead to a major increase in the federal budget deficit (73 percent);
- cutting back on government seriously weakens or eliminates environmental regulations (73 percent);
- new limits on welfare cut off benefits to poor families even when no work is available (73 percent); or
- many poor mothers have to give up their welfare benefits and send their children to orphanages or foster homes (78 percent; see Sedgwick 1995).

In line with Samuelson's observations on popular inconsistency, a Times Mirror poll conducted one month after the election found that nearly two-thirds of the public (65 percent) considered reducing the budget deficit as a "top priority" and that fewer people (as compared with five years earlier) wanted to see federal spending increased on a wide range of government programs, e.g., Social Security, health care, public education, scientific research, programs for the homeless, and so on. Yet at the same time, this diminished support for *higher* spending was offset by a jump in the proportions favoring *maintaining* current spending levels. According to the Times Mirror (1994d, p. 2), "No significant new support was found for spending cuts in 14 program areas tested, with three exceptions—environmental protection [still just 17 percent, up from 3 percent wanting less spending in 1990], farm subsidies [29 percent, up from 13 percent], and government assistance for the unemployed [23 percent, up from 14 percent]." Perhaps the Republicans will do a better job of accommodating this sort of inconsistency than the Democrats have done in recent years, but they obviously have their work cut out for them. Campaign rhetoric and the reality of governing often turn out to be two different things.

There are those in the Republican camp who aren't as worried about the specifics of governing as you might imagine. Thomas Rosenstiel recounted the story of Newt Gingrich's first day as Speaker of the House. The congressman's chief of staff was shooting a home video of the day's events, and when the aide (who apparently spent most of his time following the boss) asked Gingrich whether he should tape what was happening on the floor of the chamber, Gingrich replied that it really didn't matter.

> His lieutenants could take care of the legislative mechanics. Actually, the details of the contract weren't all that important. What mattered was the message.
>
> Think of the contract as an infomercial, one long political advertisement. Its real purpose is to transform ... "the proto-realignment of 1994" into something grander and more profound: the end of big government and the dismantling of the welfare state. To get to the conservative millennium, Gingrich and Co. must carefully reeducate a jaded electorate and gradually build trust in the Republican Party. The contract is only a symbolic first step. "It was a campaign photo op," said one GOP strategist, which was engraved after the election into party writ. That is why Gingrich is more concerned about winning votes right now than with the nuances of the legislation (Rosenstiel 1995, pp. 16–17).

To be sure, Gingrich is not the only Republican game in town. Senate majority leader Robert Dole made it clear early on that certain elements of the contract were simply not doable, at least right away (Associated Press 1995b).[1] While stressing that "[t]he most powerful idea of all is the idea of limited government," Dole seems to recognize that the GOP must "keep our promises" *and* deliver improved policy outcomes if its 1994 victory is to be translated into a long-term governing mandate (Associated Press 1995a).

On the other side of the aisle, Democrats find themselves in an even more delicate position as they try to figure out what has gone wrong and what to do about it. The seriousness of their plight was revealed by a postelection Gallup survey in which citizens indicated—sometimes by a sizable margin—that they felt the Republicans were better able to deal with several key issues and problems facing the country, e.g., the economy (54 percent to 33 percent), taxes (57 percent to 30 percent), budget deficits (52 percent to 31 percent), health care policy (46 percent to 41 percent), crime (52 percent to 29 percent), and welfare reform (55 percent to 35 percent; Ladd 1995, p. 45).[2] In terms of overall ideology, exit polls showed that the proportion of voters calling themselves conservatives jumped from 30 percent in 1992 to 37 percent in 1994 (liberals dropping from 21 percent to 18 percent, and moderates from 49 percent to 45 percent)[3]—an increase that was matched almost exactly by improvement in the Republicans' share of the total vote for the U.S. House (45.5 percent nationally in 1992, 52.4 percent in 1994· Ladd 1995, pp. 2, 17). Finally, of course, there was the bottom line: A loss by Democratic candidates of more than 50 seats in the House of Representatives (35 incumbent Democrats defeated vs. 0 Republican incumbents), 10 in the Senate, close to 500 in the various state legislatures, and 11 governorships (Ladd 1995, p. 2).

If they wish to look for the silver lining, Democrats might take comfort from the same popular inconsistency that bedeviled them throughout the first two years of the Clinton administration (and likely will bedevil the Republicans now that they are in the driver's seat).[4] Moreover, polling numbers reported by Greenberg Research, Inc. suggest that the 1994 elections did *not* represent an unqualified rejection either of the party or of its embattled leader. For example (registered voters only; see Democratic Leadership Council 1994, pp. 33–56),

- Fifty-six percent of 1994 voters said they were "trying to send a message" about their dissatisfaction with Washington politics, but nearly half of these were sending a message about "politics as usual" (45 percent) rather than about the president (15 percent), Congress (15 percent), liberals (6 percent), or Democrats (5 percent) in particular.
- Nonvoters indicated that they would have supported the Democratic candidate in their congressional district by a margin of 45 percent to 33 percent.
- Just 46 percent of all respondents felt that "Bill Clinton [was] moving the country in the right direction," but 64 percent said the president was *trying* to do so.

- Seventy-three percent said it was "too early" to render a final verdict on the Clinton administration, and 68 percent expressed hope that the president still might be successful.
- Fifty-one percent believed that it was important that government "be made more efficient so it delivers more services for less money," compared with just 25 percent who emphasized that "the government should be made smaller so it will cost and do less";[5] similarly, 69 percent agreed (either strongly or somewhat) that "we have important problems that the government must play a bigger role to help solve," and 63 percent wanted any cuts in "wasteful [or] outdated government spending" to be used for deficit reduction (33 percent) or for investment in education, training, and infrastructure (30 percent, with just 9 percent saying that savings should be used to reduce taxes).

All things considered, a reasonable conclusion might be "that Americans don't necessarily want less government [so much as they] want less inefficient and ineffective government" (Morin 1995a, p. 37).

The question therefore becomes, Which party (if either) can persuade citizens that it is more capable of achieving these goals? For now, Republicans have the upper hand. The public temper is short, however, and patience is in short supply. Symbols are important—they always have been, perhaps never more so than when Franklin Roosevelt sought to reassure a troubled nation (e.g., with his fireside chats and his insistence that there is "nothing to fear but fear itself") during the height of the Great Depression in the 1930s. But the New Deal ultimately delivered substance as well, and one suspects that the GOP will need something more than gestures such as term limits and proposals for a balanced budget in order to maintain its present advantage.

THE BROKEN CONTRACT

This book is not really *about* either the 1994 elections or the presidential contest of 1992. But it *is* about the temperament of the times that led to the electoral upheavals of the 1990s. Its origins date back to the late 1960s and early 1970s—a time when researchers began to look closely at the shifting current of American domestic politics (electoral and otherwise) and discovered a variety of changes that have subsequently helped to reshape our understanding of the relationship that exists between citizens and their leaders. The most influential study of that earlier era was *The Changing American Voter,* written by three prominent scholars (Nie, Verba, and Petrocik 1979) who saw the public being transformed as a result of new and different "stimuli offered to them by the political world: the nature of the issues, the salience of these issues, and the way in which issues are presented" (p. 151). That is, when the controversies of the day are highly charged or appear to impact on the personal lives of citizens, and when politicians address them in clear and relatively unambiguous ways, then people will respond accordingly.

Likewise, for Gerald Pomper (1975, p. 8), the essential nature of the average voter and "the influences upon his [voting] choices, are not permanent, but change with the circumstances of the times and with political events." Taken as a whole, such revisionist studies portrayed the electorate as having become more attentive to politics and to political issues (especially those relating to race, war, crime, gender, and morality) than had been the case a decade or two earlier, more sharply polarized along liberal-conservative lines, less reflexively partisan and perhaps even "ripe" for a 1930s-style realignment that would redefine the basis of national political discourse, and alienated (though modestly so) from its governmental—as well as nongovernmental (Lipset and Schneider 1987)—leaders and institutions.

As time passed, however, things settled down a bit and the lessons learned from both academic political science and real-world politics seemed to suggest that the period roughly from President Kennedy's assassination in 1963 through the election of Ronald Reagan in 1980 may have been something of an aberration. The long-awaited realignment never happened, certainly not in any traditional form that was recognizable from our past experience. Voter turnout rates continued to drop, and the "politicized" (or "responsive") electorate described by Pomper and others was in evidence only sporadically. Popular attitudes toward the parties remained less than enthusiastic, and voters split their tickets in sufficient numbers that divided control of government in Washington and in many of the states became commonplace (Fiorina 1992). But, at the same time, aggregate partisanship actually rebounded slightly during the 1980s, and there were some observers who argued that the rise in nonpartisanship between 1964 and 1980 didn't mean all that much anyway (Keith et al. 1992). As for citizen attitudes toward government, the original increase in public mistrust that began during the Johnson administration failed to provoke widespread civil unrest (antiwar protests, race riots, and occasional other disturbances notwithstanding), and by the mid-1980s, confidence levels appeared to be climbing again under the strong leadership of President Reagan.

Then came Iran-contra, Willie Horton, a nasty recession that reached deep into the middle class, and, with the 1992 and 1994 elections in particular, a renewed sense of citizen frustration, anger, and feelings of powerlessness with respect to government and the political process. Although the rise of popular discontent is a phenomenon that first attracted scholarly attention during the Vietnam era, what we are seeing today seems less a reemergence than an *extension* and *intensification* of what happened in the 1960s and 1970s—and a potentially dangerous extension at that, since the base of support at the beginning of the period was not anything to brag about. In assessing the "upbeat mood" of the early Reagan years, Lipset and Schneider (1987, pp. 411–412) concluded that

> the situation is much more *brittle* than it was at the end of the 1920s, just before the Great Depression, or in 1965, immediately preceding the unrest occasioned by the Vietnam War and the outbreak of racial tension. . . . The United States enters the 1980s, however, with a lower reserve of confidence in the ability of its institutional

leaders to deal with the problems of the polity, the society, and the economy than at any time in this century. As a result of the strains produced by the experiences of the last fifteen years, our institutional structure is less resilient than in the past. Should the 1980s be characterized by a major crisis, the outcome could very well be substantial support for movements seeking to change the system in a fundamental way.[6]

Well, we survived (more or less) the 1980s, and the 1990s have yet to present us with a "major crisis" that might spark grassroots revolutionary fervor on any kind of broad scale. It is obvious, though, that the dissatisfactions accumulating since the early 1960s have left their mark.

Moreover, as unhappy as the American public was in 1992, the political climate of 1994 seemed worse. Despite an improving economy and a reasonably impressive domestic record (Alter 1994), Bill Clinton's job-approval ratings dropped so low that Democratic candidates in every region of the country scrambled to keep their distance—while Republicans tried hard to prevent them from doing so (Merida 1994). Congress was held in even lower esteem than the president (Morin 1994), the term-limits movement continued to gain momentum (Times Mirror 1994b, p. 142), and Ross Perot urged voters to elect a Republican majority on Capitol Hill and then join him in forming a third party if the GOP failed to turn things around over the next couple of years (Associated Press 1994). Economic growth aside, more than two-thirds of the general public (up from about half at the time of Clinton's inauguration in January 1993) said they were "dissatisfied with the way things are going in this country today" (Times Mirror 1994b, p. 121).

As already noted, there are some inconsistencies in citizens' attitudes that make it difficult to know exactly what they are upset about. Even as people complain about the direction of the nation as a whole, for example, an overwhelming majority (83 percent in spring 1994; see Times Mirror 1994a) express satisfaction "with the way things are going in your personal life." But perhaps the most glaring inconsistencies—nothing new here, really—have to do with perceptions of Congress. For one thing, voters continue to rate the performance of their own representative much more highly than that of the institution (53 percent vs. 24 percent approval, respectively, in an ABC News poll[7]). And although almost two-thirds say that representatives should pay greater attention to national as opposed to local concerns, there still is a prevailing sense that members should try to (1) "direct more government spending to your congressional district where you live" (58 percent); (2) "bring federal projects to your district" (73 percent); (3) "help create jobs in your district" (90 percent); and (4) keep "voters in your district informed about issues through frequent visits to the district or through newsletters" (93 percent; see Morin 1994).

In the end, though, we are left with an electorate that "is angrier and meaner than at any time in recent history" (Morin 1994, p. 37). Why? What has brought us to this point? And what are the likely consequences if the relationship between citizens and their leaders deteriorates further in the months and years to come? Having considered these questions at length in Chapter 3 and in Craig (1993), I

want to take the opportunity here to mention just two or three of the themes that
I believe are central to an understanding of contemporary popular discontent in
the United States. In the first place, such discontent is not—or at least is not
mainly—about ideology. Back in the late 1960s and early 1970s, it appeared for a
time that public mistrust might be the result of partisan choices that were insuffi-
ciently distinct for an electorate that had been polarized by the events and issues
of the day (Miller 1974). Today, analysts are apt to be critical of parties and candidates who are *too* ideologically polarized for a mass public that is centrist in its
political orientations.

Gordon Black and Benjamin Black (1994), who argue that "the most disconnected and frustrated [voters] in the United States are basically political moderates" (p. 25), see the problem as one of public policy tending to fall "into two
unpleasant categories: policies that lead to excessive spending, far beyond what
the public would accept if it had a direct choice, and policies of governmental
inaction on issues where the public wants substantial change but powerful issue
minorities are opposed" (p. 10). Their principal solution is the creation of a new
political party of the center that would do several things: restore competitiveness
to the electoral process (by providing "viable alternative candidates" in areas currently dominated by one party); "give people a reason to participate and encourage the reentry to the political system of thousands . . . who have been driven
away by the failures and scandals of the two major parties"; encourage fiscal
responsibility in government by increasing "the electoral risk of pandering to the
needs of special-interest groups"; and "use the best of both modern technology
and grassroots politics to involve voters in the political process" while also creating "a strong incentive for the other parties to concentrate on reformulating and
strengthening their own brand images" (pp. 171–177).

In a similar vein, E. J. Dionne (1991, pp. 14–15) complains that "the false
choices posed by liberalism and conservatism make it extremely difficult for the
perfectly obvious preferences of the American people to express themselves in our
politics." That is,

> Americans hate politics as it is now practiced because we have lost all sense of the pub-
> lic good. Over the last thirty years of political polarization, politics has stopped being a
> deliberative process through which people resolved disputes, found remedies and
> moved forward. When Americans watch politics now, in thirty-second snatches or
> even in more satisfactory formats like "Nightline" or "The MacNeil/Lehrer News
> Hour," they understand instinctively that politics these days is not about finding solu-
> tions. It is about discovering postures that offer short-term political benefits. We give
> the game away when we talk about "issues," not "problems." Problems are solved; issues
> are merely what politicians use to divide the citizenry and advance themselves (p. 332).

Like Black and Black, Dionne (p. 14) presumes that most citizens are ideologically
centrist (or "ambivalent"; see Ladd 1981; Popkin 1991): They "believe in [both]

social concern and self-reliance; they want to match rights and obligations; they think public moral standards should exist but are skeptical of too much meddling in the private concerns of others."

Dionne's call for a "politics of remedy" basically follows the advice proffered by Jack Citrin (1974), who felt that the initial rise of popular mistrust in the 1960s might be resolved by politicians paying more attention to finding workable solutions than to toeing the ideological line. Lipset and Schneider (1987, p. 399) concluded along the same lines that "[the] vast majority of the population [in the 1960s and 1970s] was not unhappy because government policy did not correspond to their ideological predispositions. They were unhappy because political leadership was proving ineffective in dealing with massive social and political problems, like war, race relations, and the economy." More recently, Kevin Phillips (1994, p. 5) accounted for the grim mood of the early 1990s by observing that "[n]ever before had so many Washington regimes for so long proved so incapable of relieving the fears and concerns of the citizenry."

We should not, however, be seduced into thinking that more pragmatic and results-oriented leadership will necessarily make things right. As I pointed out in *The Malevolent Leaders* (Craig 1993, chapters 2 and 6), the perceived effectiveness of policy "results" lie, to a considerable degree, in the eye of the beholder. Whereas most citizens are neither liberal nor conservative in any strict sense, many Americans—especially those who are politically active and whose views are therefore magnified in political decisionmaking—*do* have belief systems and value structures based upon general principles. Thus, even if contemporary discontent stems largely from ineffective governmental performance over the course of three decades, one is hard pressed to imagine that the kinds of "results" that satisfy those on the right will be deemed equally acceptable by those on the left (or in the middle) of the ideological spectrum, and vice versa. With the confidence levels of liberals, moderates, and conservatives alike having taken a nosedive since the 1960s (Craig 1993, pp. 29–41), improved policy outcomes might seem to be a good place to begin searching for a solution to the problem. But it will not be enough. The "perfectly obvious policy preferences of the American people" cited by Dionne are a good bit less obvious than either he or Black and Black (with their plea for a third party of the center) believe them to be.

I do not mean to imply, of course, that performance factors are irrelevant in shaping citizens' attitudes toward government and politics. More jobs, less crime, better schools, lower taxes, a cleaner environment, progress in the war against drugs, affordable health care—discernible movement toward achieving any of these policy goals would surely be met with a positive response from the mass public. In particular, there has been much talk lately about one broad category of performance that strikes close to home for a large group of Americans. Their case was recently stated by syndicated columnist Richard Reeves (1994):

This was America's deal with me: If I kept my nose clean and paid attention in school, I could go to college, even if I had to work in the summers and part time during the school year to pay for it. Then, if I worked for a few years, I could afford to buy a house and one day make enough money to make sure my own kids got through college.

And that's what happened, for which I am very grateful. That deal, and the fact that if one screwed it up the first time there was almost always a second and third chance in the land of the free, are a good part of the reason I have always thought this was a great country. What more could you ask for?

Reeves was talking here about our nation's middle class, whose prosperity he viewed as "the heart of American democracy. If the system does not work for most of the people most of the time, there will be no wise and lucky America, only selfishness and the kinds of conflict we thought we had left behind us in the 19th century, in the 1930s, in the 1960s" (Reeves 1994).

The middle-class dream is indeed perceived (especially by those directly affected) to be imperiled—and this perception is based less on ideological quibbles than on the huge and growing discrepancies between politicians' promises and their performance once in office. According to Kevin Phillips (1994, p. 57), "Few worries change a country more or play greater havoc with the success of politics and government than economic security." Anxiety about the country's long-term economic security is, as it happens, the order of the day in American politics right now (Johnson 1994). The 1980s were not nearly as good to as many people as the aggregate numbers made them out to be (Phillips 1993; Luttwak 1993; Mishel and Bernstein 1995) and, thus far, the 1990s have not been much better. Underlying optimism somehow still prevails: A Times Mirror (1994b, p. 27) survey done in mid-1994 found 68 percent of the general public agreeing that "as Americans, we can always find a way to solve our problems and get what we want" and 62 percent denying that "there are any real limits to growth in this country today." Yet other poll results (not to mention election outcomes) suggest that such optimism entails a certain amount of "whistling past the graveyard" by individuals who are trying to sound more hopeful than they really are.

Policy "results" that reflect progress toward a more secure economic future should thus have an ameliorative effect on public confidence in government. Let us keep in mind, however, that there are a fair number of Americans who believe that the essence of national decline lies in another area altogether. Kevin Phillips (1994, p. 61) notes that

[t]o a majority of conservative leaders and pundits, *moral* and *cultural* decline far outweighs economic slippage as an explanation of the nation's 1990s trauma. Some also blame moral decline for any ebb in the economy. Are Americans' living standards down in some places? That's because of weak productivity growth, reflecting how our citizens have lost their old work ethic, especially next to hardworking Japanese, Koreans, or Chinese. Is the country's income gap widening? That's because so many high-earning wives in the top tenth now work full time. Central-city crime, in turn, doesn't reflect poverty; it reflects the breakdown of the family. (emphasis added)

Further, with liberals unable or unwilling to strike a proper balance between "programs and policies granting rights and entitlements" on the one hand and "accompanying responsibilities or ... standards of reciprocal obligation" on the other, conservatives have been able to make political hay "by focusing public attention on morality-laden 'values' issues—issues running the gamut from the lack of labor-force participation in the ghetto, to sexual promiscuity, to drug abuse, to teen pregnancy, to crime, and so on" (Edsall and Edsall 1991, pp. 278–279).

Citizens for whom such concerns are paramount will not be totally satisfied even by significant gains on the economic policy front. And those for whom economic security *is* the overriding issue (assuming they can avoid being distracted by the disingenuous rhetoric offered by politicians on both sides) likely will continue to question efforts by the right wing to transform the debate into one centered on values and lifestyle choices. In the end, broadly acceptable "results" may be nearly impossible to achieve. This is true because of the difficulty in identifying, collectively, people's "perfectly obvious policy preferences"—but also because (1) the behavioral changes urged by conservatives cannot easily be mandated and (2) the programmatic initiatives favored by liberals would cost money that simply isn't available (due to budget shortfalls combined with the aversion of taxpayers to footing the bill for new programs when the old ones don't seem to be working very well).

Finally, on top of everything else, some political analysts have concluded that the potential for meaningful policy change of *any* sort is minimized—especially in the current era of complex, interrelated problems and limited resources with which to address them—by the structure of our governmental system. Part of the argument here is familiar: that such characteristics as separated powers, bicameralism, occasionally divided government, and weak parties serve to promote the *representation* of competing (often narrow and parochial) interests in the political process at the expense of effective *governance* in pursuit of a common good. But there is more. Lawrence Dodd explains that, since the time of the Founding Fathers, it is the legislative branch that has served as our nation's principal "deliberative" body—"the only institution that addresses national policy questions through open debate and collective policy choice. The deliberative character of Congress has meant that, when faced with severe national problems, citizens could look to Congress to clarify the problems and devise broadly acceptable solutions" (Dodd 1993, pp. 419–420). Accordingly, in order "to sustain the long-term support of the public, Congress and its members must demonstrate a reasonable capacity to recognize the fundamental problems of a historical era, deliberate over the proper solutions to these problems, and enact legislation that addresses them in a credible manner" (pp. 418–419). For the most part, they have done so over the years with a fair degree of success and thereby maintained an acceptably high level of support among citizens "even in the midst of severe crises" (p. 420).

Perhaps no longer. With too many members being motivated primarily by a desire to enhance their "reelection and career-advancement" goals, Congress has become less competent both as a representative institution (shifting "away from broadly focused *issue representation* and toward narrowly focused *interest representation*"[8]) and as a deliberative assembly (designing rules, procedures, and norms that inhibit "the reasoned search for broadly understood and acceptable policy solutions; Dodd 1993, pp. 425–428, emphasis in original). As a result, today we see Americans not only expressing intense criticism of the way Congress performs its job but, more important, they are beginning to give a higher proportion of their votes to candidates who run against congressional incumbents (Jacobson 1993)—especially when the former can successfully portray themselves as "outside" the Washington establishment—and are endorsing various changes (term limits, a balanced-budget amendment) that would alter the character of the institution itself, and of government generally in the United States.

For Dodd (1993, p. 424), these circumstances constitute something close to a crisis of legitimacy that stems from growing doubts about "the problem-solving capacities of the contemporary Congress." "[T]he public's loss of faith in Congress may reflect an astute reading on the part of citizens that however well Congress manages the service state and addresses their immediate narrow interests, it is not attentive to the general issues shaping their collective well-being or their long-term future" (p. 430). Dodd (pp. 438–439) anticipates that one likely outcome of Congress's diminished stature is that it will face, and be less well equipped to resist, renewed efforts at executive dominance. Maybe so, but it appears to me that citizens are increasingly running out of patience with presidents as well as with legislators. Two of the last four incumbents (Jimmy Carter and George Bush) have lost their bids for reelection, and a third (Bill Clinton) will be sorely tested should he seek another term in 1996.

People may, at least initially, respond more readily to the leadership of a single president than to the cacophony of signals they receive from 535 representatives and senators. Still, Mr. Clinton and his successors have their work cut out for them, especially to the extent that they wish to pursue a programmatic agenda (as opposed to being satisfied with incremental changes achieved independently of legislative authorization and appropriation). The failure of health care, lobbying, campaign finance, and other reform proposals in 1994 illustrates that it often is easier for both Congress and the White House to do nothing. And the more "nothing" that gets done, the more grave the legitimacy crisis—for U.S. government as a whole, not just Congress—will become in the years ahead.

Let me say once again that my remarks should not be construed as suggesting that the absence of broadly acceptable policy "results" is irrelevant to the confidence gap of the 1990s. I simply want to point out that there are good reasons for doubting that such results can be generated very easily, very quickly, or in a way that conforms to the "perfectly obvious policy preferences of the American people"—assuming that the nature of those preferences can somehow be divined. Also, I am convinced that unsatisfactory policy outcomes are only part (and not necessarily the most telling part) of the story. Consider, for example, the recent work of John Hibbing and Elizabeth Theiss-Morse on popular attitudes toward Congress. Rejecting the notion that citizens disapprove of Congress because it is out of step with their ideological and issue preferences, Hibbing and Theiss-Morse (1994, pp. 11–12) argue that "public disaffection with institutions is largely the result of frustration with the way democracy is practiced in those institutions." Their focus-group participants generally insisted that the country would be better off if members of Congress just paid more attention to the wishes of "the people" or "the majority"—except that "they almost never connected these wishes to actual substantive content." For most Americans, in fact, "the public good is *not* specific policy outcomes; rather, it is a feeling that the government goes about its business in a manner that is sensitive to the public interest. As such, the public good is as much procedural as substantive."

This is a theme that emerged clearly in my own research (see Craig 1993 and Chapter 3 in this volume). As Hibbing and Theiss-Morse (1994, p. 12) note, "At the national level, particularly in a large, complex, and diverse society, the public's belief in the existence of consensus seems naive." Yet the belief exists, and what is so frustrating is that "[t]he reality of diverse special interests, partisanship, a ponderously slow political process, debate and compromise all seem strangely out of place to [people who are] convinced that deep down we all agree on most things" (p. 13).[9] Zeroing in on Congress, Hibbing and Theiss-Morse (p. 16) explain that "[u]nhappiness with Congress stems from the perception that it has more to do with shaping the governmental process than do other institutions as well as the perception that Congress's power is manifested primarily through obstructionism. If the public is upset when nothing seems to be done, it usually vents its spleen at the institution it believes possesses but does not employ the ability to affect significantly those conditions: the Congress. In the eyes of the people, Congress's power keeps things from getting done."

The same message came through in my conversations with citizens back in the mid-1980s and then again, even more emphatically, in follow-up interviews I conducted over the course of the presidential campaign in 1992 (see Craig 1993, chapter 4). In my case, however, I discovered that perceptions of "procedural injustice" (Tyler 1990; Hibbing and Theiss-Morse 1994) are often at the core of the anger and disappointment people feel toward *all* governmental institutions and toward the political process as a whole. Congress may be viewed as the worst offender but is far from the only one.

The most common complaint along these lines is probably that "[a] minority—the extremists, the special interests—[have] more access and influence" with politicians than do "the people" (Hibbing and Theiss-Morse 1994, p. 19). According to Kevin Phillips (1994, p. 36), "Decision making in [Washington] has increasingly come to be a polling of affected campaign donors and interest groups rather than of the people, and the money and lobbying brought to bear in the process has become a symbol of how the capacity of Americans for associations and fraternal organizations has become a political curse as well as a cultural blessing." Making matters worse for many Americans is the belief that problems of representativeness cannot be effectively redressed through traditional electoral means. The parties are regarded with either hostility or indifference (Wattenberg

1994; Black and Black 1994), and a growing number of voters are looking else-where for leaders who share their sense of outrage. The disfunction of Washington politics, says Phillips (1994, p. 37), "accompanied by the increasing incapacity of the two-party system, [is] starting to produce a new kind of outsider, antisystem, or third-party politics, exemplified by Eugene McCarthy and Ralph Nader, and Jerry Brown, Pat Buchanan, and Ross Perot. Voters [are] getting angry waiting for promised reform and renewal that never [comes]."

Ross Perot, of course, personified the "outsider" dynamic that was so evident in 1992 (Ceaser and Busch 1993), and a legion of successors took up the mantra in 1994: Michael Huffington in California, Ollie North in Virginia, Mitt Romney in Massachusetts, Bill Frist in Tennessee, George Pataki in New York, former drag-racing star and U.S. House candidate Don "Big Daddy" Garlits (who initially announced that he would run in a neighboring district because of confusion about where he lived) here in north central Florida, and others too numerous to mention. Issues and real-life problems—except for crime, which overwhelmed just about everything else that anyone might want to talk about during the campaign[10]—were less important than the ability to convey a sense of "populist estrangement" (Fineman 1994a, p. 34).

Congressional Republicans emphasized their outsider status by putting forth the dubious Contract with America; Democrats; by and large, didn't add much to the debate apart from bashing the GOP for its hypocrisy and insisting that they were against coddling criminals, too. In most races where there was enough money to do so, both sides opted for the low road by piling negative ad upon negative ad—a strategy that might not have been so offensive if only the ads had contained a little more substance (instead of relying mainly on symbolism and character assassination) and a little less distortion of the target candidate's record, policy stands, and personal integrity. As election day drew near, voters (including those who believed that a few more "outsiders" in government would help, if nothing else, to shake things up a bit) could hardly be blamed for wondering whether the foolishness they witnessed over the course of this "sullen, distraught, down and dirty" campaign season (Fineman 1994b, p. 24) had anything to do with anything that was important in their lives.

MASS POLITICS IN THE 1990s

With the politics of disaffection still going strong (and probably getting stronger), what can we say about the future? I mentioned earlier the revisionist scholarship that became prominent in the late 1960s and the 1970s. Some of the changes in citizen attitudes and behavior that took place during that period (public mistrust, party decomposition) were real enough—but others (ideology, issue voting, the generation gap) proved to be less substantial, less enduring, and a good bit less relevant than they appeared to be at the time as a touchstone for subsequent trends in the 1980s and 1990s. In assessing the present era, we should therefore be humble about our forecasting abilities. Although much of what is happening today *looks* to be a harbinger of things to come, the shape of our political future depends upon events and circumstances as yet unforeseen.

For the most part, then, my goal in putting together this book has been to take stock of where we are at the moment. Certain aspects of mass politics in the 1990s are relatively new developments (talk-show democracy, heightened grassroots engagement in the 1992 presidential election), but others reflect and build upon changes that have been under way for a while now (dealignment, the Perot phenomenon, tax revolts and term limits, group conflict based on religious values). About the only two things we know for sure are that (1) the relationship between citizens and their leaders is quite different than it was just twenty-five or thirty years ago, and (2) from all indications, the pace of change has accelerated over the past decade. In recognition of this quickening pace (and of the degree to which it challenges many of our assumptions concerning the rules of "normal" politics), each of the following chapters includes at least some discussion—however speculative—of the longer-term implications of whatever attitudinal, behavioral, or institutional patterns are reported therein. Yet our collective focus is primarily on the here and now. It is difficult enough to understand the nature, origins, and relevance of current trends without pretending that we can also anticipate the various twists and turns that undoubtedly lie ahead as we move toward the start of the twenty-first century.

The book is divided into four parts, the first of which ("Attitudes") offers a closer examination of how Americans think and feel about government. Although popular discontent is by no means the sole defining element of mass politics in the 1990s, it does seem to be the connecting thread among all of the changes that we will be considering. According to Wilson Carey McWilliams (1993, p. 194), "The clearest message of 1992 was the majority's demand for active government, engaged to relieve America's discontents and reclaim the future." The catch, even more apparent in 1994 than in 1992, is that "along with some hope, the electorate harbored an abiding doubt that government can succeed" in achieving these goals (p. 196). That citizens have mixed views about government is a familiar story, of course; at issue is whether the balance of "hopes" (expectations) to "abiding doubts" (cynicism) has tilted decisively in favor of the latter. A cautionary note is sounded in Chapter 2 by Linda and Stephen Bennett, who build upon their analysis in *Living with Leviathan* (1990) to describe the ambivalence that has been—to one extent or another—a mainstay of our political culture for over 200 years. This is followed by an update of my own work in *The Malevolent Leaders*, and by Ruy Teixeira's assessment of the problems facing the Democratic Party as it tries to reestablish credibility with middle-class voters who are increasingly skeptical of what activist government can do for them.

The essays in Part 2 ("Involvement") deal, in various ways, with politics at the grass roots. Kevin Phillips (1994, p. 14) has recently described how "[d]uring the period from 1800 to 1932, the American people did something no other nation's population has ever done—they directed, roughly once a generation, revolutionary changes in the nation's political culture and economic development through a series of critical presidential elections." To accomplish the same thing today, we are told, would be extremely difficult because of "a huge, new entrenched govern-ing elite" and "a capital city so enlarged, so incestuous in its dealings, so caught up in its own privilege that it no longer seems controllable or even swayable by the general public" (p. xiii).

Alternatively, the key obstacle to a "revolutionary" shift in power and policy (otherwise known as partisan realignment) in the 1990s may derive not from active resistance on the part of elites but rather from the fact that "political parties no longer mean as much to people as they once did," i.e., because they are consid-ered to be "less relevant in solving the most important domestic and foreign pol-icy issues of the day" (Wattenberg 1994, pp. 35, 89). The argument here is that the American public has become largely indifferent or apathetic toward the parties, focusing its attention instead on individual candidates and on the performance of specific leaders such as the president. With higher levels of educational attain-ment and "cognitive mobilization" permitting more citizens to make their voting choices independent of party cues anyway (Dalton 1984), future realignments could end up being very different (less dramatic, less durable, less likely to pro-duce lasting changes in government policy[11]) from those we have experienced in the past.

Regardless of whether this is the way it happens—and Republicans at the moment are betting that it isn't—the past thirty years have been marked by an erosion of the old New Deal coalition and by partisan *de*alignment, ticket-split-ting, electoral volatility, and divided government. Some texts continue to divide American political history into five distinct "party systems"; the evidence pre-sented by John Aldrich and Richard Niemi in Chapter 5 make a persuasive case that we are now well into a *sixth* party system characterized by partisan decompo-sition and candidate-centered elections.[12] Indeed, if one accepts the "periodicity" of realignments (i.e., that mainly due to generational turnover, the electorate finds itself "ripe" for another of Phillips's revolutions approximately every thirty to forty years; see Beck 1974), it may be time to start looking for signs of the changes that signal our move into the *next* partisan era.[13] In this spirit, the remainder of Part 2 explores three areas that are cited in most accounts of the 1992 presidential campaign: voter engagement (Randolph Horn and M. Margaret Conway), the rise of political talk shows on radio and television (Diana Owen), and the Perot movement (Lonna Atkeson, James McCann, Ronald Rapoport, and Walter Stone).

Politics is about conflict, and the chapters in Part 3 ("Groups") address several of the most significant bases of social cleavage present in the United States today. Although 1994 may not have been an overly impressive follow-up to 1992's Year of the Woman, the gender gap described by Janet and Cal Clark in Chapter 9 shows few signs of vanishing from the political landscape anytime soon;[14] there simply are too many issues that impact men and women in different ways—and on which the two sexes hold at least moderately divergent views—for this to be the case. By the same token, if gender is relevant in certain circumstances (on spe-cific issues and in close elections), religion and race represent elements of the social environment that have helped to define our politics from the beginning. The former is examined by Allen Hertzke and David Rausch in Chapter 10 (an overview of the religious factors that are lately drawing so much notice from pundits and politicians alike), the latter by Timothy Bledsoe, Michael Combs, Lee Sigelman, and Susan Welch in Chapter 11 (a case study contrasting black and white attitudes toward government and social services in Detroit). Should there be a seventh party system in our not-too-distant future, I suspect that both religion and race (along with social class; see Chapter 4) will play a large role in determining its content and structure.

The focus shifts in Part 4 ("Linkage") to political decisionmakers and decisionmaking. Glenn Parker and Charles Barrilleaux start things off by asking whether members of Congress are the "wholly reelection-motivated caricatures that frequently emerge from analyses of their activities"—and the answer suggested by their data is not one that a cynical electorate would necessarily expect. Chapter 13 is an accounting by Paul Herrnson, Kelly Patterson, and John Pitney of how the parties have tried to adapt (not altogether successfully) to the altered, predominantly candidate-centered electoral context in which they find themselves in the 1990s. The final chapter on "direct democracy" by Jack Citrin brings us, in a sense, full circle. Whereas scholars eventually came to conclude that the original upsurge in popular mistrust almost thirty years ago posed little threat to system stability, there is greater awareness today that discontent can have serious consequences even when it does not lead directly to revolutionary upheaval or civil strife.

The so-called tax revolt that began in the late 1970s was one such consequence (Sears and Citrin 1985), and the current term-limits movement is clearly another—both of these causes having been advanced through use of initiative and referendum procedures at the state and local levels. The problem, as Citrin explains in Chapter 14, is that the desire for "more" democracy is understandable (given a lack of faith in the responsiveness of elected leaders) but ultimately does little to "redefine the nature of popular control. Voters might be in a better position to chastise the professional politicians for their excesses, but the pluralist world of interest-group politics [remains] largely intact." Peter Schrag looked recently at California's experience with citizen policymaking and concluded that the various reforms enacted ("most, though not all, by the initiative route") since Proposition 13 was approved by voters in 1978 "have crippled state and local governments with so many limits and mandates and so tangled responsibility that it is increasingly difficult for representative government to function at all and nearly impossible for even well-informed people to know who's accountable for what. In effect, Californians, pursuing visions of governmental perfection, have made it increasingly difficult for elected officials to make any rational policy decisions" (Schrag 1994, p. 52). Proposition 13, according to Schrag, "set in motion a Rube Goldberg machine that has so divided and concealed responsibilities that it could do nothing but further alienate voters" (p. 52).

And therein lies the danger: As the social contract is perceived to have been broken by an ever larger proportion of the general public, Americans can hardly be blamed for wanting to take matters into their own hands. Doing so almost certainly will not resolve their main concerns, but what other options are available? Whether it is through changing party control of Congress and of the state legislatures, supporting "outsider" (including Independent and minor-party) candidates, imposing term limits, acting as citizen legislators, or something else (see Craig 1993)—we have reached the point at which, absent effective political leadership, people likely will continue doing whatever they can to keep elected officials on a short leash. Perhaps through a process of trial and error, some acceptable redress for our grievances will be found. And perhaps, along the way, more citizens will realize that they have been part of the problem all along (e.g., for expecting government to provide services that it cannot afford without additional tax revenues, for being ill informed on many issues, for rewarding candidates whose campaign appeals are simplistic and misleading) and act accordingly. However, politics does not come with the assurance of complete satisfaction or your money back. Unless and until our politicians decide to do the job they were elected to do, the democratic impulse will remain strong—and the future will remain uncertain.

NOTES

1. One example was the inability of House Republicans to pass a balanced-budget amendment that would have required a 60 percent vote in Congress to enact future tax increases.

2. A study of registered voters by Greenberg Research, Inc. also found that, among Independents, the Republicans had an edge in "having people take greater responsibility" (44 percent to 19 percent), "making America prosperous" (39 percent to 19 percent), "insisting on moral standards, that people know right from wrong" (34 percent to 16 percent), "strengthening families" (31 percent to 20 percent), and "insisting on more discipline" (45 percent to 15 percent)—though Democrats came out ahead in "respecting the ordinary person" (35 percent to 19 percent), "openness to change and innovation" (38 percent to 25 percent), "respecting people's individual freedom" (37 percent to 29 percent), "trying to make things better for people" (37 percent to 21 percent), and "understanding the financial pressures on people and families" (39 percent to 21 percent; Democratic Leadership Council 1994, pp. 49–50).

3. Perhaps surprisingly, the same exit poll cited by Ladd (1995, p. 16) found the partisan composition of the electorate in 1994 (37 percent Democrat, 35 percent Republican, 29 percent Independent) to be virtually unchanged from what it had been two years earlier (37 percent, 35 percent, and 29 percent, respectively). The survey of registered voters conducted immediately after the election by Greenberg Research, Inc. produced a similar distribution: 36 percent Democrat (45 percent with leaners included), 34 percent Republican (45 percent with leaners), and 29 percent Independent (9 percent pure Independent)—as well as statistically identical mean scores for the Republican Party (53 degrees, 50 among Independents) and the Democratic Party (52 degrees, 49 among Independents; see Democratic Leadership Council 1994, pp. 33, 35) on "feeling thermometer" questions comparable to those described in the Appendix to this book.

4. They can derive less comfort from the considerable diversity that exists within their own ranks about how to respond to the changing political climate of the 1990s. President

Clinton, seen by many voters as having fallen captive to his party's left wing, is trying to reestablish his credentials as a "new Democrat" less reflexively in favor of "big-government solutions" to social problems than he occasionally has appeared to be (especially with regard to health care reform) in the past; in fact, poll results suggest that (1) this is an appropriate strategy given the public's present mood and (2) the president has at least a fighting chance of pulling it off (Democratic Leadership Council 1994, pp. 39–41). Nevertheless, a fair number of congressional Democrats and others inside the party (Jesse Jackson, to name just one) are likely to resist any meaningful shift away from the party's traditional message (Marcus 1995).

5. These figures are from a multiple-response question in which respondents were asked to indicate which of several changes (from a list of seven possibilities) in the federal government they regarded as most important.

6. Some evidence to support the historical view offered by Lipset and Schneider: In 1937, with the country still mired in the Great Depression, 44 percent of respondents in a national survey indicated that Congress is "about as good a representative body as is possible for a large nation to have," a fairly modest 16 percent said that "congressmen spend more time thinking of their own political futures than they do in passing wise legislation"; by 1990, the first of these figures had fallen to 17 percent, and the second had jumped to 41 percent (Roper 1994). Also in the late 1930s, there was little support (less than 20 percent) among voters for a third party; by 1992, however, approximately 60 percent of the public claimed to favor "the formation of a third political party that would run candidates for president, Congress, and state offices against the Republican and Democratic candidates" (Black and Black 1994, pp. 23–25; also see Times Mirror 1994b, p. 161, in which 53 percent were reported as favoring "a third major political party in this country in addition to the Democrats and Republicans").

7. In fact, even the 53 percent approval for one's representative reflected a drop of about 9 points between March and September (Morin 1994). Although it may seem like a matter of semantics, Hibbing and Theiss-Morse (1994) have demonstrated that most Americans actually do hold the *institution* of Congress (and usually their own representative) in high regard—what they don't like is the *party leadership* and the *general membership* (members "as a collectivity") in Congress.

8. This shift, says Dodd (1993, pp. 425–426) refers to "legislators [having] come to build broadly inclusive electoral coalitions within their districts by servicing the particularized interests of all constituent groups—farmers, bankers, union members, students, the elderly, and so forth. Although such groups may disagree on the broad issues of the day, and would support opposing candidates in an issue-oriented campaign, they agree on the importance of maintaining in office an incumbent who has the power to serve their immediate individual and group interests. Incumbents thus win reelection by large and secure margins . . . while their constituents receive the assistance with their service needs that an experienced and powerful incumbent can provide." It is unfortunate that over the long haul, "both incumbents and citizens can become so dependent on the politics of service delivery that they overlook the emerging policy problems of a new era."

9. There is, in short, "little appreciation for the fact that, as Madison said, interests are naturally divided and cannot be accurately represented without representatives coming into conflict and attempting to resolve these conflicts by debating, disagreeing, and compromising" (Hibbing and Theiss-Morse 1994, p. 21).

10. For a discussion on the importance of "valence" issues—i.e., those that "powerfully move the electorate [but] do not present even two alternative positions that divide the par-

ties and candidates on the one hand and the electorate on the other" (p. 7)—in campaigns today, see Stokes and DiIulio (1993).

11. In commenting on the GOP's victory in 1994, historian Michael Beschloss (1994, p. 49) correctly observed that prior realignments (at least through the 1930s) "occurred not just when Congress changed to reflect the popular mood, but when the new majority enacted the ideas it ran on and when the public perceived them to work."

12. Looking at the previous fall's results, Ladd (1995, p. 20) concluded that "we learned in the 1994 balloting relatively little which is new about our era. It was a striking shift in political power . . . [but the Republican victory] only added emphatic punctuation to a political story which has long been unfolding." It is Ladd's contention that "[t]he United States is somewhere in the middle stages of a major political realignment" that has thus far failed to produce an unambiguous winner; in other words, the Democrats have long since lost their status as majority party, but the GOP has not yet proved strong enough to take their place (p. 28).

13. I am assuming here that citizens' attitudes toward the parties have not atrophied to the point where the very concept of realignment is rendered obsolete (Ladd 1990).

14. For example, although the number of women elected to Congress in 1994 did not change much, exit polls revealed a sizable—and perhaps even growing—gender gap in congressional voting (57–43 percent Republican support among men, 54–46 percent Democratic support among women in U.S. House races; see Bowman 1995, p. 52).

PART I

Attitudes

2

Looking at Leviathan: Dimensions of Opinion About Big Government

LINDA L.M. BENNETT
STEPHEN EARL BENNETT

Many Americans today are confused when the word leviathan is used in connection with government. Dictionaries state that it refers to something of "enormous size and power" that harks back to the "sea monster" described in the Bible. Only people who are familiar with the philosophical tome *Leviathan*, originally published in 1651 by Englishman Thomas Hobbes (1991), are likely to connect the term to notions of centralized governmental power. Yet this is the basis for our chapter's title. Its theme is straightforward: The central government in the United States has grown tremendously, and citizens are still "coming to terms" with that growth (also see Bennett and Bennett 1990).

What do Americans think about government? What do they believe government should do or not do? These are fundamental questions that tap the roots of American political culture. How a democratic society is oriented toward its national government guides the legitimate range of that government's activities. Ultimately, those activities can determine how democratic the society will remain. We believe that as our national government has grown in the complexity of its organization, the number of people it employs, the range of responsibilities it has absorbed, the breadth of activities it seeks to regulate, and the revenues it extracts from taxpayers to spend for a broad panoply of programs, there has been an accompanying shift in American attitudes toward government. Even though politicians still draw appreciative applause by assailing "wasteful spending," "dishonest politicians," and "intrusive regulations," there is growing acceptance of government's many roles in everyday life. People's orientations toward government are multidimensional and reflect more than simply an abhorrence of "bigness." Furthermore, a significant part of the change in political culture is evident in the varying orientations toward government held by individuals of different age groupings (or cohorts), beginning with those who were young adults during the Great Depression of the 1930s, and ending with today's young adults, sometimes called Generation X or, referring to the huge generation they follow, post–baby boomers.

We start our discussion with a brief reconnaissance of two significant periods in governmental growth during the twentieth century and the shifts in popular opinion about government that accompanied them. During the first period in the 1930s and 1940s, the national government in the United States grew to meet both domestic and international crises. A second major spurt of governmental growth began with the domestic reforms of the mid-1960s Great Society programs and ended in the early 1970s with American withdrawal from a controversial war abroad and visible fault lines in race relations at home.

Any consideration of changing attitudes about big government must begin with the traditional mistrust of a powerful central establishment, a suspicion rooted in Americans' revolutionary experience with King George III and his ministers in the eighteenth century. Political scientists Gabriel Almond and Sidney Verba (1963, pp. 441, 494) noted that one result of the American Revolution was that citizens tend "to be uneasy with a powerful government," and this leads to a "tendency to subject all government institutions, including the judiciary and bureaucracy, to direct popular control." Samuel P. Huntington (1981) believed that a "pervasive antipower ethic" is both an integral part of the American creed and the basis of the American preference for a weak national government. Fundamental components of the creed, such as individualism, a belief in liberty, and a desire for equality lead to a suspicion of bigness, particularly in any organization involving the structuring of power, such as government. Moreover, according to James A. Morone, the dread of powerful government as a threat to liberty has on several occasions led Americans to demand enhanced popular control over political institutions and processes. Morone contends that reforms aimed at increased popular control over political institutions have instead often "expand[ed] the scope and authority of the state, especially its administrative capacity. A great irony propels American political development: the search for more direct democracy builds up the bureaucracy" (Morone 1990, p. 1).

NATIONALIZING PUBLIC
EXPECTATIONS OF GOVERNMENT

Franklin Roosevelt and the New Deal

American government and society were forever transformed by events and trends in the 1930s and 1940s. A harbinger of inevitable change was contained in census data from 1920: For the first time, a majority of the U.S. population lived in urban rather than rural areas. The United States was no longer a nation of self-reliant farmers and small entrepreneurs. The interdependence of urban living conditioned citizens to expect services, if not from local party organizations increasingly perceived as corrupt, then from government.

The 1920s had begun with an economic boom but ended in a bust. With the stock market collapse of October 1929, there was little question that what had initially seemed to be another recession had degenerated into a full-scale depression. In retaliation, voters—particularly those most affected by the widening economic disaster—began ejecting Republicans from Congress in 1930. In 1932, they gave the Democratic Party a political power base it held for the next generation. With widespread unemployment (as high as 25 percent of the workforce) and a banking system in collapse, many people turned to a new president for help. Public expectations that Franklin Roosevelt would lead the country out of its economic morass bolstered both the national government's power and that of the presidency. Roosevelt is usually credited with ushering in a new era of president-centered politics. His energetic and highly personal leadership cemented a bond between the public and the presidency that later presidents would try to reinforce, not always successfully (Leutchenburg 1983).

In its response to an economic crisis, the national government grew in size and power. In the first three years of FDR's tenure, spending by the national government increased the national debt by 50 percent (to over $33 billion) even while receipts increased by 100 percent (to over $4 billion). During the same time period, civilian employment by the national government shot up 44 percent and Washington-based government employment skyrocketed by 75 percent (U.S. Department of Commerce 1976, p. 1105; hereafter referred to as USDC). Social ills once thought to be the appropriate province of families or private charities, such as security for the elderly, became an important part of the New Deal legacy. Along with taking on a plethora of new responsibilities, the national government moved in to provide electricity to the rural portions of the South and West and regulated the market for farm goods.

How did citizens view the expanded role of the national government? In general, they approved, though there were signs of ambivalence—a tendency that some analysts claim still exists in American public opinion (Feldman and Zaller 1992). Hadley Cantril and Mildred Strunk's (1951) volume cataloging public opinion from 1935 to 1946 shows that the public was aware that the national government's power was growing (see also Bennett and Bennett 1990, pp. 20–24). In response to a May 1939 Gallup poll question, "Do you think the federal government will have more power or less power ten years from now than it has today?" nearly half of adult Americans (48 percent) said it would have more power. Only about one in five thought the government would have less power, one-sixth of the public felt the national government's power would remain unchanged, and the rest said they didn't know.

How much support was there for the New Deal in the 1930s and 1940s? Again, public opinion was mixed. Fifty percent in a January 1936 Gallup poll said they favored the New Deal; almost as many (46 percent) claimed they did not approve. Three years later, in November 1939, 45 percent agreed with a *Fortune* magazine poll item suggesting, "Although the New Deal has not worked perfectly in many ways, it has done a lot of good and should be continued with some modification and improvements." Just months before the United States would formally enter World War II, 56 percent of respondents in a Gallup survey disagreed that "there is too much power in the hands of the government in Washington." In short, despite differences in poll methods and particularly variations in the wording and format of questions seeking to elicit public opinion, there appears to have been a slow but steady growth in support for the New Deal and for an enhanced government presence in American society. Nonetheless, even in late 1941, public opinion about the New Deal and big government remained decidedly mixed.

The transformation in national government activity, along with the shift of public expectations of government that had been shaped by a devastating economic crisis, was solidified and extended by the successful role of the United States in World War II between 1942 and 1945. A January 1945 *Fortune* poll found that from one-quarter to two-fifths of the public did not believe that national government programs went "far enough" in providing Social Security pensions, increasing low-cost housing, boosting wages, or helping the farmer "make a decent living" (Cantril and Strunk 1951, p. 986). Only small portions of the public (6–14 percent) believed the government had gone too far in these areas. Truly, as Arthur Ekirch Jr. (1969, p. viii) noted, there had been a shift in the "traditional values and attitudes of the American people, conditioning them to look, as never before, to the national state as the basic arbiter and fundamental factor in their lives." Describing the "ratcheting" upward of government size and power in response to crises, Robert Higgs (1987, p. 195) offered a darker interpretation of the period that he believes still affects American opinions today: "In place of the old beliefs there now prevails a greater toleration of, and even a positive demand for, collectivist schemes that promise social security, protection from the rigors of market competition, and very often—to be blunt—something for nothing."

Republican rhetoric scored the New Deal programs as disastrous for both the nation's economy and its moral fiber during the years when FDR and his successor, Harry S Truman, were president (1933–1953). Still, when former general Dwight D. Eisenhower was elected carrying the GOP banner in 1952, little was changed in those programs. In fact, President Eisenhower believed that a social welfare program such as Social Security "was an absolute necessity in a modern, industrialized society" (Pach and Richardson 1991, p. 56). Eisenhower appeared to understand the political consequences of shutting down programs and benefits that citizens had come to believe they were entitled to receive and warned his fellow Republicans that should any party attempt to dismantle portions of the New Deal, "you would not hear of that party again in our political history" (Pach and Richardson 1991, p. 56). Eisenhower understood that Americans had "embraced [big government] overwhelmingly" (Lowi 1985, p. 1).

The "Welfare Shift" of Lyndon Johnson

The Kennedy-Johnson years (1961–1969) brought a second major surge in domestic policymaking in this century. Lyndon Johnson became president following the assassination of John F. Kennedy in November 1963, before most of Mr. Kennedy's domestic legislative agenda had been enacted into law. LBJ undertook to secure passage of those proposals as a fitting monument to the martyred young president. Johnson also interpreted his 1964 landslide victory over Republican Barry Goldwater as a clear public repudiation of the conservative call to roll back the welfare state. So decisive was LBJ's victory that one political scientist declared that "it would be a courageous man indeed who would run on a Goldwater plat-form again" (Burns 1966, p. 311). The election results were widely viewed as a call from the American people for the national government to address a host of domestic welfare problems.

The War on Poverty and Great Society programs that Johnson proposed and Congress quickly adopted were intended as a frontal attack on social ills including juvenile delinquency, poverty, and racism. Never had all three branches of the cen-tral government moved so aggressively to regulate social relations in the United States. The predictable result of this heightened level of government activity was that during the decade of the 1960s, civilian employment in the federal govern-ment increased by 16 percent to almost 3 million and the federal budget went from a surplus of $269 million in 1960 to nearly a $3 billion deficit in 1970 (USDC 1986, p. 291). Of course, increased employment and spending resulted not only from the flurry of domestic policymaking but also from an expanded war in Southeast Asia.

Reaction to the unrest stemming from the Vietnam War and to the series of long, hot summers during which racial riots convulsed and scorched dozens of American cities eventually began to transform patterns of public opinion that had been estab-lished during the 1930s with the New Deal. People's feelings about big government and its role in society both became more complex and began to depart from what they had been from the years of the Great Depression through the mid-1960s.[1]

DIMENSIONS OF AMERICANS' ATTITUDES
ABOUT BIG GOVERNMENT

Someone seeking to describe Americans' attitudes about big government con-fronts two nagging questions. First, what do people have in mind when they express an opinion about the power of the federal government? Although politi-cians and journalists can readily think of several distinct things when asked about big government—taxes, spending, regulation, and so on—students of public opin-ion have long known that elites and masses speak in different tongues when talk-ing about politics (see Converse 1964). To complicate matters further, there is some reason to wonder if, when asked an abstract question such as "Do you think the government in Washington is too powerful?" many people simply respond with the first thing that comes to mind even though that "opinion" may actually mean nothing to them (Zaller 1992). Often such "opinions" are forgotten almost immediately so that the next time people are asked the same question, their "opinions" are completely different from those given the first time even if only a brief period has elapsed between the two measurements (see Converse 1970). Researchers refer to the tendency for survey respondents to manufacture "opinions" on the spur of the moment as "pseudo-opinions," "door-step opinions," or "non-opinions" (Asher 1992).

Concern about what Americans have in mind when they offer opinions about big government, and whether such "opinions" really mean anything to many people, is heightened by the absence of much research on these questions. One study that does look at what people mean when they think about big government is by Joan Flynn Fee (1981). She found that people responded to questions about big government in terms of four essentially independent clusters of ideas: welfare-statism, corporatism, federal control versus states' rights, and bureaucracy. Welfare-statism refers to federal spending for social programs. Corporatism entails Washington's support for big business and its looking after the interests of the wealthy. Fee argued that conservatives tended to respond to questions about big government in welfare-statist terms and that liberals thought in corporatist imagery. The federal-control dimension has to do with Washington's actions that wrest power from the states and local governments, and bureaucracy conjures up notions of growing bureaucratic structures, which are the very antithesis of popular democracy. Fee's data also indicated that the four dimensions, or "clusters of ideas about big government," are essentially unrelated to one another.

The size and composition of the samples Fee relied upon—college-educated, upper- and upper-middle class, and predominantly urban—caution against complete confidence in her results. So it is fortunate that there are two large nationwide surveys with questions on a wide variety of topics that relate to government power; we believe it would be useful to explore these surveys in order to get a better sense of what images come to mind when Americans are asked their views about big government and government's power. In 1987 and again in 1990, the Times Mirror Center for the People and the Press commissioned nationwide polls of the voting-age population. The first was done by the Gallup Organization (roughly 4,400 respondents being interviewed) and the second by Princeton Research Associates (about 3,300 interviews).[2]

On each occasion the surveys contained more than twenty questions tapping different facets of big government and governmental power.[3] Some questions touched on civil liberties issues such as whether AIDS patients' access to public places should be restricted, whether government has a right to censor media stories that may put national security at risk, whether books that contain dangerous ideas should be banned, whether government employees must submit to mandatory drug tests, whether police may search the homes of suspected drug dealers without a warrant, and whether school districts should be allowed to dismiss teachers who are homosexual. Other questions elicited opinions about various facets of government policy such as changing laws to make it more difficult for a woman to obtain an abortion, instituting a mandatory death penalty for persons convicted of first-degree murder, relaxing environmental controls to facilitate economic growth, raising taxes to reduce the budget deficit, and maintaining affirmative action programs for minorities.

Respondents were also asked about classical welfare-state issues such as government taking care of people who cannot look after themselves, helping the needy even if it requires raising taxes, and guaranteeing everyone food and a place to sleep. Finally, several questions inquired about different aspects of government power itself, such as whether the federal government controls too much of people's daily lives, whether it should control only those things that cannot be left up to other governments or to the private sector, whether dealing with a government agency is worth the trouble, whether federal regulation of business causes more harm than good, whether the federal government should be able to overrule the states, whether it is wasteful and inefficient, and whether it is run to benefit all the people or by just a few big interests protecting themselves. For each item, respondents were asked if they "completely agreed," "mostly agreed," "mostly disagreed," or "completely disagreed."

What did the nearly 8,000 Times Mirror respondents have in mind as they offered their opinions on these questions? Some possibilities are suggested by the results of a maximum likelihood (ML) factor analysis, rotated to a varimax solution. Factor analysis is a statistical technique allowing researchers to identify dimensions, or factors, that underlie an array of variables such as the ones described earlier. Although there are many types of factor analysis, they all can be used to reduce the complexity of a large number of variables to one or more underlying (but unmeasured) components.[4]

Our analysis revealed the same three dimensions to public opinion about government in both surveys. The first dimension included items tapping various aspects of *civil libertarianism*: banning books that contain dangerous ideas, denying free speech to groups such as the KKK and the Communist Party, permitting government censorship of press reports, permitting school boards to fire homosexual teachers, and so on. The second factor, or dimension, comprised items tapping *welfare-state* issues: government help for those who cannot assist themselves, preferential treatment of minorities, guaranteed food and shelter for the needy, and the like. The third dimension consisted of items tapping general beliefs about *governmental power:* The federal government is inefficient, dealing with a government agency is not worth the trouble, the federal government controls too much of our lives, government regulation of business causes more harm than good, the federal government should get involved only in things other institutions cannot solve, and the federal government is run to benefit all the people.

Table 2.1 depicts the three dimensions and identifies the types of items in each one (results are for 1987 only; the factor solution for 1990 looks almost exactly the same, however). Although the overall pattern provides some support for Fee's conclusions, our most important finding is that the American public's opinions about big government *in the abstract* form a distinct cluster that is separate from their views on more *specific issues*. Indeed, the two surveys show that the "big government" dimension is not even related to the other two identified factors.

TABLE 2.1   Dimensions of Americans' Opinions About Big Government, 1987

Variable	Civil Liberties	Welfare State	Big Government
Limit women's access to abortion	x		
Death penalty for capital crimes	x		
Drug tests for government employees	x		
Reduce environmental regulation	x		
Restrict people with AIDS	x		
Equality has gone too far in U.S.	x		
Fire homosexual teachers	x		
Ban books with dangerous ideas	x		
No free speech for extremist groups	x		
Police can search suspected drug dealers	x		
Government censors press reports	x		
Do what is necessary for equal opportunity		x	
Government cares for those who need care		x	
Government helps needy even if more taxes needed		x	
Government guarantees everyone food and shelter		x	
Give minorities preferential treatment		x	
Federal regulation of business is bad			x
Something run by government is wasteful			x
Federal government runs only what states can't			x
Federal government controls our lives too much			x
Government is run to benefit all the people			x
Dealing with federal agency not worth it			x
Increase taxes to reduce deficit[a]			
Federal government should overrule states[a]			

NOTE: Variables marked by an x loaded on the indicated factor at or above 0.30.
[a]These variables do not load at an acceptable level on any of the dimensions.
SOURCE: Gallup Poll for Times Mirror (1987).

Opinions concerning big government, in short, exist in "splendid isolation" from views on particular aspects of government involvement in U.S. society. As Lane (1962) pointed out, many people tend to "morselize" their views about government. This, more than any other reason, accounts for the inconsistencies scholars frequently describe when they talk about how the public thinks about big government in the United States. The degree of organization evident in Table 2.1 nevertheless leaves little doubt that such opinions are real—and therefore worthy of further study. It is to this task that we now turn.

OPINIONS ABOUT BIG GOVERNMENT

In order to trace public opinion about big government over a period of time, researchers must examine questions that have appeared in surveys for the entire period under consideration. The University of Michigan's American National Election Study (ANES) series has employed just such a question periodically since the early 1960s.[5] Respondents are asked the following: "Some people are afraid the government in Washington is getting too powerful for the good of the country and the individual person. Others feel that the government in Washington is not getting too strong. Do you have an opinion on this or not? [If yes] What is your feeling, do you think (1) the government is getting too powerful; or do you think (2) the government is not getting too strong?"[6] There are four possible answers here. Some individuals express no opinion, but most say either that they think government is too powerful or that they do not. In addition, a small portion in each survey volunteers the mixed response that "it depends."

The ANES question was first utilized in 1964, which happens to be the year in which Republican presidential nominee Barry Goldwater made opposition to big government the centerpiece of his campaign. It subsequently has appeared, with very little change in wording, on a more or less regular basis—encompassing a historical period when in virtually every presidential election at least one major candidate ran against one or another facet of federal government authority (including, most recently, Ronald Reagan, George Bush, and Independent H. Ross Perot in 1992).

Since we used this item for most of our analyses in *Living with Leviathan,* there is no need to repeat what was written there (see Bennett and Bennett 1990, pp. 25–35). Instead, a brief review of the years between 1964 and the late 1970s, before Ronald Reagan was elected, will suffice. In 1964, a slightly larger percentage of the public felt that the government in Washington had not gotten too strong than believed it had (35 percent vs. 30 percent). Just over 30 percent, however, had no opinion on the issue of Washington's power, and they were joined by a handful saying "it depends." Two notable trends became evident over the next decade and a half:

- First, there was substantial growth in the percentage believing that Washington had indeed become too powerful (rising to over 45 percent), and a commensurate decline in those indicating that the central government was not too strong (falling to as low as 15 percent).
- Second, although the percentage expressing no opinion remained fairly steady between 1964 and the mid-1970s, the size of this group suddenly jumped to nearly 40 percent near the end of the decade.

By 1978, then, (1) nearly 45 percent had come to believe that the federal government was too powerful, (2) just over 40 percent had no opinion, and (3) only about 15 percent did not believe Washington had gotten too strong.

There are at least a couple of reasons to pay special attention to the period between 1980 and 1992. For one thing, these are the Reagan-Bush years, regarded by some observers as having been a watershed in the public's attitudes toward government. Also important is the decision by ANES to add a follow-up question asking respondents who believed that Washington was *not* too strong whether they wanted it to become *even stronger* or remain as it is. This new item allows us to monitor public opinion with a more sensitive instrument than was available prior to 1978; now we can differentiate between citizens who are satisfied to let things alone and those who prefer Washington's power to expand even further.

Figure 2.1 depicts the distribution of responses to the revised power-of-government question from 1980 through 1992. For 1980, the first thing that strikes the eye is the large percentage saying that Washington had become too powerful. On the eve of Reagan's election, approximately half the public believed that the federal government was too powerful for the good of the nation and the individual person. Small wonder that Reagan's anti-big-government rhetoric struck a responsive chord among voters that year. Only a small percentage of the public (7 percent) felt that Washington should become more powerful, and about one-tenth was satisfied with the status quo. It is interesting that despite Reagan's having campaigned hard against governmental intrusion into people's lives—e.g., claiming that "government is the problem, not the solution"—just over a third did not care to express an opinion in the 1980 ANES survey.

With Reagan in office and seeking reelection, the 1984 figures look rather different. Of particular note is the sharp drop of 17 percentage points in the frequency of beliefs that Washington has too much power, though this is partially offset by a 10-point gain in no opinions on the issue. Overall, about one-third of the public felt that the federal government was too powerful, slightly more than two-fifths did not express an opinion, one-fifth accepted the status quo, and a tiny proportion (4 percent) favored making government stronger. In trying to interpret the shifts that occurred between 1980 and 1984, it almost appears as if, with Reagan—whom many students of American politics judged to be the most conservative president since Calvin Coolidge in the 1920s—in the White House, a fair number of citizens either decided that Washington was not too strong for the good of the nation or they simply lost interest altogether in the issue of federal power.

Data from the 1988 ANES were virtually identical to 1984, with the only significant change being a modest dip in the percentage of the public saying they were content with the status quo in regard to Washington's power. Looking back at the decade of the 1980s, two things stand out: First, during the time when Ronald Reagan was president (1981–1989), a smaller proportion of the electorate worried about big government than was true previously. Second, in the same period an average of 45 percent failed to express an opinion on the ANÉS power-of-government question. Since people are inclined to say they do not have opinions on issues they either do not care about or do not believe are personally relevant

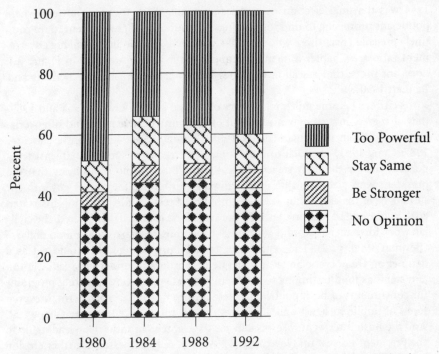

FIGURE 2.1 Opinions About Big Government, 1980–1992. *Source:* American National Election Studies, 1980–1992. Figures indicate the distribution of responses of the power-of-government questions (See Appendix for wording).

(Converse 1976–1977), one might reasonably conclude that concerns about big government were not as important to sizable percentages of the public as they had been prior to 1980.

Finally, although many commentators interpreted the outcome of the 1992 presidential election in terms of more Americans calling for activist government, results from ANES caution against such a broad-gauge interpretation. There was, in fact, an increase (to about two-fifths) in the percentage of the electorate believing that the federal government had become too powerful, as well as a slight decline (to 42 percent) in the percentage who did not express an opinion. Moreover, the level of support for a stronger central government was precisely the same as in 1980—supposedly a benchmark year for the conservative cause.

To summarize: Keeping in mind that it is always wise to guard against making too much of a single survey question, we infer from our analysis of public opinion over the past thirty years that 1964 may have been the last time when Americans saying that Washington had *not* gotten too strong outnumbered those who believed that it had. Some astute analysts of American politics have argued that

1964 was the final election in a series stretching back to 1932—an era when politicians promising to find more things for the national government to do routinely prevailed over those who said that, if elected, they would curtail big government (also see Chapter 5 in this volume). The evidence reviewed in Figure 2.1 does not prove that assertion but does lend it credence (see also Bennett and Bennett 1990).

As citizens became much more wary of federal power between 1964 and 1980, they also grew increasingly mistrustful of government in general and of government officials in particular (Bennett and Bennett 1990; Lipset and Schneider 1987; Craig 1993). Yet each of these long-term trends was reversed at least temporarily during the early stages of the Reagan era. It is no small irony that the president who pledged in his 1980 campaign to reduce the size of government should have the impact of lessening political pressure for achieving his stated goal. By the end of Reagan's tenure, "the size of the federal deficit soared, the civilian work force increased, and government spending rose to over a trillion dollars" (Berman 1990, p. 7). The yearly deficits and burgeoning debt would act as a damper on Democratic hopes to generate new programs under President Clinton and stand as loud testimony to powerful interests protecting spending programs for constituents of both political parties. During Reagan's second term, however, levels of public mistrust once again began to climb (Craig 1993; see Chapter 3). And the Bush interregnum, especially for the eighteen months or so leading up to the president's defeat on November 3, 1992, not only witnessed a further erosion of trust but also renewed anxiety among Americans about whether the government in Washington had become too strong.

The final point to be made about changes occurring between 1964 and 1992 relates to the higher proportions who are now unwilling to state an opinion on the issue of big government. Even in 1992, with Reagan four years out of power, more than two-fifths of the public declined to say either yea or nay when asked whether the government in Washington was too strong. This represents a significant shift in Americans' political dispositions. Scholars frequently note that fear of big government has been a central tenet of political culture in the United States since its birth as a sovereign nation more than 200 years ago (Almond and Verba 1963; Huntington 1981; Morone 1990). We believe that something rather basic has happened since the late 1970s, i.e, that the issue of big government no longer has much personal relevance for a substantial number of citizens. In the next section, though, we show that the changes just described did not take place equally among all segments of the public; rather, they appear to be concentrated among younger Americans—a circumstance suggesting that the transformation may not yet be complete.

Big Government and Birth Cohorts

We began this chapter by discussing significant periods of governmental growth, the premise being that the public's orientation toward government changed as government itself changed. The impact of political events since the

1930s similarly guides our analysis here as we divide the electorate into six birth "cohorts" and then examine how these cohorts differ in their views about big government during the 1980s and early 1990s. The term "cohort" is used instead of "generation" because it has a less-demanding definition. A cohort can "consist of people who experience a common significant life event within a period of one to ten years" (Glenn 1977, p. 8). A generation, in contrast, is generally assumed to have a stronger sense of conscious identification with peers of similar age than does a cohort (see Mannheim 1952). What follows is a brief description of six cohorts, any of which may or may not qualify as a generation in the more rigorous sense.

Our cohorts contain individuals who came of age in the context of a significant event (or events) that affected relations between people and government. "Coming of age" is a somewhat vague concept, but it permits the grouping of those who were young adults when a particular event occurred. Naturally, some events such as the Great Depression and World War II affected all ages, yet the most vivid imprint is presumably on the future lives of those who happen to be young adults during their occurrence. The six birth cohorts are

- *New Dealers (born 1909 to 1921)*. The older members of this cohort would have been in their early twenties when Franklin Roosevelt entered the White House in 1933. Their young adult lives were dominated by FDR's twelve-year tenure, and his death was a traumatic event for many.
- *World War II (born 1922 to 1929)*. There is a natural overlap between this group and the New Dealer cohort, yet being slightly younger put World War II in the center of these people's lives. The entire country was mobilized for the war effort, and the national mood would never return to its prewar state. These individuals ultimately became the parents of the largest birth cohort in U.S. history—the baby boomers.
- *Cold Warriors (born 1930 to 1945)*. Many of these people came of age in the period immediately after World War II, though tensions between the United States and the Soviet Union dominated both foreign and domestic policy discussions for more than a decade. During the 1950s and 1960s, the political rhetoric of Republicans and Democrats alike echoed the theme of cold war.
- *Early Boomers (born 1946 to 1954)*. The usual time frame for the baby boom is from 1946 to 1964; we have divided baby boomers into two separate cohorts of roughly equal time length. The division is not arbitrary, however, since those born in the first nine years of the unprecedented population boom came of age during the turbulent 1960s, when Vietnam and civil rights rocked the national political scene.
- *Late Boomers (born 1955 to 1964)*. The latter half of the baby boomers came of age during the 1970s, a decade of economic jolts that included oil embargoes and skyrocketing unemployment, interest rates, and inflation. The indulgent atmosphere that had enveloped their older peers was no

more. A focus on economic realities and the residues of the Watergate scandal seemed to push politics into the background for many Late Boomers.

• *Post Boomers (born 1965 and after).* These individuals share many orientations with the Late Boomers. Both groups, for example, were among the most enthusiastic Reagan supporters in the early 1980s. Diminished expectations for material success led many Post Boomers to extend adolescence by staying at home with at least one parent longer than their older peers and delaying other adult roles such as marriage. One author described this group as having a confused mixture of frustration and entitlement (Littwin 1986).

How did these cohorts differ in the way they viewed government during the 1980s and early 1990s? Figure 2.2, separated by year, provides some answers. Across the four surveys there is a clear tendency for younger voters (especially Late and Post Boomers, the latter entering the electorate only in 1984) to fret less about the government's power than do their elders. In 1980, 54 percent of New Dealers, along with 60 percent of those in the World War II cohort and 55 percent of Cold Warriors, said that the government had gotten too powerful. This high level of concern diminished somewhat over the course of the 1980s, however, and by 1992 the three older cohorts (45 percent, 46 percent, and 44 percent, respectively) were barely distinguishable from Early (41 percent) or Late Boomers (39 percent)—though they still were a good bit more likely than Post Boomers (30 percent) to be apprehensive about the extent of federal power.

In addition to their lower levels of concern throughout most of the period, younger cohorts also were consistently the least opinionated as to whether the central government had become too strong. In 1980, for example, 55 percent of Late Boomers (then the youngest of the age groups) expressed no opinion; in 1984, which was their debut in the ANES presidential surveys, 76 percent of Post Boomers preferred not to take a position on the issue. By 1992 the rate of "no opinion" answers had dropped among each of these cohorts, but they nonetheless abstained on the power question more often (44 percent of Late Boomers, 55 percent of Post Boomers) than any of the older groups.

The two middle survey years, 1984 and 1988, offer evidence that some of the cohorts wanted continuity in their conception of government's power. Levels of concern dipped from 1980 levels among all cohorts, and the percentages saying they believed government's power should stay the same were correspondingly higher. In 1984, the year of Reagan's reelection, 17 percent of both New Dealers and World War II cohorts expressed a preference for continuity; Cold Warriors, Early Boomers, and Late Boomers all hovered around the 20 percent mark in opting for no change. By 1988, probably the last year a president would share their formative memories, fully one-quarter of the World War II cohort said that they wanted government's power to remain the same. The growing desire for continuity may help to explain Reagan's reelection and the later success of George Bush in

1988. By 1992, though, there was a mild upsurge across the cohorts in those feeling that government was too powerful.

Do Americans Really Want Government Out of Their Lives?

The upshot of the data examined thus far is that despite sizable percentages that remain concerned about Washington's power, many Americans (particularly in the younger age groups) no longer feel strongly about the issue of governmental power. In fact, most people have little difficulty thinking of things they would like the central government to do. The 1976 ANES shows, for example, that Americans thought the federal government should have "a great deal" of responsibility for handling a wide variety of societal issues including the environment, crime and drugs, regulation of consumer goods, unemployment, inflation, race relations, and high taxes (see Bennett and Bennett 1990, pp. 104–105).

An Ohio Poll taken in fall 1993 indicates that Americans continue to experience little difficulty in identifying problems for the federal government to address.[7] Demographers consider the state's population to be fairly representative of the nation, so data from an Ohio Poll are probably close to what a survey of the broader U.S. public might look like. A random sample of 842 adults living in Ohio were asked the following question: "[W]hat is the *best* thing the federal government could do for you and your family? This could mean doing *more* or *less* of something the federal government already does . . . or it could be something the federal government should *begin* doing . . . or it could be something the federal government should *stop* doing." Table 2.2 depicts the results.

Several features of these data are interesting. Most obvious is that the overwhelming majority of Ohio residents were able to conjure up *something* when asked what they thought the federal government should do for them or their families. Granted, nearly 6 percent stated that the best thing the federal government could do is to "leave me alone." But even if we include those who said "none, nothing," and "don't know," roughly four-fifths of the poll's respondents had something on their minds that they felt Washington could do for them.

It would be a mistake, of course, to claim that 80 percent or so of the public wanted a more powerful federal government. Sixteen percent of Ohio residents thought that cutting taxes would be the best thing Washington could do. Eleven percent wanted lower spending, less government waste, deficit reduction, or fewer government regulations. Still another 6 percent gave a variety of "conservative" answers, supporting reductions in welfare, opposing government health care programs, and so on. In short, when asked what they think is the best thing the federal government could do, about a third of the public gives answers that would warm the cockles of Rush Limbaugh's heart.

That percentage, however, is smaller than the proportion of Ohioans who want government to do more. Thirteen percent said that government-sponsored health care reform was uppermost on their list of things for Washington to do. Six per-

38

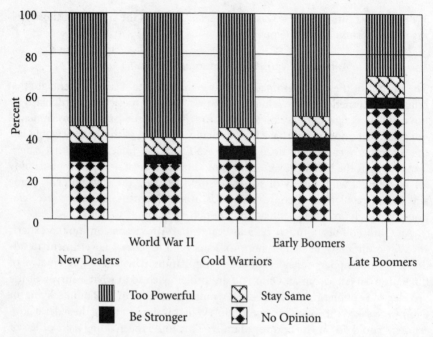

FIGURE 2.2(a) Cohorts and Big Government, 1980*.

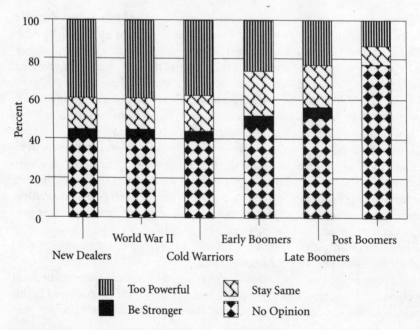

FIGURE 2.2(b) Cohorts and Big Government, 1984*.

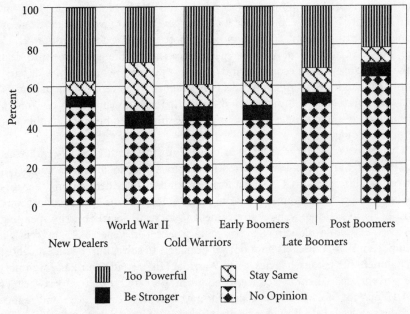

FIGURE 2.2(c)   Cohorts and Big Government, 1988*.

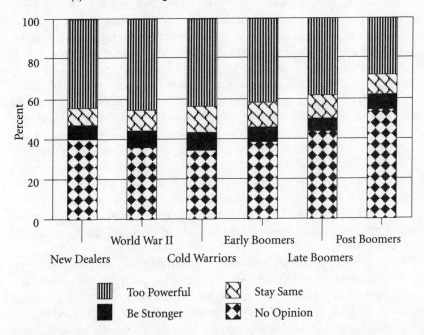

FIGURE 2.2(d)   Cohorts and Big Government, 1992*. *Source:* American National Election Studies, 1980–1992.

*Figures in 2.2 (a-d) indicate the distribution of responses to the ANES power-of-government

question (see Appendix for wording).

cent, mostly elderly respondents (see further on), wanted more spending for Social Security. Nine percent wanted increased government involvement in one or more of several domestic social programs: more spending for education, child care, the poor, and so on. A similar percentage wanted the government to deal with some aspect of the economy, and another 7 percent mentioned a wide variety of new activities that might be taken on. In short, 44 percent of respondents in the Ohio Poll had something in mind for the federal government to do—and a fair number of these people were calling for Washington to begin doing things it is not now doing.

The Ohio Poll is large enough to divide into five birth cohorts (with New Dealers and the World War II cohort combined due to low case numbers). Interesting differences in a wish list for government are evident among the various age groups. As mentioned, those in the New Deal–World War II cohort were most likely to say they wanted government to increase Social Security spending (16 percent) while reducing government spending in general (13 percent), a conundrum that politicians have not yet been able to solve. But the oldest cohort isn't alone in its inconsistencies. Cold Warriors (16 percent) and Early Boomers (20 percent) shared similar concerns about health care reform, yet between 14 and 17 percent of each cohort called for government to lower taxes and reduce spending as well. Late Boomers wanted lower taxes (26 percent) but 15 percent advocated higher spending on a range of social services such as aid to the poor, child care, and education reform. Post Boomers closely resembled Late Boomers, with 21 percent wanting lower taxes and 17 percent encouraging increased spending on social services. Reflecting patterns already discussed, 17 percent of Post Boomers said they didn't know what government could do.

All in all, the Ohio Poll data reveal how easy it is for today's Americans to think of things they want government to do. Yes, a sizable portion of the public wishes for lower taxes and less government spending; a relative few would even prefer that Washington simply let them be. Nevertheless, it remains true that more people want the national government to do things that amount to expanding Washington's reach and power. The laundry list is quite lengthy and covers issues frequently in today's news headlines such as health care reform, higher Social Security spending, and increased government involvement in several domestic social programs. The 1993 Ohio Poll demonstrates that although the relationship is sometimes uneasy, Americans have come to expect a great deal from their government.

This probably helps explain why, when asked if they want more federal spending, the same amount, or less, on a series of domestic programs, far more people call for more than for less. For example, when the 1992 ANES tapped opinions regarding federal spending in ten specific areas—Social Security, food stamps, AIDS, loans for college students, programs that help blacks, the homeless, environmental protection, science and technology, the unemployed, and public

TABLE 2.2   Ohioans' Views of "The Best Thing the Federal Government Could Do" for
Themselves and Their Families, 1993 (percent)

Lower taxes	16.1
Reduce spending, etc.	11.4
Deal with economy, etc.	8.5
Increase Social Security spending	6.1
Health care reform	12.9
Other domestic social services and programs	8.8
Reduce crime, drugs, deal with morality, religion, etc.	3.6
Reduce welfare, no health care reform, etc.	5.9
Other	6.7
Leave me alone	5.7
None, nothing	5.0
Don't know	9.4
N = 808	

SOURCE: Ohio Poll, October 22–November 2, 1993, conducted by the University of
Cincinnati's Institute for Policy Research.

schools[8]—the only one on which the percentage of the public preferring less
spending was larger than that preferring more was food stamps. In several
instances (Social Security, AIDS, student loans, the homeless, the environment,
and public schools), the percentage calling for more spending was *several times*
larger than that asking for less in federal outlays.[9]

Finally, we should keep in mind that the ANES data reviewed earlier show
large numbers of citizens not sufficiently worried about big government to offer
an opinion about Washington's power. It would appear that many Americans
have come to terms with big government by expecting it to do more—but without fully pondering the implications of such heightened activity.

THE IMPACT OF THE 1994 ELECTIONS

When voters handed control of the U.S. Senate and House of Representatives to
the Republican Party in 1994, many took the GOP's historic victory to mean that
public opinion had dramatically shifted rightward, away from dependence on big
government. That was certainly the postelection analysis on many talk-radio programs where conservative hosts celebrated the election results. Talk radio serves
as a powerful medium for those opposed to big government (see Chapter 7), and
the 1994 election results appeared to legitimize their views. Since several portions
of the Republicans' Contract with America entailed reducing the federal government's size and reach, it was inevitable that some would ask if large portions of
the public were committed to curtailing big government.

We agree that voters were determined to change the status quo in Washington
and around the country as they trudged to the polls on November 8, 1994. Sur-

veys taken shortly before and after the election, however, do not show overwhelming support for drastic reductions in Washington's power. Rather, they show the same pattern of ambivalence described previously (see also Morin 1995a). A poll conducted for the Times Mirror Center for the People and the Press shortly before the 1994 elections, for example, showed that sizable majorities of Americans were in a cynical mood toward politicians and believed that the federal government was wasteful and inefficient, that it "controls too much of our daily lives," and that "government regulation of business usually does more harm than good." But the same poll showed that well over half the public continued to agree that "the government should guarantee every citizen enough to eat and a place to sleep"; almost three-fifths of adult Americans also agreed that "it is the responsibility of the government to take care of people who can't take care of themselves," and roughly 90 percent called for "stricter laws and regulations to protect the environment" (Times Mirror 1994b).

It is therefore a mistake to believe that in the aftermath of the 1994 elections, large portions of the electorate endorsed the GOP's contract in its entirety. A *Washington Post*–ABC News poll done in January 1995 found that only 39 percent of the public were even aware of the Contract with America (Morin 1995b). Moreover, that same survey uncovered strong support (80 percent) for a balanced-budget amendment when the question was asked in the abstract—but the level of support fell precipitously when details such as cutting federal spending for either Social Security or education were mentioned. The public was about evenly divided on the desirability of a balanced-budget amendment if such an amendment would require raising federal income taxes.

A *New York Times*–CBS News poll from February 1995 cast further doubt on the proposition that Americans today are committed to significant reductions in government (see Berke 1995). It found, for example, that although four-fifths of the public favored a balanced-budget amendment, fewer than half supported an amendment if that meant cutting Social Security. Even a majority of self-identified Republicans opposed the balanced-budget amendment if it entailed cutting Social Security. Approximately two-thirds of the public said that welfare recipients should continue to receive benefits as long as they are willing to work for them, and roughly three-fifths favored providing welfare benefits to unwed mothers under the age of eighteen.

Our reading of the 1994 elections dovetails with that of Clyde Wilcox (1995). Fed up with "politics as usual" in Washington, voters performed a surgical strike on incumbent Democratic senators, House members, and even some high-profile Democratic governors. Most people do subscribe to portions of the GOP contract: term limits for federal legislators, increased spending to combat crime, an end to "welfare as we know it," and tax breaks for the middle class (however defined monetarily). Republicans risk raising public ire, however, if they interpret their mandate too broadly. Large majorities of Americans continue to believe that government is morally obligated to provide a long list of programs and services, and as polls taken after the election indicate, if Republicans in Congress wield their budgetary knife too aggressively, their hopes that 1994 was the harbinger of the long-awaited realignment may quickly dim in 1996 (see also Morgan 1995).

CONCLUSION

The short span of a chapter does not permit a full discussion of all the factors that affect the public's orientation toward the power of the central government. Still, we have attempted to provide an outline of some key elements that help to explain the dimensions of public opinion about government, and how opinions have changed in recent years.

The most significant feature of the three dimensions of opinion about governmental power (Table 2.1) is that they exist largely in isolation from each other, i.e., the orientations toward big government dimension is not linked to either the civil liberties dimension or the welfare-state dimension. Most individuals express their specific preferences about what government should or should not do without reference to broad concerns about governmental power. Therefore, when politicians attempt to implement what they believe their constituents want in terms of policy ends, they often run into resistance from those very same constituents when the coercive force of government—either through regulations or taxation—is activated in the course of fulfilling their policy desires. Instead of connecting their policy preferences to the force of government necessary for implementation, many Americans seem to believe that benefits can be maintained and new programs created by cutting waste and inefficiency in government.

The Clinton administration has hoped to assuage voter concerns about government waste with its "reinventing government" proposals, presented by Vice President Gore (Gore 1993). The report of the National Performance Review panel headed by the vice president claims savings from the proposals of $108 billion by 1999. Already encircled by those who doubt the proposals can deliver what they promise, the report remains an effort to convince voters that their concerns about waste are being addressed. The New Covenant that presidential candidate Clinton heralded at the Democratic National Convention in 1992 was intended to reassure Americans that government largesse in the form of social welfare programs would carry a concomitant responsibility. Several commentators expressed the belief that even middle-class "entitlement programs" such as Medicare and Social Security must carry the same message (e.g., Borger 1994). So far, many citizens continue to expect a great deal from government without confronting either the cost for their wish lists or the implications for expanded governmental power as Washington moves to provide a longer list of benefits and services.

Aside from the three distinct dimensions of public opinion about government, we found significant differences in opinion between age groups. From 1980 to 1992, younger Americans (Late and Post Boomers) were the least likely to believe that the national government had gotten too powerful; in fact, they were the most likely not to have an opinion at all on the subject. Is this likely to change as the young mature? Only time will tell, but if their apathy about government power continues, they will forge a fundamental shift in political culture as older cohorts fade from the scene. American political culture has traditionally exhibited an open mistrust, or at least an ambivalence, toward centralized power. But that can change as younger cohorts come to dominate the political arena. As we have stated before,

> Today, the ambivalence expressed by many Americans has become increasingly hollow. Ambivalence, or difficulty in choosing between conflicting options, makes sense in a nation with truly limited government, where citizens might be struggling with the choice of whether or not to extend government's hold on their daily lives. But when that government has grown to extend its regulations into all reaches of the private sector, economic and social . . . we are no longer talking about ambivalence but rather a distant angst. Americans are no longer struggling with a choice. They have made a choice, and it is in favor of big government (Bennett and Bennett 1990, p. 137).

NOTES

1. For further discussion, see Bennett and Bennett (1990, chapters 2–4).

2. The Times Mirror data were released directly to us by the Times Mirror Center for the People and the Press. We wish to thank Ms. Carol Bowman and her staff for their assistance.

3. Exact wording can be found in Ornstein, Kohut, and McCarthy (1988, pp. 117–134).

4. Kim and Mueller (1978a, 1978b) provide good discussions of the different types of factor analysis and their uses. Factor analysis works by first obtaining correlation coefficients that describe how each of the variables is related to every other variable included in the analysis and then by proceeding according to a statistical algorithm to identify the dimension or dimensions that are initially hidden within the correlation matrix. Maximum likelihood factor analysis enables a researcher to test hypotheses about the number and nature of dimensions undergirding an array of variables. That is why it is called "confirmatory" factor analysis. When a factor analysis is rotated to a varimax solution, the dimensions detected in a correlation matrix are unrelated to one another. One problem the factor analyst confronts is determining the "solution" that best fits the data entered into the factor analysis. How many dimensions are there, and which items best belong to which dimension? Using the procedure recommended by Wheaton and his associates (1977), the best ML factor solution for both surveys identified three underlying dimensions.

5. Anyone who wants to pursue the matter further might also want to look at a similar question appearing (occasionally) since 1964 in polls conducted by the Gallup Organization and by the Advisory Commission on Intergovernmental Relations.

6. Question wording has varied slightly over the years; this particular version is from 1992. The biennial ANES surveys are conducted by the University of Michigan's Center for Political Studies and made available by the Inter-University Consortium for Political and Social Research. We are responsible for all analyses and interpretations.

7. The Ohio Poll is conducted by the University of Cincinnati's Institute for Policy Analysis. The data are gathered by means of random digit dialing. In 95 out of 100 similarly sized samples, the results would vary by plus or minus 3.4 percentage points just by chance. We wish to thank Alfred J. Tuchfarber, director of IPR, and Andrew Smith, a staff member, for releasing the data to us.

8. See Appendix for question wordings.

9. For more information on public opinion about government spending, see Bennett and Bennett (1990, chapter 4).

3

The Angry Voter: Politics and Popular Discontent in the 1990s

STEPHEN C. CRAIG

The signs are unmistakable and they have been there for quite a long time now. They were there in 1979 when President Jimmy Carter (in an act of political mis-judgment that foreshadowed his defeat at the polls a year later) spoke to the American public about a growing "crisis of confidence" that was threatening "to destroy the social and political fabric" of our nation (see Strong 1986). And after a brief lull during the early part of the decade, they were there again in 1987 when journalist Jonathan Yardley looked ahead to the upcoming presidential race and confessed that "[a]fter more than a quarter-century as a registered voter and working journalist, I have lost virtually all interest in politics—not public affairs, but politics. . . . Where once I believed that politics is an honorable, if not noble, calling, I now see it as the refuge of opportunists and self-aggrandizers, if not scoundrels. Where once I believed that it was possible for an individual to change the course of national events, I now am deeply skeptical of messianism in all forms, left, center or right . . . " (Yardley 1987, p. 25).

The signs were there in 1988 when 63 percent of the public said that "the gov-ernment is pretty much run by a few big interests looking out for themselves" rather than being run "for the benefit of all the people" (Craig 1993); in 1990 when a plurality agreed that their own representative in Congress was "more con-cerned about getting reelected" (44 percent compared with 41 percent who believed that the incumbent was "sincerely working to solve the critical problems facing the country," see Morin 1990) and when voters in three states (Oklahoma, Colorado, and California) passed ballot measures limiting the number of terms that various elected officials could serve;[1] and once more in 1992 (see Chapter 14) when fourteen additional states enacted term limits and 67 percent of the overall public claimed that business, religious, and governmental leaders—but especially the latter[2]—were "less trustworthy and honest" than had been the case ten or fif-teen years earlier.

Popular dissatisfaction with politics and government reached something close to a fever pitch during the 1992 presidential campaign. One could hardly turn on the television set or read an election update in the local paper without encountering some new discourse on "the angry voter" (a *Time* cover story in early March) or "the American angst" (Taylor 1992) and, indeed, survey after ubiquitous survey seemed to leave little doubt that voters *were* angry. Consider the following examples drawn from Times Mirror polls conducted between January and September:[3]

- *National priorities (June)*: A resounding 88 percent believed that "we should pay less attention to problems overseas and concentrate on problems here at home" (though 91 percent took the potentially contradictory position that "it's best for the future of our country to be active in world affairs").
- *The president (June)*: George Bush's job-approval ratings dropped to 32 percent (versus 57 percent disapproval), compared with 77 percent in May 1991.
- *Congress (June)*: Only 37 percent claimed that Congress was "having mainly a good influence on the way things are going in this country" (versus 49 percent who said "mainly a bad influence").
- *Incumbents in general (June)*: Eighty-four percent agreed that "it is time for Washington politicians to step aside and make room for new leaders," and 56 percent went a step further to say that "we need new people in Washington even if they are not as effective as experienced politicians."
- *Political parties and the electoral process (June-July)*: Forty-one percent (up from 27 percent in January) weren't sure or didn't believe that either party could do a better job of handling whatever was thought to be the country's most important problem, and 24 percent indicated that it was *very* likely (plus another 30 percent saying *possibly* likely) they would vote "none of the above" if such an option were available on the fall ballot.[4]
- *Politics as a profession (June)*: A mere 27 percent said they would like to have their son, daughter, or other family member "go into politics as a career" (versus 63 percent who would not).

Of course, politics and politicians were not the only targets of citizen discontent in 1992 (cf. Lipset and Schneider 1987):

- *Direction of the country (January)*: Twenty-eight percent said they were satisfied (versus 68 percent dissatisfied) with "the way things are going" in the United States at the present time; 38 percent believed the national economy was in a depression that would "last a long time" (versus 51 percent saying "short-term recession" and 7 percent who felt that economic "recovery" was already under way).

- *Big business (June)*: Seventy-seven percent felt "there is too much power concentrated in the hands of a few big companies"; just 40 percent agreed (versus 56 percent who disagreed) that "business corporations generally strike a fair balance between making profits and serving the public interest."
- *The media (September)*: More than 80 percent maintained that members of the news media (often or sometimes) "let their own political preferences influence the way they report the news."
- *The American dream (June)*: Seventy-eight percent agreed (38 percent "completely" and 40 percent "mostly") with the statement that "today it's really true that the rich just get richer while the poor get poorer."

Voters, then, appeared to be in a fairly nasty mood as the campaign got under way—and, judging from Ross Perot's 19 percent of the presidential vote (the best showing for a third-party or independent candidate since 1912) and the 14-for-14 sweep on state term-limitation proposals, they stayed that way until the bitter end.

Nevertheless, we would do well not to jump too quickly onto the disaffection bandwagon. Incumbents who seek reelection continue to win much more often than not (Jacobson 1993; Hershey 1993) and even in 1992, when many voters initially expressed unhappiness with the entire field of presidential contenders, a majority "ended up both liking their [preferred] candidates and feeling good about the process. Although they often despaired over the available choices, by election day they were both more intrigued and more satisfied than in any recent election year" (Frankovic 1993, p. 126; also see Quirk and Dalager 1993). There also is ample evidence to suggest that the average person remains relatively satisfied with most aspects of his or her private life (including marriage, family, children's future, job, friends, housing, and neighborhood; e.g., Hamilton and Wright 1986; Inglehart 1988; but cf. Kanter and Mirvis 1989).[5]

In the June 1992 Times Mirror survey, 58 percent of the public said they were "pretty well satisfied with the way things are going for me financially" (versus 41 percent who felt otherwise).[6] As for what the future might hold, 66 percent agreed that "as Americans, we can always find a way to solve our problems and get what we want," and 58 percent denied that there are "any real limits to growth in this country today." Numbers such as these led some analysts to conclude that the latest outburst of election-year "angst" was superficial and overblown, in large measure reflecting the mass media's portrayal of a national economic climate that was bad—but not nearly as bad as people were being told. According to Everett Ladd (1992, p. 7), "[w]hen asked about things they know about through first-hand experience—how they themselves are doing economically, their satisfaction with the work they do, how things are going in their own communities, etc.—Americans appear anything but negative and pessimistic. For the most part . . . it's only when questions focus on things that people can't assess from personal observation and must rely on the pictures which the media supplies, that a marked down-turn in mood in recent months is evident."[7]

Ladd's assessment recalls that of Jack Citrin (1974, p. 984), whose examination of declining public trust in the late 1960s and early 1970s persuaded him that the cynical answers given by respondents to many standard survey questions "merely record opposition to incumbent officeholders or largely ritualistic expressions of fashionable clichés." Subsequently, Citrin and coauthor Donald Philip Green (1986; also see Miller and Borrelli 1991) attributed the temporary rise in aggregate trust levels during Ronald Reagan's first term primarily to an improving economy and to the "persona" or "perceived character" of the president—in particular, the widespread belief that Reagan was a stronger and more effective leader than his immediate predecessor.

I would argue, however, that the so-called confidence gap (Lipset and Schneider 1987) is neither as shallow as Citrin and Ladd apparently believe nor as contemporary in its origins as the steady media drumbeats of 1990 and 1992 might imply. The latter point is illustrated nicely by the trend lines for four questions used in public opinion surveys, including the American National Election Study (ANES) series employed throughout the remainder of this chapter,[8] to measure citizens' feelings of *trust in government*:

How much of the time do you think you can trust the government in Washington to do what is right—just about always, most of the time, or only some of the time?

Do you think that people in the government waste a lot of the money we pay in taxes, waste some of it, or don't waste very much of it?

Would you say the government is pretty much run by a few big interests looking out for themselves or that it is run for the benefit of all the people?

Do you think that quite a few of the people running the government are crooked, not very many are, or do you think hardly any of them are crooked at all?

The over-time trends displayed in Figure 3.1 reveal a sharp rise in aggregate levels of popular *mis*trust beginning in the mid-1960s, followed by a partial turnaround in 1980–1984—but then renewed disaffection during the second half of the decade and into the 1990s. Whereas most of this increased negativism probably reflects shifting evaluations of decisionmaking in Washington (Craig 1993), it is unlikely that any level, any branch, or any major institution of government has managed totally to escape the wrath of citizens during this tumultuous period.[9]

Perhaps "wrath"—along with "anger," "angst," "disaffection," "alienation," and their synonyms—is too strong a word for the kinds of attitudinal changes I am describing. Virtually all available evidence suggests that feelings of national pride and support for the political system as a whole remain quite robust: In the 1987

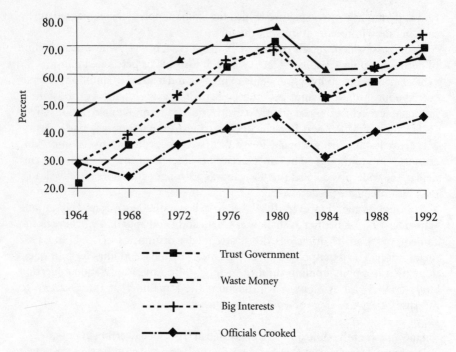

FIGURE 3.1   Trends in Political Mistrust, 1964–1992. *Source:* American National Election Studies, 1964–1992. See Appendix for question wordings. Trend lines indicate the proportion of all respondents who say that (a) the government in Washington can be trusted to do what is right "only some" or "none" of the time; (b) "a lot" of the money we pay in taxes is wasted; (c) the government is run by "a few big interests looking out for themselves"; and (d) "quite a few" of people in government are a little crooked.

ANES pilot study, more than 90 percent of those interviewed agreed with the statements that "whatever its faults may be, the American form of government is still the best for us" and "I would rather live under our system of government than any other I can think of";[10] similar proportions expressed pride in being an American and, despite some genuine misgivings about the efficacy of elections, allowed that "voting is an effective way for people to have a say about what the government does" (Craig, Niemi, and Silver 1990). When these findings are considered with the Times Mirror results presented earlier concerning personal life satisfaction and faith in America's collective future as a nation, it is tempting to conclude that the crisis of confidence in government is not much of a crisis after all. They certainly belie the notion that popular discontent in the United States significantly boosts the potential for mass mobilization and for "revolutionary alteration of the political and social system" (Miller 1974, p. 951).

What, then, are we to make of the anti-incumbency sentiment that has become such a central element of American political discourse in the 1990s? Is it simply an outgrowth of the nation's long-standing, if qualified (see Free and Cantril

1967; Bennett and Bennett 1990), commitment to the principles of individualism and limited government? Should it be viewed (if I may borrow from a particularly colorful characterization of the electorate's flirtation with Ross Perot in 1992) as something akin to "a national temper tantrum"[11]—real enough, yet lacking in intensity and based mainly on voter misperceptions, media distortions, and the rantings of opportunistic, self-serving politicians (cf. Fenno 1978)? Or can the current wave of ill feeling be understood as nothing more than the reasonable and perfectly healthy response of people living in a time when elected officials are doing an unusually poor job of dealing with important societal problems?

In his original essay on declining trust, Citrin (1974, p. 987; cf. Lipset and Schneider 1987, p. 399) employed a sports analogy to make the point that "political systems, like baseball teams, have slumps and winning streaks. Having recently endured a succession of losing seasons, Americans boo the home team when it takes the field. But fans are often fickle; victories quickly elicit cheers. And to most fans what matters is whether the home team wins or loses, not how it plays the game. According to this analysis, a modest 'winning streak' and, perhaps, some new faces in the lineup may be sufficient to raise the level of trust in government." After nearly thirty years, though, one must wonder whether we are reaching a point at which the repeated failure of U.S. leaders to mount anything close to a *sustained* winning streak (modest or otherwise) threatens to erode "even the strongest underlying bonds of attachment" among citizens (Easton 1975, p. 445). If the "new faces" of the Clinton and subsequent administrations fail to produce broadly acceptable policy outcomes—and given the scope and magnitude of problems they face, their challenge in doing so is enormous—will the American public continue to grumble and complain yet still wait more or less patiently (without ever giving up hope) for the home team to turn things around?

Maybe, maybe not. In the following section I try to provide some useful clues as to the nature and meaning of contemporary discontent by, first, showing that feelings of political mistrust have become diffused throughout the mass public since the 1960s (as opposed to their being concentrated within one narrow segment of the population) and, second, explaining (based on evidence from my previous research using open-ended depth interviews rather than the standard large-sample surveys; see Craig 1993) how such a thing could have happened. Then, with this discussion in mind, I speculate as to whether recent developments (and especially those associated with the 1992 elections) hold out any realistic hope for a restoration of public confidence in the foreseeable future.

THE ORIGINS OF DISCONTENT

The Confidence Gap, 1964–1992

My earlier analysis of ANES data from 1964 through 1988 (Craig 1993, pp. 29ff.) yielded a number of not very surprising conclusions, including that (1) liberals/ Democrats tend to evaluate government less favorably during conservative/

Republican administrations, and vice versa; (2) those who believe that major governmental actors and institutions are doing a poor job or (3) who worry about the direction of the country in general, or of the economy (and their own personal financial situation) in particular, tend to express more negative views than those who feel otherwise; and (4) individuals who attribute certain politically relevant character traits to the president (e.g., that he is a strong leader, honest, and cares about "people like me") tend to be less cynical than those who do not. Yet none of these relationships are terribly strong—and none can adequately explain why declining trust has occurred pretty much across the board (that is, within virtually every identifiable demographic and political segment of the population) since the early 1960s.

Consider, for example, the results presented in Table 3.1. Several groups were predictably more cynical than others in both 1964 and 1992: out-party identifiers (Republicans during the Kennedy-Johnson years, Democrats in the Bush administration), supporters of nonincumbent candidates for president (Goldwater and Clinton-Perot voters, respectively),[12] individuals who believed that the government in Washington had become too powerful, and those whose family financial situation had recently worsened. Yet the most compelling pattern we see here is that levels of mistrust increased sharply among *all categories* of partisan identifiers and presidential voters, among those who felt the federal government had too much power *and* those who did not, among persons whose personal finances had improved or stayed the same *and* those whose situation had deteriorated—as well as among self-reported voters *and* nonvoters, the politically involved *and* uninvolved, those who believed that either the Democrats or the Republicans were better able to handle the nation's most important problem *and* those who saw no difference between the parties, plus every one of the sociodemographic groupings listed in Table 3.1 (the young and the old, women and men, whites and blacks, those with a college education and those without). Over time, the confidence gap clearly has become pervasive in American society.

This observation is reinforced by the data in Table 3.2, which shows only comparisons drawn from the 1992 ANES survey. Although some kinds of people (e.g., those who gave the president and/or Congress poor performance ratings, those who believed that the country was on the "wrong track" or who felt the national economy was getting worse) were a good bit less trusting than others, it is difficult to find any group whose overall evaluations of government were not predominantly negative. Between one-half and two-thirds of respondents who said the country was headed in the "right direction" (55.0 percent), who approved of the job being done by President Bush (66.3 percent) or by Congress (53.2 percent), who believed that the nation's economic situation was improving (58.6 percent), or who opposed term limits on elected officials (64.6 percent) were nonetheless classified as "very" mistrustful. In addition, cynical orientations were extremely common among liberals (75.6 percent), moderates (73.7 percent), and conservatives (75.0 percent) alike; among those with pro-life (72.1 percent) and pro-

TABLE 3.1   Change in Political Mistrust, 1964 to 1992

	1964		1992	
Party identification				
Democrat	21.6%	(679)	74.3%	(738)
Independent	31.4%	(271)	77.0%	(792)
Republican	37.1%	(299)	69.2%	(529)
Presidential vote				
Democrat	17.1%	(665)	76.0%	(745)
Independent	–		79.5%	(292)
Republican	47.1%	(308)	71.3%	(516)
Does government in Washington have too much power?				
Too powerful	43.1%	(385)	85.3%	(853)
Not too strong	16.0%	(475)	65.0%	(351)
Political interest				
Most of the time	32.6%	(387)	77.8%	(554)
Some of the time	23.6%	(543)	74.0%	(883)
Only now and then	27.6%	(210)	70.2%	(436)
Hardly at all	25.4%	(126)	72.7%	(198)
Election turnout				
Voted	26.5%	(990)	75.2%	(1,586)
Did not vote	29.6%	(277)	70.1%	(492)
Which political party is better for dealing with the most important problem facing the country?				
Democrats/Republicans	26.2%	(713)	75.6%	(975)
No difference	28.8%	(260)	74.7%	(858)
Personal finances				
Better off	23.0%	(600)	68.7%	(635)
Same	28.7%	(492)	75.2%	(711)
Worse off	37.0%	(173)	77.4%	(727)
Respondent age				
17–24	23.1%	(91)	63.8%	(188)
25–39	24.8%	(404)	73.4%	(779)
40–59	26.8%	(526)	74.2%	(612)
60 and over	33.3%	(243)	78.6%	(500)

(continues)

TABLE 3.1 (continued)

	1964		1992	
Respondent education				
Less than high school	29.8%	(537)	67.1%	(365)
High school grad	23.3%	(430)	75.4%	(682)
Some college	28.0%	(293)	75.8%	(980)
Respondent gender				
Male	27.0%	(564)	73.8%	(975)
Female	27.3%	(703)	74.2%	(1,104)
Respondent race				
White	27.9%	(1,120)	75.1%	(1,751)
Black	21.7%	(138)	72.3%	(260)

NOTE: See Appendix for question wordings. Table entries, based on 100%, are the proportion of each group scoring as "very mistrustful/cynical" (16 and above on a scale with scores ranging from 4 to 20). Numbers in parentheses are raw unweighted N's.

SOURCE: American National Election Studies, 1964 and 1992.

choice (75.9 percent) views on abortion; among the rich (73.9 percent) as well as the poor (69.9 percent); among regular churchgoers (75.5 percent) as well as the least actively religious (74.4 percent); and among both working-class (76.4 percent) and middle-class (71.7 percent) identifiers.

With such consistent numbers, one might reasonably conclude that there are *many* bases for the tension that exists today between rulers and ruled in the United States, i.e., that different kinds of people are unhappy for different reasons. This does not, however, tell us as much as we would like to know about the intensity and centrality of discontent to citizens' worldviews and to their overall orientations toward government, about the reasons for the apparent staying power of contemporary discontent (especially when support for the regime and political community remains high), or about the likely consequences (presumably short of revolutionary upheaval) if effective steps are not taken to resolve the problem. In an effort to begin filling in some of the blanks, I decided to approach the topic from a somewhat different perspective than that afforded by mass opinion surveys.

Conversations with Citizens

In a report prepared for the Kettering Foundation based on focus-group sessions held around the country during 1990 and 1991, the American public was described as having experienced "a widespread public reaction against the political system. This reaction is more than the familiar attacks on individual politicians, incumbents, big government, party politics and corruption. It is a reaction against a political system that is perceived as so autonomous that the public is no longer able to control and direct it. People talk as though our political system has been taken over by alien beings." Despite having a strong sense of pride in their politi-

TABLE 3.2   Distribution of Political Mistrust, 1992

Ideological identification			Term limits		
Liberal	75.6%	(438)	Favor	77.3%	(1,518)
Moderate	73.7%	(495)	Oppose	64.6%	(336)
Conservative	75.0%	(629)			
			Views on abortion		
President job approval			Always permit	75.9%	(960)
Approve	66.3%	(855)	Restrict abortions	72.1%	(1,074)
Disapprove	79.4%	(1,186)			
			Family income		
Congress job approval			$0–$14,999	69.9%	(502)
Approve	53.2%	(588)	$15,000–$24,999	74.4%	(316)
Disapprove	83.5%	(1,348)	$25,000–$39,999	77.9%	(429)
			$40,000–$59,000	73.0%	(370)
Direction of country			$60,000 and over	73.9%	(333)
Right direction	55.0%	(342)			
Wrong track	77.8%	(1,678)	Church attendance		
			Every week	75.5%	(551)
National economy			Occasionally	72.7%	(520)
Better	58.6%	(87)	Seldom/never	74.4%	(309)
Same	66.0%	(471)			
Worse	77.3%	(1,509)	Social class identification		
			Working class	76.4%	(1,043)
			Middle class	71.7%	(971)

NOTE: See Appendix for question wordings. Table entries, based on 100%, are the proportion of each group scoring as "very mistrustful/cynical" (16 and above on a scale with scores ranging from 4 to 20). Numbers in parentheses are raw unweighted N's.

SOURCE: American National Election Study, 1992.

cal heritage, "many Americans do not believe they are living in a democracy now! They don't believe that 'We, the people' actually rule. They . . . describe the present political system as [being] impervious to public direction, a system run by a professional political class and controlled by money, not votes. What is more, people do not believe this system is able to solve the pressing problems they face" (Kettering Foundation 1991, pp. iii–iv).

The Kettering report is interesting, in part, because its conclusions were reached through a methodology—small-group discussions—that is seldom employed by political scientists (but see Conover, Crewe, and Searing 1991) and has almost never been applied to the study of discontent.[13] Also, no survey-based research with which I am familiar describes the public temper in such emphatically negative terms or places quite as much emphasis on the role of attitudes toward *participation* and *democratic responsiveness* in shaping citizens' feelings about incumbent leaders and governmental institutions.

Is the report accurate? Due to the small and unrepresentative samples involved, it is difficult to say—which happens to be the great drawback of focus

groups, depth interviews, and qualitative research in general. Yet whatever its limitations, a qualitative approach has the advantage of allowing respondents to talk
with us in ways that surveys do not, to express beliefs and opinions that are more
complex and more subtle than the traditional ANES and Times Mirror questions
can ever hope to capture. This type of research does run the risk of attributing to
the broader American public an outlook that it does not have, but the potential
for discovery is considerable. And discovery was a central aim in my earlier work
utilizing two sets of depth interviews (twenty conducted from November 1984 to
December 1986, eight during summer and fall 1992 when the presidential campaign was in full sway) with residents of the city of Gainesville and other, generally more rural areas of Alachua County, Florida (see Craig 1993).

No pretense will be made that the Alachua sample is in any way representative
of the broader American public, or even of the specific community from which it
was drawn, though special care was taken to ensure that I did not end up with a
group consisting solely of political sophisticates. In fact, few had been active to
any significant degree and these were balanced by a like number whose level of
attentiveness could be described as, at best, minimal; most fell into what might be
called the "spectator" category (see Milbrath 1965), though even here there was
substantial variation in respondents' interest, information, and understanding of
politics and political issues.

Data limitations aside, my hope is that these open-ended conversations with
ordinary citizens can help us to understand better what it means to be "mistrustful" of government in the 1990s. I should acknowledge up front that Alachuans,
almost without exception, exhibited strong support for both the regime and the
political community (Easton 1965): they were proud to be Americans (while
occasionally mentioning aspects of social or political life that they "were not so
proud of," e.g., abortion, drugs, homelessness, abuse of the environment), had
difficulty imagining they would ever leave the United States to live in another
country, and generally felt that our political system needed, at most, minor alterations (Sniderman 1981). But if there was little dissatisfaction with "the system"
as a whole,[14] Alachua County residents expressed considerable disdain for the
profession of politics (see Mitchell 1959) and for the behavior of individual incumbents, candidates, bureaucrats, campaign advisers, lobbyists, party leaders, and
others who regularly engage in it.

In seeking to identify the basis for such negativism, what I looked for in the
interviews was evidence of widely shared images or beliefs that cut across partisan, ideological, and policy lines and were not tied to relatively narrow performance judgments. My hypothesis was simply that *discontent is a function of the
perceived fit between one's expectations and the performance of political leaders,
institutions, and/or processes.* In other words, the incidence of negative orientations toward government should increase as larger numbers of citizens come to
believe that their substantive, symbolic, or procedural demands (or "politicized
values"; see Schwartz 1973) are being frustrated by governmental decisionmakers,
or by the system itself.

Along these lines, Bernard Barber (1983, p. 9, emphasis added) identified two types of demands that people often make upon their leaders: One relates to the expectation of *technically competent role performance* and the other to the expectation that leaders "will carry out their *fiduciary obligations and responsibilities, that is, their duties in certain situations to place others' interests before their own.*" Whereas Barber (p. 82) maintained that declining trust in the U.S. government probably has had more to do with the technical competence dimension (cf. Citrin 1974), Karl Lamb (1974, p. 201) concluded from his interviews with residents of Orange County, California, that suspicions about political leadership frequently centered around the notion that politics is "dirty" and the belief that too many politicians "serve specific and limited interests, including their own personal welfare, rather than the interests of the whole."[15]

My reading of the Alachua County materials follows closely Lamb's California results. Asked about the return we get on our tax dollars (see the ANES "waste money" question in Figure 3.1), virtually all respondents agreed that at least *some* money is wasted by the government, primarily due either to wrongheaded spending decisions (e.g., liberals who were offended by what they saw as the misguided priorities of the Reagan-Bush era, conservatives who wanted the government to do more about overly generous giveaway programs and social spending in general) or to simple inefficiency (e.g., too much bureaucracy and red tape, a government establishment that is too big and too complex to be run the way it should be).[16] Several Alachuans, however, saw other factors at work as well, e.g., dishonesty, pork-barrel politics, and the perquisites of incumbency ("overseas travel, social functions, lavish offices, and big staffs" in the words of one person). I also encountered the same themes, having more to do with fiduciary obligations than with technical competence, over and over again in answers to two of the other ANES trust questions ("officials crooked" and "big interests") cited earlier.

It is perhaps encouraging that neither Alachuans nor, judging from the percentages for "officials crooked" in Figure 3.1, the broader American public is of the opinion that most politicians are on the take. Yet politics is widely viewed as an arena in which thieves and scoundrels *can* ply their trade without too much danger of being caught—and even those individuals who doubt that there is rampant corruption typically have the sense that politics is somehow different, that crooks are a minority but the incidence of dishonesty is nonetheless a good bit higher than we would find in almost any other line of work. Further, there is a sizable segment for whom the real problem stems not from the desire of politicians to attain personal wealth (or power[17]) so much as from their readiness to compromise, make deals, pander to special interests, and divide up the available pork in ways that do little to benefit the country as a whole. Such behavior is often regarded as being every bit as "crooked" (and as injurious to the common good) as taking a bribe, and it clearly contributes to the perception of politics as being a less honest endeavor than citizens have a right to expect.[18]

In addition, roughly three-quarters of Alachuans explicitly stated that the U.S. government is "pretty much run by a few big interests looking out for themselves"—or, at a minimum, that certain powerful interests have a distinct advantage even though they do not always get what they want. Some respondents mentioned that it is perfectly natural for groups to pursue favorable policy outcomes and that no matter what the rest of us might think, the Constitution gives them the right to do so. But the Constitution does not compel reelection-obsessed incumbents to attend more to the needs of the wealthy and well-organized than they do to the general welfare. As one woman explained to me, groups can have influence only "if the person in government allows [them] to have influence." And it is not only pursuit of the general welfare that is important here; it is also *the obligation of leaders to be attentive to the wishes of voters who elected them in the first place.* In a political culture such as our own, where the democratic norms of popular participation and governmental responsiveness are highly valued (Almond and Verba 1963; McClosky and Zaller 1984), we can expect that "feelings of powerlessness toward public authority [will] tend to create feelings of hostility toward that authority" (Stokes 1962, p. 67; also see Madsen 1987).

Now, let me be clear: Alachuans did not feel altogether powerless to influence the actions of their elected representatives. At times, an underlying faith in the effectiveness of collective action—i.e., the belief that, sufficiently aroused, large numbers of ordinary citizens might be able to overcome the system's normal bias in favor of special interests—was manifest on answers to a variety of questions. Yet even those who anticipated a reasonably high level of governmental responsiveness on most occasions (and not all of them did) were reluctant to depend solely upon the goodwill of leaders. I was told, for example, that public officials don't really care what people think "but they know they sort of have to listen" and "they're gonna get axed" if they don't. On the surface, this "coercive" (as opposed to "voluntary"; see Craig 1993) view of responsiveness is consistent with popular expectations of governmental accountability: Politicians may not want to listen but they can be *forced* to listen as long as we are prepared to exercise our rights as citizens—first and foremost, the right to vote.

Still, I hesitate to carry the argument too far for a couple of reasons. First, many respondents were less than pleased that elites must be "coerced" into doing what is, after all, their job. And second, recent surveys show that the American public as a whole has decidedly mixed feelings about the principal mechanism through which coercion is exercised, i.e., voting and elections. In the mid-to-late 1980s, although 90 percent said that voting is "an effective way for people to have a say in what the government does," just over one-third indicated that having elections does "a good deal" to make government "pay attention to what the people think" (Craig 1993); also, 63 percent agreed that "those we [elect] to public office usually try to keep the promises they have made during the election,"[19] compared with 76 percent who believed that "to win elections, most candidates for Congress make campaign promises they have no intentions of fulfilling" (*Public Opinion* 1986, p. 22).

Based on its 1990–1991 focus groups, the Kettering Foundation (1991, p. 21) concluded that "[a]ll the hoopla, speeches, money, propaganda, and sundry other aspects of political campaigns lead Americans to one fundamental thought, which a Richmond man put this way: 'Questions do come out of campaigns . . . people begin to ask: "What's wrong with our system?"' The answer, according to group participants, is virtually everything." Among the problems cited were spiraling campaign costs, negative ads (mudslinging), candidates who duck the issues and make promises that are never meant to be kept, media coverage that is typically "driven by sound bites and negativism," and so on (pp. 21–28).

In my local sample, there were a few individuals whose faith in the coercive power of elections—and of citizen participation generally—was nearly unshakable, but most betrayed a deep *ambivalence* about the potential for democratic accountability in American politics. The electorate was seen as having superior numbers on its side, and sometimes that is enough to produce meaningful results. However, the dominant tone of these interviews was one of considerable (and possibly growing) uncertainty and doubt, more hope than conviction that our representative system is working as intended. Elections do matter, but their impact is diminished when voters are frequently bamboozled by candidates who promise what they cannot deliver and are adept at playing the public relations game. Other forms of collective action are potentially effective as well, but they require a degree of patience and perseverance that the average person does not possess. The frustration and outrage engendered by this state of affairs seems to be at the core of contemporary discontent, in Alachua County and elsewhere, and it is likely one of the main reasons that a deep mistrust of government now cuts across the entire political spectrum from left to right and everywhere in between.

Time for a Change

Alachua County respondents certainly would have welcomed a higher level of technical competence in government, including elected officials who put their native intelligence to good use (Craig 1993) and programs that give us something close to our money's worth in terms of the benefits provided. More than anything else, though, these Floridians wanted decisionmakers to live up to their fiduciary obligation "to place others' interests before their own" (Barber 1983, p. 9)—something that, by and large, they did not believe they were getting. In fact, the Alachuans with whom I spoke in 1992 were even more predisposed than their 1984–1986 counterparts to complain that today's leaders have grown out of touch with the needs and desires of ordinary citizens and (one or two exceptions notwithstanding) that their commitment to action on behalf of the "common good" is far less than it should be. There also was continuing dissatisfaction with the effectiveness of elections as instruments of popular control. For example,

Pearl Kennedy (moderate Democrat, on the intelligence of those running the government): They must be smart to get in there, saying they're gonna do all of this . . . but when they get elected, none of it happens.

Miriam Jackson (conservative Republican, on the same topic): The really smart ones, the ones who should be there, don't run because they don't want to put up with the mudslinging and go through the kind of campaigns like we're having right now . . . where they go out and dig up every bit of dirt they can about you, your uncle, your great-grandmother, and the horse-thief cousin you have, just to discredit you.

Kyle Lefferts (Independent and apolitical, on the challenge of casting an informed vote): Well, there are a lot of things that candidates promise to do, and they make so many different promises that you won't remember some of the few that really count. They sort of go, like . . . start at A and go around to Z, and by the time they get to Z you've done forgot the other half.

Frank DiPalma (liberal Democrat, on whether government is too powerful): If anything, maybe the opposite is true . . . the way they get themselves tied up with all these fringe issues. A lot of it has to do with how people are elected, having to raise so much money and being beholden to those who contribute. It really distorts the system.

Andrew Simms (moderate Democrat, on citizens using the electoral process to force change): It just seems like we're always electing the lesser of two evils—this one hasn't done anything so we'll try that one for awhile, then back and forth. And once they're in office, the Democrats end up fighting with the Republicans. . . . I mean, it's like they battle between right and wrong. They get there and all they do is clash.

Raymond Kinnick (moderate Independent, on the need for term limits): I think the people in office need to find some courage, which they haven't shown much of lately. . . . They always seem to vote whatever path will help them to be reelected. Too many of them approach it as just a job, and it's time for some fresh ideas.[20]

If anything had changed in 1992, it was the greater willingness of respondents to acknowledge that the failure of our electoral institutions may be at least partly—and maybe primarily—the fault of citizens for allowing themselves to be repeatedly hoodwinked by duplicitous politicians and for failing to stand up and insist that their voices be heard. A lack of faith in "the people" can be seen in one woman's impatience with those who do not vote ("a lot of them don't care who they put in there"); in a Perot supporter's observation that Americans often look for "instant gratification" from their elected leaders ("most people don't know what's best for the country, especially those who want something for nothing"); in a longtime state government employee's lament that much of the time, "I think we get exactly the leadership we deserve"; and in a middle-aged secretary's outright anger at the public's unwillingness to assume responsibility for their actions ("we've elected these people, we've let them run rampant, and that's why our country is in the shape it's in").

The good news is that even the most cynical Alachuans were not ready to throw in the towel completely. Some political analysts concluded after the 1992 election was over that "[i]n his bizarre way [Ross] Perot contributed more to preserving faith in the electoral process than [either] Clinton or Bush."[21] The two Perot supporters whom I interviewed agreed, as did a few of my other respondents. Miriam Jackson, in particular, managed to combine a strong sense of disaffection with a stubborn refusal to give up hope; asked whether ordinary citizens are truly able to influence the actions of decisionmakers, she replied, "Yes, if we yell loud enough and demand loud enough, and if we've got guts enough to talk with anybody who will listen. It's damn hard and most of the time you're going to beat your head against the brick wall, but if you don't do it then you're giving up."

Indeed, events in 1992—e.g., Perot's candidacy and perhaps Clinton's as well; continued momentum for the term-limits movement; the emergence of alternative media (from Larry King et al. to MTV's Rock the Vote campaign) as channels of political communication; a presidential debate in which participants were openly scolded for their failure to address issues of concern to voters;[22] the defeat or semivoluntary retirement of numerous incumbents at every level—apparently helped to persuade many Americans that their fierce commitment to representative government was not entirely misplaced. In addition to voter turnout rates going up nationwide for the first time in over thirty years (from about 50 percent to 55 percent of those eligible to cast ballots in the presidential race; see Chapter 6), an examination of the 1992 ANES survey reveals several other interesting developments (Figure 3.2):

- Although there was virtually no change in overall perceptions of governmental responsiveness between 1988 and 1992,[23] the proportion indicating that having elections does "a good deal" to *make* government pay attention to popular preferences jumped from 36.8 percent to 46.3 percent.
- More Americans exhibited a strong sense of *internal efficacy;* they believed themselves to have the necessary skills and qualifications to participate effectively in politics (apart from any reservations they might also have had about the likely attentiveness of leaders to their efforts).[24]
- Confronted with a list of four possible *future goals* for the nation (see Inglehart 1977), the proportion whose top priority was to give "the people more say in important political decisions" rose from 27.4 percent in 1988 to 34.7 percent four years later.

Shifts of this magnitude are hardly earth-shattering, but along with higher turnout, they do represent something new in American politics. It is as though a portion of the electorate said to itself, "Enough! Things are a mess and they aren't going to change unless people like me decide to do something. We are *qualified* to participate, we *need* to get involved so that leaders can be held in check, and there's actually a chance that, together, we will be able to *make a difference*." Moreover, the assertive mood of the election year carried over into 1993 and beyond with unprecedented numbers of citizens making telephone calls to the White House or to Capitol Hill, sending Western Union opiniongram messages to let

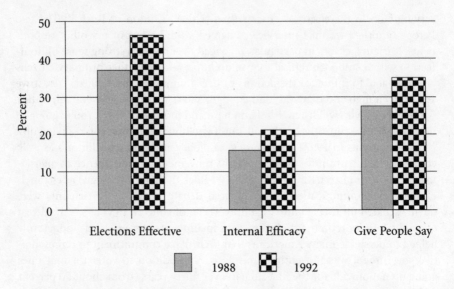

FIGURE 3.2   Change in Citizen Attitudes Toward Political Involvement, 1988–1992.
Source: American National Election Studies, 1988 and 1992. See Appendix for question wordings.
Figures refer to the proportion of all respondents who (a) say that elections do "a good deal" to make the government pay
the attention to what people think; (b) register as "highly efficacious" (8 and below on a scale with scores ranging from 4 to
20); and (c) rank giving people "more say in the important political decisions" as one of the two most desirable future goals
that the nation might pursue.

government officials know how they felt about some issue, attending town meetings in their local communities, or engaging in other limited and not-so-limited
forms of grassroots activism (see Georges 1993; Meacham 1993; cf. Greider 1992).

What remains to be seen is whether this burst of energy can be sustained, or
whether it is little more than a brief and temporary respite from our long slide
toward widespread popular estrangement from all things political. As James
Sundquist (quoted in Lipset and Schneider 1987, p. 400) has observed, "The people expect the government to control events. After all, candidates for office keep
promising that it can do so. They go on insisting that elections make a difference.
So each time an election does not, it adds to the disillusionment." For the moment, Americans still believe that the system can be made to work—at least in
extraordinary circumstances, when constituents *force* leaders to attend to their
wants and needs. The danger is that more disappointments will raise the tension
between rulers and ruled to the point at which, short of dramatic system change,
a restoration of public trust becomes almost impossible to achieve (see Easton
1975). Unless decisionmakers get that message and get it fairly soon, the call for
term limits may turn out to have been just the beginning.[25]

CONCLUSION

It is difficult to know exactly what might be done to prevent the confidence gap from becoming a permanent feature of the American political landscape. None of the "reforms" either enacted or proposed in recent years—e.g., limiting the number of terms that elected officials can serve, imposing tax ceilings on state legislatures (or passing a balanced-budget amendment to the U.S. Constitution), prohibiting Congress from awarding itself an immediate pay raise (the Twenty-seventh Amendment), making wider use of initiative and referendum elections, changing state and federal campaign finance laws (public funding, spending caps, eliminating PACs, free television time for candidates or parties), requiring strict financial disclosure from individuals who hold key government positions, using independent special prosecutors to pursue wrongdoers, etc.—are apt to have a huge effect, though some may serve the symbolic purpose of supplying an outlet for the disaffected to vent their anger at politicians who are seen as being remote and inaccessible. Nor do increased opportunities for grassroots activism appear to be a realistic solution, since even today, only a relatively small proportion of the population is ready to make the sort of personal commitment that such activism requires.

Yet in the end, responsibility for closing the confidence gap rests mainly with the people themselves. Only the people can ensure that their tax dollars are spent for quality education and health care rather than for savings and loan bailouts and costly pork-barrel projects that do nothing to advance the common good. Only the people can punish officials who vote to raise their own pay and accept favors from special interests but fail to address a budget deficit that is spiraling out of control. Only the people can do something about incumbents who spend hundreds of thousands or even millions of dollars getting reelected but have no real grasp of the problems that are troubling their constituents. Only the people can prevent candidates from promising voters expensive new programs and tax cuts as well or from running predominately negative campaigns based on gross distortions of their opponents' records. Only the people can challenge the hypocrisy of politicians who call for being tough on criminals but then fail to commit adequate resources to our already overburdened law enforcement, judicial, and penal systems. And only the people can insist that lawmakers draw legislative district boundaries in such a way that the diverse interests of different geographic areas (and of the voters living in them) are fairly represented. Citizens today expect a lot from government, and unfortunately, not everyone is going to get everything they want; this is the essential nature of politics, especially during periods when money is tight and hard choices must be made about the kinds of activities that can be supported.

Budget constraints aside, however, for broadly acceptable outcomes (Citrin 1974) to be realized in just about any area—and whatever the obstacles facing decisionmakers, there surely is room for improvement in most of them—the

public must become more fully engaged in the political process. Let me emphasize here that I am *not* necessarily calling for the creation of new participatory
opportunities; critics are naive to think that structural and procedural reforms
such as term limits, referendum elections, easier voter registration, and publicly
funded campaigns will suddenly produce a better crop of leaders than the ones we
have right now (cf. Morone 1990). It is unfair to assign all blame for recent failures of our government to "the people," but I would argue that "the people" must
share at least a portion of that blame—and, more to the point, that any restoration of trust depends upon the willingness of the politically inert rank and file to
take seriously both the rights *and* the obligations of democratic citizenship, e.g.,
the obligation to be well informed, to participate, to use one's vote to reward
politicians who pursue the common good and punish those who do not.

Even the majority of Alachuans who shied away from direct personal involvement seemed to acknowledge (if sometimes reluctantly) the effectiveness of collective action. They wished that democratic responsiveness were more easily
attained and that close supervision were not required to ensure that leaders are
technically competent and committed to fulfilling their fiduciary obligations—
but they were not totally oblivious to the centrality of their own role as citizens. In
his scathing account of Washington pork-barrel politics, Brian Kelly (1992, p.
255) concluded that taxpayer dollars will continue to be wasted "until the simple
part of the problem is addressed. Namely, the voters have to say it's time for a
change. Ultimately, the blame and the responsibility for the system belong on all
of us. . . . Or, in the famous words of Joseph de Maistre, 'Every country has the
government it deserves.' " So, too, with any hopes of putting to an end the various
other types of elite behavior that have caused Americans to lose faith in their governmental leaders and institutions: Nothing is likely to change until the public
decides that enough is enough. If and when it does, the necessary participatory
structures are already in place.

NOTES

An earlier version of this chapter was presented at the 1993 Annual Meetings of the
Midwest Political Science Association, Chicago, Illinois.

1. Such sentiment did not lead at once to dramatic turnover either in Congress or in the
states, though some voters apparently did find ways to translate their dissatisfaction into
electoral action; for example, the average vote for both Democratic and Republican incumbent House members dropped off in 1990 to its lowest level since the Watergate election of
1974 (Jacobson 1993, p. 161).

2. These data, from a postelection survey conducted by William R. Hamilton and Staff
of Washington, D.C., were made available by the Florida Institute for Research on Elections, Department of Political Science, University of Florida. Of those saying either that
leaders were less trustworthy and honest or that little had changed in recent years (14 percent of the total), 55 percent blamed the leaders of *both* major political parties (versus less
than 10 percent each for business, religious, or Democratic and Republican leaders in particular).

3. The following data were provided to the author by Carol Bowman of the Times Mirror Center for the People and the Press.

4. In this particular Times Mirror poll, Ross Perot led the presidential trial heat with 36 percent (including "leaners") to 31 percent for Bush, 27 percent for Clinton, and 6 percent other or undecided.

5. Moreover, reflecting the commitment to individualistic values that is a key element of our political culture in the United States, citizens often show little inclination to hold government responsible for many of the personal problems they do have (e.g., finding a job, seeing that the bills are paid, coping with illness or poor health; see Sniderman and Brody 1977; Verba and Schlozman 1977).

6. Still, 52 percent admitted they "often don't have enough money to make ends meet."

7. Others contend that the angst is real but point the finger of blame at the media in a different sense, i.e., by citing the excesses of post-Watergate reporting or, more generally, a "culture of scandal" that is promoted by "investigative reporters" who "view every established leader or organization chiefly as a locus of possible crime" and corruption (Garment 1991, p. 82; cf. Sabato 1991). However, the impact of changes in the news (or television entertainment programming; see Ranney 1983) on images people hold of government and politics should not be exaggerated. Whereas many scholars insist that there is indeed a relationship between exposure to unfavorable television (Robinson 1976) and newspaper (Miller, Goldenberg, and Erbring 1979) coverage and feelings of discontent, Ranney (p. 79) acknowledges that there is little support for the notion that shifting journalistic practices have been "the sole or even the main cause" of heightened negativism among the American public since the early 1960s (also see Hallin 1984; Iyengar and Kinder 1987, pp. 129–130). The media have had, after all, a steady stream of "bad news" to report over the past thirty years or so, and contemporary discontent is probably better understood as a product of that bad news than as a reflection of the manner in which it has been communicated to a gullible public by cynical, headline-seeking reporters.

8. The ANES surveys, conducted since 1952 by the Center for Political Studies at the University of Michigan, are made available by the Inter-University Consortium for Political and Social Research. Results from 1992 are based on an early ICPSR release of that particular survey. Neither the consortium nor the original collectors of the data bear any responsibility for the analyses or interpretations here.

9. The same thing can be said for the leadership of major nongovernmental institutions such as business and labor; see Lipset and Schneider (1987).

10. The public usually is inclined to blame scandals and other shortcomings on incumbent officeholders, and many who say they would like to see changes in "our whole system of government" (nearly 50 percent according to a question in the 1976 ANES) appear to have nothing more in mind than a few specific policy adjustments or the election of new leaders (Sniderman 1981; Craig 1993).

11. See the letters section in *Newsweek*, July 6, 1992.

12. Notice that Perot voters were the most cynical in 1992, but not by nearly as large a margin as one might have expected (see Chapter 8).

13. The subject of discontent has occasionally been explored through depth interviews (Gilmour and Lamb 1975; Sniderman 1981; Sanders 1990), though always with a somewhat different emphasis than that found in my own research.

14. See Sanders (1990, pp. 49–52) for a slightly different interpretation. At the same time, conventional wisdom (not yet backed by much empirical evidence) has it that an unfavorable assessment of the players can ultimately lead to a withdrawal of popular sup-

port for the fundamental "rules of the game" or even for the broader political community; see Easton (1975) and Gamson (1968, 1971).

15. Barber conceded that Watergate and related scandals dealt at least a temporary blow to expectations of fiduciary responsibility in the 1970s; William Mitchell (1959) cited concerns in both areas as contributing to the ambivalent social status of the American politician during the 1950s.

16. One might argue that describing government as wasteful is in many instances a comfortable stereotype rather than a manifestation of genuine discontent. Yet apart from their answers on the "waste taxes" question, a number of my respondents returned to this theme—often without any prompting on my part—at various other points during the interview. The notion that government wastes money may be a stereotype, but it apparently is a stereotype with teeth for many Americans.

17. Asked whether the real quest was for money or power, about half the Alachua sample emphasized the former (personal gain, greed, lining their own pockets, getting rich); the other half suspected that it was a combination of the two.

18. It is surprising that one aspect of honesty mentioned by only a few respondents has to do with candidates not keeping their promises once the campaign is over. Perhaps this particular issue is simply part of the broader complaint about the tendency for representatives to "lose touch" with the voters who elected them.

19. This figure is from the 1987 ANES pilot study.

20. Thumbnail sketches of these individuals are provided in Craig (1993).

21. This particular quote is from a former adviser to presidential candidate Pat Buchanan; see *Newsweek's* special postelection issue (November/December 1992), p. 13.

22. See Germond and Witcover (1993, chapter 1).

23. Only 12.3 percent (compared with 12.8 percent in 1988) said that government pays "a good deal" of attention to what the people think; 51.8 percent (compared with 50.5 percent four years earlier) agreed that "public officials [don't] care much what people like me think."

24. Exact wording for items composing the internal efficacy index can be found in the Appendix. In addition, there was a modest increase (from 21.2 percent to 27.0 percent) in the proportion disagreeing with the statement that "sometimes politics and government seem so complicated that a person like me can't really understand what's going on."

25. Off-year election results in 1994 suggest that matters have gotten worse rather than better (see my remarks in Chapter 1).

4

Economic Change and the Middle-Class Revolt Against the Democratic Party

RUY A. TEIXEIRA

In the previous seven presidential elections, the Democratic Party—the party of activist government in the United States since the 1930s—has averaged only about 43 percent of the popular vote, doing especially poorly among the middle class.[1] Why have so many middle-class voters lost confidence in the ability of elected leaders to deal effectively with important societal problems? The following chapter offers a provisional analysis of this question, organized into four sections. It begins by identifying what seems to be the root cause for middle-class hostility toward government in general, and toward the Democratic Party in particular, and then follows with a discussion of how the party has tried to respond to this growing hostility. In the next section I evaluate, in light of the 1992 election and its aftermath, the success of the Democrats' response. The chapter concludes with a consideration of whether and how further steps might be taken to restore middle-class faith in activist government.

ORIGINS OF THE MIDDLE-CLASS REVOLT
AGAINST ACTIVIST GOVERNMENT

Several explanations have been advanced to account for middle-class antipathy toward activist government. One argument sees it as a deep-seated, *ideological* rejection of government that has intensified over time. Supposedly, middle-class Americans now tend to have a fundamentally conservative view of taxes and of government—a view that leads them to reject the Democratic Party and most new taxation and spending proposals. There is, however, very little evidence to suggest that the middle class's ideological orientations (as opposed to its operational assessments of government) are any more conservative today than they were in the early 1960s (Bennett and Bennett 1990). Consequently, changing ideology among the middle class cannot tell us much about the origins of current hostility toward activist government and the Democratic Party.

Another argument concerns the impact of changing *values*. According to this perspective, middle-class values—for example, commitment to the welfare of family and community, belief in the value of hard work—have moved so far toward the individualistic and hedonistic end of the spectrum that public support cannot be generated for an activist approach to solving the nation's problems. Once again, though, we find little indication that core values (at least in the areas most pertinent to public policy) have changed much, if at all, over the last several decades. Yes, middle-class citizens today put more emphasis on self-expression and tend to have less rigid standards with regard to morals and sexual behavior. But when one looks at values concerning the importance of work, fairness, community, and so on, the amount of change is small (Yankelovich 1994). It is therefore difficult to see changing values among the middle class as a significant component of current antigovernment sentiment.

Still another interpretation centers around the role played by *demographic* shifts (e.g., suburbanization, sectoral employment shifts, and generational replacement) in eroding the political base for activist government and for the Democratic Party. Yet even here, where some real changes have taken place,[2] available data generally indicate that they cannot by themselves account for major transformations in American politics (Mayer 1992, p. 224).

Given these problems, I propose a different approach to understanding middle-class hostility. My approach builds on Craig's (1993) contention that citizen discontent with political institutions and leaders is mostly driven by the perceived fit between expectations that people have and the actual (or at least perceived) performance of those institutions and leaders. Once we look at matters in this way, a likely source of middle-class discontent immediately presents itself. The source I have in mind, of course, is the *economy*—specifically, the jobs, wages, and incomes of middle-class Americans. There have been dramatic economic changes in the United States since the 1960s, the net effect of which has been to produce a middle class for whom "good" jobs (i.e., with high wages and secure benefits) are increasingly scarce: Family incomes have stagnated, average wages for the non-college-educated have dropped sharply, and confidence about the country's future economic prospects is low (see Mishel and Bernstein 1995).

Such setbacks look especially serious when they are measured against the robust wage and income growth running from the end of World War II until about 1973—growth that created the middle class as we know it today and decisively shaped its economic expectations. With these expectations no longer being tenable, citizens' faith in the governmental activism that produced (or at least accompanied) the middle-class boom in the first place has been deeply shaken. This development, I contend, lies at the heart of continuing middle-class hostility toward expansive government, and toward the party (Democrats) with which an activist approach to government is closely linked.

This is not to say that values and ideology have nothing to do with middle-class disdain for activist government. Values and ideology are important because they describe the "interpretive scheme" through which the middle class tends to view the world. But this interpretive scheme has not changed much over time: Middle-class Americans were, and are, inclined to see government as a necessary evil; middle-class Americans were, and are, convinced that work should be rewarded and that no one should be given an unfair advantage. What *has* changed is that their economic problems have grown and government appears to have done little to solve them. As a result, the middle class applies its interpretive scheme to the situation and concludes that (1) government is now less necessary than evil; (2) government tax and spending policies, since they are not benefiting middle-class Americans, must be unfairly advantaging others; and (3) the Democrats are suspect, since they are associated, by and large, with more government, more taxes, and more spending.

HOW THE DEMOCRATIC PARTY RESPONDED

The Democratic Party responded to the rise of middle-class hostility with what was essentially a *marketing* approach—an approach that treated *symptoms,* rather than the causes, of popular discontent. Specifically, it was understood that the party's image had become negative in the eyes of too many voters and that, therefore, a new image was needed. Several key differences between the old ("bad") image and the new ("improved") image proposed by disgruntled Democrats are summarized in Table 4.1.

The marketing strategy was identified most strongly with a group called the Democratic Leadership Council (DLC), formed in 1985 by a group of elected officials (including Senator Chuck Robb of Virginia, Representative Dick Gephardt of Missouri, then-governor Bruce Babbitt of Arizona, and Senator Sam Nunn of Georgia) and political operatives (the central figures being President Al From and Will Marshall of the DLC's Progressive Policy Institute) within the party. Once formed, the DLC quickly became a pole of attraction for the considerable number of politicians—mostly moderate to conservative and many from the South—who felt the party's image needed a drastic overhaul.[3] Their drive to transform the Democratic Party received considerable impetus from Michael Dukakis's poor showing in the 1988 presidential contest. Despite some efforts by Dukakis to distance himself from traditional liberalism, it was widely believed that he had failed to shed the debilitating image outlined on the left side of Table 4.1. This failure helped to increase support for the DLC—even among those who found the group's specific policy ideas wrong or incoherent, or perhaps both—and for others who were pushing the necessity for a new party image.

To accelerate the hoped-for transformation, the DLC and allied forces adopted a confrontational stance against those Democrats who most adamantly opposed their ideas. As a result of this stance, they succeeded (and that was how they viewed it) in getting both the AFL-CIO and Jesse Jackson's Rainbow Coalition to picket the 1991 DLC convention in Cleveland. Later, during the 1992 presidential

TABLE 4.1   Old and New Images of the Democratic Party

Old Image	New Image
Social liberalism, for "rights"	For family, rights, *and* responsibilities
For welfare	Welfare reform
Income redistribution	Economic growth
Big government, much spending	Lean government, "reinvent" programs
Giveaways to poor and minorities	"New covenant," hand up to willing poor
Soft on crime	Tough on crime
For special interests	Against special interests
Unpatriotic	Patriotic
Against white middle class	For white middle class

primaries, Bill Clinton—who had only recently stepped down as chairman of the DLC—issued his famous denunciation of rap singer Sister Souljah at a public event in Washington sponsored by Reverend Jackson.

Indeed, by the time of Clinton's acceptance speech at the 1992 Democratic Convention, it is fair to say that those elements within the party that were most hostile to the image makeover implied by Table 4.1 had been thoroughly marginalized. The party was thus able to unite for the fall campaign around just the sort of themes summarized on the right side of the table and elaborated at great length by Clinton in his speech. With a new and more palatable image to market, Clinton succeeded in presenting himself as a viable—or, at any rate, not disastrous—alternative to an extremely unpopular incumbent.[4] The result: Enough voters deserted George Bush to hand the election to Clinton on November 3, 1992.

IS THE DEMOCRATIC PARTY RESPONSE WORKING?

Needless to say, simply managing to get a Democratic president elected was an important first step. But has middle-class faith in the party of activist government truly been restored? There are two critical problems facing the Democrats here, the first of which is suggested by Clinton's managing to win just 43 percent of the 1992 popular vote[5]—a relatively weak showing that is underscored by exit-poll results obtained on election day. That is, although Democrats more or less neutralized the Republican Party's efforts to revive its old image, they failed to consolidate the bulk of disaffected former Bush voters into a new Democratic coalition (also see Corrado 1994; Shribman 1994). Many of these people instead backed Independent candidate Ross Perot (56 percent of whose total came from 1988 Bush voters, compared with 17 percent from those who four years earlier had voted for Dukakis).

In contrast, only 25 percent of Clinton's support came from former Bush voters—a figure that is very close to the 23 percent received by Dukakis in 1988 from former Reagan backers. This suggests that the Democratic nominee's performance among Bush defectors was probably not too much different from what could be expected from normal year-to-year "churning" of the electorate,[6] rather than any particular success he may have had at wooing voters away from the other side. Nor does it appear that Clinton did unusually well in his efforts to reach Democratic defectors: He captured 53 percent of the votes cast by Bush Democrats, but Dukakis won a comparable 51 percent from Reagan Democrats in the prior election.[7]

Ultimately, the "new" Democratic voters of 1992 looked a great deal like the "old" Democratic voters of 1988. This is illustrated by the data in Table 4.2, which show that Clinton was, if anything, more likely to underperform—rather than overperform—relative to Dukakis among demographic groups thought to be critical for rebuilding the Democratic Party. For example, among those with a high school degree or some college, Dukakis received 49 and 42 percent of the vote, respectively, compared with 43 and 41 percent for Clinton. When high school graduates are broken down by gender, Dukakis won 49 percent among men and 50 percent among women, compared with Clinton's 43 percent among both groups.[8]

If we look specifically at whites—where the collapse of Democratic support has been concentrated—Clinton actually did one point worse than Dukakis, 39 to 40 percent. He scored a single point better among white men (37 to 36 percent) but two points worse among white women (41 to 43 percent). When white respondents are broken down further according to their level of education, we learn that Clinton's performance among key middle-education groups (high school and some college) was uniformly anemic.[9] He received just 41 percent of the vote from white male high school graduates, for example, and an even less impressive 35 percent from white males with some college; the corresponding figures for women were 39 and 37 percent, respectively. Similarly, the Democrats won a mere 45 percent from those with incomes in the $15,000–$30,000 range (40 percent among whites) and 41 percent from those earning between $30,000 and $50,000 (37 percent among whites).

The future success of Bill Clinton and his party thus depends, to a considerable extent, on the same kinds of people with whom the Democrats made very little (if any) headway even in recapturing the White House after twelve years of Republican dominance: middle-income, middle-education white voters. The "swing" elements of these groups[10] have been voting Republican in presidential politics for a number of years now; in 1992 they deserted the GOP, but many opted to support Perot rather than Clinton. As a result, the Democratic coalition remains weak—fatally weak unless the situation changes.

Why did this happen? Why did so many swing voters choose to vote against Bush but select Perot over Clinton? Multivariate analysis of the 1992 Voter Research and Survey (VRS) exit-poll data provides some clues. Results show that—after controlling for demographics, as well as partisanship and ideology—both short- and long-term assessments of the economy were important predictors of an anti-Bush vote. For example, individuals who said their family financial situation had gotten worse over the previous four years were more likely than those who felt otherwise to vote against the president, all else being equal. In addition, those who claimed that trade with other countries lost (rather than gained) U.S. jobs, and

TABLE 4.2   Comparing Democratic Support by Demographic Group, 1988 and 1992

	Dukakis (1988)	Clinton (1992)
Education		
High school dropout	56%	54%
High school graduate	49%	43%
Some college	42%	41%
College graduate	43%	44%
Selected other demographics		
Whites	40%	39%
Men	36%	37%
Women	43%	41%
Male high school graduates	49%	43%
Whites only	–	41%
Female high school graduates	50%	43%
Whites only	–	39%
Men, some college	38%	40%
Whites only	–	35%
Women, some college	45%	42%
Whites only	–	37%
Family income $15,000–$30,000	–	45%
Whites only	–	40%
Family income $30,000–$50,000	–	41%
Whites only	–	37%

NOTE: Table entries are percentages of the two-party vote in 1988, and of the Clinton-Bush-Perot vote in 1992.

SOURCE: CBS–*New York Times* (1988) and Voter Research and Survey (1992) exit polls.

especially those who believed the country was in a serious long-term economic decline (rather than a temporary downturn), were more likely to vote against Bush.

It was harder, though, to find ways of distinguishing *among* anti-Bush voters. For example, none of the economic evaluations previously described predicted a Perot, as opposed to a Clinton, vote given the person's initial decision to support someone other than the incumbent. Nevertheless, I did discover two areas with some predictive power in separating Perot and Clinton voters. The first is familiar to analysts of the 1992 election, the second considerably less so.

The first area centers on assessments of the role of government. Simply put, Perot voters were skeptical of the utility of increased government activism and spending; Clinton voters were much more supportive of such activism. This difference is nicely illustrated by responses to a question in the VRS exit poll: "Would you rather have government provide more services but cost more in taxes OR government cost less in taxes by providing fewer services?" Over three-fifths (61 percent) of Clinton voters called for a government that both provided and cost more, compared with just 28 percent of Perot voters.[11] Essentially the same finding holds up in a multivariate context, with an antigovernment response being a strong predictor of voting for Perot over Clinton.

Related to their reservations about government activism, Perot voters also registered substantially greater concern about the budget deficit than did Clinton voters. It is important to note, however, that the deficit *as a specific policy priority* did not discriminate well between Perot voters and Clinton voters in a multivariate model. That is, Perot voters, on the descriptive level, were more likely than Clinton voters to cite the deficit as a policy priority, but concern about the deficit performed poorly as a predictor of a Perot over a Clinton vote once other factors were held constant. This finding is consistent with evidence showing that the commitment of Perot supporters to the deficit as a specific policy priority tended to be fairly weak—substantially weaker, for example, than their commitment to improving the economy and creating jobs. Accordingly, Greenberg (1993) has concluded that the deficit plays a symbolic role for many voters, acting as a lightning rod for their negative feelings about government and about perceived national decline.

The second area with some predictive power for Clinton versus Perot voting has to do with the actual economic experience of voters as opposed to their survey responses about economic conditions. To investigate, I integrated Current Population Survey (CPS) wage data[12] covering a twenty-year time period with the 1992 VRS exit poll; this enabled me to estimate the average wage change experienced by different groups of respondents in the exit survey—for example, Clinton and Perot voters as shown in Table 4.3.

The data show a clear pattern: Both Clinton and Perot voters experienced wage losses in every time period, but Perot voters' losses were uniformly larger. The difference is one that holds up in multivariate testing: With basic control variables in place, the greater the wage loss experienced, the more likely a voter would choose Perot over Clinton. It is interesting that the pro-Perot effects of wage losses tend to be larger and more robust for the longer time periods. That is, where wage losses were relatively large over a long period (for example, 1979–1992) pro-Perot effects also are large and relatively unaffected by other variables in the model; in contrast, pro-Perot effects for shorter time periods (for example, 1991–1992) are much smaller and likely to be washed out by the inclusion of enough control variables. This fits with the idea that long-term economic decline is driving much of the bitterness toward the Democratic Party and the apparent failures of government—bitterness that prevents many whose economic interests might seem to lie with the Democrats from aligning with them.

Thus, the difficult task faced by Democrats in the 1990s is that of welding together two groups: (1) their core supporters, i.e., voters who think, with good reason, the economy needs to be fixed and believe that increased government activism is central to doing so; and (2) a group of swing voters, primarily middle-

TABLE 4.3   Comparing Clinton and Perot Voters by Change in Real Hourly Wage, Selected Time Periods

Time Period	Clinton Voters	Perot Voters
1973–1992	-0.48%	-0.57%
1979–1992	-0.44%	-0.55%
1988–1992	-0.76%	-0.87%
1990–1992	-1.04%	-1.36%
1991–1992	-1.02%	-1.35%
2nd quarter to 2nd quarter	-1.31%	-1.61%
3rd quarter to 3rd quarter	-1.07%	-1.26%

NOTE: Table entries are annualized percent changes. Wage rates were deflated using the CPI-U-X1 deflator. Exit poll sample was reweighted by education to reflect voter education distribution in November 1992 CPS voter supplement file (see Table 4.5). Voter group wage changes were estimated by assigning individual exit-poll respondents the wage change corresponding to their age/education/race/gender classification, then averaging these changes over voter groups. Due to data limitations, people aged 65 and over were omitted from calculations.

SOURCE: Voter Research and Survey (1992) exit poll and Bureau of the Census Current Population Surveys (1973, 1979, 1988, 1990, 1991, 1992).

income, middle-education whites, who also believe, with even better reason, that the economy needs to be fixed—but are skeptical that government activism can do the job.[13] The obvious solution, of course, is to fix the economy without doing anything unusual in the way of government intervention. In this way, questions about the role and size of government can be avoided while providing both segments of the intended Democratic coalition with what they presumably want: an economy that delivers a dependable and rising standard of living to the broad middle class.

But herein lies the second big problem facing Democrats, which is that the economy is no longer doing a very good job of providing the basis for rising middle-class living standards. This is happening because the real wages of American workers have been declining since 1973, leading most families to struggle (e.g., by putting in longer hours, having both spouses employed, reducing the number of children, etc.)—many unsuccessfully—simply to maintain a middle-class lifestyle. These wage trends are summarized by the data in Table 4.4, both for all workers and for men and broken down by education group.

As the data show, real-wage decline has been worst for those with low levels of educational attainment: High school dropouts and high school graduates have seen their wages decline 23 percent and 15 percent, respectively, since 1973 (27 percent and 20 percent for men[14]). However, *all* education groups—including those with two years or more of postgraduate study—experienced some decline over the time period examined. The 1980s, in particular, stand out as a disastrous decade for those without a college education[15] (over three-quarters of today's

TABLE 4.4   Change in Real Hourly Wage by Education, 1973–1993 (1993 dollars)

	All Workers				
	High School Dropout	High School Graduate	Some College	College	College and 2+ Years
Real hourly wages					
1973	$10.16	$11.63	$12.86	$16.99	$20.91
1979	$10.06	$11.23	$12.24	$15.52	$18.80
1987	$ 8.74	$10.49	$11.96	$15.98	$19.77
1989	$ 8.44	$10.21	$11.82	$15.90	$20.36
1993	$ 7.87	$ 9.92	$11.37	$15.71	$19.93
Percent change					
1973–1979	-1.1%	-3.5%	-4.8%	-8.6%	-10.1%
1979–1989	-16.1%	-9.1%	-3.5%	2.4%	8.3%
1989–1993	-6.7%	-2.8%	-3.8%	-1.2%	-2.1%
1973–1993	-22.5%	-14.7%	-11.6%	-7.5%	-4.7%
	Men Only				
	High School Dropout	High School Graduate	Some College	College	College and 2+ Years
Real hourly wages					
1973	$11.85	$14.02	$14.73	$19.41	$22.20
1979	$11.58	$13.49	$14.29	$18.10	$20.31
1987	$ 9.93	$12.24	$13.74	$18.32	$21.48
1989	$ 9.57	$11.83	$13.41	$18.16	$22.30
1993	$ 8.64	$11.19	$12.70	$17.62	$21.71
Percent change					
1973–1979	-2.3%	-3.8%	-2.9%	-6.7%	-8.5%
1979–1989	-17.4%	-12.3%	-6.2%	0.3%	9.8%
1989–1993	-9.7%	-5.4%	-5.3%	-2.9%	-2.6%
1973–1993	-27.1%	-20.2%	-13.8%	-9.2%	-2.2%

SOURCE: Mishel and Bernstein (1995), Tables 3.18 and 3.19. Reprinted with permission.

labor force), with (1) high school dropouts' wages falling 16 percent over the decade, (2) those of high school graduates down 9 percent, and (3) those of individuals with some college down 4 percent. All of these declines were sharper among men, who still provide the bulk of income in most families.

So if Democrats are to provide a secure basis for middle-class prosperity, the first thing they must do (assuming, of course, that the GOP gains of 1994 can be reversed and that Democrats can hold on to the White House in 1996) is reverse the wage trends in place since 1973. But, as Table 4.4 makes clear, they have a long way to go in accomplishing this goal, especially for the non-college-educated who were hit so hard during the 1980s. Nor do results from the early part of Clinton's administration generate confidence that a reversal is taking place. Bureau of Labor Statistics data show, for example, that real wages were essentially stagnant for both production and nonsupervisory workers (over 80 percent of the labor force) from June 1993 to June 1994[16]—a year that included two quarters of growth so strong the Federal Reserve Board felt obliged to cool down the economy by raising interest rates.

One could argue, of course, that the trends here will be extremely difficult to counter and that the less-educated segments of the population being hurt are rooted in old economic arrangements that simply are being replaced. Perhaps, then, the Democrats should concentrate mainly on appealing to groups who tend to benefit from the "new economy" (i.e., college-educated, high-skill, relatively affluent) rather than worry too much about the economic situation of those who are losing out. Some encouragement for such a view is provided by exit-poll data showing that the college-educated now constitute almost two-fifths of the electorate, with the very highest education group (individuals having a college degree plus postgraduate education) being particularly favorable toward the Democrats. Similarly, studies reveal that as much as one-third of the electorate now have family incomes over $50,000.

Yet even when we put aside any problems with the idea that the labor-market travails of the less well educated are attributable to rapid skill upgrading in the economy (see Mishel and Teixeira 1991; Teixeira and Mishel 1993; Mishel and Bernstein 1994; Howell 1994), there is a further and fatal problem with the argument: Exit-poll data almost certainly misrepresent—and misrepresent profoundly—the structure of the U.S. electorate. This can be seen by comparing exit-poll and census survey data. Specifically, as can be seen in Table 4.5(A), the 1992 VRS exit poll (which is widely reported and relied upon in political and journalistic circles) estimates that the electorate is far more upscale than indicated by the November 1992 CPS voter-supplement data. Since exit polls cannot control for the fact that better-educated and affluent citizens are more willing to fill out survey forms at polling places and the census survey suffers from no such bias, a reasonable inference would be that VRS seriously misrepresents the composition of the U.S. voting public.

According to Table 4.5, the most serious misrepresentation by education is for college graduates. The exit poll overstates the proportion of college graduates among all voters by 12 percentage points: 39 percent (almost two-fifths) in VRS to 27 percent (just more than one-quarter) in the census survey. The most serious misrepresentations by income are for the affluent group (family incomes of $50,000 or more), whose weight in the electorate is overstated in VRS by 18 points (32 percent to only 14 percent in the census survey) and the lower-middle-income group ($15,000–$30,000), whose weight in the electorate is *under*represented in the exit poll by 18 points (24 to 42 percent).

It should be noted that the income data I am using are based on figures for family income of voters in census publication P20–466 (U.S. Department of Commerce 1993), which excludes single individuals. However, were singles (who

TABLE 4.5   Comparison of Voter Estimates from Exit Poll and Census Survey Data, 1992

	Education			Family Income	
	Exit	*Census*		*Exit*	*Census*
A. All voters					
Less than high school	7%	12%	Under $15,000	14%	13%
High school graduate	25	33	$15,000–$30,000	24	42
Some college	29	28	$30,000–$50,000	30	31
College graduate	39	27	$50,000–plus	32	14
B. Clinton voters					
Less than high school	9%	15%	Under $15,000	19%	17%
High school graduate	25	32	$15,000–$30,000	25	42
Some college	27	26	$30,000–$50,000	28	28
College graduate	39	26	$50,000–plus	29	12
C. Perot voters (all)					
Less than high school	6%	12%	Under $15,000	14%	12%
High school graduate	28	35	$15,000–$30,000	27	42
Some college	32	30	$30,000–$50,000	31	33
College graduate	34	23	$50,000–plus	28	12
D. Perot Democrats					
Less than high school	8%	14%	Under $15,000	16%	14%
High school graduate	30	37	$15,000–$30,000	28	45
Some college	30	28	$30,000–$50,000	33	32
College graduate	32	21	$50,000–plus	22	9
E. Perot Independents					
Less than high school	6%	11%	Under $15,000	14%	13%
High school graduate	28	36	$15,000–$30,000	27	44
Some college	32	30	$30,000–$50,000	31	32
College graduate	34	22	$50,000–plus	28	11

SOURCE: Voter Research and Survey (1992) exit poll and Bureau of the Census Current Population Survey (1993). The income data in this table are based on data in Census Report P20–466. Preliminary analysis of census microdata has indicated that the income data in the report are faulty and that the income bias shown in the exit poll are probably not as severe as presented here.

tend to be less well off) included in our calculations, the disparity between pro-portions of the affluent in the two surveys would be *larger,* not smaller, than what we see here. In other words, my estimates of exit-poll income bias are actually fairly conservative.

If the exit poll misrepresents the composition of the voting electorate as a whole, it also misrepresents the makeup of those supporting any particular candidate. The extent of this misrepresentation can be gauged by recalibrating the exit-poll data to reflect the more accurate education and income distribution of the census data; specifically, I assume that the education and income distribution of voters in the census is the "true" distribution and that the exit poll captures the "true" relative levels of support for different candidates by education-income group.

The results for Clinton voters in Table 4.5(B) are again striking. Contrary to the hefty proportions indicated by exit polls, census data reveal that only 26 percent of Clinton's support in 1992 came from college graduates and a mere 12 percent from those with family incomes of $50,000 and above. Conversely, much more of his support was provided by high school graduates and lower-middle-income voters ($15,000–$30,000) than is shown in the exit poll.

We find basically the same story in Table 4.5(C) for Perot voters, who obviously constitute a key target group for the Democrats in 1996 and beyond. Census data portray Perot voters as being far more downscale (by both education and income) than is suggested by the exit poll. And when Perot Democrats and Independents, the segments most accessible to future Democratic candidates, are broken out—in Table 4.5(D) and 4.5(E)—the pattern is even stronger: Only 21 and 22 percent of Perot Democrats and Independents, respectively, are college graduates, and just 9 percent and 11 percent, respectively, earn at least $50,000 a year in family income. If anything, the income figures probably *overstate* the proportion of these voters from affluent backgrounds!

Our data, then, give reason to believe that exit polls overestimate by a considerable margin the weight of affluent and well-educated voters in the U.S. electorate. Therefore, to the extent that politicians and journalists rely on such polls for a sense of the composition of the electorate, they will be misled. It is even possible that certain stirrings within the Democratic Party (see Edsall 1994a, 1994b) that suggest the party might want to explore a strategy of reaching out to the college-educated[17] and better-off—while deemphasizing appeals to voters with less education and moderate incomes—are partially attributable to a misplaced reliance on exit-poll and similar data[18] that profoundly distort the socioeconomic composition of Bill Clinton's (and Ross Perot's) electoral support in 1992.

To illustrate the implications of this strategy, let us consider a two-person contest in 1996: Clinton versus the Republican nominee, but not Perot. In terms of education, if the Clinton voting rate among non-college-graduates (all those without degrees) remained at its 1992 level, the president would need 71 percent of the college vote to win (with a 51 percent popular majority). Alternatively, support for Clinton among the college-educated could remain at its previous level and the Democrats would then need only 54 percent of noncollege voters in order to be successful. If we look at income, constant levels of support from the middle class ($15,000–$30,000 family income) and the poor (under $15,000) would mean that Clinton needs 84 percent (!) of upper-income voters to stay in office. But if the president's 1996 numbers match those of 1992 among both the affluent *and* the poor, he could be reelected with just 52 percent support from the middle class.[19]

Ignoring the wage problems of the non-college-educated middle class hardly is a viable option for the Democratic Party because those doing well[20] in the new economy are not numerous enough to constitute a plausible alternative basis for

Democratic strategy. This strengthens the idea that expanding the party's electoral base and reviving wage growth are tightly linked—a point that is underscored by numerous poll results obtained since the 1992 election. For example, a survey done by the *Los Angeles Times* in June 1993 found that two-thirds of Perot voters thought that the next generation of Americans would have a worse standard of living than today's. Similarly, in a March 1994 Times Mirror poll, more than 7 in 10 Perot supporters described the country as "losing ground" with regard to the availability of well-paying jobs. Indeed, Perot voters in general have shown themselves to be consistently more pessimistic than Clinton or Bush voters about the U.S. economy's future ability to deliver the goods (see Chapter 8). If their pessimism remains in place, the Democrats' prospects for enlarging and solidifying their electoral coalition seem poor.

CONCLUSION: CAN THE DEMOCRATS REUNITE WITH THE MIDDLE CLASS?

The foregoing analysis suggests that the Democratic Party's quest to revive the middle-class base for activist government is far from over. In fact, quite the opposite: Based on 1992 election results and the difficulties posed by long-term economic trends, its task would appear to be a most formidable one. Furthermore, the very success Democrats have had in changing the image of their party—discussed earlier and summarized in Table 4.1—may prove to be an obstacle in confronting this task. The reason is that all of the internal party agreement on symbols and signals, absent a substantive approach to reversing long-term economic trends, does *not* necessarily translate into concrete help for the middle class; to the contrary, it can lead to a policy agenda driven by marketing considerations of little real benefit to the voters who are being targeted.

To illustrate my point, the "new Democrat" marketing strategy that appeared to drive the policy focus of the Clinton administration during its first two years generated few tangible benefits for the broad middle class. Indeed, such benefits were provided mainly for the poor, e.g., through the earned-income tax credit (EITC) in Clinton's 1993 budget bill. And welfare reform, were it to happen (in a form preferred by the Democrats rather than by the new GOP majority in Congress), would undoubtedly include substantial training and childcare assistance—again, helping the poor most of all. Even the president's now-defunct health care reform plan, whose inspiration owed the least to "new Democrat" marketing concerns, appeared to be of greatest assistance to uninsured low-income individuals who don't qualify for AFDC or Medicaid while providing a mixed bag to many in the middle class (health security on the one hand versus higher costs and reduced choice on the other).

To the extent that there is a Democratic strategy for restoring middle-class prosperity, it seems to be a variant of the GOP's trickle-down economics. This approach, which owes much to mainstream thinking among professional economists, combines trade liberalization (North American Free Trade Agreement [NAFTA], General Agreement on Tariffs and Trade [GATT]) with low interest rates (sustained by cutting the deficit) in an effort to promote business expansion. Business expansion will then, presumably, produce more jobs and higher wages that benefit the middle class. The questionably Democratic nature of such an approach has been noted by many, including President Clinton himself (see Woodward 1994). More to the point, however, it may not produce the desired results, since trade liberalization, whatever its other effects, probably will intensify the downward pressure on wages of non-college-educated Americans.[21] In addition, cutting the deficit is hardly a sufficient condition for low interest rates given the uncontrollability of the Federal Reserve[22] and various other economic factors[23]—nor do low interest rates automatically translate into high levels of business investment.[24]

Finally, and perhaps most important, simple expansion of the economy under today's labor-market conditions is unlikely to reverse the wage trends documented earlier. Rising wage inequality makes it possible for the economy to grow in the aggregate but without improving the situation of most members of the labor force. This disconnection between positive aggregate change and higher wages for individual workers (see Blank and Binder 1986; Blank and Card 1993; Mishel and Bernstein 1995) characterized the so-called boom of the 1980s and, absent significant changes in current labor-market conditions, will probably continue through the rest of the 1990s. Mishel and Bernstein (1995) estimate that if both aggregate economic growth and labor-market trends continue at their post-1979 rates for another ten years, wages for the median male worker will have actually dropped another 10 percent by 2005!

Under these circumstances, reliance on economic growth to ensure Democratic political fortunes seems unwise. It is perhaps no coincidence that economist R. C. Fair's (1978, 1982, 1988) presidential voting model, which relies almost exclusively on aggregate economic conditions, was so far off—it predicted a lopsided victory for President Bush—in the 1992 election. In a situation where aggregate economic growth and wage growth are disconnected, we should not expect favorable overall economic performance (as the nation experienced in the several quarters before the election) to have the same effect as it once did. Fair, as well as Bush and the Republicans, expected that this would be the case, and they were wrong. Clinton and the Democrats should be careful they don't make the same mistake.

Results of the 1994 midterm elections bear out my point. Despite a respectable level of economic growth, low inflation, and relatively low unemployment rates, the Democrats still took a tremendous drubbing, including a loss of over 50 seats in the House of Representatives. And once again the forecasting models were wrong, most of them cranking out predictions of modest Democratic losses based on the favorable economic data; the well-known model of Michael Lewis-Beck, for example, predicted that the Republicans would pick up only 5 seats in the House (see Lewis-Beck and Rice 1992; Lewis-Beck and Wrighton 1994)!

Exit polls from 1994 further suggest that aggregate growth has failed to mollify voters' pressing economic concerns and fears. The 1994 VRS exit poll showed that

57 percent of voters believed the condition of the U.S. economy was either not good or poor; those who said not good voted Republican by a margin of 60–40 percent, and those who thought the economy was doing poorly supported the GOP by 71–29 percent. Similarly, 74 percent of voters thought their family financial situation was either unchanged or worse; the unchanged group went Republican by 53–47 percent, and those who felt their family situation was worse did so by a margin of 64–36 percent.

Wage and household income data—as opposed to traditional aggregate indicators—validate voters' perceptions. Despite relatively strong GDP growth, for example, the latest census data show that median household income went *down* 1 percent between 1992 and 1993, reducing it to a total of $2,300 (or 7 percent) less than in 1989. And middle-class incomes probably did not rise in 1994, since real wages continued to deteriorate through the third quarter of that year—down 2.6 percent (3 percent among men, 2 percent among women) for the median full-time wage and salary earner since the third quarter of 1993. Thus, the Clinton administration has provided little relief to voters who, due to large long-term wage declines, have seen their economic prospects erode badly over time.

Indeed, it is precisely these voters who so massively deserted the Democrats in 1994. The party's support declined 7 percentage points among high school dropouts, 10 points among high school graduates, and 11 points among those with some college; in contrast, among those with a college degree or more, Democratic support was rock steady. The same basic pattern applies when the previous off-year election (1990) is compared to 1994. That is, the decline in Democratic support was again among the non-college-educated: down 8 points for high school graduates and 10 points for those with some college. The main difference is that the 1990–1994 comparison (unlike 1992–1994) shows no change among high school dropouts. This underscores the curvilinear nature of Democratic support today: The party is doing better at the ends of the education distribution and collapsing in the middle. Unfortunately for the Democrats, the middle is where most of the voters are.

For whites, where the decline in Democratic support between 1992 and 1994 was concentrated (black support actually went up slightly), the shift was especially pronounced among non-college-educated voters. And among non-college-educated whites, the anti-Democratic shift was sharpest among men, dropping 20 points (to 37 percent) for white men with a high school education and 15 points (to 31 percent) for white men with some college. As shown in Table 4.4, it is non-college-educated men who have suffered the largest wage declines over the past two decades. It is important to note, however, the Democratic losses among white non-college-educated voters extended to women as well—for example, a 9-point decline among both white women with a high school diploma and those with some college. Thus, to ascribe the falloff in Democratic support to "angry white guys," as many in the media did, is to miss the point. A large number of non-college-educated white men *and* women were the true culprits.

The challenge facing the Democratic Party, then, is to shift its focus away from simple aggregate economic growth (and policies with high marketing content) toward a more clearly substantive approach that can generate middle-class prosperity. This, in turn, may call for a new marketing strategy, since the party's approach probably will call for the use of greater resources and more government than many in the middle class are currently prepared to endorse.[25] Is such a marketing strategy even possible? It is difficult to say with any certainty. What *can* be said is that it is central to the Democrats' efforts that they implement programs that might substantially benefit their electoral target: white, middle-income, middle-education voters. If unable to implement these programs, they will be thrown back on the politics of symbolism—a politics well suited to defeating unpopular incumbents but poorly suited to reviving middle-class faith in the Democratic Party and activist government.

NOTES

1. In 1992, for example, American National Election Study (ANES) data show that more than 7 in 10 middle-class citizens (roughly operationalized as those with family incomes between $15,000 and $50,000) believed that the national government could be counted on "to do what is right" only "some" or "none of the time." Similarly, 1992 Voter Research and Survey (VRS) exit-poll data indicate that more than 60 percent of middle-class voters preferred a government that provided fewer services and cost less to a government that provided but also cost more.

2. Consider the following: (1) *Suburbanization.* In 1960, about one-third of the national vote was cast by suburban residents; by 1988, that share had increased to 48 percent (Schneider 1992b); (2) *Sectoral employment shifts.* The proportion of the electorate in white-collar occupations grew from 26 percent in 1960 to 37 percent in 1988 (Teixeira 1992); and (3) *Generational replacement.* According to Abramson (1983), about half the electorate is replaced every twenty years.

3. For an interesting scholarly overview of the formation and evolution of the DLC, see Hale (1993).

4. For some evidence on the electorate's unusually negative evaluations of Bush and the Republicans in 1992, see Abramson, Aldrich, and Rohde (1994, chapter 7).

5. In fairness to Clinton, it should be noted that the VRS exit poll from which these figures are taken indicated that Perot voters were about evenly divided between Clinton and Bush—suggesting a Democratic victory even if Perot had not run. The fact remains, though, that the Texas billionaire *did* run and enormous numbers of anti-Bush voters chose to support him rather than the Democratic nominee. There is no way to interpret this as anything other than electoral weakness.

6. In any given election, regardless of the incumbent party's level of public approval, a certain number of former supporters will choose to switch sides, as will a certain number of those who previously voted for the opposition. This means that even if the party stays in power (perhaps with the same *level* of support as before) the *composition* of its electoral base will have shifted at least somewhat.

7. These figures are derived from the 1992 VRS exit poll.

8. The 1992 percentages reported here and in Table 4.2 are based on the totals for all three major candidates (as opposed to just two in 1988); the fact remains that Democrats were unable to improve significantly on their numbers from four years earlier.

9. Because the 1988 exit poll was unavailable to me for separate analysis, over-time comparisons cannot be made for either education or income. Given what we already have seen, however, it is unlikely that the party's 1992 showing represented much of an improvement in any of the demographic subgroups discussed here.

10. At any given time, each party has a core of supporters that will be very difficult for the other party to reach. One might hypothetically say, for example, that the Democrats and the Republicans each have a core of about 40 percent of the electorate who can be counted on, absent drastic political events, to back the party's candidates. This leaves 20 percent of the electorate more or less "in play"—its voting decisions truly determined by the campaign and thereby deciding or "swinging" the final outcome. The exact size of the swing voter group, as well as its political complexion, will naturally change from one election to the next. Examples of swing voters include pure Independents (in any election), Reagan Democrats in the 1980s, and, most recently, Perot supporters.

11. Although this particular question elicited the sharpest split between Clinton and Perot supporters, other questions concerning the role of government showed a similar pattern.

12. The CPS is a monthly labor-market survey used by the government to determine unemployment rates and to collect other information concerning the labor force. Roughly one-quarter of respondents in any month of the CPS (those being rotated out of the sample) are asked questions about their weekly and hourly wages and hours worked. These data—typically referred to as the Outgoing Rotation Group (ORG) files—contain wage information on between 155,000 and 171,000 respondents per year. Information from the ORG files provides the basis for wage tabulations and analyses presented in this chapter; for more on the ORG files, see the appendix to Mishel and Bernstein (1995).

13. The skepticism of this group about the effectiveness of government does not necessarily translate into calls for *smaller* government. Instead, the belief is that government in general, and government expansion in particular, do not deserve support unless criteria of effectiveness and responsiveness are met. A similar interpretation of the attitudes of Perot voters is provided by Greenberg (1993).

14. It should be noted that women did not experience strong wage growth either. Indeed, the falling or stagnant wages of most women over the time period only look good relative to the sharp declines experienced by most men (see Mishel and Bernstein 1995). And since women's wages started from a much lower base than that of men, the lack of substantial forward progress is all the more vexing.

15. Individuals with a college education fared better, though their gains were modest. Those with just a four-year degree (two-thirds of college graduates), for example, saw a wage increase of about 2 percent.

16. See U.S. Bureau of Labor Statistics (1994, Table B–3).

17. In its most ludicrous version, this strategy is designed to take advantage of the "curvilinear" nature of support by education groups for the Democrats. It is true that Democratic voting is higher at the far end of the education scale—but only among those who have done postgraduate work, a segment constituting just one-third of all college graduates and 9 percent of the overall electorate (of whom half voted against Clinton in 1992 anyway).

18. Telephone surveys, relative to the census data, also tend to oversample upscale households and individuals.

19. Although I am taking some obvious liberties in comparing 1992 percentages with a hypothetical two-candidate matchup in 1996 (i.e., because at least a portion of the 1992 anti-Clinton vote will surely shift to the president if he seeks reelection), the substantive point is still valid: Clinton and the Democrats do not need to improve their performance among affluent and well-educated voters so much as to boost their standing with the broad middle class.

20. It should be understood that "well" is a relative term here. As can be seen in Table 4.3, the widening gap between higher and lower education groups is almost entirely attributable to the decline of wages for the latter—rather than increasing wages for the former. See Teixeira and Mishel (1993); Mishel and Bernstein (1995).

21. Economists estimate that perhaps 15 percent—somewhat more, somewhat less, depending on supply elasticities and time period—of the increase in college versus high school wage differential during the 1980s can be attributed to increased trade and immigration (Borjas, Freeman, and Katz 1991).

22. Largely as a result of Federal Reserve actions, interest rates had by mid-1994 climbed back to the level they were when President Clinton took office, i.e., before his deficit-cutting package was passed or even on the table.

23. On the generally weak relationship between size of the deficit and interest rates, see Eisner (1994).

24. On the weak relationship between interest rates and business investment, see Fazzari (1993).

25. See Teixeira (1995) for some specifics on what new substantive and marketing strategies for the Democrats might look like.

PART II

Involvement

5

The Sixth American Party System: Electoral Change, 1952–1992

JOHN H. ALDRICH
RICHARD G. NIEMI

Over the more than 200 years of U.S. history, there have been dramatic changes in the patterns of electoral politics. During most of the nineteenth century, for example, voters went to the polls in much higher proportions than at any time during the twentieth century; attachments to political parties were much stronger than they are today; and voters rarely split their tickets, partly because of their strong party feelings but also because—prior to 1890—the parties themselves controlled voting procedures and made it difficult if not impossible to cast votes for candidates from more than one party.

In order to make sense of the changes that have occurred, historians and political scientists often speak of "party systems," referring to periods of a generation or more in which electoral politics differ distinctly from the periods before and after. A standard interpretation (e.g., Chambers and Burnham 1975) is that there have been five American party systems, the first beginning around 1796 with the emergence of two-party competition between the Federalists and Jeffersonian Republicans, and the last starting in the early 1930s with the rise to majority status of New Deal Democrats.[1] We demonstrate in this chapter that, in fact, a new party system—the sixth party system—emerged in the 1960s and has now existed for a quarter-century. We justify our conclusions by documenting a wide variety of changes that took place as the fifth party system ended and the sixth one began.

The "critical era" between the fifth and sixth systems is unique in that it is the first transition period for which we have public opinion survey data to help us understand how attitudes and behaviors were altered.[2] For earlier cases, including the 1930s, we must rely on so-called aggregate data such as how various states, cities, or wards voted, or on the recollections of people interviewed long after the fact. Both of these techniques are useful and have given us some insight into the kinds of transformations that occurred during the New Deal realignment of the 1930s (Andersen 1979; Gamm 1989). They obviously cannot, however, provide

information about the full range of changes that are presumed to have characterized the era.

For the analysis that follows, we begin by reviewing a number of election-re-
lated attitudinal and behavioral changes that took place during the 1960s.[3] These
are called *micropatterns* because we are looking at one "indicator" (or measure) at
a time. We then collect all of these individual changes into a *macropattern*—capturing in one figure a summary of the changes discussed earlier. The latter allows
us to make generalizations about changes during transitions between party systems, that is, to draw conclusions that might apply to earlier as well as to future
transitions. Finally, because we are talking about changes in *party* systems, we discuss the role of political parties in the candidate-centered era that emerged from
the turmoil of the 1960s critical period.

FROM THE FIFTH TO THE SIXTH
PARTY SYSTEMS: MICROPATTERNS

What distinguishes a critical era between party systems is a set of rapid changes in
a broad range of crucial political variables, where these changes, once made, en-
dure. That is, we begin with a system, here a party system, at equilibrium. The
critical era is a period—a relatively short period—of disequilibrium. After this
short period, the system settles into a new equilibrium state for some period of
time, historically for between thirty and forty years. We take these two characteristics—the equilibrium–disequilibrium–new equilibrium cycle and the short but
intense duration of the disequilibrium relative to both preceding and proceeding
equilibrium periods—as the central defining characteristics of party systems and
the critical eras between them.

Changes during the 1960s can be seen in a broad range of party-and election-
related variables; collectively, the patterns outlined in this chapter confirm that
massive alterations did indeed characterize the American political universe
throughout the decade. Many of our measures are drawn from the National
Election Study surveys and therefore are available only since 1952. This gives us
three presidential elections (1952–1960) held prior to the critical era, plus five
(1976–1992) that lie beyond the critical period. The 1964 and 1968 elections are
the ones most clearly within the critical period. The most central of these critical
years is 1968, with 1964 sometimes setting patterns in motion and sometimes
marking the end of the old. In most observations, the 1972 election falls into the
new equilibrium period and is treated as such in our later summarization.

Party Identification

Partisanship of Blacks.   There were two remarkable changes in partisanship
among African Americans during the 1960s. From 1952 to 1962 the proportion of
blacks considered as "apolitical" was quite high (a steady 15–18 percent).[4] In
1964, this percentage dropped to approximately the same low level as among
whites and has hovered in that range ever since (Figure 5.1). This is a good exam-

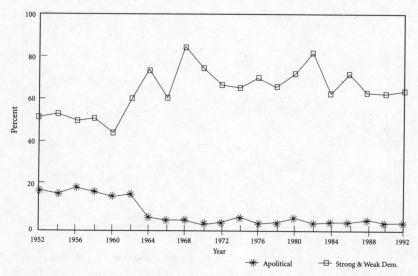

FIGURE 5.1   Partisanship Among Blacks, 1952–1992. *Source:* American National Election Studies.

ple of a shift in equilibrium levels occurring all at once. It can be attributed to the same events that made civil rights prominent on the list of what citizens regarded as the nation's most important problems (see further on).

A second change is the dramatic increase in the proportion of blacks who, beginning in 1964, identified with the Democratic Party. The pattern here is a bit more complicated, with percentages rising and falling at least partly in response to specific political events. The surge in 1968, for example, is due to a decline in the proportion of Independents—probably reflecting former Alabama governor George Wallace's use of that term in his bid for the presidency under the American Independent Party label. At any rate, Figure 5.1 reveals considerable volatility throughout the realigning period and a reasonably steady state thereafter.

Partisanship of Whites.   White partisanship also changed markedly in the mid-1960s (Figure 5.2). The proportion of "pure" Independents (i.e., those claiming not to lean toward either party) was at 9 percent or less through 1964; this was followed, however, by a substantial increase between 1964 and 1972 into what could be seen—despite the dip in 1982—as an essentially steady state since then. The proportion of *all* Independents (including "leaners") also jumped in 1966, then showed a more gradual increase through 1972, a smaller and less consistent increase through 1978, and finally a sharp decline and subsequent rebound in recent years. All Independents constituted about the same share of the electorate in the late 1980s and early 1990s as in the early- to mid-1970s; in every measurement, they registered well above levels observed in the 1950s. Thus, once again, a major increase over the 1964–1972 period appears to have given way to a more or less steady (and higher) rate of independence as time passed.

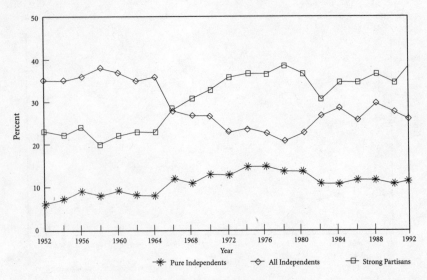

FIGURE 5.2   Partisanship Among Whites, 1952–1992. *Source:* American National Election Studies.

We should take special note of the 1966 election because it represents both the first and largest rise in independence during the critical era and the point at which total Independents initially outnumbered strong partisans—a "crossing" that endured through 1992. As shown in Figure 5.2, the proportion of strong partisans (Republicans and Democrats combined) varied little from 1952 through 1964. It declined sharply, though, in 1966—the largest change in any two-year period under examination—and then continued to sag through 1978, before climbing back to about where it was in 1966 (still well below the 1950s level).[5]

Party Support Coalitions.   The biggest shift in this area is the declining support of southern whites for the Democratic Party, beginning in earnest around 1962 or 1964. A useful long-term perspective can be obtained by calculating "incremental probabilities" that show, on average, how much more likely it is that a person will be a Democrat (rather than a Republican) because he or she happens to be a native southern white; they can be thought of as comparing persons with an identical set of other characteristics—e.g., religion, union membership, or social class—and then determining the relative likelihood that the native southern white will be Democratic. These probabilities hovered close to 0.42 from 1952 through 1960, then dropped precipitously to about 0.20 in 1968. Thereafter, they never reached more than half their early value before declining to an all-time low of 0.05 in 1990 and 1992 (Stanley and Niemi 1995).

Another important change has to do with the percentage of the Democratic coalition claiming to be working class (see Appendix for question wording). Through 1960, the working class made up between 65 and 70 percent of all Democratic identi-

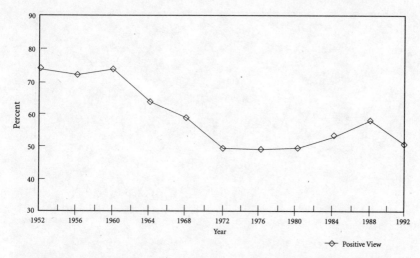

FIGURE 5.3   Party Images, 1952–1992. Shown is the percentage who view at least one party positively. *Source:* Wattenberg (1987 and personal communication).

fiers; following declines that occurred throughout the 1960s, this proportion has hovered around 55 percent through 1992 (see Stanley and Niemi 1995).

Party Images.   Coincidental with the weakening of partisanship was a sharp change in affect toward the political parties (Figure 5.3). In response to open-ended questions concerning what they liked and disliked about the Democratic and Republican parties (see Appendix), nearly three-quarters of ANES respondents through 1960 viewed at least one party favorably.[6] That percentage dropped 10 points by 1964 and another 15 points by 1972. It remained at roughly the same level for several elections before rising somewhat in the 1980s and then dropping back again in 1992.

Issues

Most Important Problems.   One indicator of the issues that parties and politicians face is provided by individuals' assessments of the most important problem facing the nation (see Appendix). The specific problems cited are highly variable, but most can be categorized as referring to either domestic or foreign policy. Figure 5.4 provides the distribution of domestic versus foreign problems between 1952 and 1992. It shows a major change beginning just before 1968 and continuing through 1974, with short spikes thereafter. The pattern is one of a reasonable balance between domestic and foreign concerns from 1952 to 1967, but a predominantly domestic agenda after 1974. If one "subtracts out" Vietnam—an issue described as "intermestic" by some observers (e.g., Hess and Nelson 1985) because it combined domestic impact with foreign policy—the change took place at the height of the critical period, about 1965 or 1966.

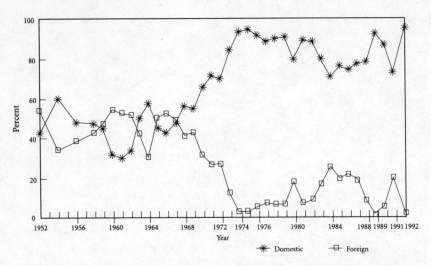

FIGURE 5.4   Most Important Problem, 1952–1992. Shown is the percentage citing foreign vs. domestic, polls averaged Nov.–Oct. Gallup data (Stanley and Niemi 1994, p. 164).

The Basis of Issue Conflict.   Carmines and Stimson (1989) have developed impressive evidence of changes in the direction of racial attitudes during the 1960s (Figure 5.5). With respect to the electorate, they showed, first, that the clarity of party stands on racial issues—as measured by the degree to which citizens perceived the Democrats as more liberal than the GOP with regard to desegregation—increased dramatically between 1960 and 1964. Despite some fluctuations, clarity remained well above 1950s levels thereafter;[7] the Carmines-Stimson series ended in 1980 at almost the exact point reached in 1964. They also showed something called "net public affect"—in other words, the extent to which racial liberals and conservatives had different overall evaluations of the parties. Here, too, there was a sharp increase between 1960 and 1964: In the 1950s, racial liberals and conservatives liked the two parties about equally well; beginning in the early 1960s, however, affect toward the parties quickly became related to issue positions (conservatives being more favorable toward the Republicans, liberals toward the Democrats). Fluctuations after that remained at a level clearly above that of the earlier decade.

Issue-Party and Candidate Linkages.   There has been considerable change over time in the extent to which issues are linked to parties versus candidates. In response to "likes" and "dislikes" questions about parties and candidates (see Appendix), some respondents link issues to both of these actors and some link issues to only one. Figure 5.6 reports the percentages of those mentioning domestic policies *only* in evaluating the political parties or *only* in evaluating the candidates (the remainder mentioned both). What is remarkable is the high incidence of linking issues to parties but not candidates before 1964—and the abrupt change in 1964 to an even mixture of the two. After 1964 there were fluctuations, but

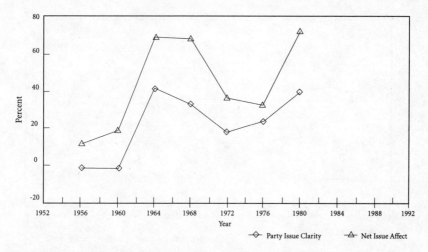

FIGURE 5.5   Clarity of Party Racial Issue Stands and Public Affect Toward Parties, 1956-1980. *Source:* Carmines and Stimson (1989, p. 165).

always with a more even balance between issue-party and issue-candidate connections. Parties were the linkage between issues and voter choices before 1964; over the next thirty years, presidential elections became much more candidate centered.

Geer (1992, p. 52, and personal communication) reported an analogous measure of issue and party-candidate linkages but focused just on New Deal issues (e.g., employment, social welfare programs, agricultural and labor policy, housing, education, and the like). Use of New Deal themes in evaluating the *parties* declined sharply from 1952 to 1956, remained about the same through 1968, then droppd again in 1972 and remained steady through 1992. Use of New Deal policies in evaluating presidential *candidates* climbed steadily from1952 to 1972, except for a sharp drop in 1968; if we set aside a large increase that took place in 1984, use of such policies remained at about the same level through 1992. The pattern is not exactly as one might expected. Yet it is notable that New Deal issues were used primarily when referring to parties prior to 1972—and about equally for parties and candidates since then.

Interest and Involvement

When thinking about critical electoral eras, we need to consider political interest and participation. Indeed, V.O. Key (1955) claimed that increased interest and involvement are hallmarks of critical elections but that signs of heightened popular engagement should decline to more normal levels once the critical period has passed. Only two of the three measures examined in this section follow Key's prediction; the one that does not nevertheless reflects an important feature of mass politics in the sixth party system.

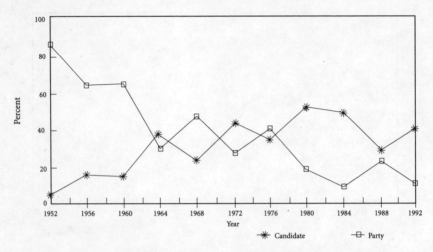

FIGURE 5.6   Party-Candidate Linkages on Domestic Issues, 1952–1992. *Source:* Wattenberg (1980, pp. 84–85, and personal communication).

Interest in the Presidential Campaign.   The public's level of interest (see Appendix) jumped sharply in the no-incumbent presidential race of 1960 from what it had been during the two Eisenhower elections. It stayed high in 1964 despite the presence of an incumbent and a one-sided contest, then rose again in 1968. After that, there was a decline to 1950s levels—except for 1976, when higher interest may have been an aftereffect of the Watergate scandal. Notwithstanding the influence of incumbency and of election-specific events, a pattern of greater interest at the height of the critical era emerges.

Protest Behavior.   Questions about signing petitions, participating in marches and demonstrations, and so on, were not asked in national surveys until the 1970s. Yet surely in the 1960s the level of "unconventional" behavior was greater than at any time since perhaps the 1930s and at any time since. Large-scale participation in the civil rights movement began with the Freedom Riders in 1961, escalated with the March on Washington in 1963, and continued with numerous smaller demonstrations and marches that took place throughout the remainder of the decade. Protests over the Vietnam War were greatest in connection with the presidential election of 1968, though they began a year or two earlier and did not stop until the United States withdrew the last of its troops in January 1973. Active, visible participation was therefore at its height during the entire critical era.

Voting Turnout. Voting is yet another form of participation, and if it were taken as simply a measure of involvement, we would expect an increase during the critical period and then decline once the period ended. But there are many factors that affect turnout (e.g., strength of partisanship in the electorate, feelings of political efficacy or inefficacy,[8] legal requirements for voting, etc.)—plus one, the structure of political parties, that is central to our account of the critical period and its aftermath

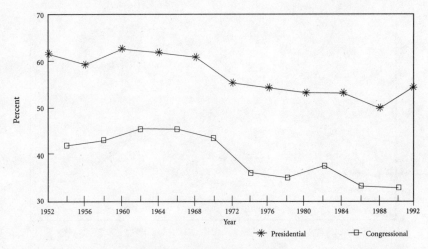

FIGURE 5.7   Turnout in Presidential and Congressional Elections, 1952–1992. *Source:* Ornstein, Mann, and Malbin (1992, p. 48), updated by authors.

(see further on). As a result, the pattern here is expected to be more consistent with the other micropatterns analyzed than was true for either general interest or protest.

Figure 5.7 shows that turnout rates in presidential elections were at a postwar high in 1960, at which point a long-term slide began. The biggest part of the decline was completed by 1972, though there was a further notable decline in 1988 followed by a rebound in 1992 (see Chapter 6). Turnout in off-year congressional elections increased moderately during the early 1960s before dropping to a new level after 1970. Hence, most of the decline in both presidential and congressional voting had occurred by 1974.

Voting and Election Outcomes

Split-Ticket Voting.   Split-ticket voting increased greatly over the period observed. A steady state existed from 1952–1960 in state and local races, with ticket-splitting at 26–31 percent (Figure 5.8). This figure jumped to over 60 percent by 1974 and, though it fell after that, it remained far above 1950s levels. Two other measures of split-ticket voting also were very nearly constant from 1952 to 1960 with (1) about 15 percent supporting different parties for president and the House and (2) roughly 10 percent doing the same in House and Senate races. In 1964, Senate-House ticket-splitting nearly doubled to 18 percent; it again increased sharply in 1978, then fell back to about the level of 1974. The president-House measure did not change much until after 1964, a big jump occurred between 1968 and 1972, and in later years it stayed fairly steady at about 25 percent.

Party-Line Voting.   Besides looking at split-ticket voting, one can assess the relevance of partisanship by examining directly its relationship to the vote (i.e., the extent to which citizens support the candidate of their preferred party in an elec-

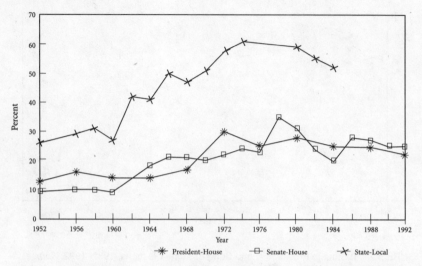

FIGURE 5.8   Split-Ticket Voting, 1952–1992. *Source:* Stanley and Niemi (1994, p. 446).

tion). For presidential voting, this relationship declined sharply during the 1960s and then rose back to its original level after 1972. In 1956 and 1960, the simple two-party correlation between partisanship and presidential vote choice was strong (Pearson's r = 0.68 and 0.70, respectively). In 1964 and again in 1968 it weakened noticeably (0.62 and 0.50), and remained at the same low level (0.51) in 1972 (Nie, Verba, and Petrocik 1979, p. 165). It quickly bounced back, however, climbing to 0.63, 0.66, 0.70, 0.71, and 0.74 between 1976 and 1992. Although not truly representing a *new* steady-state value, the pattern here is consistent with an out-of-equilibrium relationship in the critical period leading to a lower-than-usual relationship between partisanship and the vote; this was followed by a redefined basis of partisanship and, hence, a reequilibration between party identification and the vote during the new steady-state period.

For House and Senate voting, the patterns are somewhat volatile, but there was clearly a rise in party defections during the 1960s (Stanley and Niemi 1994, p. 142). On the House side, there was another smaller and temporary increase in 1978. It is helpful to our argument that in both houses, the defection rate in 1992 was almost exactly that of 1968.

Presidential Coattails.   Another sign of the disjuncture between presidential and House voting has to do with the erosion of presidential coattails, i.e., the ability of a popular candidate for president to attract votes for other candidates running on the party's ticket. Looking just at House races, the coattails of both Republican and Democratic standard-bearers weakened initially and then became stronger over the period from 1956 to 1964. Between 1968 and 1980 they fluctuated somewhat—but, except for the Reagan landslide in 1980, at a clearly reduced

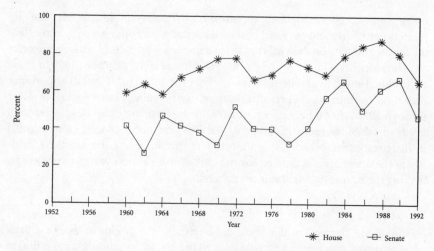

FIGURE 5.9 Percentage of Incumbents Gaining Sixty Percent of the Vote or More, 1960–1992. *Source:* Stanley and Niemi (1994, pp. 128–129).

level compared with earlier years (Calvert and Ferejohn 1983, p. 416). This particular analysis has not been extended beyond 1980, though most election experts concluded that presidential coattails also were relatively "short" in 1984, 1988, and 1992.

A related measure is the percentage of split-district outcomes, referring to the number of congressional districts that vote one way for president and the other way in House or Senate contests. These figures lend less support to our argument than others, with a fairly steady increase in split-district outcomes being evident from 1952 to 1972 (Stanley and Niemi 1994, p. 147). Still, over the entire span from 1964 to 1992, only twice has the proportion dipped as low as 30 percent—its highest point in the earlier period.

House Incumbent Security. The collective safety of House incumbents can be measured by the proportion with "landslide" victories (where landslide victories are defined as those in which the winner receives at least 60 percent of the two-party vote). The number of such races was fairly substantial by 1964, but it nonetheless increased further in the years that followed (Figure 5.9). The first big jump came between 1964 and 1972 as the proportion of safe seats went from about 60 percent to 80 percent. This percentage fluctuated from 1972 through 1984, then rose to new heights in 1986–1988 before dropping back again. On the Senate side, there seems to be little pattern that might be traceable to the critical era.

One can also examine the extent to which high return rates for incumbents are due to personal factors (reflecting positive voter evaluations of the representative himself or herself) versus party or presidential fortunes (over which the individual representative usually has little or no control). Alford and Brady (1989a, 1989b) developed measures of "retirement slump" and "sophomore surge,"[9] and using these components, they apportioned the safety of incumbents seeking reelection to party and personal bases. Historically, party has been a positive factor for incumbents because most of them come from districts in which a majority of voters identify with their party. Alford and Brady show that from 1848 to 1986, party ebbed and flowed with no obvious change in terms of its overall importance over time. In contrast, the personal status of the incumbent was a negligible factor through 1958—but it became a positive value in 1960, increased steadily through 1970, and then fluctuated; after 1970, party and incumbency were close to equal in their respective values.[10] It is unfortunate that for our purposes, the Alford-Brady measures are not defined for two out of five election years in any decade, making them unsuitable for our later analysis.

Confidence in Government

As shown in Chapter 3 of this book and elsewhere, the origins of today's climate of popular discontent can be traced back to the 1960s. Specifically, a collection of items thought to measure trust or confidence in government revealed a dramatic loss of trust after 1964 (see Figure 3.1); in light of the Watergate scandal, it is not surprising that these measures continued to slide throughout the next decade as well. Although confidence was partially restored during the early 1980s, this short-term gain was reversed between 1984 and 1992. At no time did any of the indicators return to anything close to 1950s levels.

FROM THE FIFTH TO THE SIXTH
PARTY SYSTEMS: THE MACROPATTERN

Central to our argument is that the patterns discussed thus far in a variable-by-variable fashion are consistent across a wide variety of measures. In particular, we contend that (1) there was an equilibrium in the fifth party system, (2) this equilibrium was disrupted during the 1960s, and (3) a new equilibrium had emerged by 1972. The final stage of our analysis provides an overview of this process, combining most of the indicators used in the previous section into a single model.

Our data are presidential-year values for twenty-seven of the measures previously shown; each of the twenty-seven has values for all or most of the election years from 1952 to 1992.[11] These variables are measured on very different scales and with widely varying ranges, so in order to combine them for an assessment of the overall pattern, we first standardized them such that each had a mean of 0 and a variance of 1 across the eleven elections.[12] We next set the "polarity" (i.e., multiplied the standardized measure by −1 where appropriate) so that low (negative) standardized values were expected before 1964 and high (positive) values were expected from 1972 to 1992. Finally, the standardized measures were combined into a single variable with 268 observations (297 minus missing data).

Figure 5.10 charts the mean score of this combined, standardized set of measures for each election year. It is quite evident that the annual means are low and comparable in the pre-1960s elections and that they increased dramatically and almost linearly in 1964, 1968, and 1972. After 1968, there were only small changes in the election-year averages. The pattern of means in the sixth party system (1972–1992) is, like that in the fifth (1952–1960), nearly flat. The difference between the average on our measure before 1964 (−1.24 in standardized units) and at the new equilibrium, beginning in 1972 (0.66), is quite large and obviously statistically significant.

Another way to look at the standardized measure is shown in Table 5.1, where we report for each presidential election year the number of instances in which the measure is positive and negative. Prior to 1964, all 73 observations are negative; there is, in other words, not a single instance for the entire period in which the value for any of the variables is at or above the mean. Beginning in 1972, 88 percent of the cases are positive (only 17 of 141 falling below the mean level). For the two realigning elections, however, we find exactly the same number of cases above and below average: 26 percent (7 of 27) above average in 1964, 74 percent (20 of 27) in 1968.[13]

In sum, the data support our contention that there was major and systematic change in a wide range of variables over the period in question. Moreover, this change is almost exactly the kind we would expect if the equilibrium account is correct: Substantial stability is followed, during the realignment, by massive change—which is in turn followed by substantial stability in the postcritical era.

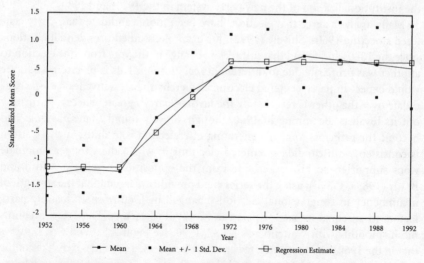

FIGURE 5.10   Macropattern, 1952–1992. Shown are mean and +/−1 standard deviation of 27 standardized variables. *Source:* Calculated by the authors.

TABLE 5.1   Number of Times the Standardized Summary Variable Is Above or Below the Mean, by Year

	1952	1956	1960	1964	1968	1972	1976	1980	1984	1988	1992
At or above mean	0	0	0	7	20	24	22	25	19	17	17
Below average	21	25	27	20	7	3	4	2	2	3	3

NOTE: This table is based on the 27 measures used to construct Figure 5.10. See text for further discussion.

SOURCE: American National Election Studies, 1952–1992.

INSTITUTIONALIZATION OF THE
CANDIDATE-CENTERED PARTY SYSTEM

Our empirical analysis provides strong evidence of the cycle of equilibrium–disequilibrium–new equilibrium that is at the heart of changes in party systems. The many series of micropatterns, along with the macropattern displayed in Figure 5.10, vividly demonstrate the rapid, fundamental change in the political order that took place in the 1960s. Just as striking is the portrayal of a new equilibrium in the 1970s and 1980s. Instead of continuing instability, which some believe to be characteristic of this period, we see a degree of stability quite similar to the supposedly quiescent 1950s. It is our view that the current equilibrium era represents a distinct sixth party system—one that we call the "candidate-centered party system." This section proceeds with three claims, two made rather briefly. We begin by pointing to the rise of candidate-centered elections in the 1960s, note several aspects of a policy basis to that critical era, and then argue in more detail about the institutionalization of the new party system in the 1970s and 1980s.

Many analysts agree that elections have been more candidate than party centered since the 1960s. Shively (1992), for example, studied presidential elections since the 1840s and found that until 1960, change in the vote from one election to another was primarily due to differential *mobilization*. This is precisely what one would expect in party-centered elections, whereby the attractiveness of one candidate over the other is revealed by the favored party's greater success in turning out its loyalists. Beginning in 1960, though, Shively found that *conversion* had become the principal force in generating interelection vote shifts. Such a pattern is consistent with candidate-centered elections in which the stronger candidate woos supporters to his or her side from the opposition. Similarly, Alford and Brady (1989a, 1989b), using the series cited previously, argued that the strength of incumbency in congressional elections changed in 1960 from exclusively party factors to an equal impact of party and individual factors. These two accounts mesh smoothly with Wattenberg's (1987, 1990; see Figures 5.3 and 5.6) findings that in the 1960s and thereafter, fewer citizens expressed *any* likes *or* dislikes of the parties on standard ANES open-ended questions (see Appendix); this was interpreted by Wattenberg as an indication of the increasing irrelevance of parties to voters' assessments of candidates, issues, or contemporary politics in general.

Studies such as these conclusively document the candidate-centered nature of elections today, a pattern that first became evident in the critical era of the 1960s. It also appears that a "policy realignment" occurred at about the same time. On the domestic side, Carmines and Stimson (1989), Edsall (1991), and others have described dramatic changes in the parties' stands on civil rights, racial, and other domestic issues during the 1960s; they also have noted the extent to which this new alignment was perceived clearly by the electorate. In foreign affairs, the 1960s witnessed a breakup of the bipartisan consensus over the Cold War and relations with the Soviet Union (see Destler, Gelb, and Lake 1984)—a breakup due to the Vietnam War, which led to a new partisan cleavage over foreign and defense policies at both the elite level and that of the mass public.

But although mass (and elite) opinions and behavior fit closely with the equilibrium–disequilibrium–new equilibrium cycle, and significant policy realignment can also be found in the 1960s, we differ from those who saw largely instability and dealignment (e.g., Jensen 1981; Silbey 1991) in our belief that what has happened since the critical era involves a new *form* of political parties: the "candidate-centered" parties. Moreover, this new form has become sufficiently institutionalized since the early 1970s to conclude that this period saw the emergence of a new, and quite different, party *system*.

Let us consider, then, the form of party that this new party system replaced. Created in the 1830s, the earlier party was a *mass-based* party centered mainly on winning elections—i.e., on mobilizing voters to get to the polls and support the party's candidates on election day. Accounts from the "golden age" of parties in the late nineteenth century use such terms as "armies" and "religious movements" to describe the intense feelings that surrounded partisan election campaigns. In particular, candidates relied on the parties to carry their message (see Chapter 13); it was not until the turn of the century, for example, that presidential nominees actually campaigned in person. With the secret ballot not adopted in most places until at least the late 1880s, parties distributed their own "party strip" ballots—which meant that incumbents' reelection fortunes usually depended as much on the overall success of the party as on their own personal strengths. As a result, the freedom to maneuver after being elected was constrained by the knowledge that they would have to depend on help from the party if they wanted to win another term (see Burnham 1970).

Although U.S. parties became progressively weaker throughout the twentieth century, their basic form (mass organizations designed to get out the vote) remained that set down in the Jacksonian era. In contrast, the current party is configured very differently: Elections center on the individual candidates, and the "party-in-the-electorate" has greatly deteriorated as an unnecessary and often irrelevant loyalty. The critical era of the 1960s was, therefore, critical for the party as well as the polity as a whole. Both parties reformed their institutions and practices after (and even during) this critical era.

The most visible action on the Democratic side began with the adoption of rules changes proposed by the McGovern-Fraser Commission in 1972; numerous other reforms followed, primarily affecting the selection and instruction of delegates to the national nominating convention (see Crotty and Jackson 1985). Some critics (e.g., Polsby 1983) have argued that these reforms undermined the party by wresting control over presidential nominations from party elites and moving it to voters, candidates, and the media. Yet Reiter (1985) has convincingly demonstrated that the supposed ill effects of the new rules largely predated their adoption. Thus, it is better to see Democratic reforms of the 1970s as adjusting the party to the new realities of candidate-centered elections—or, at most, as pushing it further along that path. Perhaps more consequential was a different aspect of these and related changes, i.e., the fact that they imposed national rules over those developed by the state parties and, at times, over laws passed by state legislatures. That is, the reforms were an important step in the process of *nationalizing* political parties.

The GOP generally followed, if often far more weakly than the Democrats, a similar path toward procedural reform. However, Republicans took the lead in making changes that served to further nationalization in other ways (while at the same time strengthening state and local party organizations)—and this time, it was the Democrats who played catch-up. What we are referring to are efforts in both camps to professionalize, institutionalize, and build up the resource base of "parties-as-organizations" (Herrnson 1988; Kayden and Mahe 1985). To a greater degree than ever before, party organizations no longer ran campaigns; doing so became the responsibility of individual candidates. But they did begin to provide critical *services* and technological *expertise* to candidates, from recruiting and training them to providing assistance in polling, media operations, direct mail, fundraising, assistance with legal requirements, and the like. In addition, under campaign finance legislation enacted by Congress in the 1970s, parties were able to contribute at least limited direct funding (as well as additional "soft money") to assist campaigns; they also created such devices as "bundling" gifts from political action committees and channeling this money to candidates.[14] In fact, evidence gathered over the years indicates that party organizations have indeed become stronger, more professionalized, better financed, and more fully institutionalized at the national, state, and local levels (Cotter et al. 1984; Gibson et al. 1983; Herrnson 1988).

A third component of the political party is the "party-in-government." With the Democratic majority in Congress deeply divided during the 1960s and 1970s over civil rights, Vietnam, and other issues, typical measures of the "strength" of parties as legislative voting blocs declined and the so-called conservative coalition (where a majority of Republicans and southern Democrats are pitted against a majority of northern Democrats) came to rival party as the principal basis of congressional voting. At about the same time, reform efforts within Congress began to gain increasing support from members. According to David Rohde (1991), changes enacted in the mid-1970s provided the institutional basis for "conditional party government" by, among other things, strengthening the role of the Democratic caucus (the name given to meetings of all Democrats in the chamber) and of the House and majority party leadership.[15] By "conditional," Rohde meant that an American version of party government was made more feasible through these reforms, provided that a key condition was met. The condition was simply that party members must have sufficient interests in common to desire acting collectively to achieve common policy goals. In the late 1970s and 1980s, this condition began to be satisfied more fully—with the result that the voting strength of party increased dramatically and, by some measures, reached highs unsurpassed since early in the century.

Growing satisfaction of the conditions necessary to sustain conditional party government (i.e., greater intraparty agreement and more pronounced interparty divisions on policy goals) was an indirect consequence of the critical era of the 1960s. For example, one of the great achievements made possible by the parties' policy shift on civil rights was passage of the Voting Rights Act in 1965. This legislation effectively enfranchised blacks and dramatically increased their proportion of the voting public, especially in the South. And as we saw earlier, blacks realigned to become overwhelmingly Democratic in their party affiliations during the 1960s while significant numbers of native white southerners moved to the GOP. The result was that, particularly in presidential and congressional elections, Republican candidates found themselves able to compete with mounting success in southern politics.

For many southern Democratic politicians, the inclusion of blacks and the defection of large numbers of conservative whites led to electoral and reelectoral coalitions that were more liberal than in the past. Accordingly, as Rohde shows, there were some instances in which formerly conservative southern Democrats in Congress began voting much like their northern counterparts. Especially in districts where public opinion leaned to the right, Democrats were often replaced by conservative Republicans; in other districts, moderate and even liberal Democrats succeeded their conservative predecessors. By the late 1970s and 1980s, the southern Democratic congressional delegation had started to look more like northern Democrats. Because these two groups tended to have numerous policy views in common, the conditions of conditional party government were more fully satisfied. Thus, the party-in-government eventually strengthened as a result of the critical era of the 1960s and internal reforms in Congress.

Denise Baer (1993, p. 2), in trying to "codify and define an emerging consensus among a variety of party scholars concerning the institutionalization of party," has suggested that the contemporary "institutionalized parties are characterized by an integrative party community, the development of stable factions, increased organizational interdependence, and an increased organizational vitality" (p. 28). We may fairly conclude that today's political party is institutionalized as the representational vehicle for the sixth party system, but the new party is far different from its predecessor, which for all intents and purposes collapsed in the critical era of the 1960s. The old party was designed to control elections and therefore to control access to office, and to use that access for securing the spoils needed to maintain a well-oiled and effective machine. The quintessential example of this form of party was the local machine, led by someone who might or might not hold office himself but who sought to control the fates of those who did (see Chapter 13). The new form of party is not such a machine. It is, instead, an organization designed to serve the interests of its central actors—its candidates and officeholders. Although well-financed and professionalized, the organization no longer dominates campaigns; candidates do. The party stands in service to its candidates, and it is the candidates whom the voters see and evaluate.

We might say that, in effect, the decaying "party-in-the-electorate" has been replaced by a vital "party-in-elections." Whether in elections or in government, the modern party organization serves its officeseekers and officeholders—thereby making the candidate-centered election system viable and facilitating the exercise of a version of party government, provided the necessary conditions are met. As noted, the key condition for party-in-government to be effective is that its officeholders find common policy ground among themselves. In office, as in elections, this is a defining characteristic of the politician-centered party. And the critical era of the 1960s, in partisan terms, is marked above all by a fundamental transformation to just this sort of party system.

CONCLUSION

It is time to declare the existence of a sixth American party system. The United States experienced a critical-election era in the 1960s, as is amply demonstrated by the collection of changes we have reviewed. It was a change unlike previous realignments, but all such periods are in some ways unique. As anticipated, there is a new equilibrium in the same indicators that were so stable in the 1950s and changed so dramatically in the 1960s. It has taken a series of elections for this to become clear, but it is now amply apparent.

The last major analysis of an entire spectrum of descriptors of the American electorate was in *The Changing American Voter* (Nie, Verba, and Petrocik 1979; originally published in 1976). Covering as it did the previous equilibrium, the realignment period, and the first of the postrealignment elections—and being written in reaction to the masterful description of the 1950s in *The American Voter* (Campbell et al. 1960)—it is not at all surprising that what the authors emphasized was the change that racked the electorate as well as our theoretical understanding of public opinion and voting. With the decline in partisanship, which had been regarded as the bedrock of the electorate's understanding and evaluation of parties and candidates, it is small wonder that dealignment and volatility became the new catchwords.

Just as *The Changing American Voter* heralded a revised view of voters and elections based on the data then available, it is time for a reassessment based on the entire period from 1952 to the present. What such a review indicates is (1) an equilibrium period for 1952–1960 as was described in *The American Voter*; (2) a period of turmoil documented in *The Changing American Voter* that can now be properly interpreted as a realignment of numerous features of the electorate; and (3) a not previously recognized equilibrium period since 1972. The new equilibrium is unlike the old—the curve in Figure 5.10 shows no hint of a return to the previous level—but that is not surprising. Reestablishment of the old order is not a characteristic of any of the previous critical eras.

There seems to be consensus on the appropriate name for the sixth party system. What most clearly characterizes the period since the 1960s is the decline of parties in the electorate and the rise of candidate-centered parties. When partisanship gave way as the underpinning of electoral decisions, candidates came to the fore. Parties did not merely stand aside, however, and preside over their own decay. They changed their representative character and the ways in which they related to candidates and emerged as still viable institutions in the American electoral world.

The sixth American party system—the candidate-centered party system—has been with us since 1972. Changes that occurred during the 1960s were so great and so pervasive that they cry out to be called a critical-election period. The new system of candidate-centered parties is so distinct and so portentous that one can no longer deny its existence or its character. With this recognition, we have come full cycle in our study of the American electorate. We began in an equilibrium period; lived through, documented, and observed a critical realignment; and can now, with the perspective of time, recognize the new stability.

When the periodicity of American electoral history first became apparent to scholars, we might have thought that this completed our understanding of voting behavior. What we realize instead is that each new critical era establishes patterns that are unlike the old and that need analysis and interpretation of their own. So our study of voting behavior is not complete. Still, we have reaffirmed the view that voters, parties, and their interaction—including macropatterns of electoral history—can be understood using many of the concepts that have been developed over the decades since the Columbia and Michigan groups first began the empirical study of electoral behavior and since V.O. Key Jr. (1955, 1964) wrote his brilliant studies of political parties and introduced critical elections as a central concept for understanding American political history.

THE 1994 CONGRESSIONAL ELECTIONS

The 1994 elections were arguably the most dramatic and surprising in at least a generation. Republican success in winning control of Congress for the first time in forty years, along with the GOP's capture of numerous state legislatures and governorships, was the stuff of which realignments are made. These changes seemed all the more impressive because they were largely unanticipated, even by party leaders, right up until election day. A case can thus be made for 1994 as the beginning of a new critical election period—this time including the long-awaited realignment of political parties.

That the sixth party system was, by the early 1990s, roughly three decades old served to fuel such speculation. The periodicity of earlier party systems had been between thirty and forty years, thereby reinforcing the belief that the existing party system was aged and nearing, if not at, its end. The social basis of the vote begun in the 1930s and sustained even as parties weakened during the 1960s and 1970s became so altered by 1992 that one of the authors of this chapter wrote afterward, "[I]t is time to declare the New Deal coalition dead" (Stanley and Niemi 1995, p. 237). The emergence of a new generation of leaders, replacing the World War II cohort that had held power since the 1960s, was another sign of change; in Washington, only Senate Majority Leader Robert Dole remained of the World War II group. Likewise, the fact that all of the Republican leadership in Congress (again excepting Dole) came from the South was a truly striking indicator of the altered electoral coalitions of the two parties.

A transformation could also be seen in the sharpened degree of conflict (especially outside the nation's capital; cf. Ceaser and Busch 1993) along the "insideroutsider" dimension of politics. From all appearances, voters' long-time disenchantment with politics as usual had finally produced a new power distribution that would lead in turn to significant changes in (1) the way Congress governed itself, (2) substantive policies regarding welfare, affirmative action, and so on, and (3) relations between Congress and the states. Last, the Republican Contract with America was closely analogous to a national party platform, an approach that stood in sharp contrast to the candidate-centered elections of the sixth party system.

Despite all of these developments, a note of caution is appropriate. For one thing, the narrow Republican majority in Congress (less than 20 seats in the House) and the relatively small shift in the aggregate vote that occurred from 1992 to 1994 (about 5 percentage points) remind us that GOP domination is not yet secure. The resentment and cynicism of voters that brought Republicans into power could just as quickly remove them if there is insufficient progress made toward implementing the contract (for example, with respect to term limits); or if Democrats succeed in portraying Republican policies as helping the rich at the expense of children, the poor, and others who are defenseless; or if seniors become disenchanted as Republicans come face to face with the problems of Social Security and Medicare; or if the Republican leadership is perceived as being too cynical and self-aggrandizing. Intraparty resolve and unity could also dissolve quickly as leaders compete with one another for the 1996 presidential nomination.

Moreover, we must remind ourselves that critical eras are not defined solely by realigning partisanship and that other indicators examined in our analysis have not necessarily changed a great deal. Although few of the measures we employed in this chapter are currently available for comparison, it would appear that many remained quite stable in 1994. Popular cynicism toward politics and government persisted at a high level. Images of the political parties, and of issue-party versus issue-candidate linkages, probably changed very little despite the contract. The country's most important problems continued to be viewed as lying mainly on the domestic front. Racial issues still sharply divided Republicans and Democrats. Voting turnout remained low by historical standards. And the possibility of greater consistency between congressional and presidential voting was not an issue in 1994.

The 104th Congress may therefore be the first of a new era (perhaps like the Republicans emerging and becoming the leading party in Congress in 1855 but failing to become the new majority party nationwide until 1960). Or it might turn out to be the last Congress fighting the politics of the sixth party system, with the shape of the seventh party system not well formulated for another several election cycles. Alternatively, current party institutions may prove to be incapable of establishing and maintaining a stable era that would constitute a new party system like those we have known in the past. Or minimally, it is possible that the United States is entering into a seventh party system unlike anything in our previous experience as a nation. The only certainty about the future when seen from the vantage point of an old and aging alignment is that the future is entirely uncertain—and that conflict in the emerging critical era remains, for the moment, a fiercely contested effort to define the politics of the next generation.

NOTES

This chapter was begun while the authors were fellows at the Center for Advanced Study in the Behavioral Sciences. We are grateful for financial support provided by the National Science Foundation (grant no. BNS87-00864). Most of the data are drawn from the University of Michigan's American National Election Study series, made available by the Inter-University Consortium for Political and Social Research. We would like to thank David Brady, James Stimson, and Martin Wattenberg for providing us with information or updates about their work, and Morris Fiorina, Franco Mattei, and Harold Stanley for their comments on an earlier draft.

1. The first party system began with the creation of the earliest U.S. political parties—Federalists and Jeffersonian Republicans—in the 1790s; it was in disarray by the 1820s. The second party system emerged with the rise to power of Jacksonian democracy and the mass-based parties of the 1820s and 1830s, and it lasted into the 1850s. The third party system was fully in place by 1860 with the election of the first Republican president, Abraham Lincoln; it was characterized by close competition between Republicans and Democrats. The fourth party system was formed in 1894–1896 as the GOP achieved a level of dominance that remained largely unbroken until the Great Depression. The fifth party system was forged in the 1930s as Democrats became the dominant party. For additional details, see Sundquist (1983), Clubb, Flanigan, and Zingale (1980), Brady (1988), Reichley (1992), Aldrich (1995).

2. The election(s) that usher in a new party system may constitute a "realignment," in which the minority party at the time becomes a majority (winning most of the votes cast and capturing most elective offices at all levels); this happened most clearly in the 1930s. But changes in party systems also may be realized as fundamental shifts in partisan institutional arrangements, e.g., when an altogether new party comes onto the scene (like the Republicans in the nineteenth century). For this reason, we prefer the more general term "critical election" or "critical era." See Aldrich (1995) for a more thorough discussion of the earlier party systems and the critical eras between them.

3. Our analysis does not exhaust all possible measures, but we believe that it does tap each of the major components proposed by "realignment" theorists as they apply to the mass electorate. Moreover, we have not selected only the best-fitting measures; indeed, a

few are discussed that do not fit very well at all (e.g., salience of New Deal issues, presidential and House split-district outcomes), although these are included in the macroanalysis even after establishing their lack of fit.

4. The ANES classifies as "apolitical" those individuals who express neither a partisan preference nor an attachment to independence; as their name implies, apoliticals tend to be uninterested, uninvolved, ill informed, and generally unconnected to the world of politics and government. See the Appendix for exact wording of the party-identification question.

5. The decline in numbers of strong partisans (and parallel increase in Independents) that occurred in 1992 was, we suspect, a short-term response to events—especially Ross Perot's presidential bid.

6. Favorable evaluations are indicated when the number of likes exceeds the number of dislikes for a particular party.

7. Changed popular perceptions were, in fact, rooted in reality: In Congress, a racial liberalism index based on members' roll-call votes shows Republicans in both houses to have been more liberal than Democrats from 1945 through 1964. But a dramatic reversal occurred in the mid-1960s, followed by a further increase in party differences during the 1970s (Carmines and Stimson 1989, p. 163).

8. On the concept of political efficacy and its relation to voter turnout, see Craig, Niemi, and Silver (1990), as well as Chapters 3 and 6 in this book.

9. Retirement slump reflects the tendency for the in-party's candidate to fare less well in an open-seat contest immediately following the retirement of an incumbent. Sophomore surge refers to the tendency for incumbent congressmen to do better in their first bid for reelection than they did when they won initially.

10. A similar trend is evident in the Senate, but these conclusions apply most clearly to House races (where smaller, more homogeneous constituencies give representatives a greater opportunity to interact and communicate with potential voters).

11. Excluded are interest in campaigns (because it is theoretically expected to have a different pattern) and Alford and Brady's measure of retirement slump and sophomore surge (because of its unmeasurability in 40 percent of the cases). Of the various ANES items that tap citizen feelings of trust and external efficacy, only "public officials don't care" (see Appendix) was included because it was the only one asked in presidential surveys prior to 1964. To avoid redundancy, we used the percentage of all Independents for whites (but not pure Independents), the racial liberalism of House and Senate Democrats (but not Republicans), and the item in Figure 5.6 (but not the numbers from Geer).

12. This is a common form of standardization, used to make items comparable when they are measured on different scales. It uses the formula $Z = (x_i - \bar{x})/s_x$ where x_i stands for each of the values across the eleven elections and $s_x = \sqrt{(1/(n-1))(x_i-\bar{x})^2}$ The values (i.e., the x's) are thus measured in terms of standard deviations above or below the mean of that variable across time.

13. We can also summarize the progression of the twenty-seven individual measures over time via a simple regression. The standardized measure is regressed on a realignment variable that is 0 for the fifth-party-system years, 0.333 for 1964 and 0.667 for 1968 (in order to capture the apparently linear change over the course of the realignment), and 1 for the sixth-party-system years. The result is as follows:

Standardized summary variable = $-1.169 + 1.870(X)$,
(.063)   (.083)

where X = 0 for 1952–1960, 0.333 for 1964, 0.667 for 1968, 1 for 1972–1992. (Standard errors in parentheses.)
Adj. R^2 = 0.656; N = 268

The predicted difference between the fifth and sixth party systems is a very substantial 1.9 standardized units.

The fit of this model is superior to one that assumes a linear increase (adjusted R^2 = 0.58), and it is nearly as good as one that allows each year to assume its actual mean value on the standardized measures. The latter had an adjusted R^2 of 0.69, which is the maximum possible obtainable from any combination of election-year values. We also estimated models with a linear "drift" within a given party system, but the estimate of change was not significant in either system.

14. For further information on campaign financing (including such practices as "soft money" and "bundling"), see Sorauf (1988), Alexander (1992), and Magleby and Nelson (1990).

15. These reforms were adopted primarily (but not exclusively) by Democrats in the House of Representatives. They included giving the Democratic caucus more say in choosing committee chairs and the Speaker greater control over assigning bills to committees and scheduling legislation, among numerous others.

6

Public Judgment and Political Engagement in the 1992 Election

RANDOLPH C. HORN
M. MARGARET CONWAY

In 1992, a three-decade-long trend in declining voter turnout was reversed. Although turnout rates did not reach the level attained in 1960 (see Chapter 5), various estimates confirm that a greater proportion of the electorate voted in 1992 than in recent presidential elections. One possible explanation for this is that higher turnout reflected a significant increase in the public's degree of political engagement during the 1992 campaign.

By "political engagement" we mean interest in and attention to politics. Indicators of engagement might include having a general interest in governmental and political affairs, following political campaigns, discussing political issues and candidates with friends or family, and consuming the mass media's political content regardless of the format through which that content is conveyed. In this chapter we examine political engagement, comparing a variety of measures from 1992 with patterns occurring in prior presidential elections and in the 1990 midterm. Also discussed are possible explanations for the patterns of engagement observed in 1992.

MODES AND LEVELS OF POLITICAL ENGAGEMENT

Were levels of political engagement among the mass public higher in 1992 than in previous presidential election contests? Comparisons based on a number of indicators suggest that the answer is yes. Although Americans did not raise their low opinions of government officials during the campaign season (see Chapter 3), they nevertheless appear to have become more engaged in or connected to the political process. The most obvious indication of this is the substantial increase in voter turnout, with just over 55 percent of the voting-age population making it to the polls on election day (up from about 50 percent four years earlier).[1] It seems unlikely that a highly alienated public would make such an impressive showing.

Rather, the increase points to an increasingly engaged, albeit skeptical, public that believes the political process to be important.

This same public pushed the campaigns to take positions on issues. For example, in a conversation with one of the authors, one senior Clinton adviser recalled the seriousness confronted by the Arkansas governor's campaign in New Hampshire during that state's primary: "Those people wanted no part of the media sideshow; they wanted to know what the candidates were going to do about the economy." The same seriousness and attention to issues was evident in the second 1992 presidential debate, which was held in Richmond, Virginia, and employed an unusual town hall format; audience members that night virtually pleaded with the candidates to abandon character assassination and mudslinging tactics and to provide a meaningful discussion of problems such as unemployment, crime, and the national debt that affected all citizens (see Germond and Witcover 1993, chapter 1). Most journalistic accounts of the 1992 campaign, from New Hampshire to election day in November, emphasized that voters were indeed attentive to what the candidates were saying and anxious to hear their ideas about how to deal with key policy issues. The earnestness implied by these largely anecdotal accounts is evident in survey results from 1992 as well.

Increased Levels of Political Engagement

Data from the American National Election Studies (ANES) series support the perception of increased popular investment in the political process.[2] Table 6.1, for example, presents figures for the past four presidential-year surveys. One clear sign of heightened engagement is the greater proportion of 1992 respondents claiming to have followed the campaign very closely (see Appendix for exact question wordings). The three previous presidential campaigns had sparked levels of interest only slightly higher than in off-year contests, hovering around 25–30 percent of the electorate. In 1992, however, the percentage saying they were "very much" interested increased by more than 10 points over 1988, and the percentage "not much" interested dwindled to 17.4 percent (down from about 25 percent between 1980 and 1988). Although such interest could conceivably stem from a fascination with the soap-opera-like adjuncts to the substance of the campaign, this does not appear likely given the intensity of issue interest and concern over the outcome also evident in 1992 (discussed further on).

Increased interest in the campaign was accompanied by a modest rise in the number of respondents saying they generally "follow what's going on in government and public affairs" whether there's an election going on or not. Attention to politics remained fairly static during the 1980s, but in 1992 people shifted into the more attentive categories. The proportion indicating that they followed politics "most of the time" increased from 22.4 percent in 1988 to 26.5 percent (almost identical to the levels observed in 1980–1984), the proportion who did so either "most" or "some of the time" increased from 59.3 percent to 67.9 percent (up five points from the previous high in 1984). These figures suggest that Americans were

TABLE 6.1   Levels of Political Engagement and Concern, 1980–1992

	1980	1984	1988	1992
Follow election campaign				
Very interested	29.8%	28.4%	27.8%	38.8%
Not interested	26.0%	24.8%	25.0%	17.4%
Pay attention to politics				
Most of the time	26.4%	26.4%	22.4%	26.5%
Most or some of the time	61.3%	62.8%	59.3%	67.9%
Care about election outcome				
A good deal	55.9%	64.8%	61.0%	75.7%
Economic evaluations				
National economy better	3.7%	42.8%	18.8%	4.6%
Personal finances better	32.4%	43.3%	42.4%	30.3%
Follow campaign through media				
Radio	46.9%	45.2%	31.2%	36.7%
Newspaper	70.7%	76.9%	63.6%	65.4%
Magazine	34.6%	34.8%	24.5%	22.7%
Television	85.9%	86.1%	n/a	88.9%
Sample N =	1,614	2,257	2,040	2,487

NOTE: See Appendix for question wordings.
SOURCE: American National Election Studies, 1980–1992.

at least somewhat more attuned to political events in 1992 than they had been in over a decade.

The data in Table 6.1 are consistent with the engagement thesis in yet another way: People cared more about the election outcome in 1992 than they had throughout the 1980s. From 1980 to 1988, the proportion of respondents saying they cared "a good deal" who won the presidential contest fluctuated between 55 and 65 percent. In 1992, that number climbed to almost 76 percent, more than 10 points higher than the apex of recent elections—and almost 20 points higher than the nadir in 1980. Clearly, the American public felt that it mattered who won the race for the White House.

One reason for such concern probably had to do with citizens' anxiety over the economy, which was evident from the very beginning of the campaign through the general election in November. Specifically, many more people in 1992 thought the economy was worse relative to a year earlier (72.3 percent) than had been true in either 1984 or 1988; only 4.6 percent thought the economy was improving. Respondents' worries about national economic conditions also hit close to home, with only about 30 percent feeling that their *personal* financial situation had improved in the preceding twelve months (substantially lower than the proportion in 1988). Although this figure implies that people's personal economic evaluations were perhaps more positive than their national economic assessments, it does not imply true satisfaction. Indeed, taken as a whole, respondents' evaluations of their personal financial situation were marginally lower than in 1980—the last time an incumbent president was turned out of office.

It is curious that despite citizens showing greater concern over the election outcome, their appetites for news about the campaign did not increase substantially. Only slightly more attention was paid to radio reports about the campaign in 1992 (36.7 percent) than in 1988 (31.2 percent), and this modest increase seems even less impressive when one notes that both figures are substantially below those recorded in 1980 (46.9 percent) and 1984 (45.2 percent). Attention to newspaper stories rose slightly in 1992, with 65.4 percent saying they read newspaper articles about the campaign (up from 63.6 percent in 1988)—though, once again, higher levels were registered in both 1980 (70.7 percent) and 1984 (76.9 percent). Finally, rates of magazine readership were actually lower in 1992 (22.7 percent) than in any other recent election.[3]

There is, however, another side to the story. Notwithstanding the downward trend in involvement with older news formats, more than 85 percent of those watching TV news indicated that they paid at least some attention (54 percent either "a great deal" or "quite a bit") to television coverage of the campaign. Moreover, the proportion saying they watched the campaign on television increased slightly over previous election years, from about 86 percent in 1980–1984 to almost 89 percent in 1992. Although this latter figure might not represent a major change, it is important to remember that television coverage was more accessible than ever before—especially with all of the major candidates appearing on popular talk shows, and both Bush and Clinton appearing on MTV. Thus, the sheer amount of viewing attention may not have increased much, but the likelihood of what was viewed being "user friendly" was enhanced by the presence of a wider variety of television formats.

The greater variety of sources for campaign information in the most-used media platform (television) and the heightened level of overall interest should have had mutually reinforcing effects on potential voters' information about the campaign. On the one hand, the cost of obtaining appropriate (to the recipient) information was significantly reduced; viewers did not need to change their habits because news about the candidates—and often the candidates themselves—was available on programs they probably would have watched anyway, or at least were more likely to watch than the stodgy Sunday-morning public affairs programs. On the other hand, people may have been more willing to bear the increased cost for information gathering because they were more interested in the campaign and cared deeply about issues and the outcome of the contest.

Political Engagement and Mass Media Use

Without question, candidates in 1992 exploited a broad range of alternative channels of communication between themselves and the mass public. These had the advantage of enabling officeseekers to address directly what they perceived to be the electorate's concerns, bypassing the distorting filters imposed by journalists' own professional interests and goals. In the most obvious case, formats such as infomercials, radio and television talk shows, and entertainment programs—as well as some of the rules governing debates (e.g., the town hall setting in Richmond)—gave the presidential contenders an opportunity both to extend the reach of their campaigns in new and innovative ways and, in certain instances, to communicate with segments of the electorate not usually reached by network news coverage or traditional forms of electronic media-based political advertising.

Some analysts disparaged the "soft" content of radio and TV talk shows, but surveys conducted during the 1992 campaign indicated that this particular type of media was drawing attention from a significant proportion—approaching 50 percent (see Chapter 7)—of the electorate. In fact, a poll done on behalf of the Times Mirror Center for the People and the Press (1992a, p. 3) found that one-quarter of those tuning in to talk-radio programs such as Larry King or Rush Limbaugh claimed to have heard things about the election or candidates that they had not learned from other sources. People with household incomes over $50,000 and men aged 30 and older were among the most likely to obtain new information from talk-radio shows.

Late-night comedy provided another source of political information, especially for younger adults who tended not to pay close attention to politics through traditional channels. According to the Times Mirror surveys (1992a, p. 2), approximately one-third of audience members under age 30 obtained new information about the campaign from late-night comedy programs—compared with just one-fifth of those in the 30–49 age group and one-eighth of viewers aged 50 and over.

Despite Ross Perot's pioneering and extensive use of infomercials, these and other forms of paid political advertising received mixed reviews from the electorate. Although 72 percent of a Times Mirror (1992d) sample felt they learned a lot from Perot's half-hour presentations, just 40 percent said the infomercials made them more likely to vote for the Texas billionaire. Moreover, 59 percent described political ads in general as being "not too" or "not at all" helpful in deciding which presidential candidate to support (vs. 38 percent "very" or "fairly" helpful), and 74 percent (up from 63 percent in a 1990 survey) evaluated news reports more favorably than paid ads (22 percent vs. 28 percent in 1990) as a source of information about the candidates' policy positions. And although the latter did help some voters to get a better idea of what the candidates were like personally, news reports (58 percent vs. 35 percent for advertisements) were preferred even in this regard (Times Mirror 1992d, pp. 3–4).[4]

Age, Education, and Political Engagement

Higher turnout rates and overall interest in politics notwithstanding, levels of engagement in 1992 varied with both age and education. A Times Mirror survey administered in late May and early June asked people how much thought they had

TABLE 6.2   Measures of Political Engagement by Age, 1992

Age	Quite a Lot of Thought[a]	Plan to Vote[b]
18–24	36%	56%
25–29	45%	68%
30–34	50%	69%
35–49	62%	81%
50–64	64%	81%
65-plus	58%	81%

Sample N = 3,517

[a]Question: "How much thought have you given to the coming presidential election—quite a lot or only a little?"

[b]Question: "Do you yourself plan to vote in the election this November?"

SOURCE: Times Mirror (1992c, p. 35).

given to the upcoming presidential election: Fifty-five percent of all respondents (and 63 percent of registered voters) answered "quite a lot."[5] Yet, as shown in Table 6.2, younger citizens were considerably less likely than their elders to have given "quite a lot" of thought to the election—and less certain that they would make it to the polls on election day. The data also indicate that individuals with a high school education or less, regardless of age, were relatively disinclined to plan on voting in 1992 (Times Mirror 1992c, p. 38).[6]

Along the same lines, sizable age- and education-related differences can be seen from the 1984–1992 ANES data displayed in Table 6.3: Older citizens and those with higher levels of educational attainment tend to be more engaged in terms of (1) their interest in and concern about the outcome of the current campaign and (2) the attention they normally give to government and public affairs in general. What is striking, however, is the much greater interest and concern exhibited by *all* age and educational-attainment groups in 1992 as compared with the elections in 1984 and especially 1988. Also, the proportion who reported following government and politics most or some of the time rose in 1992—if sometimes by a modest amount—among all age groups except for those aged 65 to 75, and among all education categories except those with a college degree.

Given our findings in Table 6.3(B), it comes as no surprise that declining levels of turnout over time have been concentrated among certain population subgroups. One of the Times Mirror surveys provides evidence of escalating political *dis*engagement among the less well educated, with reported voter registration among those with a high school education or less dropping by 17 percentage points since 1960. Similar rates of turnout decline from 1964 to 1992 among citizens with less schooling are revealed in a series of postelection surveys done by the Bureau of the Census (U.S. Department of Commerce 1993).

116

TABLE 6.3   Political Engagement by Age and Education, 1984–1992

A. *Political Engagement by Age*

	18–24	25–34	35–44	45–54	55–64	65–75	76-plus
Follow election campaign:							
very interested							
1984	16.5%	22.0%	27.6%	31.8%	36.4%	41.4%	33.8%
1988	14.5%	20.9%	27.1%	30.6%	35.3%	39.2%	36.6%
1992	19.5%	36.6%	37.8%	42.1%	41.8%	47.5%	47.6%
Care about election outcome							
a good deal							
1984	56.5%	65.8%	66.3%	66.8%	68.1%	62.6%	68.9%
1988	47.9%	57.4%	63.5%	65.7%	68.5%	63.4%	58.3%
1992	63.9%	76.5%	74.7%	78.9%	75.6%	78.1%	79.6%
Pay attention to politics							
most or some of the time							
1984	46.9%	58.7%	64.0%	70.1%	67.9%	73.8%	63.2%
1988	45.9%	48.9%	62.4%	64.5%	63.5%	74.6%	57.7%
1992	52.5%	63.8%	67.2%	74.4%	74.4%	75.2%	68.0%
N = 1984	286	558	421	284	281	264	138
1988	196	490	480	248	252	232	133
1992	221	606	526	386	265	296	186

B. *Political Engagement by Education*

	Grades 0–8	Grades 9–11	High School Graduate	Some College	College Graduate
Follow election campaign:					
very interested					
1984	23.5%	20.7%	24.9%	30.7%	41.4%
1988	21.7%	17.1%	20.9%	33.6%	43.8%
1992	28.1%	24.7%	31.8%	42.1%	55.8%
Care about election outcome					
a good deal					
1984	59.0%	61.1%	61.7%	68.1%	74.3%
1988	56.6%	51.2%	55.2%	66.7%	73.8%
1992	66.0%	64.1%	73.3%	77.9%	84.6%
Pay attention to politics					
most or some of the time					
1984	46.2%	51.7%	57.0%	69.0%	82.0%
1988	40.0%	39.7%	53.1%	67.1%	80.6%
1992	49.7%	56.9%	60.5%	74.1%	82.4%
N = 1984	238	271	799	554	374
1988	198	240	714	450	397
1992	192	274	814	572	570

NOTE: See Appendix for question wordings.
SOURCE: American National Election Studies, 1984–1992.

Political Engagement and
Satisfaction with the Political Process

In addition to higher levels of engagement among some segments of the electorate in 1992, surveys indicate greater satisfaction with the political process than was present four years earlier. A Times Mirror poll conducted the weekend after the election, for example, found that 77 percent of the public believed they had learned enough during the campaign to make an informed choice among presidential candidates (see Chapter 3; cf. Frankovic 1993); in contrast, only 59 percent expressed such a sentiment in 1988. Credit for this shift can perhaps be given to the heightened role of issue discussion, as evidenced by the fact that 59 percent saw the campaign as being more policy oriented in 1992 than had been true in 1988. Perceptions of increased issue focus did vary, however, with the candidate one happened to support, i.e., Clinton (67 percent) and Perot backers (58 percent) perceived greater discussion of policy matters than did Bush voters (48 percent). Issue positions taken by the candidates also were more likely to be cited as the reason for vote choice by Clinton and Perot supporters than by those favoring Bush (Times Mirror 1992d, p. 1).[7]

Popular satisfaction with the political process in 1992 extended to the presidential debates, with 70 percent saying the debates had been helpful to them in making their vote choice (compared with 48 percent responding similarly in 1988). The debates were especially helpful to younger voters (81 percent of those under 30 and 73 percent of those aged 30–49); in addition, younger voters were more likely to feel they had learned enough from the campaign to make an informed choice among candidates in the presidential contest (81 percent of the under-30s and 79 percent of the 30–49 group, but only 72 percent of those aged 50 and older; see Times Mirror 1992d).[8]

It is interesting that although the youngest cohorts were less politically engaged in 1992, older citizens not only had stronger reservations about the choices available to them in that election (or, to be precise, about the information that could be utilized for making a vote decision) but also exhibited higher levels of discontent with government and with the political process in general. On a Times Mirror question asking whether "it is time for Washington politicians to step aside and make room for new leaders," widespread dissatisfaction with national leadership was present in all age groups (e.g., 80 percent agreement among the youngest respondents, 87 percent among the oldest). On the other hand, just 45 percent of those aged 18–24 (and 48 percent of the 25–29s) agreed that "we need new people in Washington even if they are not as effective as experienced politicians"—a figure that rose steadily to 62 percent for age 50–64 and 67 percent for those 65 and over (Times Mirror 1992c, p. 14).

Age differences aside, the Times Mirror surveys include several other measures that point to a growing unhappiness in recent years with government and politics. Comparing responses to a series of questions asked in both 1990 and 1992, we learn that a higher proportion of citizens in 1992 (1) believed that "elected officials in Washington lose touch with the people pretty quickly" (84 percent in 1992 vs. 78 percent in 1990); (2) rejected the idea that "most elected officials care what people like me think" (62 percent in 1992 vs. 53 percent in 1990); and (3) disagreed with the statement that "the government is really run for the benefit of all the people" (54 percent in 1992 vs. 45 percent in 1990). In contrast, a *higher* proportion (49 percent in 1992 vs. 42 percent in 1990) disagreed with the proposition that "people like me don't have any say about what the government does" (Times Mirror 1992c, p. 13; see Chapter 3). That enhanced perception of personal efficacy could well have been a significant factor leading to greater political engagement and higher turnout in 1992.

ALTERNATIVE EXPLANATIONS FOR
PATTERNS OF POLITICAL ENGAGEMENT

What might account for the seemingly higher levels of political engagement that were observed among the American public in 1992? We have suggested that one possible explanation lies with the increase in accessible information and a growing sense that the presidential contest involved a more meaningful choice and outcome than had been the case in a number of years. Evidence presented earlier supports this interpretation, and additional findings along the same lines will be offered momentarily. Nevertheless, there are other explanations that may contribute to our understanding of citizen engagement in the 1992 election.

Consider, for example, the impact of age-related differences in political engagement and of changes in age-distribution patterns that have developed over time. Low levels of engagement among the young are in part a function of these citizens' relative disinterest in politics—and of their failure to view voting as a sufficiently compelling civic obligation to stimulate turnout in the face of such disinterest (Times Mirror 1992c, pp. 4–5). The under-35 cohort also tends to have a weaker sense of political efficacy, is less likely to perceive elections as politically "effective" (Times Mirror 1992c, p. 40), and, to an even greater degree in the 1990s than previously, consumes less political content from the mass media than do older Americans (Times Mirror 1992c, p. 45). The critical point we want to make, however, is that younger people constituted a smaller proportion of the voting-age population in 1992 than in the three previous presidential elections.[9]

Another possible explanation is based on alternative processes of political mobilization and the extent to which they were present in 1992. Mobilization by social organizations is often credited with having helped to create the higher levels of engagement that existed during earlier historical eras in the United States. In particular, a traditional role once ascribed to political parties was the mobilization of their supporters. Party election-district organizations were charged with identifying supporters and making sure they were eligible to vote (including being registered in those areas where voter registration was required); on election day, the party's task was to contact these same supporters and provide assistance where needed to get them to the polls (see Chapter 13). Although parties in different areas of the country may not always have been effective at performing such tasks (and are much less effective today than in the past), the assumption underlying the task description itself may still be valid: Because citizens vary to a significant degree in their respective levels of political engagement, mobilization by others—the party, individual candidates, interest groups, or social organizations—is frequently viewed as necessary to stimulate participation by some proportion of the electorate. Perhaps, then, external mobilization efforts are one of the keys to heightened popular engagement in 1992.

A final contributing factor is suggested by Elisabeth Noelle-Neumann's (1993) "spiral of silence" theory. The theory posits that observations made in one context often spread to another; that is, individuals are encouraged to state their views—or to refrain from stating them—until, in a "spiraling" process, one perspective comes to dominate public discourse and adherents of alternative points of view end up suppressing expression of their opinions. Those who support nondominant positions, in other words, tend to remain silent so as to prevent being socially isolated. Moreover, according to Noelle-Neumann (p. 124), the more polarized the situation, (1) the less discussion that occurs on an issue and (2) the further apart are citizen estimates of the distribution of views on it. With these patterns in mind, we can see that Noelle-Neumann's (p. 153) argument places special importance on the structuring of attention through issue selection in the public-opinion-formation process.

What we are talking about here is *agenda-setting*, a function normally credited to the mass media (Iyengar and Kinder 1987) but one that also can be performed by political candidates over the course of an election campaign. Candidates' efforts to set the agenda occur mainly through personal appearances (which by their nature can only reach a small segment of the potential electorate), through paid ads, and through the filter of news media coverage. Because the latter is highly selective in the material presented, it may color perceptions that people have of both candidates and the policy agenda in general. Research studies demonstrate, for example, that news coverage of campaigns tends to focus primarily on the "horse race" and, to a somewhat lesser extent, on the personal characteristics of candidates (Patterson 1988). Only in a limited way does news content present issue stands and illuminate policy differences.

The situation was different in 1992, however. Alternative media formats employed by the candidates, in combination with new and innovative rules for presidential debates, provided more extensive and less filtered exposure to issue positions than is normally the case—as well as an opportunity for many individuals to realize that they were not alone in their issue priorities and preferences. Ross Perot's candidacy, in particular, appears to have had such an effect. We therefore agree with Ragsdale and Rusk (1993) that the *context* of an election can significantly impact information, interest, and news media use levels among prospective voters. Specifically, it is possible that the altered campaign context of 1992 may

TABLE 6.4   Perception of Party and Candidate Differences by Political Engagement, 1992

	Low Engagement	Medium Engagement	High Engagement
See important differences in what Republicans and Democrats stand for	35.7%	55.0%	77.3%
Believe one candidate would do a better job at handling nation's economy	54.4%	64.8%	74.9%
Believe one candidate would do a better job at making health care more affordable	63.6%	75.6%	80.5%
Believe one candidate would do a better job at reducing budget deficit	54.8%	55.9%	62.1%
Closer to either major party candidate on the abortion issue	61.2%	74.4%	84.1%
N =	296 (13.3%)	896 (40.1%)	1,040 (46.6%)

NOTE: See Appendix for question wordings. Political engagement is measured with an index built from items measuring campaign interest and general attentiveness to public affairs.

SOURCE: American National Election Study, 1992.

have worked to enhance both self-mobilization and the effectiveness of efforts by others (party and candidate organizations, interest groups, etc.) to mobilize citizens to political attentiveness, involvement, and even activism.

Political Engagement and Perceptions of Candidate and Party Differences

It is reasonable to expect that those who are more fully engaged in the campaign will perceive greater differences between leading presidential candidates and the parties they represent. Using an index of "political engagement" created from the 1992 ANES measures of campaign interest and general attentiveness to public affairs (see Table 6.1 and Appendix), we tested for these effects.[10] The data in Table 6.4 indicate that more-engaged respondents do indeed tend to make sharper distinctions between both parties and candidates. Most dramatically, 77 percent of the highly engaged—compared with about 36 percent of the least engaged and 55 percent of those in between—believe there are "important differences in what the Republicans and Democrats stand for."

A similar pattern is found with regard to perceived candidate differences in specific policy areas. The most engaged in 1992, for example, were much more likely (74.9 percent) than the least engaged (54.4 percent) to suggest that one of the major presidential contenders would do a better job at handling the nation's economy. A slightly smaller gap between these two groups (80.5 percent to 63.6 percent) existed on the question of whether one candidate would do a better job at making health care more affordable. We suspect that the higher overall degree of differentiation on health care is a function of the extensive treatment given to this issue during the campaign, especially on the Democratic side (with approximately 9 out of 10 Clinton voters able to discern a difference, and 56 percent of all those who did prefer one of the major candidates voting for the challenger).

Finally, high-engagement respondents were only somewhat more inclined (62.1 percent vs. 54.8 percent for the least engaged and 55.9 percent for the middle category) to believe that either Bush or Clinton[11] would do better at reducing the budget deficit. Given the vagueness of candidate rhetoric concerning how this might be accomplished, it is not too surprising that the percentages here are smaller than for the other two policy areas examined, i.e., people (especially those in the high- and medium-engagement groups) had a more difficult time choosing sides.

The last set of entries in Table 6.4 provides what we feel is a more rigorous test of the effect of engagement on one's ability to distinguish between candidates. In this case, the question is not whether respondents anticipate superior *performance* from one candidate but, instead, whether they are able to identify concrete *policy differences* on an issue of widespread public concern. The divisive issue of abortion rights seems particularly suitable for such a test because most Americans have an opinion and both major candidates were clear about where they stood on abortion during the 1992 campaign. Our results are consistent with what we saw previously: Only about 22 percent of all respondents failed to perceive a difference between Bush and Clinton, but the fully engaged (84.1 percent) were clearly more likely than other groups to do so (61.2 percent low engagement, 74.4 percent medium engagement).

If levels of engagement help to explain voters' ability to distinguish between candidates and parties on the important issues of the day—an ability that presumably makes the vote choice a more meaningful one—do they also have an independent effect on the *likelihood* of voting when differential perceptions and various of the other factors discussed are held constant? Table 6.5 presents a multivariate model of turnout that sheds light on this question and, in addition, provides some clues as to whether the pattern of turnout in 1992 was a departure from recent historical norms.[12]

Our findings confirm much of the conventional wisdom concerning turnout, with many of the variables upon which scholars have typically relied to explain voter turnout being effective in this model as well. For example, older people, the better educated, those who are "rooted" in their communities (married, owning a home; see Teixeira 1992), newspaper readers, and the politically efficacious were

TABLE 6.5   Logistic Regression of Voter Turnout, 1992

Variable	B	Variable	B
Respondent age	.2947 (.0434)	Party differences	.1322 (.1414)
Respondent education	.4412 (.0577)	Home ownership	.4330 (.1413)
Campaign: newspaper	.4825 (.1516)	Marital status	.1632 (.1375)
Campaign: radio/TV	.1103 (.1222)	Candidate: economy	.4218 (.1562)
Follow talk shows	−.0208 (.1405)	Candidate: health care	.0817 (.1727)
Campaign contacts	.2723 (.0707)	Candidate: Deficit	−.0784 (.1531)
Political engagement	.1789 (.0335)	Predict close race	−.0399 (.1391)
Express preferences	.3971 (.0913)	People have no say	.1404 (.0498)
		Constant	−4.3920 (.3699)

	Chi-Square/Degrees of Freedom	Significance
−2 Log likelihood	1436.792 / 1843	1.000
Model chi-square	522.799 / 16	.0000
Improvement	522.799 / 16	.0000
Goodness of fit	1841.912 / 1843	.5028

NOTE: Entries in this table are logistic regression coefficients, with standard errors in parentheses. See Appendix and text for question wordings and description of indices.
SOURCE: American National Election Study, 1992.

among the most likely to turn out at the polls on election day.[13] At the same time, however, our combined index of engagement also has significant explanatory power of its own, with individuals who followed the campaign and paid relatively close attention to public affairs voting at higher rates than did those who were less fully engaged. The basic relationship reported here is similar to that which existed in prior years (1980–1988), but we must not forget that the aggregate *level* of engagement was higher in 1992 than it had been in the past several elections. Thus, increased turnout appears to be partly attributable to a shift in the degree to which citizens were psychologically "involved" in the political process as a whole, and in the particular choices offered to them during the 1992 campaign.

Two added features of our model should be noted. First, as one might expect, it shows that turnout was higher—even after controlling for the effects of other variables—among people who did not mind sharing their political views ("express preferences"), i.e., among those who discussed politics, tried to persuade friends and family how to vote, wore campaign buttons and put bumper stickers on their cars, attended campaign rallies, or otherwise worked actively for one of the parties or candidates.[14] Citizens in 1992 evidently put their money where their mouths were, or at least voted if they talked. A final aspect of the model in Table 6.5 is that individuals who articulated a preference for one presidential candidate on the economic management dimension were more likely to participate than those who did not. Although this was not the case for the two other performance areas included in our analysis (making health care affordable and reducing the deficit), having a meaningful choice on the major issue of the 1992 campaign apparently did help to get voters to the polls.

CONCLUSION

Despite variations by generation and educational attainment, it seems clear that the overall level of political engagement was substantially higher among the American public in 1992 than in any recent presidential election. We believe that this change cannot be attributed solely to demographic shifts in the population, such as an aging cohort of baby boomers (whose natural progression through the life cycle is leading to greater involvement in politics; see Verba and Nie 1972) or increased educational attainment; to the contrary, heightened engagement was evident among *all* age and education groups in 1992. Other factors appear to have been at work, including an expanded information environment (made possible largely through the rise of alternative media formats), greater citizen concern with the election outcome (and satisfaction with the available choices in that election), enhanced feelings of political efficacy among prospective voters, and, perhaps, more effective mobilization efforts by organized groups such as parties and candidate organizations. Further, our multivariate analysis suggests that the higher level of engagement was likely one key factor helping to stimulate voter participation in the 1992 presidential contest.

It remains to be seen whether this newly elevated state of popular involvement in the political process will persist. The pall of apathy and alienation that has hung over American politics since the early 1960s may not yet have lifted, but recent experience at least demonstrates that it is potentially liftable: Given a stimulating campaign and a reasonable array of options to choose from, the public is willing and able to respond accordingly. It is possible, of course, that the sense of excitement that emerged from the 1992 campaign will prove to be fleeting. Having chosen a new set of leaders, the public's desire to keep those leaders on something of a "short leash" may create problems of effective governance that ultimately lead to a new wave of discontent and disillusionment (Gamson 1968; Easton 1965).

By the same token, there is no guarantee that elected officials will respond to the challenge that confronts them by becoming more "statesmanlike" and politically courageous. The implications of 1992 for our leaders seem fairly straightforward: Be serious, hardworking, and do your best to deal with the nation's most serious problems. Yet, if anything, precisely the opposite is happening today as national politics continues to grow ever more fractious and rancorous in tone. With press coverage focusing increasingly on legislative battles (process more than content), sideshow events, and personal peccadillos (Sabato 1991; Garment 1991), the result could be a public fascination that sustains the trend toward heightened engagement—or it could be a revulsion that stifles that trend. Only time will tell.

CITIZEN ENGAGEMENT IN THE 1994 CONGRESSIONAL ELECTIONS

Were levels of engagement higher in 1994 than in earlier midterm elections? Because voter turnout in 1994 (38.7 percent) was slightly higher than in either 1990 (36.5 percent) or 1986 (36.4 percent; see Ladd 1995, p. 18), we might expect levels of political involvement to have been higher as well. The evidence is mixed, however, with some indicators suggesting increased engagement and others a decline.

In October 1994, 45 percent of the public—compared with 28 percent in 1990 and 26 percent in 1986—reported following politics most of the time.[15] But even though citizens may have been more attentive in 1994, the level of thought they gave to the elections did not match that exhibited during the 1990 midterm races. A preelection survey done in October 1994 found that 36 percent of respondents claimed to have given a lot of thought to the November elections, lower than the 43 percent reporting the same level of consideration to their choices in 1990 but higher than the 29 percent who did so in 1982 (Times Mirror 1994d, p. 24).[16] In addition, the proportion of voters satisfied that they had learned enough to make an informed decision was lower in 1994 (48 percent) than in either 1992 (77 percent) or 1990 (54 percent; Times Mirror 1994d, p. 29).

Alienation in the political system also continued at high levels in 1994 (see Chapter 1). The statement that voting gives people "some say over how the government runs things" was endorsed by just 66 percent of the electorate in 1994 compared with 73 percent in 1990. Similarly, there was a drop in the proportion believing that "most elected officials care what people like me think" (33 percent in 1994 versus 36 percent in 1992 and 44 percent in 1990) and an increase in the proportion rejecting the statement that "the government is really run for the benefit of all the people" (57 percent in 1994 versus 54 percent in 1992 and 45 percent in 1990; Times Mirror 1994b, p. 23).

Thus despite the higher turnout evident in 1994, several indicators of political engagement provide a mixed picture of the level of involvement among citizens. More people claimed to follow politics, but with less thought to the choices and greater dissatisfaction with the information obtained from their attentiveness. In fairness, though, the dispersed nature of congressional, senatorial, and state elections probably contributed to this dissatisfaction—especially when contrasted with the highly concentrated media focus and the saturated coverage of candidates and issues in 1992.

NOTES

1. This calculation by the Center for the Study of the American Electorate is based on valid votes cast for president. Alternatively, the Bureau of the Census Current Population Survey estimated that 61.3 percent of the voting-age population voted in the 1992 presidential election—a figure that, like those derived from other opinion surveys, undoubtedly reflects some degree of misreporting.

2. These biennial surveys are conducted by the University of Michigan's Center for Political Studies and made available by the Inter-University Consortium for Political and Social Research. Most results from 1992 are based on an early ICPSR release of that particular survey; earlier information is drawn from the ANES Cumulative Data File, 1952–1990. Neither the consortium nor the original collectors of the data bear any responsibility for the analyses or interpretations here.

3. All of the percentages reported here are based on simple yes-no questions asking respondents whether they read or heard or watched any stories about the campaign in a given medium. See the Appendix for exact wordings.

4. An earlier poll (Times Mirror 1992c, p. 51) actually showed a much wider gap (74 percent for news reports, 22 percent for paid ads) on the personal-qualities dimension; in fact, the final postelection margin of 58–35 percent was lower than in either 1988 (67–24 percent) or 1990 (65–26 percent). It also should be noted that despite the candidates' efforts (especially those of Bill Clinton and Ross Perot) to make extensive use of alternative media formats in order to reach the electorate, the effects of those efforts on turnout—as well as on vote choice—have been questioned. See, for example, Knack (1993) and Rosenstone et al. (1993).

5. In contrast to most of our findings, the 63 percent for registered voters did not represent much of a change from 1988 (61 percent).

6. A postelection survey done by the U.S. Department of Commerce (1993, p. 35) revealed that patterns of registration and turnout in 1992 did indeed vary considerably among educational attainment groups: Only 35 percent of those with less than an eighth-grade education voted, compared to 58 percent of high school graduates and 81 percent of college graduates.

7. Those who were younger expressed greater concern with the costs of housing and education; older citizens were more concerned with access to health care. The largest generation gap on issues occurred in regard to abortion policy preferences (with gender differences also existing among the under-35 age group in their concern about this issue (see Times Mirror 1992d, pp. 11–12).

8. There were generational differences in political engagement levels, but all age groups identified jobs and the economy as the "most important problem" facing the nation in 1992. Both age and gender differences did exist, however, in the perceived salience of other issues (see Times Mirror 1992c, pp. 11–12).

9. For example, the proportion of the electorate aged 18–24 dropped from 17.1 percent in 1980 to 13.1 percent in 1992. Figures here are calculated from census data contained in U.S. Department of Commerce (1993).

10. Although we are treating perceived differences here as an independent variable, it follows from our previous discussion that this variable's relationship with engagement is probably reciprocal, i.e., higher levels of engagement may sensitize people to the choices before them, but perception of a meaningful choice also may heighten levels of public engagement and concern.

11. Although it was not an explicit response option, a small number of individuals volunteered that Perot would do a better job in each of the three areas discussed in this paragraph.

12. The logistic regression reported here (based on our use of a dependent variable that is dichotomous) bears some similarity to multivariate techniques with which some readers may be familiar. Whereas ordinary least squares (OLS) regression estimates the effect of independent variables on the predicted level of the dependent variable, logistic regression estimates the effect of independent variables on the odds that the dependent variable will have a particular value.

Although this may seem complicated, it is easy to get the gist of the model. For example, the parameter estimate of each independent variable refers to that variable's partial contribution to explaining variation in the dependent variable (turnout), i.e., the effect of the independent variable on the predicted value of the dependent variable after controlling for all other variables in the model. When the parameter estimate shown in Table 6.5 is positive and significant, the independent variable has a direct relationship with the dependent variable; as values of the independent variable increase, the probability that the dependent variable has a value of 1 also increases. When the parameter estimate is negative, the relationship is inverse: As values of the independent variable increase, the probability that the dependent variable has a value of 1 decreases. Readers interested in technical details are encouraged to consult SPSS documentation (e.g., Norusis 1985) or Liao (1994).

13. Sense of political efficacy is tapped by the "people have no say" question (see Appendix).

14. The other variable in our model that probably requires explanation is "campaign contacts"; this is a multiple-item index reflecting whether a respondent has been approached (1) during the campaign by a party or candidate organization or (2) over the past year by someone soliciting a financial contribution (on behalf of a party, candidate, or issue group). See Appendix for exact wordings.

15. Estimates for 1994 are from Times Mirror (1994d, p. 29) and for 1986–1990 from the American National Election Studies Cumulative Data File. Since question wording in these two surveys is slightly different, it is worth noting that Times Mirror also shows an increase in attentiveness between 1990 (39 percent) and 1994 (45 percent in October, 46 percent in July).

16. No figures for 1986 are available.

7

Who's Talking? Who's Listening?
The New Politics of Radio Talk Shows

DIANA OWEN

Over fifty years ago, Frank Capra brought to the motion picture screen images of ordinary Americans finding their political voice outside of formal governmental and corporate institutions. The message that common folks could reassert their place in a democratic system that had become inaccessible to them, and corrupted by elites, resonated loudly with depression-era audiences. In films such as *Mr. Smith Goes to Washington* and *Meet John Doe,* mass communication played a pivotal role in effecting change. Populist heroes used alternative media, including radio and newsletters, to compete with the mainstream press in their crusade to put politics back into the hands of the people. Although the good guys did not always win in the end, their efforts generated hope and energized a discouraged citizenry.

Until very recently, however, alternative sources of political information were oriented so as to exclude, rather than engage, the mass public. In keeping with the tone of privileged cliquishness set by government leaders in the 1980s, especially, the "highbrow" nature of most nonmainstream political media (e.g., *Meet the Press* and *The MacNeil-Lehrer News Hour*) discouraged citizens from seeking more comprehensive information than they received from nightly network television news programs. As a result, Americans earned a reputation for being poorly informed about politics (Bennett 1988).

Yet there is evidence that Capra's vision of a media-supported populism is not entirely lost in today's political environment. Since the 1992 presidential election, Americans have been turning increasingly to nontraditional channels of political communication to learn about government leaders and issues, and to make themselves seen and heard. Entertainment programs have developed into political forums that offer the public fresh access to the polity. Talk radio and television talk shows, in particular, have become mainstays of many average citizens' political media diet. In the process, politicians are finding it difficult to avoid engaging the public in political dialogue.

But is the new media populism for real? Do the new talk-politics media truly give rise to a more politically conscious and activist public, or do they simply provide another outlet for those already engaged in the political process? To better comprehend these issues, it is important to understand who makes up the audience for these new-style political media. In this chapter, I focus on characterizing the audience for politically oriented talk shows. What are the demographic characteristics of the talk-politics audience? How do the political attitudes and behavior of talk-show audience members compare to those of people who don't watch or listen? What motivates people to tune in to these programs? And finally, do the mass media tastes of talk-politics devotees differ from those of citizens who have not gotten on the new media bandwagon?

Whereas talk politics is an important phenomena on both radio and television, it has manifested itself most intensively on radio. Radio is more directly accessible to community members than is television, and opportunities for both attending to and participating in programs are greater. Thus, most of the attention here is focused on talk radio. Using data from opinion surveys conducted on behalf of the Times Mirror Center for the People and the Press, I conduct an empirical investigation that compares talk-radio callers and listeners to nonlisteners on a variety of demographic, political, and mass-media variables with the goal of devising a broad profile of the talk-radio audience.

TALK POLITICS AND THE NEW MEDIA POPULISM

The populist movement in political media has been in the works since the early 1980s, especially where talk radio is concerned. Call-in radio programs have emerged as the fastest-growing segment of the radio market, accounting for nearly 10 percent of all programming (Fineman 1993). Advances in satellite technology have made it cost effective for stations to use talk-radio feed more liberally. Demographic trends also have helped the radio industry. As listeners age, especially baby boomers, they begin to favor talk over music (Cutler 1989; Fineman 1993).

The new-style talk radio, which was predominantly the province of A.M. radio, cut its teeth on highly charged local issues in cities such as New York, Chicago, Boston, and Los Angeles. However, a series of dramatic events expedited talk politics' surge in popularity and brought it into the realm of national politics. Talk jocks honed their skills while stimulating public debates about events such as the Persian Gulf War, the Clarence Thomas–Anita Hill hearings, and the William Kennedy Smith trial, cultivating devoted audience members in the process. Although attentiveness to talk programs peaks during periods of political turmoil, each event draws new disciples into the fold.

The 1992 presidential campaign firmly established a new type of relationship between politicians, citizens, and the press. In addition to using the traditional strategy of staging pseudoevents that news organizations would be obliged to cover, candidates often circumvented the mainstream press and took their messages directly to the voters via popular media formats, especially talk radio and television. "Hard news" organizations begrudgingly covered the "soft news" generated in these channels rather than risk being scooped. Thus, a new populist era in political media was ushered in.

Recognizing the potential for reaching and even mobilizing untapped segments of the voting population, presidential candidates competed actively for airtime on talk television and radio programs. Ross Perot set the trend by declaring his willingness to be drafted as a candidate by the American people on *Larry King Live,* thereby initiating an unprecedented letter-writing campaign to bolster this effort. Bill Clinton soon joined in with an aggressive talk-media strategy, including his landmark saxophone-playing appearance on the late-night *Arsenio Hall Show.* Even George Bush, who resisted going the populist media route until the very end of the campaign, made an uncomfortable attempt to court the youth vote on MTV. Voters appeared to enjoy this new form of entertainment politics, which following the election became something of a new spectator sport.

Since the election, talk radio and television have become ensconced as popular cultural phenomena. Americans have developed a passionate and personal relationship with talk shows that is similar to their preoccupation with music, television sitcoms and soap operas, movies, magazines, and novels. Talk shows have all the elements of personal drama, scandal, and intrigue that the public has come to expect from entertainment cultural fare. Fans know the "stars," they follow the "story lines," and they themselves can even participate in the productions.

From all appearances, then, talk shows seem to represent the perfect avenue for heightened citizen activation. Call-in programs convey the constantly unfolding tension and conflict in a way that allows those who tune in to feel as if they are part of the inside world of politics. But do talk radio and television really offer empowerment to those whose political voice has previously remained silent? Let us turn now to an analysis of the talk-radio audience in an effort to shed some light on this question.

To explore the issues just raised, I employ data from surveys provided by the Times Mirror Center for the People and the Press. Most central to my analysis is a national telephone survey of 1,507 adult members of the mass public fielded between May 18 and 24, 1993; this particular study contained an oversample of individuals who had called in to talk-radio programs. Times Mirror also commissioned interviews of 112 radio talk-show hosts during the period May 25–June 11, 1993. In addition to demographic data, the surveys contain extensive information about mass-media use and political orientations of the general public and talk-show hosts.[1]

Respondents can be placed into three categories: *Callers,* constituting 12.5 percent of the sample, are individuals who are regular listeners and have called into a talk-radio program at one time or another. *Listeners* (49.5 percent) are people who tune in either regularly or sometimes to talk shows but have never actually called in. *Nonlisteners* (38 percent) rarely or never attend to such programs. One limitation of this typology, which is used for most of the analysis to follow, is that it reflects whether a person has called into or regularly listens to *any* type of talk-radio program; it does not distinguish between political and nonpolitical shows.

I also employ data from a Times Mirror survey of 1,301 adults conducted between April 30 and May 3, 1992. This study contains a number of useful items concerning the 1992 presidential campaign, although the talk-radio variables are somewhat more limited in scope than is true for the later poll. Most important, they enable us to classify respondents only into categories of people who listen to any type of talk-radio program and those who don't tune in (i.e., callers cannot be separated from noncallers).

TALK RADIO AND THE MASS AUDIENCE

The Hidden Popularity of Radio

When radio was first introduced to the American audience, a media revolution was sparked almost overnight. Word that results of the 1920 presidential election had been broadcast over the radio airwaves stimulated an almost incomprehensible public demand for radios that could not be met by manufacturers. Broadcasters quickly seized the moment; the number of stations grew chaotically and exponentially from less than a dozen in 1920 to almost 600 in 1922 (Siepmann 1950).

So much has been made of television replacing radio as Americans' medium of choice that there is a tendency to underestimate radio's popularity today. Yet radio is a pervasive presence even in the television era. Americans own more radios—over 580 million—than television sets (DeFleur and Dennis 1991); 99 percent of households have at least one radio, and the average home contains five. Furthermore, over 80 percent of the population listens to radio at one time or another every day (Roberts 1991). Between 6 A.M. and 6 P.M., citizens spend *49 percent* of their media time listening to radio, compared to 33 percent watching television, 12 percent reading the newspaper, and 6 percent reading magazines (Cutler 1989), although television dominates during the evening hours.

Call-in shows are the fastest-growing segment of the radio market.[2] Every day, approximately 15 million Americans tune in to at least a portion of a talk-radio program, and a growing number of these people are calling in. As recently as two years ago, only 1 or 2 percent of listeners would phone in to talk shows. Today, with the proliferation of talk-radio offerings and the rise in the number of car phones, this figure is increasing rapidly. A CBS News poll broadcast on February 16, 1993, reported that 16 percent of listeners called in to talk programs either on radio or television during the 1992 presidential election.

The 1993 Times Mirror study provides further evidence of the escalating popularity of talk radio: Over 40 percent of those surveyed reported listening to talk radio either regularly or sometimes. Taking into consideration that callers were oversampled, we can still deduce from the data that millions of listeners either have spoken on air or have attempted to do so (Kohut 1993). There is also evidence that talk radio in the age of entertainment politics has become important to citizens as a source of information not available from other sources. The Times Mirror election data indicate that 57 percent of listeners reported learning something about the candidates from talk radio that they had not heard before. This constitutes 25 percent of all respondents in the survey.

Nevertheless, in spite of its newfound fame, talk radio still does not command as large an audience as mainstream political media. The 1993 Times Mirror data indicate that 93 percent of the public watches local television news and 88 percent watches national evening news either regularly or sometimes. Similarly, 85 percent of Americans report that they read a newspaper with some frequency.

Radio and the Development of Pseudocommunities

At the time of its inception, radio was an entirely new communications experience for the mass public that ignited its popularity. In addition to satisfying the basic mass-media functions of informing and entertaining that print media provided, radio fulfilled a variety of latent functions. Individuals formed psychological attachments to radio because of its ability to serve as a surrogate for human companionship. As Mendelsohn (1964, pp. 241–242) pointed out, "Radio's overall role is one of an 'important and versatile presence' that can stimulate, and yet relax; that can be intimately companionable, yet unobtrusive; that can bring into focus the great events of the world outside, and at the same time admonish Junior to wear his galoshes because of the imminence of a storm."

A handful of studies conducted in the 1970s and 1980s concluded that the primary function of talk radio was to serve as a surrogate community for citizens who were largely alienated from the social and political realm. Talk radio offered companionship to people who were lonely, isolated, stationary, single, and detached from formal organizations (Turow 1974; Bierig and Dimmick 1979; Trammer and Jeffres 1983; Armstrong and Rubin 1989). Rather than providing individuals with a point of access to the polity, talk radio offered an escape from boredom and a feeling of connectedness to an otherwise unfriendly world.

The new talk-radio community has a decidedly different character in that it is less escapist and more instrumental. Whereas the audience of a previous era found personal solace in the local talk-radio ghetto, the current generation of talk-radio fans engages in both local and national conversations. The early audience used talk radio as a mechanism for dealing with individual isolation. The new talk-radio audience uses the medium to contend with social isolation— where interpersonal contacts may be many but close relationships are few. The old talk radio produced close-knit families of hosts, callers, and listeners. The new talk radio orchestrates large-scale political dramas designed to amuse, outrage, enlighten, and cajole a neighborhood of strangers.

DEMOGRAPHIC PROFILE OF THE
NEW TALK-RADIO COMMUNITY

Just who populates the new talk-radio community? It is perhaps more accurate to speak in terms of talk-radio *audiences* who have different demographic characteristics, as well as social and political tastes, rather than a single, undifferentiated mass. The people who religiously tune in to ultraconservative talk-show host Rush Limbaugh, for example, are a markedly different breed than those who gravitate toward the liberal newcomer to the scene, Jerry Brown. Keeping this in mind, however, I wish to make generalizations about the character of the talk-radio audience as a whole.

A good starting point for our empirical investigation of the new talk-radio community is with a demographic composite of audience participants. Previous studies have shown that talk-show fans tend to be somewhat older, disproportionately male, better educated, and more likely to fall into the middle- and upper-income brackets (Cutler 1989, 1990; Roberts 1991) than is true for the nonlistening public. The Times Mirror data in Table 7.1 generally support these trends. There also are significant regional differences in the proportions of those who attend to talk radio and those who do not, with southerners and westerners being more inclined to tune in than easterners and midwesterners.[3] Successful local talk-radio stations were established relatively early in the South and West (especially in Atlanta and Los Angeles), thereby anchoring audience support for the medium in these two regions.

Further, there is an interesting pattern based on race. Whites are only slightly more likely to listen to talk radio than are nonwhites—but members of racial minority groups are somewhat more inclined to call in.[4] This finding is not surprising. Talk-radio programs aimed at blacks and other minorities have been springing up in record numbers nationwide, attracting large audiences and devoted callers who welcome the opportunity to sound off. In places like New York, Los Angeles, and Chicago, black talk stations have generated controversy, persuaded listeners to take political action, and forced politicians to take notice (Schmidt 1989; Warren 1989).

POLITICAL PROFILE OF THE
TALK-RADIO AUDIENCE

The political profile of talk-radio callers and listeners is intriguing and complex. Members of the talk-radio audience tend to fit the profile of the classic good citizen—they have a strong sense of civic responsibility, keep informed, and participate actively in politics through conventional avenues. They also have a more well developed sense of political identity than do nonlisteners. Yet both callers and listeners appear to be largely disaffected from governmental institutions. It is in spite of these attitudes that they feel it is their right and responsibility to engage in the political process.

TABLE 7.1   Demographics of the Talk-Radio Audience, 1993

	Callers	*Listeners*	*Nonlisteners*
Age			
18–30	16%	29%	25%
31–40	31	23	20
41–55	22	16	19
56-plus	31	32	36
Gender			
Male	58%	50%	42%
Female	42	50	58
Education			
< High school	16%	13%	22%
High school graduate	31	33	38
Some college	33	28	23
College graduate	20	26	17
Income			
< $15,000	18%	16%	21%
$15,000–$19,999	9	13	17
$20,000–$29,999	21	21	17
$30,000–$49,999	26	22	21
$50,000 and over	26	27	24
Region			
East	19%	17%	25%
Midwest	23	26	26
South	39	34	32
West	19	23	17
Race			
White	80%	88%	85%
Nonwhite	20	12	15
N = 1,507			

NOTE: Each set of column figures sums to 100 percent.
SOURCE: Times Mirror Center for the People and the Press.

Political Identifications

Talk-radio fans differ from nonlisteners in their basic political identifications. The findings reported in Table 7.2 indicate that callers and listeners are more likely than nonlisteners both to identify with a political party (as opposed to being Independents) and to place themselves at either end (rather than in the middle) of the left-right ideological spectrum. Within this broader pattern, members of the talk-radio audience are decidedly Republican and conservative in their orientations, with callers being more conservative—but not necessarily more Republican—

TABLE 7.2   Political Identifications of the Talk-Radio Audience, 1993

	Callers	Listeners	Nonlisteners
Party identification			
Democrat	32%	37%	33%
Independent	26	23	39
Republican	42	41	28
Ideology			
Liberal	15%	14%	16%
Moderate	48	59	64
Conservative	37	27	20
N = 1,507			

NOTE: Each set of column figures sums to 100 percent.
SOURCE: Times Mirror Center for the People and the Press.

than listeners. Nonlisteners, in contrast, lean more toward the Democratic Party than toward the Republicans (33 percent to 28 percent) and are only slightly more conservative than liberal (20 percent to 16 percent) in their ideological outlooks.

Attitudes Toward Politics, Government, and Business

Audience members positioned across the partisan and ideological spectrums share some fundamental opinions about the state of American politics. Whether liberal or conservative, talk-radio listeners are fairly united in their strong anti-government sentiments—sentiments that are often conditioned and reinforced by talk-show hosts. For example, talk jocks associated with right- and left-wing politics frequently adopt populist positions such as opposition to big companies and government bureaucracies (*Economist* 1989; Roberts, 1991). Hosts, as revealed by the Times Mirror study, also believe that their callers are angry at the government and critical of the president and Congress (Kohut 1993). The hosts themselves are far more hostile in their attitudes toward political institutions than television, print, or radio news journalists (Coursen 1993).

A variety of indicators from the 1993 Times Mirror mass public database can be utilized to explore more fully the attitudes of callers, listeners, and nonlisteners toward politics, government, and business institutions. General orientations toward the political process are measured in terms of one's sense of *citizen duty*, *political efficacy*, and *alienation from politics*. An index of *national optimism* is designed to tap individuals' belief in the idea of "American exceptionalism," i.e., that there is no limit to the ability of our country to expand its horizons internally and to solve its problems. An indicator of *government alienation* measures feelings of dissatisfaction with governmental intervention in citizens' lives, and *business alienation* assesses the degree to which people feel that too much power is concentrated in corporations. Finally, we examine respondents' perceptions of their own *financial security*. Mean scores on these variables have been computed for each audience-member category.[5]

The results in Table 7.3 reveal that members of the talk-radio audience have a stronger sense of political commitment than nonmembers, but they feel less capable of influencing government. That is, callers and listeners score higher on our measure of citizen duty than do nonlisteners but exhibit lower levels of political efficacy. We also see that callers are the group that is most alienated from the political process and least optimistic about the ability of this country to solve its problems.

I find it interesting that talk-radio fans are more alienated from political institutions but less alienated from business institutions than are nonlisteners. One possible explanation for this finding is rooted in the demographic composition of the talk-radio audience, i.e., the fact that the new breed of listener tends to be positioned near the upper reaches of the socioeconomic ladder (see Table 7.1). We therefore might deduce that talk-radio fans have stronger connections to business and are more likely to have benefited directly from the business community than from government. The argument here is especially compelling for callers, who report the highest level of personal financial security among our three audience groups.

Political Activity

The most distinctive political characteristic of the talk-radio audience (and especially callers) is its high level of political participation. In keeping with their enhanced sense of civic duty, talk-radio listeners are somewhat more likely (1) to be registered to vote (89 percent of callers, 83 percent of listeners, and 78 percent of nonlisteners) and (2) to turn out in elections than are nonlisteners (90 percent of callers and listeners vs. 84 percent of nonlisteners report that they "nearly always" make it to the polls). However, the most impressive differences between audience groups have to do with types of political activity other than voting.

Table 7.4 depicts the percentage of callers, listeners, and nonlisteners who have participated in a range of activities—including letter writing, attending public meetings, contributing to political organizations and candidates, joining political organizations, and registering their opinions—over the previous year. The most striking finding is that callers participate far more actively than either listeners or nonlisteners in *every one* of these forms of political action.[6] Talk-radio listeners do tend to be more involved than nonlisteners, but differences in the level of activity are not nearly as stark as for callers. For example, 50 percent of callers claim to have written a letter to their representative in Congress, compared to 30 percent of listeners and just 22 percent of nonlisteners. Fifty-two percent of callers have attended a city council meeting; 32 percent of listeners and 23 percent of nonlisteners have done so. Forty-three percent of callers have joined a political organization, in contrast to 28 percent of listeners and 22 percent of nonlisteners.

TABLE 7.3   Attitudes Toward Politics, Government, and Business by Talk-Radio Use, 1993

	Callers	Listeners	Nonlisteners	Statistical Significance[a]
Citizen duty Range of scores: 1–4	3.74	3.61	3.55	A,B,C
Political efficacy Range of scores: 2–8	5.29	5.20	5.42	B,C
Political alienation Range of scores: 1–4	3.22	3.14	3.11	B
National optimism Range of scores: 2–8	5.30	5.47	5.40	A
Government alienation Range of scores: 2–8	6.15	5.90	5.72	A,B,C
Business alienation Range of scores: 2–8	5.85	5.87	6.17	B,C
Financial security Range of scores: 2–8	5.36	5.08	5.18	A,B

N = 1,507

NOTE: Table entries are the mean score for a particular measure (see note 6). High scores reflect high citizen duty, efficacy, alienation, etc.

[a]The statistical significance of group differences ($p < .05$ based on a t-test) is indicated as follows:

A = significant differences between callers and listeners.
B = significant differences between callers and nonlisteners.
C = significant differences between listeners and nonlisteners.

SOURCE: Times Mirror Center for the People and the Press.

Attitudes Toward Political and Mass Media
Actors and Institutions

The 1993 Times Mirror survey also allows for an examination of citizens' feelings about specific political leaders, mass-media personalities, formal institutions, and the press. In general, respondents (regardless of whether they listened to talk radio) were not overwhelmingly satisfied with public figures and institutions: Except for the military, the church, and their daily newspapers, fewer than 25 percent gave a "very favorable" rating to any of the sixteen leaders and institutions they were asked to evaluate. Still, there were a few noteworthy differences in attitudes expressed by the three categories of audience members (data not shown).

None of the four political leaders mentioned in the survey—Bill Clinton, Hillary Rodham Clinton, Robert Dole, and Ross Perot—received very high marks.

TABLE 7.4   Political Participation by Talk-Radio Use, 1993

	Callers	*Listeners*	*Nonlisteners*
Written elected official	47%	27%	21%
Written newspaper editor	22%	12%	8%
Sent letter to White House	17%	11%	9%
Sent letter to Representative	50%	30%	22%
Attended public hearing	44%	26%	17%
Participated in town meeting	38%	24%	21%
Attended city council meeting	52%	32%	23%
Contributed to PAC	28%	19%	16%
Contributed to candidate	30%	18%	13%
Joined political organization	43%	28%	22%
Joined Perot's organization	11%	6%	3%
Participated in opinion poll	54%	42%	29%
Called/mailed questionnaire	44%	18%	12%
Dialed 800 number	50%	20%	17%
Called TV/cable to complain	30%	11%	8%

N = 1,507

NOTE: Table entries are the percentage within each group who report engaging in the activity.

SOURCE: Times Mirror Center for the People and the Press.

Callers tended to be slightly more positive than either listeners or nonlisteners in their evaluations of the three male leaders. But the opposite was true for Hillary Clinton; nonlisteners held significantly more positive feelings toward her than did talk-radio devotees.[7] This could be due to the fact that politically active women do not receive especially good coverage on talk radio. Popular conservative host Rush Limbaugh, for example, refers to them as "feminazis," a term that has become ingrained in the vocabulary of his "ditto head" fans; Hillary Clinton, in particular, has been the object of repeated talk-radio and -television bashings. Alternatively, the patterns observed here may simply reflect the negative views that many in the talk-show audience have of women like Ms. Clinton in the first place (with the talk shows themselves serving to reinforce such views rather than engender them).

Overall, the talk-show personalities included in the Times Mirror study scored about as well (or, depending on how you want to look at it, as badly) with the public as did politicians. It is not surprising that talk-radio listeners and callers were somewhat more favorably disposed than their nonlistening counterparts toward radio and television hosts Larry King, Rush Limbaugh, and Howard Stern. Limbaugh's much stronger showing among callers (23 percent "very favorable") than among nonlisteners (8 percent "very favorable," with listeners in between at 17 percent) suggests that he is indeed, as some critics have noted, an acquired taste.

There is no evidence that talk radio has an impact on the generalized feelings of dissatisfaction with political institutions currently exhibited by a majority of Americans (see Chapter 3). Favorability ratings of Congress, the Supreme Court, and the Democratic and Republican Parties are already so low that talk-radio banter can do little to suppress them any further; in fact, less than 20 percent of the Times Mirror sample granted any of these institutions a "very favorable" rating. Respondents as a whole were more generous in their assessments of the church, the military, and (marginally) the United Nations than they were toward explicitly political institutions, though differences between talk-radio fans and nonlisteners tended to be negligible. The one interesting distinction is that callers—despite their relatively conservative outlooks (Table 7.2)—were slightly less positive toward the military than nonlisteners. Since military issues happen to be a recurrent topic of critical evaluation on talk radio, this finding is perhaps to be expected.

Regarding the press, talk-radio audience members were somewhat less inclined to award "very favorable" ratings to newspapers and to network television news (26 percent and 22–23 percent, respectively, for callers and listeners) than were nonlisteners (29 percent for newspapers and 25 percent for television). These differences, modest as they are, do not come as a surprise given that much of the appeal of talk radio to listeners is that it offers an alternative to so-called mainstream media.

Attitudes Toward Candidates in the 1992 Presidential Election

One outgrowth of talk-radio listeners' dissatisfaction with existing political institutions and leaders is expressed in their attitudes toward Independent candidate Ross Perot during the 1992 presidential election campaign. Perot took to the airwaves with an unorthodox style that appealed to an audience striving to distance itself from big government and formal institutions.

Times Mirror data collected in spring 1992 demonstrate that talk-radio listeners were significantly more attracted to "outsider" candidate Perot than were nonlisteners (see Table 7.5). First, respondents were asked for whom they would vote if the election were held on the day of the survey. A slightly higher proportion of talk-radio listeners said they would cast their ballot for Perot (32 percent) than for any of the other candidates; by comparison, nonlisteners were more inclined to support Bush (30 percent) and Clinton (29 percent, versus 26 percent for Perot). In addition, people were asked if they would *consider* voting for Perot in the general election. Forty-one percent of listeners reported that they would entertain this possibility, in contrast to just 34 percent of nonlisteners.[8]

One striking difference between talk-radio listeners and nonlisteners had to do with the level of attention each group paid to Ross Perot. Survey participants were asked to report how much they knew about Perot's stands on issues and, more generally, how much they had heard about his candidacy. Sixty-four percent of respondents who claimed to know a great deal about Perot's issue positions were

TABLE 7.5   Candidate Preference by Talk-Radio Use, 1992

	Listeners	*Nonlisteners*
Candidate preference		
George Bush	30%	30%
Bill Clinton	25	29
Ross Perot	32	26
Undecided	13	15
Would consider voting for Ross Perot		
Yes	59%	66%
No	41	34

N = 1,285

NOTE: Each set of column figures sums to 100 percent. This survey was conducted from April 30–May 3, 1992.

SOURCE: Times Mirror Center for the People and the Press.

talk-radio devotees, and just 36 percent were nonlisteners. The situation was almost exactly reversed for those who knew nothing about Perot: Only 34 percent were listeners, 66 percent nonlisteners. A similar pattern was found for the question tapping how much people had heard about the Independent candidate.

The evidence thus far appears to suggest that talk-radio listeners were drawn to Perot because of his eccentric manner and anti-institutional rhetoric. Yet the talk-radio audience tends to view politics and politicians with a jaundiced eye; dissonance and controversy are integral to the format's popular appeal. Therefore, even candidates favored by talk-radio listeners do not escape tough scrutiny. This is especially likely to be true when following a renegade candidate becomes a talk-radio obsession as it became with Ross Perot. Members of the community may have been more attracted to Perot than to other candidates, but they were not uncritical in their evaluations of him. His candidacy was welcomed as an anti-establishment alternative, but it was greeted as well with a healthy degree of skepticism in the talk-radio neighborhood.

A division of sentiments is clearly revealed as we probe further into the Times Mirror data. Talk-radio devotees did *not* consider Ross Perot to be the most qualified candidate either to handle the racial situation (16 percent of listeners) or to improve conditions for the middle class in the United States (25 percent). Instead, it was Bill Clinton who fared best with the public—and with the talk-show audience (32 percent on race, 36 percent on the economy)—with respect to both of these issues. George Bush also ranked higher than Perot on the race question (23 percent of listeners felt he was best able to handle the problem), though not on the economic-conditions item (18 percent). The latter result is to be expected given that voters were disappointed in the president's handling of the economy at the time of the election.[9]

Political Profile in Summary

A large portion of the talk-radio audience is unhappy about the state of political affairs in this country; callers, in particular, are often impassioned and relentless in protesting politics as usual. Yet most of these citizens register their disapproval in a manner that poses little or no threat to the established order. That is, talk-radio callers and listeners are generally willing to work within boundaries established by the very institutions they decry. They tend to have a highly developed sense of civic responsibility (which tempers their apprehensions about governmental authorities), combined with a relatively weak sense of political efficacy (which diminishes any sense of empowerment about being able to change things on their own). As a result, the dissident political voice of talk radio does not readily translate into radical political action. Instead, it goes hand in hand with listeners' heightened inclination to take part in the political process in conventional ways. At least so far, they are content to express their disaffection by supporting political outsiders whose rhetoric extols the virtues of the American system— while at the same time decrying the evils of those currently holding office.

MEDIA-USE PROFILE OF THE TALK-RADIO AUDIENCE

Historically, studies have found that individuals who regularly listen to the radio are part of an overlapping audience for a variety of mass media (Lazarsfeld and Kendall 1948). This fact, considered in conjunction with the evidence that listeners are more intensively engaged in the political process than nonlisteners, leads us to expect that the talk-show audience will be attentive to political news disseminated through a wider range of information sources than are those who don't tune in. Given their affinity for politicians and institutional entities outside the mainstream, one would also expect that listeners would be less favorably disposed than nonlisteners toward mainstream forms of political communication.

The Times Mirror data support the proposition that talk-radio subscribers continue to be part of an overlapping audience for a wide range of communication formats. Table 7.6 shows callers once again to be distinctive in their behavior; they are substantially more attentive than ordinary listeners to both print and broadcast media of all types. For example, callers are much more likely than other members of the mass public to read a daily newspaper and news magazines regularly—though they are only slightly more inclined to read personality magazines with political content, such as *People*. Further, callers tune in with greater frequency to network television news, local television news, television news magazines, CNN, C-SPAN, and *The MacNeil Lehrer News Hour*. Ordinary listeners are only marginally more likely than nonlisteners to be regular users of print and broadcast media other than radio. It is interesting, however, that neither callers nor average listeners tune in to television talk shows, including *Larry King Live*, in proportions much different from those of nonlisteners.

TABLE 7.6   Media Attentiveness by Talk-Radio Use, 1993

	Callers	*Listeners*	*Nonlisteners*
Print			
Daily newspaper	72%	67%	63%
News magazines	36%	23%	20%
Personality magazines	14%	10%	12%
Broadcast			
Network TV news	63%	59%	59%
Local TV news	84%	77%	75%
TV news magazines	62%	52%	49%
CNN	42%	36%	32%
C-SPAN	14%	14%	9%
MacNeil-Lehrer News Hour	18%	10%	8%
Larry King Show	6%	5%	5%
TV talk shows	28%	22%	26%

N = 1,507

NOTE: Table entries are the percentage within each group who report attending to the medium.

SOURCE: Times Mirror Center for the People and the Press.

Although talk-radio devotees are attuned to a multiplicity of mass communication sources, conventional wisdom dictates that they are suspicious of institutional journalistic sources and attend to talk-radio as an alternative. This speculation is reinforced by the fact that talk radio hosts often are a breed apart from their counterparts in other areas of the press, especially in their more pronounced hostility toward government leaders and institutions (Coursen 1993). The 1992 Times Mirror survey reported earlier lends some, though not unqualified, support to the supposition that talk-radio users are indeed more critical of the mainstream press than nonusers, even as they are more attentive to it (data not shown).

Respondents were asked to evaluate the press's coverage of the most important issue of the day (which they had identified in a previous question), as well as coverage of the presidential election campaign. The findings reveal an interesting inconsistency. First, talk-radio listeners were harsher in their evaluations of the press's coverage of important *non*election news stories than were nonlisteners: Forty-eight percent of nonlisteners, compared to just 41 percent of listeners, felt the press did an "excellent" or "very good" job in its noncampaign news coverage. But the pattern was reversed for election news: Fifty-three percent of nonlisteners, versus 62 percent of listeners, graded election coverage as "excellent" or "very good."[10]

One possible explanation for this disparity may have to do with the perception that the public was being presented with a new and improved populist style of campaign reporting in 1992 but that coverage of other issues and events followed the same old format—a format whose conventionality and inability to accommodate two-way communication with the audience is sometimes held in contempt by talk-radio fans. As we have seen, talk-radio listeners tend to follow news about politics in a wide array of channels. At the time of the survey, the election was the lead news story; hence, the realization that election coverage was not "news as usual," plus the sheer pervasiveness of campaign stories, may have produced a more positive evaluation among listeners. Conversely, they may have felt that other important issues were being slighted and not receiving the kind of media treatment they deserved.

Another explanation for the discrepancy in evaluations of nonelection versus election news coverage lies in the talk-radio audience's active role in making campaign news. Call-in radio and television dictated the news agenda for the mainstream press to a significant extent during the 1992 presidential campaign. Members of the talk-radio audience could therefore look more favorably upon election coverage of a campaign in which they were themselves a continual and important part of the story than they could upon reporting of other news events.[11]

In addition to being multimedia users, the talk-radio audience is considerably more attentive to current affairs than are those who do not tune in. Respondents in the 1992 Times Mirror survey were asked to rate how closely they followed ten news stories on a scale where 4 is coded "very closely" and 1 represents "not closely at all." The news stories covered a wide variety of topics including the presidential election, AIDS, abortion, the economy, the execution of a killer, the verdict in the Rodney King trial, and the stock market crash in Japan. Talk-radio listeners followed every news item, except for Earth Day, with greater intensity than did nonlisteners.

Audience Motivations for Tuning In

Detractors like to dismiss talk radio as yet another form of mass entertainment, high on sensationalism and low on substance. Given its political profile, however, the talk-radio audience seems unlikely to be sustained on a diet of pablum. In fact, talk-radio devotees are motivated to tune in far more by a desire to keep up on political issues than by the entertainment value of the medium, or of a particular host. According to Table 7.7, callers—even more so than listeners—are driven by the desire to develop a deeper understanding of issues. It is curious that neither callers nor listeners are overly concerned about using the information they gain from radio in conversations with others. Perhaps this need is met vicariously through the on-air dialogue.

TALK RADIO IN 1994 AND BEYOND

Talk radio has garnered a sizable audience of listeners and callers who tune in regularly to engage in this new form of political discourse. But does the medium have staying power or is it just a passing fad? It is too early to say for sure, but there are indications that talk radio is settling in for a long-term run. Although

TABLE 7.7   Major Reasons for Listening to Talk Radio, 1993

	Callers	*Listeners*
Keep up on issues	81%	69%
Learn what others feel about issues	85%	69%
Learn more about what I found out elsewhere	65%	57%
Pick up information for conversation	36%	32%
Entertainment	42%	41%
Like host of show	34%	26%
N = 1,507		

NOTE: Table entries are the percentage within each group who report that this is a major reason for listening to radio talk shows.
SOURCE: Times Mirror Center for the People and the Press.

the novelty had worn off somewhat, talk radio was a formidable presence during the 1994 midterm elections. Some observers, including Speaker of the House Newt Gingrich, argued that talk radio was a significant factor in the GOP victory that year as conservative candidates, in particular, used the airwaves to advertise their Contract with America, denounce opponents, and generally mobilize supporters of the conservative cause (Kurtz 1995). Moreover, the evidence suggests that talk radio will continue to be a factor in the 1996 presidential contest.

It is unlikely, however, that talk radio will be as strong a voice for conservatives and Republicans in 1996 as it seemed to be in 1994. First, the ideological range of talk-show offerings is expanding in response to a diverse and volatile audience. There are new populist and left-oriented programs establishing themselves in national markets, and Democratic politicians such as Mario Cuomo, Gary Hart, and Douglas Wilder have become part of the talk scene (Sifry and Cooper 1995).

Further, Republicans are discovering that it is difficult to use talk radio to rally the troops behind specific legislative initiatives, including those central to the Contract with America. Talk radio appears to be most successful in serving as an opposition force, i.e., it works best when registering public dissatisfaction with candidates, proposed policies, or presidential appointments. Politicians have generally had difficulty translating talk into action on behalf of a cause rather than against one. In addition, the proliferation of talk shows may serve to ignite tensions within the political parties, especially on the Republican side. Talk radio allows politicians to speak to the public directly without having to tow the party line. It is difficult to drum up support for policies when members of the same party are presenting opposing views on the air (Kurtz 1995).

CONCLUSION

Talk radio has become an established fixture of the American political process, as well as a bona fide cultural phenomenon. As Michael Harrison, editor and publisher of *Talkers,* a talk-radio industry newspaper, observes, "Information is replacing popular music as popular culture." As such, political talk shows provide information to the public in a format that satisfies the expectations of an entertainment-oriented society. But to return to the issue framing this discussion, does talk politics really work to draw individuals meaningfully into the political process—especially those who have not been involved previously?

The evidence presented here suggests that the new media populism has indeed worked to bring some Americans closer to the world of politics and government. Talk shows have the potential to further democratic goals and aims, especially in their ability to provide people with an opportunity for sounding off on issues about which they care deeply. Citizens can become more personally engaged with political problems and this, in turn, can inspire participation. And even though the potential for talk shows to mobilize citizen action is probably much greater at the level of local politics than it is in instances where national issues are involved, even the latter possibility cannot be dismissed altogether.

However, my findings also imply that excitement about the talk-politics phenomenon should be tempered with caution. Talk radio may serve as a surrogate for political community, but unlike in the past, the people in this neighborhood are not bored, immobile, or highly alienated from society. To the contrary, the new media populism provides a forum for those whose voices are already well represented in the political process. The overall profile of talk-radio devotees highlights their upscale demographic characteristics, their strong sense of civic commitment and engagement, and their propensity to seek out political information from a wide range of sources.

Because members of the talk-show audience are often disaffected from big, formal governmental institutions, they seek ways of accessing politics from within the confines of their own milieu—and they do so with substantially more regularity than do nonlisteners. Talk shows add a somewhat new dimension to the litany of political activities in which many listeners already engage. They provide fans with a means of expressing their disaffection in a way that is more captivating, more novel, and more open than what is allowed through voting, letter writing, contributing to political causes, joining political organizations, or even attending local meetings.

The most cynical interpretation of the new media populism is that rather than encouraging legitimate political engagement, its influence is illusory. Talk politics, critics say, substitutes words for action; it mistakes sounding off for acting out. As a result, it depresses meaningful political participation by giving the false impression that voicing a wide array of opinions at a high-decibel level is the equivalent of inspiring or enacting real political change. One also might argue that the power of talk is only as formidable as politicians allow it to be. Unlike the mainstream press, talk shows are granted legitimacy primarily by the willingness of politicians to appear on them and to respond to opinions voiced on air. Once leaders stop taking talk shows seriously, their influence will abate quickly.

In many ways, the newly emerged media populism does not differ greatly in character from Frank Capra's depression-era populist vision. The people, then as now, still had faith in the superiority of the American system of government even though they had lost confidence in political leaders and were estranged from political institutions. They continued to believe that it was possible to buck the established media order and get their message out. But, then as now, without a formal mechanism for having opinion translate into action, voices sound hollow and messages fall on deaf ears.

NOTES

I would like to thank the Times Mirror Center for the People and the Press for providing me with the data used in this chapter. I am also grateful to Steve Farnsworth for his valuable research assistance.

1. Sampling error for the general-public survey is plus or minus 3 percentage points and is plus or minus 10 percentage points for the talk-show-host survey. Additional information about the two surveys is contained in Kohut (1993).

2. Adult contemporary (soft rock, New Age and jazz) and country music are the two most popular radio formats. Talk radio is the third most popular format (Cutler 1990).

3. Callers and listeners combined constitute 67 percent in the West, 62 percent in the South, 59 percent in the Midwest, and just 51 percent in the East.

4. Fifty percent of whites are callers, 11 percent are listeners; the figures for nonwhites are 41 percent and 17 percent, respectively.

5. Individual scores on the variables described in this paragraph were determined by responses (ranging from completely agree = 1 to completely disagree = 4) to the following items: (1) *Citizen duty*. I feel it's my duty as a citizen to always vote; (2) *Political efficacy*. People like me don't have any say about what the government does. Most elected officials care what people like me think; (3) *Political alienation*. Generally speaking, elected officials in Washington lose touch with the people pretty quickly; (4) *National optimism*. As Americans we can always find a way to solve our problems and get what we want. I don't believe that there are any real limits to growth in this country today; (5) *Government alienation*. When something is run by the government, it is usually inefficient and wasteful. The federal government controls too much of our daily lives; (6) *Business alienation*. There is too much power concentrated in the hands of a few big companies. Business corporations make too much profit; (7) *Financial security*. I don't often have enough money to make ends meet. I'm pretty well satisfied with the way things are going for me financially. Where appropriate, scores were recoded to accommodate differences in direction of wording.

6. The last two items listed in Table 7.4 refer to respondents (1) calling an 800 number to register their opinion on some issue and (2) calling a television station or cable company to complain about a TV program they didn't like.

7. Seventeen percent of callers and 18 percent of listeners granted Hillary Clinton a "very favorable" score, compared to 25 percent of nonlisteners.

8. Favorability ratings of the three presidential contenders provide yet another indication of the talk-radio audience's affinity for Perot. Voters who attended to talk radio were more likely to grant Perot a favorable rating and less inclined to rate him unfavorably than were nonlisteners. The data show no clear patterns or statistically significant relationships for Bush or Clinton.

9. There is further evidence that the talk-radio audience was ambivalent about Ross Perot's ability to perform as president: Of the survey respondents who believed that Ross Perot would make "few" mistakes while in office, 53 percent were talk-radio listeners—but so were 52 percent of those who anticipated that he would make "many" errors.

10. Differences between listeners and nonlisteners were negligible in terms of the proportions saying that coverage was "poor" in either area.

11. It is perhaps also worth noting that the Times Mirror survey from which these data are derived was conducted in spring 1992, before Ross Perot's withdrawal and subsequent reentry into the presidential race—and before the media began to focus on his inconsistencies and occasionally strange behavior.

8

Citizens for Perot: Assessing
Patterns of Alienation and Activism

LONNA R. ATKESON
JAMES A. MCCANN
RONALD B. RAPOPORT
WALTER J. STONE

In the 1992 presidential election, nearly one out of every five votes cast went to Texas billionaire H. Ross Perot. Never before in America had a political neophyte risen so far so quickly. In a political culture dominated by the Democrats and Republicans for almost a century and a half, and in which third parties still have significant legal and organizational hurdles to overcome, Perot actually led both major-party presidential candidates for a time in the polls. The 19 percent he received on election day surpasses the percentage vote for all third-party (or independent) candidates except popular ex-president Theodore Roosevelt, who ran on the Bull Moose ticket in 1912. Perot received nearly three times the percentage of John Anderson, the former Republican who challenged Jimmy Carter and Ronald Reagan in 1980, and almost half again as much as George Wallace did running as an "American Independent" in 1968 against Richard Nixon and Hubert Humphrey. To put Perot's 19 percent showing into perspective further, only five other third-party or independent candidates have received even 5 percent of the national vote (see Table 8.1), although there have been such candidates in every presidential election this century.

As impressive as the final vote tally was, perhaps the most striking accomplishment of the Perot movement was the mobilization of hundreds of thousands of political activists who lent their efforts to his campaign. Volunteers mobilized virtually overnight to staff state and local campaign headquarters, campaigners mounted petition-signing drives to put Perot on the ballot, and an extensive grassroots electoral movement began to take shape. These volunteer activists were essential to the movement's early success, especially in getting Mr. Perot's name on the ballot in all fifty states, and their involvement supported his claim that he was leading a spontaneous popular crusade.

TABLE 8.1   Third-Party Candidates with over 5 Percent of the Vote Since 1900

Year	Candidate	Party	Vote	Percent
1912	Theodore Roosevelt	Bull Moose	4,119,538	27.4
	Eugene V. Debs	Socialist	900,672	6.0
1924	Robert LaFollette	Progressive	1,157,326	16.6
1968	George C. Wallace	American Independent	9,906,473	13.5
1980	John Anderson	Independent	5,720,060	6.6
1992	H. Ross Perot	Independent	19,721,433	18.9

SOURCE: *Presidential Elections Since 1789,* 5th ed. Washington, DC: CQ Press.

What accounts for the surge toward Perot among this activist cohort? To date, scholars, journalists, political leaders, and other commentators have offered a variety of explanations for the Perot success (e.g., see Balz 1993; Cook 1993; Faucheaux 1993; Luntz 1993; Hamilton and Mealiea 1993; Harwood 1992). One strand of conventional wisdom holds that much of the Perot bloc was deeply cynical about government and previously disengaged from the political process. For example, after conducting a series of in-depth interviews with Perot supporters, Richard Harwood (1992, p. 7) concluded that "these people, like so many Americans, were responding to a politics that had left them cold, frustrated, and for some completely alienated from the system." The emphasis on alienation from politics as a factor in mobilizing third-party support is not, of course, unique to Perot. Wallace voters and activists were far more cynical toward political institutions than supporters of the major parties in 1968 (Canfield 1984; Carlson 1981); in fact, most general theories of third-party emergence and third-party support emphasize alienation as a major determinant of electoral success (Rosenstone, Behr, and Lazarus 1984; Mazmanian 1974; Smallwood 1983; Gillespie 1993).

In this chapter, we concentrate on the mobilization of support for Perot. Our focus is on a key, but often overlooked, facet of the movement: the hundreds of thousands of activists who, moved by the candidate's appeal for help on *Larry King Live* and other venues, called his toll-free number to get information about or to volunteer for the campaign. Who were these volunteers? Where did they come from? And how did alienation affect their involvement? As our analysis shows, Perot's followers were indeed disaffected from conventional political institutions. Their beliefs about the major parties, the U.S. Congress, and President Bush were as hostile as the candidate's rhetoric, despite the fact that many came to the movement after having had significant histories of involvement in past campaigns of the two parties.

RESEARCH DESIGN

Because of the significance of the Perot movement in 1992, we conducted a study of potential activists in order to understand their motivations, backgrounds, and behavior in the campaign. Our study is based on a survey of a national sample of callers to Perot's 800 number, which was maintained during spring and summer 1992. Not all of the people who called became involved with the campaign; some were merely expressing interest and, for whatever reason, never participated further. Others became quite intensively involved. We consider members of our sample to be "potential activists" for Perot because calling to express interest requires a greater degree of initiative than merely signing a petition or voting for a candidate.

By the time Perot dropped out of the race in July 1992, these citizens numbered close to half a million. Our sample consists of 1,901 potential Perot activists who were sent a mail questionnaire in September 1992; of this group, 1,334 sent back responses for a response rate of 70 percent. Immediately following the election, we mailed respondents a follow-up questionnaire which was returned by 945 individuals (71 percent of the first-wave respondents). In these surveys, people were asked about their demographic attributes, their involvement in the Perot-Stockdale movement during the pre- and postconvention stages of the campaign, their participation in various special-interest political groups, and their attitudes and perceptions about candidates, parties, and the political system as a whole.

The individuals we are looking at here constitute an important group in American politics, since they clearly were predisposed to work for the candidate and may well become the core of any future Perot organization. Our goal in this chapter is twofold: first, to understand what distinguishes the Perot potential activists from other potential party activists and from the electorate as a whole; and second, to understand what it was that transformed some individuals from potential Perot activists into fully involved Perot activists. In approaching the first issue, we compare the Perot respondents with samples of Democratic and Republican state caucus participants from 1992 (citizens having a similar propensity to support their candidate plus the initiative to attend caucus meetings), and with the overall American electorate.[1] As for the second question, we examine the role of alienation in distinguishing between those who actually became active in the presidential campaign for Perot and those who became active for one of the major-party candidates.

A PROFILE OF POTENTIAL PEROT ACTIVISTS IN 1992

Demographic Comparisons

We begin with a demographic profile of the Perot sample. In general, party activists are significantly wealthier, better educated, and older than the population at large (Rapoport, Abramowitz, and McGlennon 1986), and they are more likely to be white. But because younger voters—who also tend to be less wealthy—are likely to have loose ties to the major parties and their candidates, we might expect at least some of these attributes to be less distinctive among the Perot group. Table 8.2 compares potential Perot activists with the national electorate and with Democratic and Republican caucus participants in terms of income, education, age, and race, as well as gender.

Looking at income and education levels, we see that the same social-class biases often noted within conventional parties characterized the Perot sample as well. In fact, potential Perot activists were scarcely distinguishable in this regard from either Democratic or Republican caucus participants—though they differed sharply from the national electorate: Over 4 out of 10 Perot supporters (along with nearly as many caucus attenders) reported family incomes of $50,000 or more, compared with less than a quarter of eligible voters as a whole; and more than twice the percentage from the Perot sample had a college degree (49.6 percent) compared to all voters (23.5 percent). Also, the Perot group resembled major-party activists in that very few were under age 30 (8.5 percent, compared with almost 1 in 5 for the national electorate).[2]

Gender is one trait on which the Perot sample was actually far less representative of the electorate than Democratic caucus participants—and slightly less representative than GOP caucus attenders. Roughly half of all eligible voters (and of the Democratic activists) were female; women constituted just 40.6 percent of the Republicans and 37.9 percent of Perot supporters. This underrepresentation in the potential activist sample was, not surprisingly, reflected in the low vote that Perot received from women (who provided just 41 percent of his total[3]) on election day.

Political Involvement

Because the Perot sample resembled the party activist samples in its demographic makeup, we might expect that Perot activists would have extensive backgrounds of political activism in campaigns and political interest groups. But given the nature of Perot's antiparty campaign, we might just as well assume that the Perot movement appealed primarily to those with little or no prior political involvement, that is, individuals who (as one Perot supporter put it) "just came out of the woodwork—people who had never been involved, people who had never ever thought about having their voice heard" (Harwood 1992, p. 7).

As is so often the case, the truth lies somewhere in between. Table 8.3 shows that many of Perot's potential campaign workers did come out of the two-party system: Nearly 15 percent had participated in the Dukakis-Bentsen campaign of 1988, either by convincing friends to support the ticket, contributing to the cause, attending a meeting or rally, fundraising, or canvassing neighborhoods. An even higher percentage of the Perot sample worked for the Bush-Quayle ticket in 1988,

TABLE 8.2   Demographic Characteristics of the Samples, 1992

	National Electorate[a]	Perot Sample	Caucus Attenders	
			Democrat	Republican
Income				
<$30,000	50.3%	25.2%	26.4%	33.8%
$30,000–$49,999	25.0	27.3	30.9	32.2
$50,000 and over	24.5	47.5	42.6	34.1
Education				
High school graduate or less	51.9%	15.9%	19.8%	22.9%
Some college	24.6	34.5	21.2	29.8
College graduate or postgraduate	23.5	49.6	58.9	47.3
Age				
Under 30	19.6%	8.5%	6.6%	8.1%
30–50	43.4	42.1	42.6	38.3
50–60	12.1	18.3	18.1	19.2
Over 60	24.9	31.1	32.7	34.3
Percent female	53.4%	37.9%	50.1%	40.6%
Percent nonwhite	15.3%	4.4%	5.9%	1.3%
Sample N =	2,487	1,334	764	385

[a]Data from the American National Election Study, 1992.

with nearly a quarter participating in some way. Altogether, about a third of the Perot sample had some involvement in one or the other of the 1988 general-election presidential campaigns. By the same token, two-thirds did not.

Turning to 1992, we see that efforts by these citizens on behalf of candidates other than Perot actually exceeded their total level of 1988 general-election activity; fully 4 in 10 performed some sort of campaign work for one or more of the major-party contestants. Most supported either Bill Clinton or George Bush, though almost half as many became involved for (1) ex-Massachusetts senator Paul Tsongas as for Clinton (an especially strong showing in light of the former's early exit from the campaign) and for (2) conservative commentator Pat Buchanan as for President Bush. Overall, then, many who called Perot's toll-free telephone number had ties either to the Democrats or to the Republicans, but a fair number of them exhibited their frustration with "politics as usual" by backing one of the major-party insurgents at some point along the way.

In the middle of Table 8.3, we find further evidence of the Perot sample's history within the parties. Roughly 1 out of 10 reported having held a Democratic party office (e.g., serving on a local committee, chairing a committee, being a dele-

TABLE 8.3   Campaign and Party Activism Among Perot and Major-Party Supporters, 1988 and 1992

| | Perot Sample | Caucus Attenders | |
		Democrats	Republicans
General election 1988			
Dukakis-Bentsen	14.4%	61.4%	1.7%
Bush-Quayle	22.9%	7.5%	68.4%
Nomination activity 1992			
George Bush	11.4%	1.5%	76.5%
Pat Buchanan	4.9%	0.0%	4.4%
Bill Clinton	17.2%	53.0%	1.8%
Jerry Brown	7.1%	9.1%	0.6%
John Kerry	2.1%	3.5%	0.0%
Tom Harkin	2.0%	28.3%	1.2%
Paul Tsongas	8.0%	9.0%	0.6%
Party office			
Democratic office held	10.3%	29.2%	1.0%
Republican office held	7.8%	0.3%	31.4%
Either party office held	16.2%	29.3%	32.2%
Sample N =	1,334	764	385

gate to a state convention), and nearly as many reported the same type of participation on the Republican side. Altogether, about 1 in 6 had actually held party office—an activity occurring at only trace levels in the mass electorate. Although these measures of campaign and party activity are far below the level exhibited by Democratic and Republican activists, they are nonetheless impressive considering the antiparty rhetoric and nature of the Perot movement.

The real question, of course, is not what Perot supporters did for others but what they did for their own candidate. How successful was Perot in mobilizing those who were initially interested in his message? The answer is found in Table 8.4, which shows the extent to which callers worked for Perot both before the party conventions and during the general-election campaign. More than 70 percent became active in some way prior to Perot's departure from the race in July—a degree of participation far above what is typically found within the mass public (Conway 1991). Looking down the list of activities we learn, for example, that (1) nearly two-thirds tried to persuade friends and associates to support Perot, (2) 32 percent participated in the drive to put his name on a state ballot, and (3) 11.6 percent reported doing neighborhood canvassing.

After Perot dropped out and then reentered, participation levels did drop somewhat during the fall. Nevertheless, supporters' continuing commitment to the campaign (almost 80 percent of those active before his exit remained in-

TABLE 8.4   Types of Campaign Activity Among Potential Perot Activists, 1992

Activity	Percent Performing
Preconvention	
Involved in any way for Perot	72.9%
Tried to convince friends/associates to vote for Perot	64.2%
Collected signatures for petition drive	32.0%
Attended meetings or rallies	28.7%
Canvassed door-to-door or by telephone	11.6%
Organized meetings	4.0%
Sample N (preelection wave) =	1,334
General Election	
Involved in any way for Perot	56.9%
Voted for Perot in the election	53.9%
Tried to convince friends/associates to vote for Perot	49.9%
Attended meetings or rallies	21.3%
Contributed money to the Perot effort	15.1%
Canvassed door-to-door or by telephone	11.6%
Sample N (postelection wave) =	945

volved) is remarkable given their candidate's vacillation about whether he was even going to run. In addition, there is the fact that Perot's emphasis during the October phase was on mass-media events and infomercials rather than the labor-intensive task of mobilizing followers and getting on the ballot—activities that had taken precedence in the campaign's early stages. As a result, there simply may not have been as many opportunities for rank-and-file citizens to participate as had existed in the spring and summer before Perot stepped aside.

Nonparty Group Involvement

Although party activity is an obvious avenue to presidential campaign activity, it is not the only one. Participation in nonparty political and nonpolitical groups also can produce the skills, experience, and social networks that encourage and facilitate campaign involvement (Verba and Nie 1972; Rosenstone and Hansen 1993). Indeed, our data show that potential Perot activists gained much of their political and organizational experience through involvement in groups of this sort. Many groups have long-standing ties with one or both of the major parties, and yet the Perot sample as a whole participated as frequently in a variety of nonpartisan organizations as did Democratic and Republican caucus attenders. In all three samples, more than two-thirds were active during the previous year in at least one group—and more than 40 percent were active in two or more.

It is interesting to note the particular kinds of organizations in which Perot supporters were involved. As Table 8.5 illustrates, large numbers of them had at some point been active in business, veterans, environmental, nonpartisan, and labor groups. In fact, more of the Perot sample claimed to be active during the preceding year in business and veterans groups—traditional factions within the Republican Party coalition, but two groups heavily identified with Perot as well— than among the set of Republican caucus attenders. Furthermore, roughly equal proportions within the Democratic and Perot blocs had been active in environmental, nonpartisan, and labor organizations.[4]

Important differences among the three samples become clear when we turn to those groups representing ideological and issue groups of the right and left— groups that are heavily represented in the Republican and Democratic caucus samples, respectively. For example, over 25 percent of the Republican caucus attenders had some involvement with antiabortion groups, and nearly as many were connected to religious-right and conservative-ideology organizations. On the Democratic side, between 20 and 25 percent had involvement with civil rights, women's, or liberal-ideology groups. For all six types of organizations, however, the degree of activism among Perot supporters was considerably less (ranging between 6.6 percent and 14.9 percent). Thus, although the level of overall group participation is very similar for our three samples, the configuration of groups varies quite a bit across the three.

Patterns of Alienation

We have seen that the Perot sample exhibited demographic traits and levels of group involvement common to party activists, but it is important to keep in mind that only one-third of them had been active in the 1988 general-election campaign. In contrast, more than four-fifths were active in 1992—heavily for Perot. It is important, therefore, to identify the factors mobilizing them to independent campaign activity and causing them to reject the two major parties and politics as usual. High levels of voter dissatisfaction with the major parties or their candidates, and voter alienation from the political system in general, have both been found to enhance third-party support in the past (Rosenstone, Behr, and Lazarus 1984; Carlson 1981; Canfield 1984).

Among Perot sample respondents, both factors operated to produce high levels of support for Perot. In the first place, Table 8.6 shows that potential Perot activists were remarkably low in their partisan loyalty:[5] Roughly 60 percent of those in the sample identified themselves as Independents, and more than one in five refused to indicate so much as a leaning toward one party or the other.[6] To put this into perspective, only about half as many (11.7 percent) in the national electorate described themselves as "pure" Independents. Under the circumstances, it is little surprise that when asked to evaluate the two parties separately,[7] Perot supporters generally gave low marks to each: Republicans and Democrats alike received favorable ratings ("above average" or "outstanding") from under 10 percent of our sample, and about two-thirds viewed them unfavorably ("below aver-

TABLE 8.5   Group Activity Among Perot and Major-Party Supporters

	Perot Sample		Democrats		Republicans	
Type of Group	Ever Member	Active Member in Last Year	Ever Member	Active Member in Last Year	Ever Member	Active Member in Last Year
Business	38.8%	23.3%	22.1%	10.8%	34.1%	16.9%
Veterans	25.9%	18.5%	17.0%	10.0%	19.7%	12.5%
Environmental	36.3%	26.4%	35.6%	21.4%	10.9%	5.5%
Nonpartisan	27.8%	16.7%	32.8%	15.8%	18.2%	10.3%
Labor	25.4%	12.3%	29.7%	12.1%	16.8%	3.8%
Religious Right	6.6%	4.5%	0.7%	0.0%	21.0%	17.2%
Antiabortion	9.2%	7.3%	4.4%	2.4%	25.4%	21.6%
Conservative ideology	11.9%	8.1%	2.2%	0.8%	21.7%	15.6%
Civil rights	11.7%	6.3%	25.4%	15.5%	3.2%	0.6%
Women's	14.9%	10.0%	21.1%	11.0%	5.8%	3.6%
Liberal ideology	10.4%	6.3%	20.7%	11.1%	1.3%	0.6%
Sample N =	1,334		764		385	

age" or "poor"; see Table 8.7); fewer than 1 in 6 (16.4 percent) scored *either* party as "above average" or "outstanding."

Even among the 79 percent leaning toward or identifying with one side or the other, the parties were not especially well regarded. Of Democratic Party leaners and identifiers, only 22.2 percent rated it as "above average" or "outstanding" (vs. 34.9 percent "below average" or "poor"); and of Republican identifiers, only one in eight (16.3 percent) scored the GOP "above average" or better (vs. 45.7 percent "below average" or "poor"). Perot supporters' lack of partisan attachment probably helped to push them away from backing either of the major-party candidates for president in 1992. But it is also likely that Perot contributed to this disaffection with his rhetoric specifically indicting the parties for their past failures and touting himself as an independent candidate who was of and for the people.

In addition to their low regard for the parties, potential Perot activists were also very dissatisfied with the major-party nominees. We see in Table 8.7 that George Bush received particularly harsh evaluations despite the higher proportion of Republicans over Democrats within the sample; two-thirds rated Bush "below average" or "poor" (vs. 12.2 percent "above average" or "outstanding"). Even among Republicans, more than twice as many rated Bush unfavorably as favorably. Bill Clinton fared only slightly better, with just 1 in 5 rating him "above average" or "outstanding" (vs. almost half "below average" or "poor"). These figures contrast sharply with the much more favorable assessments by the national electorate, a majority of whom gave positive scores to both Bush (50.9 percent) and Clinton (56.5 percent).[8] The difference in evaluation between the two sam-

TABLE 8.6   Party Identification, 1992

Party Identification	National Electorate[a]	Perot Sample
Strong Democrat	18.2%	7.3%
Weak Democrat	17.7	9.6
Leaning Democrat	14.5	19.7
Independent	11.7	21.1
Leaning Republican	12.5	19.7
Weak Republican	14.3	13.0
Strong Republican	11.2	9.7
N =	2,446	1,267

[a]Data from the American National Election Study, 1992.

ples makes clear the general dissatisfaction with major-party candidates that existed among Perot supporters.

If we go beyond the electoral setting, potential Perot activists also expressed decidedly negative views toward the institutions of American government in general. As unpopular as the parties were, for example, Congress received significantly lower scores from these respondents (less than 2 percent "above average" or "outstanding" vs. 86.2 percent "below average" or "poor"); and the Supreme Court, which is usually isolated from normal partisan politics, got just an 11.7 percent favorable rating (vs. 59.7 percent unfavorable). Compared with the Perot sample, eligible voters as a whole were much less likely to register disapproval of the presidential nominees, their respective parties, and the formal institutions of government. In fact, there is no instance in which the national electorate gave any of these political actors more negative than positive ratings. Even Congress, despite doing rather poorly relative to the others, received only 36.5 percent in unfavorable evaluations from the general public.

There was, of course, one political figure who scored better with the Perot sample than with the national electorate, and that was Ross Perot himself. Two-thirds of the potential activists judged him favorably, only 1 in 7 unfavorably. Among the national electorate, however, Perot was rated lower than Congress or anyone else—actually receiving more negative (40.9 percent) than positive (35.4 percent) evaluations.

A final indication of the degree to which Perot supporters were alienated from the institutions and policies of the U.S. government is seen in their answers to the question, "How much of the time do you think you can trust the government in Washington to do what is right —just about always, most of the time, some of the time, or almost never?"[9] As reported in Table 8.7, an overwhelming 95 percent (vs. 71 percent of all citizens; see Chapter 3) felt that Washington could be counted on to do the right thing only some (55 percent) or almost none (41 percent) of the time. The Perot group also was more likely than the electorate as a whole (97

TABLE 8.7 Evaluations of Individuals and Government Institutions, 1992

	National Electorate[a]	Perot Sample
Overall Evaluation of:		
George Bush		
Above average/favorable	50.9%	12.2%
Below average/unfavorable	35.0	66.3
Bill Clinton		
Above average/favorable	56.5%	19.1%
Below average/unfavorable	28.9	48.1
Ross Perot		
Above average/favorable	35.4%	65.3%
Below average/unfavorable	40.9	14.2
Republican Party		
Above average/favorable	45.1%	7.8%
Below average/unfavorable	34.2	69.1
Democratic Party		
Above average/favorable	58.3%	9.4%
Below average/unfavorable	24.0	64.1
Rate Both Parties		
Below average/unfavorable	5.3%	43.6%
Congress		
Above average/favorable	42.5%	1.7%
Below average/unfavorable	36.5	86.2
Supreme Court		
Above average/favorable	–	11.7%
Below average/unfavorable	–	59.7
Trust government to do what is right:		
All of the time	3.2%	0.1%
Most of the time	26.1	4.8
Only some/almost never[b]	70.6	95.1
Sample N =	2,487	1,334

[a]Data from the American National Election Study, 1992. Ratings of candidates, parties, and institutions are based on ANES "feeling thermometer" questions (see Appendix and note 8).

[b]See note 9.

percent vs. 79 percent) to say that our government was run by a few big interests looking out for themselves rather than for the benefit of all the people. Coupled with potential activists' hostility toward the major parties and their candidates, these findings suggest that activists may have been attracted to Perot precisely because of his outsider status and because his candidacy represented a direct challenge to established political institutions and practices. We consider this possibility more closely in the next section.

Political Alienation and Campaign Behavior in 1992

To repeat: Potential Perot activists were much more mistrustful of the government and unfavorable toward the major parties and their candidates than was the national electorate (or our Democratic and Republican caucus participants for that matter). It is possible, though, that these various measures of dissatisfaction do not indicate a *cumulative* alienation from government and its institutions. In other words, individuals who mistrust Congress may not be the same ones who mistrust the Supreme Court, and those who never trust government to do what is right might not be any more negative toward political parties than the sample as a whole. Such a pattern would cast some doubt on the alienation hypothesis, since respondents' alienation would tend to be more specific and less generalized.

This, however, is not the case. What we find instead (especially among Perot supporters) is that attitudes toward particular institutions and toward government *are* cumulative, and together they do seem to tap a broad-based alienation from politics. As a rule, the individuals who mistrust government in general also mistrust Congress, the people who mistrust Congress also give both parties low ratings, and the ones who give parties low ratings also express dissatisfaction with the Supreme Court. Respondents who say they almost never trust government to do what is right, for example, are over 20 percentage points more likely than those who trust government "most of the time" to evaluate Congress and the Supreme Court as "below average" or "poor"; and people who rate Congress unfavorably are almost 40 points more likely than those who express average or positive assessments to score both political parties as "below average" or "poor."

It is congruent with our understanding of third-party support that citizens who are highly alienated or disaffected from government and politics will be the most likely to consider an alternative candidate (Rosenstone et al. 1984)—a pattern that obviously is consistent with the findings for potential Perot activists. Remember, though, that the Perot sample was drawn from a population of people who were initially attracted to the Perot movement *whether or not they eventually became active in it.* Even *within* this sample of individuals who exhibited an early interest in the candidate, we find that activity as well as voting for Perot are closely related to one's level of alienation.[10]

As shown in Figure 8.1, participation in both Perot and major-party campaigns were affected (albeit in opposite ways) by respondents' feelings of political alienation. The more alienated, the more likely the potential Perot supporter was to be active for Perot-Stockdale; the less alienated, the more likely she or he was to support Bush-Quayle or Clinton-Gore. Among the least-alienated quarter of the sample, activity on behalf of the Democrats or Republicans actually surpassed that for Perot—but among the most-alienated quarter, Perot activity was four times the level of involvement for one of the major parties. The same effect is evident for voting behavior: Among the least alienated, Perot received less than a third of the vote (badly trailing Clinton; see Figure 8.2); his vote exceeded 70 percent among the most-alienated group.

Thus, it would appear from our analysis that the Perot sample was clearly influenced by its members' attitudes toward government. Their anger and cynicism about particular political actors and institutions came together in a generalized sense of political alienation, which in turn provided Perot with a large group of citizens who were receptive to his unorthodox, nonpartisan appeal. Ross Perot ran for president as someone who was independent of the parties and independent of established government. For those who were mistrustful of government insiders, his candidacy provided a definite and viable alternative.

CONCLUSION: LOOKING AHEAD

We can only speculate on whether the potential activist base for the Perot movement in 1992 can persist or develop into a full-fledged third-party movement in 1996, but our findings are suggestive. First, the Perot sample was weakly attached to the two major parties. Since there does not seem to be anything on the horizon to encourage a massive return to them among those who are independent or weakly affiliated, it is likely that a significant proportion of the potential activists will remain relatively open to appeals from Perot in the future. Second, discontent with the traditional parties, their candidates, and the political process generally seems to have become an enduring feature of U.S. national politics, and this also bodes well for continued support of Perot (or a similar type of candidate) among our sample population. Finally, we should understand that these people, despite their discontent, feel relatively efficacious[11] and possess many of the skills necessary to carry on either as a quasi–third party or as a more narrowly defined interest group.

Probably the most important factor is Perot himself. Activists were attracted to him, in part, because of the "push" away from the parties and their candidates in 1992—but they were also strongly "pulled" to Perot for the positive qualities he had to offer. Furthermore, their affection for him, although strong in our September wave, was even stronger *after* the election, when about three-quarters rated him as "outstanding" or "above average" (and less than 10 percent as "below average" or "poor"). In contrast, evaluations of Perot among the general public had begun to decline by late 1993 and continued to drop in 1994. Whether this decline in support reached into the ranks of the more politically involved individuals in our sample is uncertain, and the resilience exhibited by Perot throughout his 1992 campaign was truly remarkable. In any case, the Perot constituency of

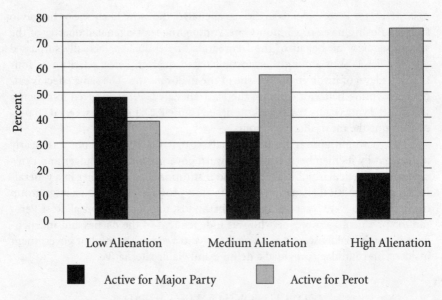

FIGURE 8.1   General Election Activity by Level of Alienation, 1992. Figures indicate the proportion of potential Perot activists of various levels of alienation (see note 10) who participated either for Ross Perot or for one of the major parties during the 1992 campaign (N=812).

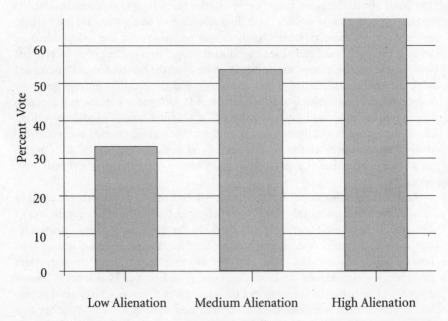

FIGURE 8.2   Perot Vote by Level of Alienation, 1992. Figures indicate the proportion of potential Perot activists at various levels of alienation (see note 10) who voted for Ross Perot in 1992 (N=792).

alienated voters and activists, particularly should there be an economic downturn, is one that both parties need to be concerned about.

Naturally, without candidate Perot, transferring the popular appeal of his movement into a third party would be an extremely difficult task. Although Perot's United We Stand America organization has rated candidates and publicized surveys of members as to their candidate preferences, there has been almost no interest in making nominations on an official United We Stand America ticket. Moreover, our sample was less unified in its support for UWSA than it was for Perot the man: More than one-third were not sure of their views toward the organization, and of those with clear opinions, positive attitudes outnumbered negative by only about 3 to 1 (compared with a better than 7:1 ratio for Perot personally).

At the time of the November 1992 survey of potential activists, however, UWSA was still a relatively new entity, and its long-term prospects were unclear. To get a better idea of our sample's orientation toward future political activity, we specifically asked respondents in the postelection survey what they planned to do over the next four years. The answers to these questions are less a prediction of what they actually will do than an indication of their state of mind once the campaign was over.

As Table 8.8 shows, about 20 percent declared their intention to work in a third party, and another 37 percent indicated an interest in continued political involvement but "not within any party." Only about 13 percent said they would drop out of political activity altogether. Notice, by the way, that there is a relationship between what respondents said they would do in the future and what they did in the 1992 election. The percentage saying they intended not to do political work at all is almost three times as high for those not active in 1992 as for individuals who participated in any of the other campaigns. In fact, only about 10 percent of those active for any ticket expected to be politically *un*involved in the future. Of particular interest is the fact that by far the highest percentage planning to work within a third party comes from the Perot-Stockdale activist group. Together, these findings suggest that for most of the Perot sample, their experience was a positive one and that an active constituency for Perot's continued involvement in the political process does exist.

But creating an insurgent political movement around individuals alienated and mistrustful of political leaders is far easier than sustaining such an organization, and the Perot movement is no exception. Although we have not yet gathered additional data on our Perot sample, collateral evidence from the membership of United We Stand America and from various surveys of 1992 Perot voters points out both the resilience of the movement as a continuing force *and* the fragility of its loyalty to any particular candidate (Perot included). For example, 1992 Perot voters displayed far less warmth toward the Texas billionaire by the time of the 1994 midterm elections than they had two years earlier. In the 1992 American National Election Study, 90 percent of those who backed Perot rated him posi-

TABLE 8.8   Prospective Future Political Activity Among Potential Perot Activists, 1992

Expected Activity Over Next Four Years	Full Sample	Not Active	For Perot-Stockdale	For Bush-Quayle	For Clinton-Gore
			1992 Activity[a]		
Work within Democratic Party	6.0%	2.9%	3.3%	0.9%	22.6%
Work within Republican Party	3.2	3.5	1.7	16.8	1.0
Work within third party	19.9	6.9	30.5	12.1	4.6
Work but not within a party	37.1	33.3	35.9	35.5	43.1
Will not be involved in politics	12.8	28.3	8.8	10.3	9.2
Unsure	21.0	24.9	19.8	24.3	19.5
N =	911	173	521	107	195

[a]Because some respondents were active for more than one campaign in 1992, there is a small amount of overlap among these groups.

tively, and his mean score on the feeling thermometer was an impressive 76 degrees. This level of support remained fairly constant through April 1993, but by November 1994, fewer than half of self-identified Perot voters gave him a positive evaluation—and his mean score on the 100-point feeling thermometer had plummeted to 54 degrees (Democratic Leadership Council 1994, p. 53). A similar decline was reflected in the number of people affiliated with United We Stand America, whose membership dropped from an estimated 1.3 million in 1993 to only about 300,000 by election day 1994 (L. Phillips 1994).

Even so, the Perot movement seems to have had a clear impact on 1994 races in terms of votes. The level of alienation, already high in 1992–1993, actually went up in 1994, when higher percentages of Perot supporters believed that "government always manages to mess things up" (81 percent agree in October 1994 versus 72 percent in April 1993), public officials don't "usually care what people like me think" (71 percent versus 67 percent), and "you really can't trust the government to do the right thing" (69 percent versus 66 percent; Democratic Leadership Council 1994, p. 55). This anger was turned largely toward the incumbent president—not surprising given the "gridlock" that characterized Bill Clinton's first two years in office, the president's inability to make good on health care, his endorsement of the North American Free Trade Agreement (NAFTA), and other frustrations. According to the 1992 ANES, more than twice as many Perot voters rated Clinton positively as negatively, and he had a mean score of 56 degrees on the feeling thermometer. In contrast, by November 1994, the situation had reversed such that twice as many Perot voters rated the president negatively as positively and his overall mean on the thermometer had dropped almost 20 points (to 38 degrees; Democratic Leadership Council 1994, p. 53).

Unfortunately for the Democrats, the anger of Perot voters was not localized to a single individual. Half again as many of them rated the Democratic Party favorably as unfavorably in the 1992 ANES, but almost twice as many rated it unfavorably as favorably by November 1994 (ratings of the Republican Party actually improved slightly during the same period; Democratic Leadership Council 1994, p. 54). From all appearances, these comparative evaluations translated directly into votes: Perot supporters in 1992 divided their congressional ballots almost evenly between the parties (50.5 percent Republican versus 49.5 percent Democratic), but in 1994 they were twice as likely to vote Republican as Democratic (67 percent to 33 percent).[12] The 17-point swing in favor of Republicans, among 19 percent of the electorate who voted for Perot for president, produced a net swing of 3.4 percentage points. With the total net increase in GOP votes between 1992 and 1994 being between 4 and 5 points, the Perot contribution to it obviously was substantial.

What is more difficult to determine is the direct role played by Perot and UWSA in stimulating the Republican mobilization in 1994. The group published ratings of sitting members of Congress, with devastatingly one-sided results: Of 172 House incumbents given failing marks, only two were Republicans. By the same token, whereas Perot encouraged his supporters to give the GOP "a turn at bat," he nevertheless left himself an opening for 1996 by promising that if the Republicans were not successful, "I will give you every ounce of everything I have and we will create a third party that will deliver" (Seelye 1994, p. 22).

Given his drop in mass support and a corresponding decline in the number of people who are formally affiliated with USWA, it remains to be seen whether Perot will be able to keep this promise; the likelihood of his doing so ultimately may depend more on Republican performance than on the candidate's own actions. As a result, the manner in which supporters of the 1992 Perot movement will participate in the political process in 1996—through UWSA, a third party, or one of the major parties—is hard to predict. The existing parties are remarkably adaptive and resilient institutions, and we expect that both the Democrats and (especially) the Republicans will continue trying to absorb the Perot legions. In fact, each has already been forced to pay attention to Perot agenda issues they might otherwise have ignored.

But the success of these appeals is unclear. Let us not forget that Perot's movement has attracted partisans as well as independents, with many in both groups expressing grave doubts about the major parties and their elected representatives in 1992 as well as 1994. If the Republicans fail to deliver on their pledges, Perot is waiting in the wings. Regardless of the 1996 scenario, however, it is quite certain that the Perot voter, like the Reagan Democrat of the 1980s, will provide an important battleground over the next few elections

NOTES

1. Comparisons with the national electorate are drawn from the 1992 American National Election Study (ANES); these data are based on surveys conducted by the Center for Political Studies at the University of Michigan and made available by the Inter-University Consortium for Political and Social Research. Comparisons with party activists are based on surveys with samples of 1992 Iowa and Virginia Democratic caucus participants and 1992 Iowa Republican caucus participants, all of which were carried out after the November election. We do not argue that our caucus states somehow represent the entire nation, but we have found that cross-state variations within party samples are fairly small, especially on most of the indicators of interest in this chapter (see Abramowitz, McGlennon, and Rapoport 1983; Stone, Abramowitz, and Rapoport 1989).

2. The racial makeup of the Perot group reflected a similar bias vis-à-vis the national electorate, as did the Democratic and Republican caucus participant samples, i.e., it was heavily white. We should point out that the combined mean incomes of Iowa and Virginia are very close to the national average, as is the overall nonwhite proportion in these two states (23 percent in Virginia and 3 percent in Iowa, for an average of 13 percent).

3. This figure is based on data from the 1992 American National Election Study.

4. This latter coalition would emerge again in 1993 as Perot lobbied against the North American Free Trade Agreement (NAFTA).

5. The measure of party identification used in our mail questionnaires was based on the ANES version (see Appendix) but with slight variations in wording to accommodate the nonverbal format.

6. We should note that it is Republicans who claim the larger share of identifiers, if only marginally (42 percent vs. 37 percent). This makes the Perot sample not only much more independent than the national electorate but substantially more Republican as well.

7. The specific question here asked for an "overall evaluation" of the Republican and Democratic parties.

8. Ratings by the general public in Table 8.7 are based on the ANES "feeling thermometer" questions (see Appendix), with scores above 50 degrees being "favorable" and scores below 50 degrees being "unfavorable."

9. This is based on one of the standard ANES "political trust" measures (see Chapter 3), the principal difference being that ANES does not offer "almost never" as an explicit response option.

10. Using various measures of alienation (most prominently trust in government, evaluation of the Supreme Court and Congress, and evaluation of the more highly rated major party), we created a scale of alienation. The scale was then trichotomized so that one-quarter was placed into the most-alienated category, one-quarter into the least-alienated category, and the remaining half into an intermediate grouping.

11. For example, 58.9 percent of the sample agreed that they could "do a better job in public office than most people."

12. Data on the congressional votes of Perot supporters are from the *New York Times*, November 5, 1992 (p. B9) and November 10, 1994 (p. B4).

PART III

Groups

9

The Gender Gap: A Manifestation of Women's Dissatisfaction with the American Polity?

JANET CLARK
CAL CLARK

The declining levels of trust described in Chapters 1 and 3 imply that something is amiss in the American polity. Clearly, the public believes that its "ownership" of democratic government in the United States has become quite tenuous. And if government has "broken a contract" with the nation's citizens, it is reasonable to expect that relatively marginal groups in society would be the ones who feel betrayed and alienated the most. In this chapter we argue that the rise of the so-called gender gap in the 1980s represented such a "broken contract" for women in America, since the growth of a distinctive women's perspective on political issues arose, essentially, because the polity failed to respond to several basic needs facing different types of women in modern society.

THE GROWTH OF THE GENDER GAP

Up through the mid-1970s, the voting behavior and most political attitudes of men and women appeared to be remarkably similar. Table 9.1, for example, presents the gender gap in presidential and congressional voting and in party identification from 1952 to 1992.[1] For most of this period, there was little systematic difference between the sexes in terms of their voting or party preference; in fact, women leaned toward the Republicans during the Eisenhower era. During the 1980s, in sharp contrast, women became substantially less supportive of Republicans than men in presidential voting; by mid-decade, a gender gap of almost 10 percentage points had opened up between men and women in terms of both their voting for and approving the presidential performance of Ronald Reagan. A somewhat earlier gap had emerged for identification with the Democrats as women stayed loyal to the more liberal party in the face of significant male defections during the 1970s and 1980s. (The absence

TABLE 9.1   Gender Gap in Voting and Party Identification, 1952–1992

Year	Presidential Vote		(% Republican) Gender Gap[b]	Gender Gap: Congressional Vote (% Republican)[b]	Gender Gap: Party Identification[a]	
	Male	Female			% Republican[b]	% Democrat[b]
1952	53%	58%	5%	-1%	4%	1%
1956	55%	61%	6%	9%	8%	-1%
1960	48%	51%	3%	-2%	3%	5%
1964	40%	38%	-2%	0%	2%	3%
1968	43%	43%	0%	0%	-2%	5%
1972	63%	62%	-1%	1%	1%	6%
1976	45%	51%	6%	1%	5%	6%
1980	53%	49%	-4%	3%	1%	7%
1984	64%	55%	-9%	-5%	-1%	8%
1988	57%	50%	-7%	-5%	-1%	10%
1992	38%	38%	0%	-3%	-5%	8%

[a]Unlike voting, where only a miniscule percentage of Americans do not vote for either of the major parties, a substantial number of citizens identify with neither party. As a result, the gender gaps in Democratic and Republican identifications are not always symmetrical (i.e., about the same size but in different directions).

[b]A positive gender gap means that women were more supportive; a negative gap shows that men were more supportive.

SOURCE: Bendyna and Lake (1994, p. 242); Clark and Clark (1993, p. 33); Kenski (1988, pp. 44, 50, 55); Pomper (1993, p. 138); *Public Perspective* (1993, p. 99).

of a corresponding gender gap for Republican allegiance stems from higher rates of "independence" among men as compared to women.) In contrast, the gender gap in congressional voting was slightly less pronounced because of the much more local nature of campaigns for the U.S. House of Representatives.

In the 1992 presidential election, the gender gap in voting shrank somewhat— Bill Clinton ran 5 percentage points better among women than men; Ross Perot, 4 points worse; and George Bush, 1 point worse. At first blush, this narrowing is surprising, since the socioeconomic strains that shaped the election should have, if anything, exacerbated the gender gap. However, this appears to have been an idiosyncratic function of the salience of the abortion issue in the 1992 election, which led pro-life women, who might otherwise have supported him, to vote against Clinton (Clark and Clark 1994). Unlike the 1988 election, when views on abortion had little association with presidential vote, the 1992 campaign brought this issue to the fore; it clearly had a significant impact at the polls (e.g., Clinton received 58 percent of the votes of pro-choice citizens but only 39 percent from pro-life ones). Yet despite a slight narrowing of the gender gap in presidential voting, there was little change in its other manifestations. The 1992 gender gap in party identification with Democrats remained at the level of the 1980s, a significant gender gap on identification with the Republican party emerged for the first time, and women's approval rates of President Clinton's performance were generally 5 to 8 points higher than men's throughout the first year of his administration (*American Enterprise* 1993, p. 83; and 1994, p. 83). It thus appears that a persistent gender gap had been formed in which women were more supportive than men of Democrats and of many liberal issues.

This gender gap in voting and partisan affiliation seemingly reflected important changes in the way men and women viewed the central issues in American politics. Until the 1970s, women and men had similar attitudes on most political issues. There were a few notable exceptions, such as women's greater concern for morality issues, support for some "traditional" values, and opposition to policies that threatened to involve the United States in violent conflict. Since then, in contrast, significant differences in political attitudes between the sexes emerged or expanded in such areas as "social compassion," support for minority rights, protection of the environment, and basic economic issues to greatly augment the previous limited attitudinal gap concerning peace and morality (see Bendyna and Lake 1994; Baxter and Lansing 1980; Clark and Clark 1993; Giles 1988; Kenski 1988; Klein 1984; Poole and Zeigler 1985; Shapiro and Mahajan 1986; Smith 1984; Stoper 1989).

The gender gap of the 1980s has often been attributed to women's distinctive values and ways of thinking, which emphasize interpersonal relationships more than power and community more than conflict (Gilligan 1982). These values, in turn, became increasingly salient politically during the 1970s and 1980s due to women's changing role in American society as denoted by the growth of the women's movement, women's increased entrance into higher education and the workplace, and most recently the significant gains that women candidates have made at the polls (Baxter and Lansing 1980; Darcy, Welch, and Clark 1994; Klein 1984; Mueller 1988; Sapiro 1983; Sinclair 1983). Thus, as women were able to broaden their horizons and escape the confines of traditional socialization, they began to realize that their basic values applied to a broader range of issues such as helping the less fortunate, supporting racial equality, protecting the environment, and most especially demanding equal rights for women. Susan Carroll (1988), for example, has explicitly argued that women's increased economic and psychological independence from men is a major cause of the gender gap. Furthermore, the basic socioeconomic and political changes that have occurred in the United States over the latter part of the twentieth century, such as rising divorce rates and falling welfare expenditures, have contributed to a "feminization of poverty," giving women an additional "self-interest" in being liberal on social welfare issues (Erie and Rein 1988).

By the early 1990s, therefore, the gender gap had become a persistent feature on the American political landscape. Women held somewhat different perspectives from men on a wide variety of important political issues—issues that clearly had been slighted during the Reagan-Bush years (and during previous, less conservative administrations as well). If the American public as a whole was increasingly alienated from or apathetic toward its government, the gender gap indicated that women in particular perceived a broken contract between public officials and their ostensible constituencies.

GENDER DIFFERENCES IN THE 1990s

The Core of the Gender Gap:
Ideology, Partisanship, and the Role of Government

Most discussions of the gender gap focus on ideology and partisanship, since these are the political attitudes most directly related to electoral outcomes. In addition, ideology and partisanship often hinge on views about the role of government—e.g., whether it is more desirable to have a strong government that can provide aid to its citizens or a weak government that cannot oppress its citizens. We therefore begin our survey of the gender gap in 1992 by examining these three sets of general orientations toward political life; Table 9.2 presents data on the nature of American public opinion and the extent of the gender gap in these areas.

In terms of general ideological and partisan predispositions, the gender gap has remained quite stable compared to the trends over time depicted in Table 9.1. In 1992, men were more likely than women to identify themselves as Republicans and as conservatives by almost identical margins (44 percent to 36 percent and 45 percent to 37 percent, respectively), producing a gender gap in partisanship and

TABLE 9.2   Gender Gap on General Orientations, 1992

	Male	Female	Gender Gap
Ideology/partisanship			
Conservative	45%	37%	-8%
Republican	44%	36%	-8%
Role of Government			
Government should expand responsibility	55%	70%	15%
Government should become more powerful	29%	44%	15%
Strong government over free market	64%	76%	12%
Government involved in what people should do for themselves	45%	31%	-14%
Government increase services vs. cut spending	32%	42%	10%
N = 2,487			

NOTE: See Appendix for question wordings.
SOURCE: American National Election Study, 1992.

ideology of 8 points—about equal to the gender gap in these two areas that has existed since the early 1970s. Once again, the enduring nature of the gender gap indicates that it taps some basic value and role differences between men and women in American society.

Americans' views about the role of government in the early 1990s appear a bit schizophrenic. On the one hand, about two-thirds of the citizenry wanted government to take on more responsibilities and preferred a strong government over a free market (which would appear to be the antithesis of the Reagan revolution).[2] On the other hand, only a third wanted the government to become more powerful; the desire for increased government services over cuts in government spending was held by a narrow plurality of 37 percent to 31 percent, and almost 40 percent believed that the government has already become involved in things that people should do for themselves. Americans are thus ambivalent about their government and about "living with leviathan" (Bennett and Bennett 1990; also see Chapter 2 in this volume). Evidently, they want it to do more for them, but they are also afraid of what it might do to them.

In terms of the gender gap, women take an even more distinctive position from men on these issues—consistently in a pro-government direction—than they do on ideology. For example, women were 15 percentage points more likely to believe that the federal government should take on additional responsibilities and become more powerful (70 percent to 55 percent and 44 percent to 29 percent, respectively), and 14 points less likely to say that government had become involved in matters that people should take care of themselves (31 percent to 45 percent); there also was a gender gap of at least 10 points on the other two government role items (prefer a strong government to the free market and increase government services rather than cut spending). Women apparently see themselves and others with whom they identify as being disadvantaged groups in America who do not necessarily benefit from the operations of free-market capitalism. Consequently, they support an expansive role for government as a means for promoting social equity.

Social Forces Generating the Gender Gap

Several sets of social forces are generally credited with producing the gender gap in ideology and partisanship. First, some have suggested that the women's movement generated a feminist consciousness about women's special needs and interests (Klein 1984; Sinclair 1983). Second, the unfortunate recent trend toward the feminization of poverty may have created a self-interest in increased social protection (Erie and Rein 1988). Finally, there is the possibility that women's traditional roles engendered both compassion, in the sense of helping the less fortunate, and pacifism, in the sense of fearing both internal and external violence (Shapiro and Mahajan 1986; Stoper 1989). In this section we consider the gender gap for three sets of issues that can be used to test the strength of these dynamics—women's issues (feminism), help for other marginal groups (self-interest and compassion), and threats of violence (pacifism).

The data on women's issues presented in Table 9.3 contain a mixture of results in terms of both overall attitudes toward women and the degree of gender differences on these issues. In some regards, Americans have moved a long way toward accepting women as social equals. Approximately two-thirds to three-quarters of the citizenry expressed (1) the opinion that women should enjoy equal rights in running business and government (as opposed to "staying at home"), (2) a high interest in women's issues, (3) pride in women's accomplishments, and (4) anger at the way women are treated at times; almost 60 percent said that (5) women should form groups to press their political priorities. There are, however, significant qualms about the changing role of women as well. Only 1 in 3 felt that sexual harassment is a serious problem, and less than half (44 percent) had a positive view of the women's movement. In addition, the public was deeply divided on abortion, with just 46 percent taking a pro-choice stance. These mixed findings probably reflect women's status in contemporary society fairly well: Although there has been substantial progress, women remain far short of achieving true equality.

Even more striking than the inconsistency in overall opinion is the fact that the size of the gender gap also varied across women's issues—i.e., on four there was a considerable differential of 11–13 points, but on the other four women and men expressed almost the same views. This is surprising, since the "feminist hypothesis" would predict a substantial gender gap on each of the attitudes examined here. Still, the pattern is consistent with a more subtle version of the feminist perspective. Three of the four issues for which a gender gap exists—views on the

TABLE 9.3   Gender Gap on Women's Issues, 1992

	Male	Female	Gender Gap
Positive view of women's movement	38%	49%	11%
Sexual harassment a serious problem	25%	38%	13%
Pro-choice on abortion	46%	46%	0%
High interest in women's issues	77%	80%	3%
Pride in women's achievements	61%	72%	11%
Anger at women's treatment	61%	63%	2%
Women have equal rights to lead business and government vs. staying at home	75%	75%	0%
Women should form groups vs. acting on their own	53%	64%	11%
N = 2,487			

NOTE: See Appendix for question wordings.
SOURCE: American National Election Study, 1992.

women's movement, sexual harassment, and the formation of women's groups—concern women's actual progress in the economic and political worlds and, thus, should be especially controversial and likely to bring out a feminist versus antifeminist division of opinion. In contrast, a significant gender gap exists on only one of the three less obviously charged opinions about women's status: pride in women's achievements (a gap) as opposed to anger at the treatment of women and interest in women's issues (no gap). Perhaps surprisingly, the question about giving women an equal role in running business and government produced a similar "halo effect" (it was supported by 75 percent of both women and men); on such issues, a cynic might say, male support for women is fairly "cheap."

Finally, abortion, on which 46 percent of both men and women adopted a pro-choice position, is clearly a very different sort of issue. It does, however, involve such a complex concatenation of religious, moral, and personal considerations that many women obviously do not see it as a women's issue at all—for example, only a bare majority even of feminist women are pro-choice (see the next section). Although the lack of a gender gap on a matter of central importance to the women's movement may seem unusual, it is consistent with earlier findings from the 1970s and 1980s. This results from the fact that women's distinctive values slightly crosscut normal liberal-conservative lines. In other words, most "women's values" lead women to take a liberal position, but their concern with moral issues and traditional values also creates groups of conservative women on issues such as abortion (Bendyna and Lake 1994; Shapiro and Mahajan 1986; Sears and Huddie 1990).

A stereotype of the "Reagan revolution" is that America, especially middle-class America, forgot the poor and dispossessed as the 1980s became the "decade of greed" (Phillips 1990). Yet the data on aiding marginal social groups in Table

TABLE 9.4   Gender Gap on Aiding Marginal Social Groups, 1992

	Male	Female	Gender Gap
Increase Social Security spending	41%	55%	14%
Increase spending for poor	48%	61%	13%
Increase spending for homeless	68%	77%	9%
Increase child care spending	44%	56%	12%
Increase AIDS spending	61%	63%	2%
Increase public school spending	62%	69%	7%
Increase college aid	59%	61%	2%
Increase spending on unemployed	35%	44%	9%
Increase spending for blacks	23%	27%	4%
Increase welfare spending	13%	21%	8%
Increase food stamp spending	15%	21%	6%
Positive view of poor	53%	64%	11%
Support government on school integration	40%	50%	10%
Positive view of gays	13%	18%	5%

NOTE: See Appendix for question wordings
SOURCE: American National Election Study, 1992.

9.4 shows that this image is hardly true in the 1990s. Almost 60 percent of Americans had a positive view of the poor (i.e., gave them a score of at least 60 on a scale of 0 to 100), approximately twice the number that were similarly disposed to big business (about 30 percent)—hardly a set of perceptions that one would associate with a Reaganaut society. Strong majorities, in addition, supported increased (as opposed to constant or decreased) spending for the homeless, the poor, public schools, college aid, and AIDS; and strong pluralities favored raising government expenditures for child care, Social Security, and the unemployed, as well as supporting an activist government role in school integration. Clearly, Americans as a people are willing to extend compassion to many of the less fortunate members of their society. Just as clearly, however, significant limits exist on this compassion for certain groups. In particular, less than one-fifth of the population favored increased funding for welfare or food stamps or had a positive view of gays; and only a quarter supported increased spending for blacks.

Both compassion and self-interest might be expected to stimulate women's support for other disadvantaged and marginal groups in the United States. Table 9.4 indicates that this is so, since a significant gender gap existed on a wide variety (but not quite all) of the attitudes toward such groups with women invariably taking the more compassionate or liberal viewpoint. A marked gender gap of 8–13 points exists in descending order on attitudes about the need to increase public spending for Social Security, the poor, child care, the homeless, the unemployed, and welfare; similarly, women were more likely to express a positive view of the poor and to support government's role in promoting school integration by about 10 percentage points. There was also a moderate gender gap of 4–7 points on increasing spending for public schools, food stamps, and blacks and on taking a positive view of gays. In contrast, there was no gender gap concerning spending for AIDS or college aid. Furthermore, given the marked aversion of Americans to helping current welfare recipients, the moderate gender gap that exists in this area represents a more sizable proportionate difference.

Women, then, certainly emerge as more compassionate than men, as we hypothesized. Several of the largest gaps are in areas of special concern for women, such as Social Security (because many women outlive their spouses) and child care, implying a component of self-interest as well. However, equally large gaps exist for spending more on the poor and the homeless and for promoting school integration, where women do not have a special self-interest. It is also interesting to note that women's traditional emphasis on education seems to have moderated.

Citizen attitudes toward war and violence were tapped by a variety of issues relating to war in foreign affairs, and crime and the environment on the home front, that are reported in Table 9.5. On these issues, opinion strays all over the spectrum. President Bush received extremely strong support for the Gulf War and for his overall foreign policy. Nevertheless, using military force in general and raising defense spending gained little favor, and just over 50 percent of Americans felt that the draft avoiders during the Vietnam War were right. In domestic affairs, there was exceptionally strong support for the death penalty and for increased spending on crime—yet the populace favored using improved social services, rather than police power, to combat urban unrest. In short, the public is (1) far from militaristic in the post–Cold War era but strongly supported the Gulf War; and (2) clearly disturbed by the high crime rate yet willing to implement both liberal and conservative policies to provide a safer society.

The hypothesized gender gap on these issues can be discerned quite easily, although a couple of caveats need to be added to the idea of women's greater pacifism. In terms of war and foreign affairs, there was a substantial gender gap of about 10 points on the three items referring to specific events (Gulf War, Bush's foreign policy, and avoidance of the draft during Vietnam) but almost no difference between men and women on more abstract issues (defense spending and the principle of military force). It would appear, then, that men's militarism needs explicit personalized issues to activate it (Clark and Clark 1989). Women's compassion and pacifism also can be seen on the crime issue—they were significantly less supportive than men of the death penalty (74 percent to 86 percent) and of using police power as the principal response to urban unrest (21 percent to 29 percent) but quite sensitive to crime and actually more supportive of increased spending to combat criminal activities (73 percent to 67 percent).

We have thus far examined the gender gap on three sets of issues that relate to widely assumed causes for male-female differences: feminism, self-interest from the growing feminization of poverty, and compassion combined with pacifism. All of these theories found a considerable amount of support; yet simply compar-

TABLE 9.5   Gender Gap on War and Violence, 1992

	Male	Female	Gender Gap
Approve Bush Gulf War policy	71%	59%	-12%
Approve Bush foreign policy	67%	58%	-9%
Endorse military force in foreign affairs	25%	21%	-4%
Favor death penalty	86%	74%	-12%
Increase spending on crime	67%	73%	6%
Increase defense spending	20%	19%	-1%
Draft avoiders right	47%	56%	9%
Police vs. social services to control urban unrest	29%	21%	-8%
Increase environmental spending	59%	63%	4%
N = 2,487			

NOTE: See Appendix for question wordings.
SOURCE: American National Election Study, 1992.

ing the attitudes of all women with all men can provide only a fairly crude picture of the presumed dynamics. The next section therefore provides more sophisticated analyses that should allow a better evaluation of the impact of feminism, self-interest, and compassion on the gender gap by examining whether the attitudes of several groups of women who are normally assumed to make special contributions to the gender gap really do differ from those of women in general.

Differences Among Women: Feminism, Self-Interest, and Compassion

The contention that feminism and/or self-interest explain at least part of the widening gender gap is based on the assumption that social change led to a shift in the attitudes of certain types of women. During the 1960s and 1970s, according to this logic, the growth of the women's movement and the feminization of poverty created a significantly larger proportion of women who, respectively, considered themselves feminists and were poor. Because feminists and poor people (either female or male) tend to be more liberal on many issues than women in general, the two social processes supposedly helped to generate a gender gap by creating larger numbers of women with left-leaning preferences—thereby causing a greater separation between the aggregate attitudes of men and women. The compassion hypothesis rests on a somewhat different dynamic. Women who would normally be expected to be conservatives, such as affluent ones, are said to adopt more liberal attitudes on issues concerning aid to the less fortunate because of their social compassion. The adverse economic trends during the 1970s and 1980s (Phillips 1990; Reich 1991; Thurow 1992), it is assumed, made social suffering more salient and thus increased the opportunities to extend compassion.

TABLE 9.6   Impact of Feminism, Disadvantaged Single Parenthood, and Affluence on Women's Attitudes, 1992

	All Women	Feminist	Disadvantaged Single Parent	Affluent Family
Total N	1,328	319	103	248
Percent of all women	100%	24%	8%	19%
Conservative identification	37%	23%	27%	41%
More government responsibility	70%	77%	89%	56%
Increase government services	42%	49%	60%	32%
Women equal role in government and business	75%	85%	79%	85%
Pride in women	72%	85%	75%	74%
Like women's movement	49%	77%	67%	44%
Women should form groups	64%	77%	71%	56%
Sexual harassment serious problem	38%	50%	54%	29%
Pro-choice on abortion	46%	55%	31%	64%
More spending on welfare	21%	31%	52%	11%
More spending on poor	61%	69%	81%	47%
More spending on child care	56%	67%	77%	56%
Approve Bush on Gulf War	59%	48%	60%	68%
Approve death penalty	74%	65%	74%	82%

NOTE: See Appendix for question wordings.
SOURCE: American National Election Study, 1992.

We can test these arguments by comparing the views of three distinct groups of women with the views of all women on several of the attitudes previously discussed. Table 9.6 presents our results. Column 1 displays the percentage of all women holding a particular attitude (and is the same as reported in the gender-gap findings in Tables 9.2 through 9.5); columns 2–4 present similar percentages for feminists, women who are disadvantaged single parents, and women from affluent families. Comparing the latter with column 1 indicates whether any of the narrower groups make a special contribution to the gender gap. Specifically, though differences should vary by issue area, we expect to find that (1) women who consider themselves feminists hold much more liberal or nontraditional views than those without a feminist identity, especially on women's issues; (2) disadvantaged women—defined here as single parents who have a low family income (under $15,000) or are on welfare (receiving AFDC [Aid to Families with Dependent Children], food stamps, Medicaid, or unemployment insurance)— favor redistributive programs out of self-interest; and (3) affluent women (with family incomes of over $50,000) deviate from their normal conservatism on issues of compassion, but not on others.

Several scholars have argued that the gender gap is primarily a function of the differences in attitude between men and the quarter of women who consider themselves feminists (Conover 1988; Rinehart 1992). That is, the beliefs of non-feminist women are fairly similar to those of men, such that the observed gender gap reflects the impact feminists have in pulling the average for all women in a liberal direction. Results in the second column of Table 9.6 are consistent with this line of argument. Feminists were considerably more liberal than other women on all fourteen of the items included here. Furthermore, the expected special concern of feminists with women's issues is clearly evident; relative to all women, they were much more positive on five of these six issues by 12–28 percentage points (and by 9 points on the other)—women should have an equal role in running government and business, pride in women's achievements, positive view of the women's movement, women should form groups, sexual harassment is a serious problem, and pro-choice on abortion. Especially striking is the fact that feminists, as opposed to women as a whole, expressed positive feelings toward the women's movement by a margin of nearly 30 points (77 percent to 49 percent). They also were considerably less likely to be conservatives (23 percent to 37 percent), indicating the expected ideological impact of feminism. In contrast, their liberal bias was significantly less pronounced (7–11 points) for the other three sets of issues—role of government, spending on the needy, and war and violence—which are related, but less directly, to the central thrust of feminism.

Feminists' (and others') views on abortion, though, are worthy of closer scrutiny. The fact that there is no gender gap on the abortion issue—46 percent of both women and men were pro-choice (see Table 9.3)—suggests strong support among traditional women for the pro-life position. This would imply a large cleavage between feminists and nonfeminists. However, this does not occur, as the "feminist gap" here of 55 percent to 46 percent is the smallest for any of the six women's issues included in Table 9.6. In addition, the positions of the other two groups under consideration are striking as well. Single mothers in poor financial conditions were only two-thirds as likely as all women to be pro-choice, perhaps reflecting their "choice" to have children. Affluent women, in contrast, were considerably more pro-choice (64 percent) than even feminists, despite the former's reputed conservatism. Thus, in addition to the question of women's rights, attitudes on abortion apparently stem from a complex set of religious and moral values that confound expectations based on gender and feminism alone (Cook 1992; Shapiro and Mahajan 1986).

The self-interest theory concerning the feminization of poverty assumes that women (and men) in distressed economic situations will be much more supportive of social spending and expansive government than others who are financially secure. This hypothesis also receives strong support from our data. The relatively small category of disadvantaged single parents (one-twelfth of all women) was between 20 and 30 points more likely than women as a whole to favor increased spending on the poor, welfare, and child care, and to express a positive view about expanding federal government responsibility—compared, for example, to a 7–11 point gap between feminists and all women. The liberalism of this lower-status group on economic issues, relative to other women, stands out even further when it is compared to the much smaller differences that exist in several other areas usually associated with liberal-conservative cleavages, e.g., violence and war (where disadvantaged single parents almost exactly mirrored women in general). These findings underline the self-interest element of attitudes about government role and spending policies, with the overall degree of liberalism among disadvantaged single mothers being somewhat less than among feminists (who took left-of-center positions on a wider array of issues)—but still well above that of the average woman.

Relating economic stress to women's issues also produces some interesting results. There is no reason to expect that economic problems will necessarily affect how one views women's issues; and in fact, disadvantaged single parents were only marginally more liberal than the average woman on the "symbolic" issues of pride in women's achievements and believing that women should have an equal role in running government and business. In contrast, significant differences do exist on the other three more concrete attitudes, although they are substantially less than for feminists. First, economically distressed women were more likely than others to feel that sexual harassment was a serious problem, almost certainly denoting their greater vulnerability to such pressures. Second, they also were more apt (along with feminists) to believe that forming groups was important for women. This might be considered surprising because socioeconomic status tends to be negatively associated with participatory behavior (Rosenstone and Hansen 1993), though the relationship suggests that disadvantaged women recognize the importance of organizing to pursue their political and social goals. Finally, disadvantaged single parents were almost 20 points more likely than women as a whole to express appreciation of the women's movement. This indicates an awareness of gender-based disadvantages and the benefits of collective efforts to secure a better status for women in American society.

The compassion hypothesis suggests that wealthy women might be less conservative than expected on the basis of their socioeconomic status alone because of their feminine values. Although such a conclusion might seem justified by the fact that women from families with incomes over $50,000 (who constitute a fifth of all women) were only marginally more conservative than average (41 percent to 37 percent), a closer examination of the fourth column in Table 9.6 demonstrates that this probably results from self-interest rather than compassion. Specifically, wealthy women did not differ from the average on support for child care spending, since many presumably need this service, but they were noticeably conservative on spending more for the poor and especially for welfare. Likewise, affluent women were as liberal as feminists on the question of whether women should have an equal leadership role in business and government and slightly more willing than average to express pride in women's achievements (perhaps implying a link to the professional careers that many of them pursue). Yet they were significantly more conservative than all woman on attitudes relating to the women's movement and to women forming groups for promoting and protecting their interests. In short, despite their obvious career concerns, affluent women tended to be leery of the feminist movement. Finally, women from high-income families were fairly conservative on issues dealing with violence and the role of government. The observed drift of affluent women away from conservatism thus appears to be fueled far more by concerns of their professional lives than by compassion for the dispossessed.

It is clear, then, that not all women contribute equally or in similar ways to the gender gap. Previous scholarship has emphasized the role of feminism, and our findings certainly support this interpretation. However, two other groups also make distinctive contributions: Financially stressed women are quite liberal, especially in the realm of economic issues; and affluent women are surprisingly liberal on some issues, evidently reflecting experiences and frustrations encountered during their professional careers. These effects, by the way, are mostly independent of each other. Only 10 percent of female single disadvantaged parents were feminists, and only 18 percent of feminists came from high-income families. Thus, as Bendyna and Lake (1994) argued, there is not a single gender gap but rather a concatenation of several that have been generated by a variety of social processes.

CONCLUSION

A considerable gender gap exists on a wide range of issues in the United States of the 1990s. It can be traced to a variety of factors including (1) the rise of feminism, (2) self-interest generated by the feminization of poverty and by an increasing number of affluent women who are pursuing professional careers, and (3) the imputed compassion that cuts across most categories of women. Each of these elements makes a distinctive contribution to the gender gap because each reflects a separate "constituency" that is disappointed, to some extent, with current U.S. socioeconomic conditions and political policies. The gender gap can therefore be taken as a sign that—high incumbent reelection rates notwithstanding—the "social contract" between citizens and their rulers has indeed been broken. It indicates that women, in particular, are unhappy with what they perceive as their marginalized position in society and have become increasingly alienated from the polity as a result.

This interpretation can be applied to the image of 1992 as a watershed election symbolizing the Year of the Woman in American politics. Despite Bill Clinton's moderate margin of victory over George Bush, his victory was seen as a decisive rejection of business as usual in government's handling of the national economy; moreover, the major jump in women's representation in Congress appeared to be one important break with the past (Pomper 1993) that could be linked, in theory,

TABLE 9.7   Gender Gap in Voting for U.S. House, 1994

Year	Male	Female	Gender Gap
1978	55%	56%	1%
1980	56%	53%	-3%
1982	54%	57%	3%
1984	51%	56%	5%
1986	51%	55%	4%
1988	49%	54%	5%
1990	50%	54%	4%
1992	51%	54%	3%
1994	43%	54%	11%

NOTE: Percentages in the first two columns show the proportion of each group voting Democratic. A positive gender gap means that women were more supportive; a negative gap shows that men were more supportive.

SOURCE: Kenski (1988, p. 55); Ladd (1995, pp. 48–49, 54).

to the gender gap. Subsequent reflection yielded more sober conclusions, however. Women's representation in U.S. government remained quite low compared to most other advanced industrial nations, and women's electoral gains in 1992 were more the latest point in a gradual trend than a dramatic breakthrough—especially since the congressional results were given added impetus by a combination of difficult-to-replicate factors that produced an unusually high number of "open seats" (Cook, Thomas, and Wilcox 1994).

It seems likely from our review of women's attitudes and social situation that the gender gap will be a continuing, if not expanding, feature of electoral politics for years to come. The 1994 congressional results are in line with this projection, as gender-based partisan preferences in voting for the U.S. House of Representatives diverged sharply—from a gap of 3 percentage points in 1992 to one of 11 points in the subsequent midterm, the latter figure being more than twice the size of any differential observed since 1978 (see Table 9.7). What happened in 1994 was that women did not follow men's defection from the Democrats to the Republicans, very probably because of their greater sensitivity to the social forces and problems discussed earlier in this chapter. Moreover, since the gap was significantly wider among those under 30 (15 percentage points) than in any other age cohort (about 9–10 points; Bowman 1995), it is possible that ongoing generational replacement will contribute to a widening gap in the future.

Thus, if early declaration of the Year of the Woman was overstated, the gender gap in the early 1990s suggests that pressures for fundamental change in our polity—a reworking of the social contract if you will—may be an enduring fact of American political life for years to come. Whereas the gender gap arose because a substantial portion of society felt marginalized and unrepresented, women (who now cast the majority of ballots in most elections) should constitute an important force for change as the new century approaches. By the same token, though, the multiple origins of today's gender gap serve as a warning that remaking the social contract will be a complex process. What apparently is needed is for women to achieve some measure of true equality (in line with feminist values and the somewhat narrower goals of professional women) and for untoward social conditions (the feminization of poverty) to be ameliorated. For the latter to happen, of course, feelings of compassion among the rich and powerful must increase from the levels indicated by our analysis of affluent women.

NOTES

An earlier version of this chapter was presented at the 1993 Annual Meetings of the Southern Political Science Association, Atlantia, Georgia.

1. These and other data in this chapter are drawn from the American National Election Study surveys conducted by the Center for Political Studies at the University of Michigan and made available by the Inter-University Consortium for Political and Social Research. Neither the consortium nor the original collectors of the data bear any responsibility for the analyses or interpretations presented here.

2. Exact wording for these and other questions from the ANES surveys can be found in the Appendix.

The Religious Vote in American Politics: Value Conflict, Continuity, and Change

ALLEN D. HERTZKE
JOHN DAVID RAUSCH JR.

Throughout American history religious currents have flowed powerfully through elections, defining partisan attachments and shaping voting behavior.[1] Still, until the rise of the Christian right in the late 1970s, many modern scholars discounted religion as a key influence in contemporary voting behavior. They did so, in part, because they were guided by the theory of *secularization,* developed by some of the West's great scholars, which posited the inevitable decline of religion as societies modernize. To Karl Marx, Émile Durkheim, Max Weber, and their followers, secularization constituted "an iron law" predicting the "elimination of religious influence in contemporary culture" (Wald 1992, p. 4; also see Kellstedt 1993).

Yet not only has religion proven to be "stubbornly persistent" in the modern world (Shupe 1990, p. 18), its political influence seems to be greater, in some respects, in the mid-1990s than it was just a couple of decades prior. This stubborn persistence probably can be explained by the universal human need for transcendent explanations of life and its hardships (see Freud 1961). But the political assertiveness of religion may arise from a dynamic identified by Ronald Ingelhart, who suggested that in a postmaterialist age, value conflict could replace class or economic interest as the defining characteristic of modern politics (Inglehart 1977). Thus religion, as the root of many value differences, becomes more salient in politics as immediate material concerns recede.

In this chapter, we chart the voting patterns of the key religious groups in the electorate—Catholics, evangelical Protestants, "mainline" (or "oldline") Protestants,[2] black Christians, Jews, and secularists—in order to present evidence for the existence of value-based cleavages in the American electorate. The differences observed are real and politically important, though we caution against exaggerating their magnitude or political significance. Value conflict does not necessarily imply a deep-seated "culture war." Moreover, our analysis suggests some enduring continuities in addition to changing alignments; that is, value conflict has not entirely replaced other cleavages.

CONTINUITY AND CHANGE IN THE POSTINDUSTRIAL ERA

From the 1960s on, American politics has seemed especially fluid. Our focus here is on the impact of cultural forces, which have fractured old party ties and produced new voting alignments while also contributing to *de*alignment in the electorate, e.g., with voting rates declining, partisan loyalties weakening, and citizen discontent being far greater than was the case in the 1960s (see Chapters 3 and 5). To understand these developments, we must take into account the evolving response of religious constituencies, since in the United States religious attachments often provide the cultural bedrock for electoral behavior.

Catholics at the Strategic Center

For at least a century and a half, the dominant religious factor in U.S. elections was the Catholic-Protestant cultural divide. From the mid-1800s onward Catholics, as a cultural minority, were loyal Democrats, just as northern Protestants gravitated heavily to the Republican side. These sharp partisan differences continued into the New Deal era of the 1930s, when Catholics at every socioeconomic level were far more likely to identify themselves as Democrats and to vote that way than were Protestants similarly situated (Ladd with Hadley 1975). A core Democratic constituency, white Catholics generally provided more than a third of the total Democratic presidential vote from the New Deal through the early 1960s (Axelrod 1986; Hanna 1979).

The 1960 election illustrated how strongly the Catholic-Protestant divide could affect voting. John Kennedy (only the second Catholic ever to be chosen by a major party as its presidential nominee) increased the normally high Catholic Democratic vote to an amazing 80 percent—but his candidacy also provoked Protestant rumblings that were reminiscent of nineteenth-century broadsides against "Romanism" and "papists" (Menendez 1977). All told, Kennedy probably lost about 1.5 million votes because of his religion, as his gains among Catholics were more than offset by losses among a larger group of traditional Democratic Protestants (Converse 1966). Kennedy's presidency and martyrdom, however, coupled with changes in the Catholic Church with Vatican II,[3] largely put to rest the deep schism that had long existed between Catholics and Protestants. Although some partisan cleavage lingers, far more important today is what *kind* of Catholic (or Protestant) the voter is, as we shall see.

Kennedy's election also represented the high-water mark for the Catholic Democratic vote, and for Catholic interest in politics. The decay of loyalty to the Democratic Party, and to politics generally, can be traced to many of the same factors that reduced Catholic-Protestant tension. Many Catholics moved out of ethnic enclaves to the suburbs (where they often sent their children to public schools for the first time), began saying mass in English instead of Latin (or stopped going to mass entirely), and generally were mainstreamed into American social life. Some, at least, became predictably Republican on class lines. But equally important was the emergence of crosscutting issues such as busing to achieve school integration, crime, abortion, and school prayer—issues that chipped away at Catholic support for the Democratic Party or led to disillusionment with the political process as a whole. As the Democrats became associated in some voters' minds with weakness on crime and defense, or as favoring social engineering, relativistic morality, and indifference to religion, Republican campaign consultants began to make hay. Indeed, that was the thesis of Kevin Phillips's widely cited book, *The Emerging Republican Majority* (1969), in which it was argued that Catholics were ripe for the picking (also see Edsall with Edsall 1991). The landslide victory of Richard Nixon in 1972 seemed to corroborate Phillips's thesis, with some 60 percent of Catholics voting Republican in the presidential contest.

Subsequent elections suggested a more complex picture. Catholic Democratic support weakened, to be sure, but Catholics did not exactly rush headlong into the Republican camp. On a number of issues, Catholics were and are more liberal than either oldline Protestants or evangelicals. Thus, although clearly unhappy with the direction of the Democratic Party, many Catholics do not feel entirely comfortable with the GOP. Such ambivalence helps to explain why their turnout rates are down from 1960, and why they have become the quintessential swing voters of the 1990s.

An evaluation of Catholic voting patterns from 1976 to 1992 confirms that the Catholic vote is now up for grabs. As seen in Table 10.1, Jimmy Carter received a majority of the Catholic vote (54 percent) in 1976, though his margin was far below that commanded earlier by Kennedy or Franklin Roosevelt. More significantly, in the next two elections Ronald Reagan gained increasing shares of the Catholic vote against his Democratic opponents; his 54 percent majority in 1984 even led some commentators to believe that a permanent realignment might be under way. Four years later, however, George Bush succeeded only in splitting the Catholic vote with Michael Dukakis (it was so close that a different exit poll from the one used here gave the Catholic edge to Dukakis).[4] Bush's fortunes with Catholic voters then took a dive from 1988 to 1992, when Democrat Bill Clinton reversed the pattern of the previous three elections and decisively bested his Republican opponent. Bush, the blue-blood Episcopalian Yankee, as one scholar put it, "never did speak Catholic" (Leege 1993), but the picture was muddied by the Independent candidacy of H. Ross Perot, who attracted 20 percent of the Catholic vote and thus kept Clinton from achieving a majority. Clearly, Catholics remain a voting constituency that cannot be taken for granted by either party at the presidential level.

At the congressional level, erosion of Democratic voting loyalty has been less pronounced, though some slippage is evident from New Deal highs. Whereas

TABLE 10.1 Comparison of White Protestant, White Born-Again Christian, and Catholic Presidential Votes, 1976–1992

Percent of 1992 Total	1976		1980			1984		1988		1992		
	Ford	Carter	Reagan	Carter	Anderson	Reagan	Mondale	Bush	Dukakis	Bush	Clinton	Perot
White Protestants — 49	58%	41%	63%	31%	6%	72%	27%	66%	33%	46%	33%	21%
White born-again Christians — 17	50%[a]	50%[a]	63%	33%	3%	78%	22%	81%	18%	61%	23%	15%
Catholics — 27	44%	54%	50%	42%	7%	54%	45%	52%	47%	36%	44%	20%
Total vote — 100	48%	50%	51%	41%	7%	59%	40%	53%	45%	38%	43%	19%

[a]See Lopatto (1985).

SOURCE: Exit polls conducted by CBS News (1976), CBS News and *New York Times* (1980, 1984, and 1988), and Voter Research and Survey (1992); assembled by the *New York Times*, November 5, 1992, p. B9. Copyright © 1992 by The New York Times Company. Reprinted by permission.

upward of 70 percent of Catholics commonly cast ballots for Democratic candidates during the Roosevelt era and beyond (Ladd with Hadley 1978), by the 1980s and early 1990s that figure was closer to 60 percent.[5] Still, this means that Catholics remain a critical Democratic constituency for members of the House and Senate, and in state and local politics as well. Moreover, even when Republicans do well among Catholics, the partisan gap with Protestants remains. At just about every level and region, Catholics are less inclined to vote Republican than are white Protestants of whatever theological stripe. Volatility also exists, so that Catholics remain a swing congressional constituency just as they are at the presidential level. For many Republicans, then, achieving an even split of the Catholic vote is sufficient to win their seats.

When we peer beneath aggregate figures, the value-based dimensions become clearer. In 1960, the Catholic electorate was largely white, but by the 1990s nonwhites constituted upward of a fifth of Catholic voters (especially Hispanics, but also black Americans, of whom nearly a tenth now are Roman Catholics). Nonwhite Catholics are far more Democratic in their voting loyalties (with the exception of Asians) than are their white counterparts. Thus, their growing numbers have masked an even greater slide in white Catholic support for Democratic candidates. In 1984, for example, Walter Mondale received 45 percent of the total Catholic vote—but only 40 percent from white Catholics. Clinton did comparatively better among white Catholics than Mondale but still received relatively fewer votes from them than from Catholics as a group. Similar gaps can be found in the congressional votes of Catholics.

An intriguing dimension here is that white Catholics, who constitute nearly a quarter of the electorate, have become the median voter group in American politics. Classic ticket-splitters, their tendency in recent years has been to support Republicans at the presidential level—but, like voters in general, to give the edge to Democrats in congressional contests. Indeed, since the 1970s, white Catholics have hovered very close to the national average in vote totals: e.g., Mondale received 40 percent of the overall vote and an identical 40 percent of white Catholics in 1984; Clinton won 43 percent overall and 42 percent of white Catholics in 1992. And so it goes.

It should be noted, by the way, that race and ethnicity are not the only cleavages that exist *within* the Catholic electorate. Table 10.2 reveals a generational split as well, with older Catholics being far more likely than younger ones to identify with the Democratic Party. In fact, white Catholics under 30 years of age are now at least as Republican (and perhaps a bit more so) as they are Democratic in their affiliations—a remarkable departure from the New Deal pattern. A majority of Catholics over 60, in contrast, still identify themselves as Democrats, with the middle groups falling somewhere in between (Ladd 1993). Should this pattern continue, we would expect white Catholics as a whole to tilt more toward the GOP as the older, New Deal cohorts die off. Nevertheless, much can change to disrupt such an occurrence, so we must be cautious in making predictions.

Table 10.2 also illustrates the importance of church attendance. One of the most important developments since Vatican II has been the marked decrease in attendance at mass by American Catholics. Lapsed Catholics, who attend mass

TABLE 10.2 Presidential Vote, Congressional Vote, and Party Identification by Age and Attendance at Religious Services, 1992 (white Catholics only)

	1992 Presidential Vote			1992 Democratic House Vote	Party Identification	
	Clinton	Bush	Perot		Democrat	Republican
All respondents	43%	33%	23%	57%	42%	30%
Frequent church attendance	40%	38%	22%	55%	42%	30%
Ages 18–29						
All respondents	42%	34%	24%	56%	35%	36%
Frequent church attendance	35%	43%	22%	53%	34%	37%
Ages 30–44						
All respondents	42%	32%	25%	55%	38%	29%
Frequent church attendance	39%	37%	24%	54%	39%	29%
Ages 45–59						
All respondents	40%	35%	25%	56%	44%	30%
Frequent church attendance	37%	40%	23%	51%	42%	31%
Ages 60 and over						
All respondents	52%	31%	17%	62%	55%	25%
Frequent church attendance	49%	34%	17%	61%	53%	26%

N = 1,847

SOURCE: Voter Research and Survey exit poll, general election, November 1992.

infrequently if at all, constitute a sizable group of those who identify themselves as Catholics. Attendance at services, we think, is a fairly good indicator of whether individuals are being regularly exposed to religious teachings, religiously based values, and cues from ministers and fellow parishioners (Gilbert 1993; Wald, Owen, and Hill 1988). As a result, sorting this out may tell us something about the political consequences of religiously based values on political behavior.

Among whites, Catholics who attend mass regularly tend to be less Democratic in their partisan leanings and voting choices than are those who attend infrequently or not at all. The pattern is most marked among younger Catholics, with older frequent attenders remaining solidly Democratic—though the figures do reveal something of a paradox: Older Catholics, although mostly Democrats, also happen to be the most strongly pro-life, which explains why they might be turned off by the choices presented to them in the contemporary era.

Table 10.3 elaborates on the issue positions of Catholics (compared with other religious traditions), thereby giving us a sense of how distinctive the Catholic electorate is. Both lapsed and faithful attenders appear to be fairly liberal on a number of issues. Regularly attending Catholics, for example, were found to be more likely to support government health insurance, environmental protection, women's rights, and gay rights than either oldline Protestants or evangelical Protestants; in addition, Catholics joined oldline Protestants in being more liberal than evangelicals in advocating defense-spending cuts. Only on abortion were regularly attending Catholics less liberal than their counterparts in the oldline Protestant churches. In a way, this sentiment reflects pretty well the positions of the American bishops, who have blended conservative stands on abortion and educational vouchers with liberal positions on welfare and defense. Something of the "seamless garment,"[6] therefore, exists at the parish level.

One reason for the swing character of the Catholic vote, consequently, is that Catholics themselves (both young and old) are more subject to cross-pressures and therefore more likely than other groups to be affected by particular candidates, issues, or short-term forces. To the extent that this is true, Catholics will continue to present a challenge for both political parties. Republican laissez-faire policies on the economy and health care, for example, may displease them just as much as supposed Democratic moral relativism on certain cultural issues. Or, as E. J. Dionne (1991) might put it, many Catholic voters may be especially turned off by the way ideological choices are framed for them by the parties and their candidates. Some might even be inclined to disengage from politics altogether.

Evangelical Protestants: A Pietist Revival for the GOP

Most Protestants in the nineteenth century were "pietist" evangelicals, heirs of the Puritan spirit. Orthodox in belief and frankly moralistic in their understanding of religion and society, they felt led to attack the evils of the day. Whether the perceived evil was slavery, alcoholism, or gambling, pietists were comfortable bringing their desire to reform society into the public realm—just as modern-day

TABLE 10.3   Issue Positions by Religious Tradition and Church Attendance, 1992

	Abortion Pro-Choice	Favor Women's Rights	Favor Gay Rights	Support Government Health Insurance	Protect[a] Environment	Cut Defense Spending
White Evangelical Protestant[b]						
All respondents	29%	64%	44%	41%	53%	31%
Frequent church attendance[c]	15%	52%	32%	34%	43%	29%
White oldline Protestant						
All respondents	56%	75%	59%	42%	56%	50%
Frequent church attendance	49%	73%	53%	38%	48%	44%
White Roman Catholic						
All respondents	43%	83%	67%	55%	61%	51%
Frequent church attendance	28%	81%	69%	52%	57%	44%
White secular[d]						
All respondents	71%	85%	69%	61%	70%	53%
Black Protestant						
All respondents	46%	74%	72%	61%	66%	52%
Frequent church attendance	36%	62%	78%	63%	60%	67%
Jewish[e]						
All respondents	93%	86%	82%	56%	62%	67%

NOTE: This table uses data from the 1992 American National Election Study. See Appendix for question wordings.

[a]The pro-environment position includes respondents who favor increased federal spending for "improving and protecting the environment."

[b]Evangelical Protestants (see note 2) are differentiated from oldline Protestants using criteria suggested by Kellstedt (1993, p. 300) and Kellstedt and Green (1993).

[c]Frequent attenders are persons who attend church at least once a week.

[d]Seculars are those respondents who reported never attending religious services and did not claim any religious affiliation.

[e]Because of limitations due to small sample size, Jewish frequent attenders could not be separated from other Jewish respondents.

SOURCE: Adapted from Kellstedt, Smidt, and Guth (1993); additional analysis provided by Lyman A. Kellstedt.

pietists do not hesitate to advocate government intervention on abortion, pornography, or television violence.[7]

Generally Republican in the North, some evangelicals were attracted to the Democratic Party by fellow pietist and populist William Jennings Bryan at the turn of the century, and later by Franklin Roosevelt. Though we tend to associate evangelicalism with conservatism today, in the past its reformist energies could blend cultural traditionalism and economically progressive stands (Hertzke 1993). In the South, of course, religious factors were submerged by the politics of race and regional pride. The Republican Party was identified with the northern army of occupation and Reconstruction. To be a loyal southerner one had to be a Democrat, and most loyal southerners were Protestant evangelicals.

Early in this century pietists lost ground in the Protestant world, especially in the North as the mainstream denominations moved away from religious orthodoxy or pietistic enthusiasm in order to embrace a more "modern" faith. Evangelicals laid low for a few decades, but conditions led to their reemergence in the 1970s—most visibly with the growing political notoriety of such activists as Jerry Falwell and Pat Robertson, and with long-term voting shifts at the mass level that are now clearly discernible.

Two momentous developments in the evangelical world have left their mark on contemporary voting behavior and party alignments. The first is the growth of evangelical churches since the 1960s and the corresponding decline of oldline denominations. In 1960, over 40 percent of all white adults claimed membership in the historically mainline denominations—twice that in evangelical and fundamentalist churches. By the 1990s, however, mainline affiliation was down to around 22 percent, barely equal to an evangelical membership that approached one-quarter of the nation's population. Moreover, since regular church attendance is much lower in mainline churches than in evangelical ones, the 20 percent figure exaggerates the actual number of people embedded in church life. Thus, the mainline (or, as we prefer, oldline) denominations are increasingly "sideline" in American society, replaced by evangelical churches as the strategic center of Protestantism (Green 1993; Leege 1993; Kellstedt et al. 1994).

The second key development is the strengthening political alignment of evangelical Protestants with the Republican Party—an alignment made all the more significant by the first trend. These two changes have dramatically altered the dynamics of internal GOP politics. Whereas the old Republican Party was an alliance of business interests and oldline Protestants, the new GOP relies more heavily on its evangelical constituency (Guth, Green, and Kellstedt 1993). This reliance has helped shaped politics in the Democratic Party as well by solidifying Jewish and secular support for Democrats. Clearly, one must understand evangelical voting to appreciate modern American politics.

For much of this century many Baptists, pentecostals, and other evangelicals were Democrats and voted accordingly in spite of general Protestant loyalty to the Republicans. It may seem strange today to think of theological conservatives as

Democrats, but there are several explanations. First, many evangelicals, especially conservative Baptists and Methodists, lived in the South, where loyalty to the Democratic Party reflected the Civil War legacy. Second, a class dimension reinforced Democratic tendencies. During the New Deal, for example, lower-status Protestants (heavily evangelical) were more likely to vote for Roosevelt than were their upper-class counterparts, who belonged to the theologically liberal oldline denominations. Thus, pentecostals, independent Baptists, and other evangelicals were more likely than Presbyterians, Episcopalians, United Methodists, and Congregationalists to be Democrats. We must also remember that however radical Roosevelt was viewed by the monied class, his agenda was far less threatening to orthodox religionists than is the case with the liberal social agenda today. Roosevelt, in fact, appropriated religious imagery in his speeches much in the populist tradition of Bryan, which appealed to many pentecostals, evangelicals, and fundamentalists.

Things began to change in the 1960s. White southerners, most of them Protestants, began voting Republican at the presidential level as the Democratic Party embraced the aims of black civil rights and voting rights. But race was not the entire story. The same cultural issues that weakened Catholic ties to the Democrats would even more strongly erode evangelical loyalty. At the same time, of course, evangelicals and fundamentalists were becoming more suburban and affluent themselves, thus reinforcing their Republican ties. Still, we find evidence for a values-based realignment as theologically conservative Protestants became even more heavily Republican over the period than higher-status oldline Protestants.

We should note that Jimmy Carter, a born-again Baptist from the South, temporarily stalled the evangelical movement into the Republican Party with his 1976 presidential victory. Analysts concluded that Carter probably did better among evangelicals than he did among oldline Protestants.[8] Yet many evangelicals felt betrayed by Carter's liberal White House, and simmering cultural forces helped to foster the emergence of a militant new Christian right just on the eve of the 1980 presidential election. Ronald Reagan skillfully courted the evangelical constituency and this, combined with a bad economy and Carter's foreign policy problems, led many evangelicals to abandon their born-again brother.

The real story, then, is the solidifying Republican alignment of evangelicals (as Table 10.1 dramatically illustrates). Whereas the born-again vote was indistinguishable from the broader white Protestant group in 1980, it became increasingly more Republican over the next two elections. In 1988, for example, George Bush garnered over 80 percent of the evangelical vote—a margin approaching the high level of black loyalty to Democratic candidates. The 1992 contest was muddied by the independent candidacy of Ross Perot, but even so, we see that most evangelicals remained loyal to the Republican nominee. Although Bush received only 46 percent of the total white Protestant vote, he won 61 percent among white born-again Christians. This fact, coupled with the president's weak showing among other groups, meant that evangelicals constituted Bush's largest single constituency, upward of two-fifths of his total (Green 1993).

A fundamental shift in the partisanship of evangelicals is indicated by the generational breakdowns of voting and party affiliation depicted in Table 10.4. Just as we would expect from realignment theory (see Sundquist 1983), it is younger white evangelicals who have become the most solidly Republican in their identification. Fifty-nine percent of those aged 18–29 identify with the GOP, as opposed to just 42 percent of those aged 60 and over. Another indication of true realignment is voting below the presidential level, and we see this as well: House Democrats received a mere 35 percent of the evangelical vote in 1992, with younger evangelicals at 32 percent and the over-60 group at 43 percent. Of course, the Democratic ticket of Clinton and Gore, two southern Baptists, did slightly better among evangelicals—and especially young evangelicals—than was the case for the Democratic ticket in 1988. But this does not diminish the evidence for continued GOP loyalty among the evangelical electorate. As the older generation is gradually replaced, we would expect increasing Republican identification and voting loyalty.

It is important to note that "evangelical" is not synonymous with "Christian right." Indeed, not all evangelicals currently support the rhetoric or agenda of Pat Robertson—just as many declined to align themselves with Jerry Falwell a decade earlier. A fair number of southern Baptists, for example, look askance at pentecostal practices and have been less than thrilled as Robertson's charismatic followers flooded Republican Party meetings at all levels in the late 1980s and early 1990s (Hertzke 1993). Realignment has thus resulted from a series of waves in which different, sometimes competing, evangelical groups moved (at their own pace and for their own reasons) into the Republican fold.

The significance of the evangelical constituency to the Republican Party is by now well recognized in professional campaign circles. Not only do groups like the Christian Coalition distribute millions of voter guides through church networks but Republican get-out-the-vote drives have had increasing success in targeting the evangelical constituency. In an analysis of the role of the Christian right in the 1992 election, John Green (1993) found that 54 percent of Bush's evangelical supporters had been contacted and urged to vote. In an atomized mass society with supposedly weak local party structures (see Chapter 13), this is a remarkable figure and suggests that combined mobilization by party organizations and religious groups is solidifying and mobilizing the evangelical realignment.

Now that many evangelicals are solidly middle class and suburban, they share the economic concerns of other Republicans. This was acknowledged by Christian Coalition leader Ralph Reed, whose own surveys showed the importance of such issues as taxes and the budget deficit to evangelical voters (Reed 1993). We saw earlier in Table 10.3, for example, that evangelicals are among the most conservative segments of the electorate on a host of issues, from abortion and gay

TABLE 10.4   Presidential Vote, Congressional Vote, and Party Identification by Age (white evangelical Protestants only), 1992

| | 1992 Presidential Vote | | | 1992 Democratic House Vote | Party Identification | |
	Clinton	Bush	Perot		Democrat	Republican
All respondents	23%	60%	18%	35%	23%	50%
Ages 18–29	25%	58%	17%	32%	19%	59%
Ages 30–44	20%	62%	18%	32%	19%	54%
Ages 45–59	22%	59%	19%	38%	24%	44%
Ages 60 and over	34%	53%	13%	43%	39%	42%
N = 1,120						

SOURCE: Voter Research and Survey exit poll, general election, November 1992.

rights to health care reform and national defense. Still, the cultural dimension remains prominent. Contrary to voters as a whole, evangelicals were more concerned with the social nexus of abortion and family values than with economic issues (according to the VRS exit poll) in 1992. Moreover, the salience of social issues rises among frequent church attenders and among the middle-aged groups who are most involved with raising children.

Aware of these complex currents, Christian right leaders and Republican operatives in the 1990s are attempting to merge social conservatism with traditional business opposition to taxes and "big government." Increasing the tax credit for children, removing the so-called marriage tax that penalizes some couples, and expanding parental choice in education and health care are seen as issues that can unite pro-family evangelicals and pro-business Republicans. Cultural and economic forces have thus begun to converge in the evangelical camp. During the New Deal, Democratic liberalism meant jobs and economic support for poor and working-class citizens—a large number of whom were evangelical Protestants. To many modern evangelicals, however, Democratic liberalism means abortion rights, gay rights, and secularization of the schools, as well as high taxes on families that have achieved middle-class status. Consequently, both values and economics pull in the same direction.

In summary, the movement (beginning in the 1960s and continuing through the 1990s) of evangelical Protestants into the Republican fold represents a return to nineteenth-century patterns—patterns that had been interrupted by civil war and by populist and class-based cleavages. Modern-day pietists have become heavily Republican again, many just since the 1980s and some as recently as the 1990s.

Oldline Protestants and the Emerging Secular Vote

In one sense there is great continuity in the voting behavior of oldline Protestants: Methodists, Presbyterians, Episcopalians, Congregationalists, and northern Baptists tilt toward the Republicans today, just as they have for more than a century. But three key changes emerge from our analysis. First, we noted earlier the precipitous decline in membership and attendance among the oldline denominations. This decline has dramatically decreased the relative vote yield for the Republican Party among oldline adherents. Second, decline in the oldline is even more severe than it appears because of the rise of a secular voting group, i.e., people who seldom attend church but still identify themselves to pollsters as Methodists, Presbyterians, Baptists—nominal religionists who are then lumped together for analysis with those who continue to serve actively as members of congregations. Recent research suggests that although faithful oldline attenders remain pretty strongly Republican, a number of lapsed Protestants have joined with others to form a growing secular segment of the electorate that tends to favor the Democrats (Green 1993). Heightened secular voting is common in Europe but rare in American history, and it bears watching.

A third, though less pronounced, change has been the erosion of oldline support for the Republican Party. Even among faithful attenders, oldline Protestants are now less Republican by far than evangelicals. In 1992, for example, Bush won only a plurality (41 percent) of the oldline vote, versus 34 percent for Clinton and 24 percent for Perot.[9] Part of the explanation here may have to do with widespread dissatisfaction over the president's handling of the economy. But it also likely reflects the fact that oldline Protestants tend to be socially liberal, if moderately conservative on economic issues, and thus cross-pressured by the apparent Republican embrace of the Christian right.

Figures for church attendance are instructive as well. Though self-reporting undoubtedly inflates estimates of actual church attendance (Hadaway, Marler, and Chaves 1993), we are interested in *relative* differences among the religious groups, and they are huge. White evangelicals show the highest church attendance, with 74 percent reporting saying they go at least once a week, followed by white Catholics at 48 percent and black Christians at 46 percent. Trailing far behind are white oldline Protestants at 34 percent, Jews at 22 percent, and, of course, seculars (VRS exit poll). In other words, many of those listing affiliation with oldline denominations are not very church-rooted at all. This pattern of church attendance probably helps to explain some (though not all) of the value-based differences in voting. White frequent attenders, whether Catholic, oldline Protestant, or evangelical, are more likely to vote Republican than are their less frequent attending counterparts and are more likely to identify themselves as conservatives. But, as Table 10.5 shows, the ratios vary among frequent attenders, with evangelicals as the most Republican (and conservative), followed by oldline Protestants and then Catholics (the only white Christian group of frequent attenders to give Clinton a plurality).

These voting patterns make sense when we consider the contrasting policy views across religious traditions, outlined in Table 10.3. The data show that among white Christians, church attendance moves voters in a more conservative direction across the board—an effect that is generally compatible with partisan differences based on church attendance. Nevertheless, the precise nature of the relationship varies from issue to issue and among the religious groups. On abortion, for example, oldline Protestants were the most liberal of the white Christian groups (and even more liberal than black Protestants). Oldline Protestants did, however, take a far more conservative position on government-guaranteed health care than did either white Catholics or black Protestants and were only slightly less conservative than evangelicals on that particular issue. Thus, whereas Democrats represent oldline sentiment on abortion, Republicans better articulate their position on health care. Oldline Protestants are therefore cross-pressured in almost the exact opposite direction as white Catholics, who are more conservative on abortion but liberal on health care and the environment. Once again, the modern political landscape presents snares for both parties and dilemmas for voters.

TABLE 10.5   Presidential Vote for White Christians Overall and by Frequent Church
Attendance, 1992

	Clinton	Bush	Perot
Evangelical Protestant	23%	60%	18%
Frequent attendance (74%)	20%	67%	13%
Oldline Protestant	39%	36%	25%
Frequent attendance (34%)	35%	44%	22%
Catholic	43%	33%	23%
Frequent attendance (48%)	40%	38%	22%

NOTE: Due to poor question wording, these figures probably inflate the true oldline support for Clinton. The VRS question used to identify evangelicals asked respondents whether they considered themselves to be born-again/fundamentalist Christians. Because some evangelicals will not answer a question that classifies them as "fundamentalists," by default they end up in the oldline category. And since evangelicals mostly supported Bush, their inclusion as oldline Protestants has the effect of inflating Clinton's total.

SOURCE: Voter Research and Survey exit poll, general election, November 1992.

As we noted before, declining church attendance since the 1960s (especially among the oldline denominations) is a factor in the rise of secular voting in the United States. This has been a quiet, mostly unheralded, trend—but one of potentially great significance for partisan alignments. In 1960, Americans were a decidedly churchgoing society: Democrats depended on churchgoing Catholics and some evangelicals to offset Republican strength among the oldline Protestant faithful. Only a tiny percentage of the public stated no religious preference, and because such individuals often were less socially connected, their voting rates tended to be low compared to the church-based population. As a result, the secular segment was a negligible influence in American elections. By the mid-1990s, however, diminished church attendance combined with an increasing share listing no affiliation to produce a larger, more distinctive secular voting group. At least a portion of that secular group is an educational and economic elite, heavily concentrated on the coasts and very likely to vote (Times Mirror 1987).

Estimates of the size of the secular group today range from 15 to 30 percent of the total electorate—the difference being how narrowly one defines secular.[10] When low church-attendance rates and other measures of nominal religious salience are taken into account, the secular segment looms rather larger than previously thought (Green 1993).

Generally speaking, secular voters are socially liberal and economically moderate, lean toward the Democratic Party (though not overwhelmingly), and are volatile in their electoral behavior. Some have clearly libertarian views and would vote for Republican candidates (or for Independents like Perot) who emphasize limited government but shy away from conservative stands on abortion and social issues. With the strengthening Republican tie to evangelical Christians, however, seculars have moved toward the Democrats in the past few elections. Bill Clinton, for example, got a strong majority vote of those who listed no religious affiliation, as well as a plurality of those whites who said they never attend church. But Ross Perot also demonstrated an appeal to the secular electorate. John Green (1993, p. 14) concluded that "Perot voters were drawn from the least committed members of each religious tradition ... disaffected Mainliners, Catholics, and Seculars."

With its apparent increase in size, the secular electorate is likely to be courted more assiduously by consultants and some candidates in the future. Positioned on the opposite side of the cultural divide from evangelicals, this constituency may be viewed as a check on the power of the religious right. As such, natural allies will be the majority of American Jews, with their historical commitment to the secular state and antagonism toward evangelical conservatives.

Jews, Liberalism, and Continued Democratic Loyalty

In one sense American Jews have always been in the vanguard of a secular vision for American politics. The vast majority are theological liberals, not Orthodox, and they celebrate the Enlightenment ideal of a nonsectarian state. Most of them are thus like secular voters, only more so—very socially liberal and intensely loyal to the Democratic Party. But Jews, even the most secular ones, have distinct reasons for their partisan attachments that appear independent of mere secularization. Moreover, their commitment to liberalism extends beyond the social realm to encompass civil rights, the welfare state, and economics.

Jewish voters remain one of the true paradoxes of American politics. It is only a slight exaggeration to say that although they look like Episcopalians in economic status, they vote like blacks. Here we see the impact of a kind of value-based voting independent of social class. And in this case, the values in question are liberal ones, rooted in tradition and in a history of persecution. To Jews, support for a more egalitarian, more tolerant society is the best protection against anti-Semitism. Thus, as Lee Sigelman put it, liberalism constitutes a kind of "lay religion" among American Jews. On civil rights (including feminism and gay rights), peace and defense, as well as the environment, Jews are among the most liberal voting groups in the country (Sigelman 1991). This is illustrated nicely in Table 10.3, where we see that Jews are liberal across the board; indeed, they are more liberal on abortion, school prayer (not shown here), and homosexuality than blacks as a group. In addition, as we see in Table 10.6, Jews are far more likely to describe themselves as liberals, despite the "L" word having taken on such negative connotations that many Democrats now shun it.

This commitment to liberal ideals helps to explain the loyalty that many Jews feel for the Democratic Party, even though their relative prosperity might other-

TABLE 10.6   Comparison of Ideological Self-Identification by Religious Tradition, 1992

	Liberal	*Moderate*	*Conservative*
Jewish	42%	49%	9%
White secular	42%	45%	13%
Black Protestant	26%	55%	21%
Catholic	22%	54%	24%
White	21%	54%	25%
Black	31%	58%	11%
White oldline Protestant	19%	53%	28%
White born-again Protestant	8%	38%	54%

SOURCE: Voter Research and Survey exit poll, general election, November 1992.

wise cause them to favor the GOP. In fact, Democratic attachments among Jews solidified during the New Deal (when Roosevelt won roughly 85 percent of the Jewish vote), continued through the 1960s (when John Kennedy, Lyndon Johnson, and Hubert Humphrey also received over 80 percent), and remain strong in the 1990s (Sigelman 1991).

Beginning in the mid-1970s, however, Republicans did begin to see opportunities for making inroads into the Jewish electorate and, by implication, into the network of Jewish financial support that has long been a mainstay of the Democratic Party. In 1976, for example, Jimmy Carter received 64 percent of the Jewish vote—a solid margin but far off that registered by other Democrats, leaving Republicans with a healthy 34 percent. At the time, Jewish neoconservative intellectuals had started to chip away at the liberal vision. Even more important was the issue of U.S. support for Israel. Carter's "relatively even-handed approach to the Middle East discomfited many Jews" (Sigelman 1991, p. 193), and that, coupled with economic and foreign policy crises during the Carter administration, produced a wide-scale abandonment of the Democratic incumbent by Jews in 1980. Not only did Republicans get 39 percent of the Jewish vote but the partisan gap narrowed to only 6 points (Democrats receiving just 45 percent of the Jewish vote and Independent candidate John Anderson garnering 15 percent).[11] Hopes for realignment were buoyed in the 1980s by Ronald Reagan's support for Israel and platform provisions adopted by Republicans that were celebrated by the pro-Israel lobby. In the Democratic camp, Jesse Jackson's rise created discomfort for many Jews, who saw Jackson as sympathetic toward the Arab cause, supportive of Louis Farrakhan,[12] and insensitive toward Jews.

The hoped-for realignment did not occur. Democrats rebounded in 1984, gaining 67 percent of the Jewish vote, which dropped only slightly to 64 percent in 1988 and then jumped up dramatically to 78 percent in 1992. What happened? For one thing, Jackson did not make it onto the Democratic ticket in the 1980s, thus allaying Jewish fears. Moreover, no clear partisan cleavage emerged on support for Israel. The Reagan and Bush administrations were not always uncritical of Israel, and many Democratic leaders, in spite of Jackson's efforts, remained steadfast in their support. But most important, the increasing Republican tie to the evangelical constituency, especially with the prominence of such figures as Jerry Falwell and Pat Robertson, raised the specter of historical anti-Jewish bigotry in the heartland. Even though Pat Robertson is strongly supportive of Israel, all the talk by some fundamentalists of America as a "Christian nation" has been unsettling.

In 1992, conservative Patrick Buchanan reintroduced a more virulent strain of nativist politics with real anti-Jewish overtones, thereby producing a visceral reaction among Jews. Simply put, the two Pats—Robertson and Buchanan—appear to scare the daylights out of many Jewish voters. Bill Clinton, in sharp contrast, skillfully touched on issues close to Jewish concerns (including tolerance, civil rights, a caring society) and did better than any Democrat since Humphrey in 1968. Thus, in 1992, even those who had been voting Republican in the 1980s abandoned the GOP, which got a paltry 12 percent of the Jewish vote. Also, contrary to the pattern with white Christians, Jews who attend religious services regularly were slightly more supportive of Democrat Clinton than those who do not.

We do not have good data on breakdowns within the Jewish community, but it is likely that a good share of the vote Republicans got came from the small number of Orthodox and ultra-Orthodox Jews, who share many of the conservative attitudes of traditional Christians and who have been tending toward the Republican Party for the past few elections. Even so, Clinton likely did better among this group than had his recent predecessors.

More analysis is needed on why 1992 was such a bad year for Republicans among the Jewish constituency. What we can say with certainty is that Jews, along with secular voters, represent the flip side of the evangelical shift toward the Republican Party. Despite vigorous attempts by GOP leaders to court Jews, and despite a sustained effort by Jewish neoconservatives, Jewish voters have not abandoned the Democratic Party. They remain firmly on one side of the cultural divide.

Black Christians

Notwithstanding the public visibility of Louis Farrakhan's Nation of Islam and the growth of orthodox Islam among African Americans, black voters remain overwhelmingly Christian and predominately Protestant. And in a sense they present a paradox equal to the Jewish case, but in the opposite direction. Blacks are heavily evangelical in their religious orientation but liberal and almost monolithically Democratic in their voting behavior. For example, well over half of all African Americans regard themselves as born-again Christians and biblical literalists, and a majority claim to watch religious programming on television.[13] The salience of religion in general is high among blacks: Nine out of ten say that religion is very important in their lives (more than is true for any other demographic or ethnic group), and over half say they pray several times a day (see Hertzke 1993, chapter 6).

Part of the paradox of black politics can be explained by the unique American tradition of black Christianity, which blended evangelical pietism with prophetic and liberationist messages.[14] Black churches were, and are, infused by a keen identification with the biblical narratives of captivity and freedom, of God's judgment on oppressors and succor for the downtrodden. Many African American Christians, and especially their leaders, see themselves chosen as carriers of God's prophetic message of justice to a troubled land. What this means is that black voters often combine religious and moral traditionalism with economic and political progressivism. Thus, blacks surpass whites in their overwhelming support for school prayer and are less liberal by far than Jews, secular voters, and oldline white Protestants on abortion. At the same time, they also are far more liberal than others in their support for social welfare policies, government jobs programs, government health care, and civil rights.

This fascinating blend is often not treated seriously in voting studies of blacks because their monolithic support for the Democratic Party leaves no variance to explain. Blacks are loyal Democrats because it was the party of the civil rights revolution in the 1960s and remains, however imperfectly, the carrier of the New Deal creed of positive government and egalitarian economic policy today.

Black church life, however, is important in political behavior in ways that aggregate voting studies cannot capture. First, because the black church is the central social institution in the African American community, it continues to be the focus of political organizing, voter registration drives, political cues, and overt campaigning. In a very real sense it is the precinct for black politics. Jesse Jackson's two presidential drives were heavily church based, with leadership, forums, and fundraising being centered within congregational networks. Other Democrats now routinely campaign in black churches—most recently Bill Clinton, who sings gospel music and speaks fluently the argot of evangelical redemption and prophetic justice. The point is that almost uniquely in the black community, church membership connects people to politics and increases voting participation (see Wald, Kellstedt, and Leege 1993; Peterson 1992). Church members are far more likely to vote than nonmembers, partially compensating for the lower voting rates we tend to see among people of lower socioeconomic status. And contrary to the pattern for whites, higher church attendance, although it may increase conservatism on some social issues, tends to increase Democratic voting and turnout. Church life is thus positively linked to Democratic support. One need only attend congregational services near election day to see why. Cues from pastors can be pretty clear, and endorsements from the pulpit are not at all uncommon.

This fact is connected to another key development: the expansion of the black electorate. From the 1970s through the 1990s, black voting support has hovered around the 90 percent range for Democratic presidential candidates. What such figures do not tell us is the relative size of that electorate and its impact on national politics. Though the Voting Rights Act of 1965 officially enfranchised black voters, its promise was not fully realized until the mid-1980s, when black registration figures mushroomed, especially in the South. Many organizations were a part of the effort, but black churches and Jackson's campaigns in them were central to galvanizing African American political energy. As the black electorate grew, it profoundly altered the political calculus of numerous political figures and enhanced the clout of black leaders in the Democratic Party (Hertzke 1993).

There is a final sense in which black religious conviction has implications for contemporary American politics. On certain issues—school prayer, abortion, homosexuality, school vouchers, and the like—blacks are being courted by white religious conservatives as allies in their culture war against "secular elites." These efforts are based on the premise that although blacks vote for Democrats, many can be mobilized in letter-writing campaigns, local nonpartisan campaigns, referenda battles, and so on. And there is some evidence that such a strategy sometimes works. Black parents turned off by condom distribution in the schools, for example, can be recruited to join in Christian right school board initiatives—just as they were in the New York school board elections of 1993. Moreover, Republicans hope that black alienation from secular trends might even lead a portion of them to join the Republican ranks. They note that increasing the GOP black vote from 10 percent to 20 percent would change the fortunes of many congressional and senatorial candidates.

On some issues, white Christian conservatives may find allies among black pietists. Pat Robertson, as it happens, is more popular among blacks than among whites, and his charismatic followers share a language and set of religious experiences with many black pentecostals (Hertzke 1993). But Republican inroads are hampered by the continued temptation of candidates and consultants to play the race card, as they did in 1988 with the Willie Horton ad, and as Jesse Helms (R.–N.C.), a darling of the Christian right, did in his recent U.S. Senate race against Harvey Gantt (see Diamond and Bates 1992). Until that temptation ends, Republican hopes to break the Democratic lock on the black vote will fail, however much some blacks share conservative cultural attitudes with white evangelicals.

THE RELIGIOUS VOTE IN THE 1994 ELECTIONS

The stunning Republican victory in 1994 midterm races flowed from an intensification of trends already discussed. First, and most obvious, was the strong support of white evangelical voters for the GOP: An estimated three-quarters of white Protestant evangelicals cast their ballots for Republican congressional candidates (Kellstedt et al. 1995). Equally significant, intense get-out-the-vote efforts by such evangelical groups as Christian Coalition and Focus on the Family, coupled with the galvanizing effect of disgust for President Clinton among many of these individuals, helped to increase the white evangelical share of the national electorate. Estimates vary, but evangelicals made up from a quarter to a third of all voters in 1994—figures that do not include allied religionists such as Mormons.[15] This surge in pietist voting swept into office numerous conservative evangelical candidates, an historically underrepresented group in Washington. In the 104th Congress, the Republican freshman class contained a significant share of newcomers with membership in an array of evangelical churches, including, for example, Nazarene, Assembly of God, Southern Baptist Convention, Evangelical Methodist, Christian Missionary Alliance, United Brethren, unaffiliated Baptist, and nondenominational Christian.[16]

An unheralded but equally noteworthy factor in the 1994 outcome was the unprecedented Republican success among Catholics. As we noted earlier in the chapter, although Catholic support for Democratic presidential candidates has been eroding, support for congressional Democrats remained strong through the early 1990s. The party's control of the House of Representatives for four decades thus rested, to a considerable degree, on continued Catholic majorities voting for Democrats. That changed in 1994, as GOP candidates received about half to slightly more than half of the total Catholic vote[17]—a major departure from voting habits that go back into the nineteenth century. In addition, white Catholic support for Republicans was at least 53 percent (Kellstedt et al. 1995), reflecting an increase of about 10 points from the 1992 election. Not surprisingly, several Catholic Republicans were elected to Congress in 1994.

On the other side of the cultural divide, Jewish voters and blacks remained intensely loyal to the Democratic Party, casting nearly 9 in 10 votes for Democratic congressional candidates. Just as one would expect, secular voters also strongly supported the Democrats. Oldline Protestants, in contrast, split their votes between the two parties, with faithful church attenders being the more strongly Republican (Kellstedt et al. 1995).

What these patterns suggest is an emerging churchgoing (largely white) Republican base opposing a Democratic coalition of more secular voters and minorities. We examine the implications of this alignment, as well as other features of culture-based politics, in the following section.

CONCLUSION:
ASSESSING THEORIES OF RELIGIOUS VOTING

The foregoing analysis helps us to sort out some of the competing claims being made about the nature of American politics and voting alignments. No interpretation of religion and politics gets more attention today than the "culture wars" thesis, which asserts that a deep cultural divide separates religious traditionalists (of whatever denomination) from a progressive coalition of liberal Christians, Jews, and secularists. Thus, according to some scholars, politics increasingly has become a war over the culture—with skirmishes being fought locally over control of school boards and city councils, and nationally in presidential elections and congressional lobbying (Wuthnow 1989; Hunter 1991). Activists on both sides of the divide have adopted the language of *Kulturkampf* and are seeking allies in the war. Religious conservatives, for example, speak of building an "ecumenism of orthodoxy" that would unite evangelical Protestants, conservative pro-life Catholics, Orthodox Jews, pietist blacks, and even Muslims (who tend to be very conservative on social issues) in a crusade against "liberal secularists."

Our analysis indicates that whereas value conflict exists in the electorate, it is not always as divisive or as neatly defined as the culture-wars argument implies. In the first place, we doubt that many rank-and-file voters see themselves as engaged in a battle in which some of their neighbors, presumably, would be mortal enemies. Second, voters (unlike elites; see Converse 1964) do not typically think about politics in consistent ideological terms, nor do they vote that way. Many oldline Protestants continue to vote Republican even though they are strongly pro-choice on abortion, and many Catholics still vote Democratic even though they are pro-life. And the majority of blacks are born-again Protestants yet remain loyal Democrats. Even if such patterns reflect, as they almost certainly do, a blend of views and cross-pressures, that fact merely illustrates that the cultural divide is not as neat as some would have us believe.

We do find evidence of a softer version of value conflict in the electorate. Among whites, for example, as church attendance goes up, Republican support increases regardless of tradition, suggesting that religious salience is an increasingly important cultural division in American society (see Table 10.7). Moreover, orthodox religionists—whether Protestant or Catholic, Jewish or African American—tend to be more conservative on social issues than their theologically liberal counterparts. And with the exception of blacks, they are more Republican than their liberal sisters and brothers as well. We also see evidence of value conflict in the marriage gap. As Everett Ladd (1993) observed, a plurality of married voters supported Bush in 1992; single, divorced, separated, and widowed persons all backed Clinton by wide margins. We know that as people get married, and especially have children, they are often drawn back to churches; lifestyle differences thus reinforce religious differences to produce a distinctive cultural experience and set of concerns. But economic factors also converge with cultural ones. The need for government support is greater among the poor, the young, single parents, and among the widowed or retired; hence, the Democratic leanings of these groups is hardly a surprise. Married couples with children, in contrast, are most likely to feel the pinch of taxes and to be concerned about unhealthy cultural influences on their kids. As a result, they tilt toward the Republicans.

This role of church attendance in defining partisan attachments was not apparent even as recently as the mid-1970s, and its presence in the 1990s has led some to conclude that a kind of European-style party alignment may be emerging in the United States (Kellstedt et. al. 1994; Guth, Green, and Kellstedt 1993; Green 1993). Such an alignment, which would pit a Christian right-of-center party (Republicans) against a more secular left-of-center party (Democrats), is plausi-

TABLE 10.7   Presidential Vote, Congressional Vote, and Self-Identified Ideology by Attendance at Religious Services (whites only), 1992

| | *1992 Presidential Vote* | | | *1992 Democratic* | *Ideology:* |
	Clinton	*Bush*	*Perot*	*House Vote*	*Conservative*
Attend at least					
once a week (39%)	33%	48%	18%	45%	41%
Do not attend at					
least once a week (61%)	47%	28%	25%	58%	21%
N = 7,028					

SOURCE: Voter Research and Survey exit poll, general election, November 1992.

ble and it is partially supported by the data. There are, however, some problems—beginning with our discovery that many voters are not so neatly placed as the European model (secular-left versus Christian-right) might lead us to expect. Furthermore, the single most loyal Democratic constituency (African Americans) is also one of the most solidly Christian, orthodox, and church-rooted; to a degree, the same pattern holds for Hispanic Catholics. Although minority attachment to the Democratic Party can be explained on economic and historical grounds, that does not diminish the departure from the European norm. In the United States, at least, there is a more robust progressive Christian tradition to draw upon than in Europe.

Quite obviously, modern politics confronts religious constituencies with keen dilemmas and cross-pressures. E. J. Dionne (1991) has suggested that voters do not always like the way activists tend to frame issues in dichotomous terms—e.g., feminism versus family—and as political discourse becomes ever more polarized in this fashion, many are turned off by the whole process. Our analysis puts Dionne's argument in a slightly different light by showing how particular religious constituencies often face unsettling choices between candidates and parties; it is not surprising that the effect of those cross-pressures is greater volatility, split-ticket voting, disenchantment, and disengagement from politics. Gone are the days, for some, when elections offered unambiguously appealing choices.

Finally, our findings leave little doubt that a kind of postmaterialist, value-based voting is an important feature of contemporary American politics, with churches and religious beliefs playing a vital role in producing and shaping those values. On the eve of the twenty-first century, religion remains a defining characteristic of American political life, contrary to the predictions—and in some cases the wishes—of scholars.

NOTES

1. Notable here is the work of Paul Kleppner (1970 and 1987), who analyzed the role of ethnoreligious forces in nineteenth-century politics; Paul Lopatto (1985), who focused on religion and presidential elections; and Albert Menendez (1977), whose work summarized religion and voting from the founding era onward.

2. We have chosen to use the term "oldline" to designate Protestant denominations— Presbyterians, Methodists, Episcopalians, Congregationalists, Lutherans (Evangelical Lutheran Church of America, or ELCA), and northern Baptists—that for many years enjoyed the appellation of "mainline." These theologically liberal denominations have so declined in membership and church attendance since the 1960s that the term "mainline" is no longer accurate. Indeed, as the narrative in this chapter makes clear, the center in American Protestantism has shifted toward the more theologically conservative evangelical churches.

3. Vatican II is shorthand for the Second Vatican Council of the world's bishops, convened by Pope John XXIII in 1962 and continuing through 1965. As a result of Vatican II, church teachings and practices were substantially modernized (including changing from the Latin mass to the vernacular of the people).

4. The CBS–*New York Times* survey had Catholics giving 52 percent of their votes to Bush, and the ABC News exit poll reported 51 percent for Dukakis. These results recommend caution in interpreting close margins. Though the news organizations often note that their surveys should be accurate within certain confidence limits—usually plus or minus 3 percentage points—commentators (and consumers) are tempted to treat surveys as hard and cold facts.

5. Kenski and Lockwood (1987) found a pattern of strong but diminished Catholic support (roughly 60 percent) for Democratic congressional candidates in the early 1980s, and our own analysis of VRS surveys in 1992 showed a further drop to just under 60 percent in the U.S. House races that year.

6. The metaphor of the "seamless garment" was coined by Cardinal Bernardin of Chicago, who argued that Catholic teaching emphasized a seamless garment of concern for life that encompassed not just abortion but opposition to capital punishment, peace issues, and economic-justice concerns. Thus, Bernardin argued that opposition to abortion was perfectly consistent with opposition to the MX missile, support for welfare programs benefiting children, and so on.

7. For further information on pietists, see Kleppner (1970, 1979).

8. Lopatto's (1985) analysis suggested that Carter split the evangelical vote with Ford but lost among the broader Protestant constituency.

9. These results (along with the patterns described in the preceding paragraph) are based on an analysis of the 1992 American National Election Study, which, unlike the VRS, breaks Protestants down into specific denominations.

10. Previous analyses had included as secular only the 10 percent or so who listed no religious affiliation at all.

11. Figures here are from the *New York Times*, November 5, 1992, p. B9.

12. Farrakhan is leader of the Nation of Islam, a militant and separatist black sect whose highly unorthodox theology suggests, among other things, that whites are a race of devils. His followers should not be confused with the growing number of African Americans who have become orthodox Muslims.

13. This is according to the 1992 American National Election Study survey.

14. An excellent summary of black Christianity is provided by Lincoln and Mamiya (1990). For a review of the politics of the black church, see Fowler (1985) and Hertzke (1993); for a discussion of the role of churches in the civil rights movement, see Branch (1988) and Garrow (1986).

15. Using a relatively expansive definition, the Christian Coalition's own survey showed that white evangelicals constituted about 33 percent of the 1994 electorate, up from 24 per-

cent in 1992 (Peyton 1994). Employing a more restrictive definition, scholars (drawing upon national exit polls; see Kellstedt, Green, Guth, and Smidt 1995) estimated the Protestant evangelical share at about a quarter of the electorate, also an increase from 1992.

16. The Christian Coalition identified 38 GOP freshmen (over half the incoming class's total of 72) as "pro-family" and "pro-life." The largest share of these 38 were evangelical Protestants, followed by conservative Catholics, conservative oldline Protestants, and Mormons. See Hook (1995).

17. The Voter News Service exit poll (as reported in Baumann 1994) found 53 percent of Catholics voting Republican in the congressional races, but the 1994 Election News Service put that figure at just under half (see Kellstedt, Green, Guth, and Smidt 1995).

11

The Social Contract in Black and White: Racial Differences in Evaluations of Government

TIMOTHY BLEDSOE
LEE SIGELMAN
SUSAN WELCH
MICHAEL W. COMBS

Central to all social contract theories[1] is the idea that individuals come together freely to establish a framework that will allow them to interact with one another in mutually beneficial ways. Through the contract, certain rights are reserved to individual citizens and protected against encroachment by either fellow citizens or government.

The idea of a social contract, which really represents little more than a pledge of citizens' loyalty in return for fairness of treatment, implies a joint commitment between citizens and government. Government commits to provide citizens with certain rights, services, and protection against foreign and domestic threats. Martin Luther King, in his historic "I Have a Dream" speech, referred to these rights under a social contract: "One of the first things we notice in this dream is an amazing universalism. It does not say some men, but it says all men. . . . And there is another thing we see in this dream that ultimately distinguishes democracy and our form of government from all of the totalitarian regimes that emerge in history. It says that each individual has certain basic rights neither conferred by nor derived from the state."

The "basic rights" that King referred to were almost certainly limited in number, but they were crucial in importance: the right to vote (and to fully participate in the democratic process) and civic equality, or an end to racial discrimination. The rights sought for African Americans by King would fall far short of those to which perhaps the most prominent modern social contract theorist, John Rawls (1971), and others would declare them entitled. Indeed, many contemporary theorists would argue that government also has an obligation to provide a social safety net that minimizes hunger and homelessness, provides health services, and offers public education. Citizens, as their part of the contract, commit to following laws passed by their representatives, participating in the democratic process, and (according to most theorists) channeling any discontent through established political procedures.

Applying the notion of a social contract to blacks is troubling because of the issue of *consent*. The ancestors of most other Americans came into the country freely and therefore might be said to have freely entered into this abstract contract. But the ancestors of most African Americans were forcibly brought here and kept as slaves during the time that the social contract was being established. Under the circumstances, they can hardly be thought to have offered their consent. Still, although separatist sentiment has held sway among some American blacks from time to time, an important goal for most blacks has been to secure equal rights within the existing civil society.

Our purpose in this chapter is to explore the degree to which black and white Americans share a mutual evaluation of government and political processes today as compared with 1968, only a few years after the moment when Dr. King electrified the huge crowd on the mall—and the nation—with his "I Have a Dream" speech. In 1968, the President's Commission on Civil Disorders (Kerner Commission 1988), in its report on the urban riots that swept many U.S. cities during the mid-to-late 1960s, envisioned the development of two separate societies in America: one urban, black, and poor, the other suburban, white, and affluent. Instead of having a single social contract, America seemed to be dividing along racial lines. A little over a quarter-century after that report was issued, we attempt to assess the accuracy of its predictions. To what extent have separate and unequal societies developed, and of what consequence is such inequality for any sort of social contract between government and all its people, both white and black?

By analyzing citizen attitudes in metropolitan Detroit in 1968 and 1992, we seek to determine whether, within this one urban area, whites and blacks have grown more similar or more dissimilar in their evaluations of government, or whether no substantial change has occurred. In other words, we seek to determine whether whites and blacks now share the fruits of a similar social contract in a way that they obviously did not prior to the civil rights movement of the 1960s. For answers, we look primarily at local government and local policies, though our findings almost certainly have relevance for blacks' and whites' views of other components of the political system as well.[2]

Detroit is similar to most other large metropolitan areas. It is an old industrial city of the frostbelt that peaked in population at about 2.5 million residents in the mid-1950s. Most of its residents at that time, black and white, lived together in the central city; many of today's suburbs were little more than villages, and some were still pastureland. But the Detroit area boasts of having the first modern expressway and claims the first enclosed shopping mall, and few things either facilitate or embody the suburbanization of American cities more than express-ways and shopping malls. So it is that between the 1950s and the 1990s—but par-ticularly after 1967—the suburbs grew as thousands of Detroiters left the city for the suburbs and most newcomers settled in the suburbs rather than the city. Significantly, most of those leaving the city and most of the newcomers settling in suburban communities were whites. Detroit's population now barely tops the 1 million mark, but its suburbs in the immediate three-county area are home to more than 3 million residents. The city is overwhelmingly black and the suburbs are overwhelmingly white.

In the mid-1990s, two decades after the first African American was elected mayor of what was then the nation's fifth largest city, the Detroit metropolitan area is one of the most highly segregated in the nation. Massey and Denton (1993) go so far as to maintain that the current segregation of poor blacks in cen-tral cities and affluent whites in suburbs is tantamount to a system of American apartheid, a strict and willful separation of the races that results in the subjuga-tion of blacks and perpetuation of privilege for whites. A system of apartheid, if that is an accurate depiction of racial segregation today, would clearly contradict the notion of a universally shared social contract.

THE SURVEYS

Our analyses are based on two opinion surveys, one conducted in 1968 and the second in 1992. The first survey, directed by Angus Campbell and Howard Schuman, was part of the Kerner Commission study of the urban riots and included Detroit among its fifteen cities. This survey sampled approximately 200 black residents of the city of Detroit, 200 white city residents, and 200 white sub-urban residents. The roughly equal number of white city and suburban respon-dents approximated the population split between city and suburbs at the time. The 1992 survey, funded by the National Science Foundation, was conducted by Wayne State University's Center for Urban Studies. Respondents included ap-proximately 300 blacks and 230 whites in the city of Detroit, 230 whites in the suburbs, and (though limited use is made of their responses in this chapter) over 350 black suburbanites.[3]

Five scales were developed for analyzing the two surveys using similar, and occasionally identical, survey questions. Of course, no matter how similar the questions may be, even slight differences in context and wording can produce substantial differences in response patterns (e.g., Schuman and Presser 1981). We therefore focus much of our attention on the *size* of the racial divide. By this we mean the magnitude of the difference between blacks and whites in the late 1960s compared to the magnitude of the difference today. In other words, how has the gap between blacks and whites in evaluations of government changed in the quar-ter-century since the Kerner Commission study was conducted? Admittedly, this approach does not entirely eliminate problems posed by differing contexts or inconsistent question wording, but it greatly lessens problems of comparability.

In addition to dealing with different question wording, we are also faced with different response categories, different numbers of response categories, and even different numbers of items that can be used to measure some of the concepts of interest to us. For three of our five concepts we have but a single indicator for each time period, but for two other concepts we combine two survey questions into a single indicator. To facilitate comparisons across all five items, we constructed standardized measures for our concepts, including those measured by a single survey question.[4] These standardized measures provide at least a partial solution to the problems mentioned and facilitate comparisons of racial differences over time.

RACIAL EVALUATIONS IN 1968 AND 1992

Evaluations of Police

No right is more fundamental to the social contract than that of safety and security in one's home and neighborhood. Indeed, according to John Locke, the original compact among individuals first entering into society was based on the regulation and preservation of property, and on employment of force by the community to that end (quoted in Sabine 1961, p. 532). The most basic right to protect person and property originally belonged to each individual, but upon formation of a civil society, this right was transferred to the community as a more effective way of protecting natural rights in general (p. 532). In theory, then, individuals relinquish their individual police powers to the community. How well does the community protect these rights in practice? And to what extent does race affect the ability or the willingness of the community to offer protection?

These are difficult questions, though we can begin to answer them by examining responses to questions about the effectiveness of police services in protecting neighborhoods. Obviously, such assessments depend not only on the perceived quality of the police force but also on the seriousness of crime in the neighborhood. That is, some neighborhoods need greater police protection because of higher crime rates, and others may be relatively free of serious crime.

We do not need surveys to tell us that crime is a problem that especially plagues minorities in central cities. But are blacks more likely today than in 1968 to feel they lack adequate police protection? Has the racial divide in perception that law enforcement agencies keep them safe from crime increased? The question taken from the 1968 Kerner study reads as follows:

I'd like to ask you how satisfied you are with some of the main services the city is supposed to provide for your neighborhood. What about the quality of police protection in this neighborhood—are you generally satisfied, somewhat dissatisfied, or very dissatisfied?

The question in the 1992 Detroit survey was:

Are you [well satisfied, more or less satisfied, or not satisfied at all] with the police protection provided for your neighborhood?

Both of these questions refer specifically to the interviewee's neighborhood and both use the term "police protection." Although the two questions are not identical, we see no problems comparing responses to them.

Figure 11.1(a) graphically portrays the racial divide in 1968 and 1992 in evaluations of the police and in the assessments that are defined further on. The bar on top of the horizontal line represents the size of the gap, anchored on one end by the placement of the average, or mean, white score and on the other end by the average black score. Where racial differences are minimal, the bar is shorter; where they are greater, it is longer. The midpoint for all interviewees in a given year is shown by the broken line, with positive scores on the dimension to the right of the midpoint and negative scores to the left. Again, all scores must be understood in relative terms, since they are the products of the standardized measurement procedure outlined in note 4.

The 1968 survey excluded people over 69 years of age, so for purposes of comparison, we exclude such respondents for 1992 as well. Also, in 1968 whites were interviewed in both Detroit and the suburbs—but blacks only in Detroit. Again for comparative purposes, we omit suburban blacks from our main analyses, though we mention them if the distinction between African Americans in the city and those in the suburbs proves interesting.

Looking at citizen evaluations of police protection in 1968 and 1992, we see an increase in the racial divide. Blacks felt less secure than whites in the police protection provided their neighborhoods in 1968 and, relative to whites in the Detroit area in 1992, felt even less secure. What is not apparent from this simple comparison of blacks and whites is the dramatic importance of *location* on evaluations of police protection. In sharp contrast to the situation of 1968, today there is no racial difference in evaluations among Detroit residents—blacks and whites offer identical evaluations of the police. But far more whites live in the suburbs today than did so then, and suburban whites are far more positive in their assessments of the police than city whites. The suburbanization of whites has, in this case, served to expand the wide chasm that separates blacks and whites in their evaluations of police.

White suburbanization has also served to confuse the issue of equal access to basic public services. On the one hand, the gap that divided white and black Detroiters in the 1960s is gone. On the other hand, the racial difference that was spawned by the movement of tens of thousands of whites to the suburbs and that resulted in a resegregation of black city and white suburbs looms even greater than the gap that separated black and white city residents twenty-five years ago. Clearly, the relocation of many whites to suburbs in recent decades, in Detroit and in other American cities, cannot reasonably be ignored in assessing overall political and policy differences between blacks and whites. The racial divide that separates blacks and whites in what must be considered a fundamental clause of the social contract—the right to feel safe and secure in the police protection provided their neighborhoods—has grown since the 1960s. This growth can be explained entirely in terms of the disproportionate suburbanization of white citizens.

Evaluations of Schools

If there is a "public service" that touches the life of every citizen to the same degree that the police do and that has similar social importance, it is the educational system. Public schools share with other basic social institutions the responsibility for turning children into productive and successful workers and competent citizens. Moreover, even more than with police service, schools have been the subject of widespread criticism for failing to carry out their responsibilities effectively. The public appears, for example, to be quicker to assign blame to the school system for poorly educated and unemployable young adults than blame for high crime to the failure of the police.

Horace Mann (1855) referred to education as "the great equalizer of the conditions of men . . . the balance wheel of the social machinery." In fact, the United States was a world leader in recognizing access to free public education as a universal and basic right. An egalitarian notion of equality of opportunity runs deep in the American people, and in theory they place a high priority on effective schooling. But does equal access today really serve as a social "balance wheel," to borrow Mann's term, given that the fortunes of birth seem to yield *un*equal access to *effective* schooling? More particularly, does race shape how individuals view the effectiveness of their schools?

In the 1950s, landmark court cases sought to ensure equal educational opportunity regardless of race; and in the 1960s, public schools were desegregated and students bused in an attempt to redress the differential quality of black and white schools. However, in an important 1974 case that ironically originated in Detroit (*Milliken v. Bradley*), the U.S. Supreme Court ruled that forced busing of students could not take place across district boundaries unless intentional segregation could be proven in both city and suburb. Given the trends of white suburbanization previously mentioned, it is not surprising that in metropolitan Detroit in the 1990s a racial imbalance of remarkable proportions exists in schools: Ninety percent of whites live in suburbs where schools average 90 percent white, and 90 percent of blacks live in the central city, where schools average 90 percent black. And according to the *Milliken v. Bradley* decision, the line that divides city from suburbs cannot be crossed by buses carrying children to help lessen racial differences between city and suburban schools.

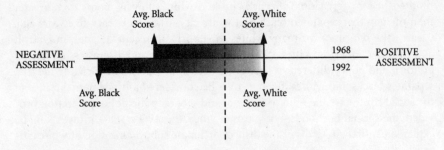

FIGURE 11.1a   Race Differences in Evaluations of Police Protection, 1968 and 1992

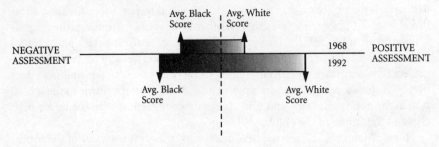

FIGURE 11.1b   Race Differences in Evaluation of Schools, 1968 and 1992

To guide our analysis of blacks' and whites' assessments of the public schools, we rely on one question from the 1968 Kerner Commission study and one from our 1992 survey. The 1968 question reads:

What about the quality of public schools in this neighborhood—are you generally satisfied, somewhat dissatisfied, or very dissatisfied?

The 1992 question reads:

Do you think schools here in your community need lots of improvement, some improvement, or are they pretty good as is?

Unlike the 1992 question, the one in 1968 refers specifically to public schools and to "neighborhood" schools; the 1992 question refers to schools generically rather than to public schools, and to schools in the community rather than the neighborhood. Moreover, the 1968 item asks about the existing quality of schools and the 1992 item asks about whether schools need improvement. Clearly, whereas both questions tap assessments of the quality of public education, they are not quite parallel.

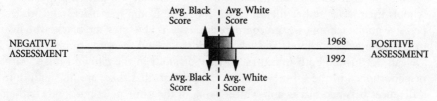

FIGURE 11.1c   Race Differences in Local Political Efficacy, 1968 and 1992

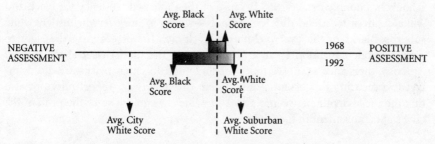

FIGURE 11.1d   Race Differences in Trust of Local Government, 1968 and 1992

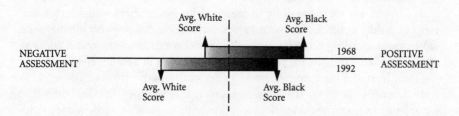

FIGURE 11.1e   Race Differences in Perceptions of Urban Unrest, 1968 and 1992

As shown in Figure 11.1(b), the responses to our survey items indicate a larger increase in the racial divide from 1968 to 1992 than in any of the other areas considered here. Even in 1968, whites had a higher regard for the quality of public schools, with an average rating of 0.16 as opposed to –0.31 for blacks. But this difference of 0.47 points was less than half of today's difference: In 1992, white evaluations stood at 0.58 and black evaluations at –0.40. Further, as was the case with evaluations of the police, the change over time among whites is entirely attributable to the twin facts that suburban schools are more favorably viewed than city schools (by a wide margin) and that more whites live in the suburbs today than did so in the 1960s.

To show that these racial differences are a result of the differing quality of schools themselves rather than a racial difference in the way blacks and whites perceive public schools, we can compare evaluations of whites and blacks who live in the same neighborhoods and whose children attend the same public schools. We can do this for both mixed-race neighborhoods in the city and mixed-race neighborhoods in the suburbs. The results confirm that there are no significant differences between blacks and whites living in the same neighborhoods (either city or suburbs) in how they evaluate their public schools.[5]

Blacks and whites differ tremendously in their evaluations of schools because, in large measure, their children attend different schools in different settings. Moreover, the relative gap between whites and blacks in their evaluation of schools has doubled since 1968 because of the increased tendency for black and white children to attend different schools—whites in the overwhelmingly white suburbs, blacks in the overwhelmingly black city. If we recognize the right to quality public education as an essential part of the modern social contract in America, then once again we must conclude not only that blacks are disadvantaged in securing this essential instrument of equality of opportunity but also that the racial divide between blacks and whites has grown since the peak of the civil rights movement in the 1960s.

Local Political Efficacy

A recent study showed that citizens value different levels of government for different reasons. Those who place the greatest value on the national government cite its importance in critical war and peace issues. Those who place greater value on state government are more likely to mention the effectiveness with which it carries out public policies. But the roughly one-third of people who identify local government as being most important to them do not mention grand issues or effective policies; instead, they emphasize the closeness of people holding office at the local level and their immediate and personal responsiveness (Bledsoe 1993). Indeed, one of the things that local or municipal government can do better than other levels of government is offer an opportunity to exercise participatory rights of citizenship that are often forgotten in today's mass democracy. By participatory rights of citizenship, we mean the opportunity to have direct personal contact with elected officials and come away with the feeling that the contact has in some way been beneficial.

In other words, to the extent that a successful social contract has been forged, citizens should feel that their government is responsive to their needs and actions. Citizens who feel this way are said to have a well-developed sense of *political efficacy*, i.e., they believe that when they request something of local government, there is a reasonable expectation that local officials will respond.[6] In the 1968 Kerner Commission survey, two questions tapped such feelings:

1. If you have a serious complaint about poor service by the city, do you think you can get city officials to do something about it if you call them?

2. Have you ever called a city official with a complaint about poor service?

In the 1992 survey, the counterpart questions were

1. If you had a complaint about a local issue and took that complaint to a member of your city council, would you expect him or her to pay a lot of attention to what you say, some attention, very little attention, or none at all?

2. Have you ever personally gone to see, spoken to, or written to some member of the local government or some other person of influence in your present community about some need or problem?

The two pairs of questions are similar in that one refers specifically to getting local officials to respond to a complaint, and the other seeks information about personal contact with a local official. They differ in that the first Kerner Commission question inquires about an ability to obtain action from local officials, but the more recent item refers somewhat vaguely to getting officials to pay attention to a complaint. The second Kerner Commission question refers specifically to a complaint about poor service; the second 1992 question makes a broader reference to "some need or problem." Notwithstanding these differences, we would expect summary responses to the two sets of questions to offer similar indications of citizen feelings of efficacy relative to local government.

According to Figure 11.1(c), blacks in 1968 scored somewhat lower on our efficacy measure than whites, with means of −0.11 and 0.04 respectively. In 1992, there was the same 0.15 gap: The white mean was +0.08, the black mean −0.07. Local political efficacy is unique among the five dimensions of local political attitudes analyzed here in the irrelevance of race as a source of difference once other individual-level factors are controlled for. Indeed, racial differences can be completely explained simply by taking differing levels of education into account. Whites and blacks of similar educational attainment have similar levels of local political efficacy regardless of local political context. Better-educated individuals tend to have substantially higher levels of efficacy, and whites in the Detroit area tend to have higher levels of educational attainment than blacks do.

Curiously, racial differences in local political efficacy in the 1960s were linked to educational differences in an entirely different way. Then, as now, efficacy was higher among better-educated whites. But for blacks in the 1960s, efficacy was actually higher among those with *less* education. That is, better-educated blacks were less likely to consider local government accessible and responsive than less well educated blacks. The fact that educational attainment is now associated with *higher* levels of efficacy among blacks may point to a significant change in the nature of local government. In the 1960s, the most educated—and presumably the most knowledgeable and best informed—among Detroit blacks felt alienated from local government. Today, the same kind of people feel the greatest sense of empowerment relative to local government.[7]

Residential location is another factor that may account for racial differences in political efficacy. Suburbanites hold greater feelings of local political efficacy than central city residents. This was true in 1968 as well as in 1992, and it was true for blacks as well as for whites; in fact, blacks living in predominantly black suburbs have the highest average efficacy scores of either race in the city or its suburbs. Those who are residents of a large central city have lower political efficacy, as the sheer size of local government becomes daunting to many. Thus, more blacks than whites face the prospect of alienation from politics simply because of the growing concentration of blacks in Detroit and other large central cities.

Trust in Local Government

If we understand the modern social contract to entail a reasonable level of citizen trust in government, there are at least some indications that black citizens are at a disadvantage here as well. No dimension of racial differences in local political perspectives has been examined more carefully than trust in government (e.g., Abney and Hutcheson 1981; Ellison and Gay 1989; Herring, House, and Mero 1991; Kleiman 1976), and yet there is little consensus among researchers about how to measure trust. Perceptions of corruption, of efficiency or effectiveness, and simple expressions of approval have all been used at one point or another to tap the concept of trust in government.

The Kerner Commission study created a three-item index of "government distrust" by summing responses to an identical question asked about local, state, and federal governments. We use the local-government item, which reads:

> Do you think the mayor of [name of central city] is trying as hard as he can to solve the main problems of the city, or . . . is he trying fairly hard to solve these problems, or not hard at all?

Our 1992 measure of trust is very similar to one of several items employed by Howell and Fagan (1988). It reads:

> How much of the time do you think you can trust local government here in [name of city] to do what is right—just about always, most of the time, only some of the time, or almost never?

Although both items can claim to measure trust, they obviously differ in some important respects. The first specifically mentions the mayor but the second refers to "local government" generally. Also, whereas the Kerner Commission question taps feelings toward government in the central city (meaning that people living in the suburbs evaluated the government of Detroit), respondents in the more recent survey were asked about their own local government. We must therefore be cautious in interpreting differences based on responses to these questions, especially in comparing suburban residents.

Figure 11.1(d) reveals that blacks' and whites' assessments of the trustworthiness of city government did not differ much during the 1960s. Whites overall scored higher (0.01) than blacks (−0.07), but not by much; city and suburban whites also differed little from one another in their trust of Detroit city government. By contrast, racial differences abounded in 1992. Overall, whites were much more trusting of their local government—whatever government that might have been—than blacks were. Whites averaged 0.11 on our trust measure, compared to −0.34 for blacks. But differences *between* blacks and whites are substantially less than differences *among* whites. Suburban whites average 0.17 on this scale but city whites score an abysmal −0.61, far below black residents of the city. City blacks average −0.34 compared to suburban blacks' scores of −0.14. Whites in the black-dominated city were about as alienated from their local government as they could possibly be. It is interesting that even black suburbanites living in predominantly white communities had greater confidence in their local government than blacks living in Detroit—a city where blacks held most political power.

In evaluating these findings we must take into account the prevailing political climate at the time of this study. The mayor of Detroit, Coleman Young, had held office for some eighteen years. His administration was clearly on the wane, and a year later he would announce his retirement. The city's black population had become frustrated with the failure of municipal services to keep pace with greater demands resulting from an increasingly poor population. Whites in the city had voted in the 80–90 percent range for Mayor Young's opponent every time he stood for reelection; they would maintain that pattern in the election to choose his successor, supporting the opponent of the candidate Young endorsed. The African American candidate who received this bloc of white votes, Dennis Archer, won the election even though he received a bare majority of the black vote. His challenge clearly is to restore confidence in local government among both blacks and whites. As the first mayor elected to office in over twenty years who received a majority of both black and white votes, he may have a chance of succeeding where the previous regime failed.

Perceptions of Urban Social Protest

We have seen that, compared to whites, blacks have a lower regard for the quality of two vital local services (schools and police protection), a somewhat lower level of political efficacy, and significantly less trust in their local governments. Furthermore, there are indications that on three of these four dimensions the gap between black assessment and white assessment has grown between the 1960s and the present.

In the face of this unhappiness with essential services, general distrust of local officials, and perceptions of inability to affect change, we must consider the potential for substantial differences in the views of blacks and whites toward extraordinary forms of political participation—violent social protests. If people become disillusioned with their social and economic progress, if they are unhappy with their personal situation and disappointed with the ability of government to address their needs, if they do not believe they can exercise any political voice that will be heard in the corridors of power, or if they lack confidence in the willingness of public officials to act on their voice even when it is heard, then they may resort to acts of violent political protest. We saw this in Detroit in 1967 when a police raid on an after-hours black nightclub sparked several days of death and destruction in that city, in Newark the same summer, in many cities following the assassination of Dr. Martin Luther King the following year, and in Los Angeles after the acquittal of police officers by an all-white jury in the original Rodney King beating trial in 1992. Social outrage resulted in violent social protest. Here we look to see if blacks and whites share a common understanding of the reasons for protest and the result of protest, and whether the racial gap in understanding acts of violent protest was as great in 1992 as it was following the Detroit riots of 1967.

For the examination of racial differences in orientations toward social protest, we have the luxury of comparing survey questions where an effort was made in 1992 to replicate the original Kerner Commission questions. Replication was not exact, as conditions have changed in the intervening quarter-century, but the questions are similar enough to enhance confidence in the comparisons reported here. The Kerner Commission survey included the following questions about the urban riots in 1967:

1. Some people say these disturbances [which occurred in Newark and Detroit in summer 1967] are mainly a protest by Negroes against unfair conditions. Others say they are mainly a way of looting and things like that. Which of these seems more correct to you?

2. On the whole, do you think the disturbances have helped or hurt the cause of Negro rights, or would you say they haven't made much difference?

Our 1992 questions repeated the Kerner Commission questions with only slight modification:

1. Some people say these disturbances [which occurred in Los Angeles] are mainly a protest by blacks or African Americans against unfairness of the system. Others say they are mainly a way of looting and things like that. Which of these seems more correct to you?

2. On the whole, do you think the disturbance [which occurred in Los Angeles] has helped or hurt the cause of blacks or African Americans in securing their rights, or would you say they haven't made much difference?

Certainly blacks and whites differed in their understandings of the causes and consequences of the 1967 civil unrest, even to the point of blacks and whites using very different terms to describe the violent episode. Whites called it a "riot" and saw it as nothing more than rampant lawlessness and senseless destruction. Blacks preferred to call it a "rebellion" and saw it more in terms of a civil insurrection against an oppressive regime.

Responses to these questions reveal sharp racial differences in perspectives regarding the civil strife of 1967. Our two-question measure of perceptions of the 1967 rioting yields a mean of –0.23 for whites and 0.47 for blacks. No important subgroup of the black population—divided by age, income, gender, or education—produced a majority with a negative impression of the rioting, and no portion of the white public had a majority with a positive impression of it.

But as different as black and white Detroit area residents were in assessing the civil unrest of 1967, they may have been even more different in their assessments of the 1992 rioting following the acquittal of police officers in the Rodney King beating case. The average for whites on this measure was –0.48, for blacks it was 0.35. The gap between blacks and whites thus appears to have widened somewhat in perceptions and understandings of urban social protest as represented by our two cases. Blacks see in these instances of social protest an appropriate, and even just, response to a political system that has left them with few alternatives. Whites see a breakdown of law and social order and a violation of citizens' social contract with one another and with government.

THE 1994 ELECTION AND ITS AFTERMATH

The midterm elections of 1994 have been characterized as representing the revolt of the white male. Indeed, the gender gap in voting was pronounced, with men exceeding women in their support for Republican congressional candidates by at least 10 percentage points (see Chapter 9). But the real story of 1994, in our view, can be seen in the racial distribution of the vote: Nationwide, whites exceeded blacks in their preference for the GOP by 48 points. This figure compares to a mere 28-point disparity in 1990 and is one of the largest racial gaps ever recorded for congressional elections.[8]

Underlying the sharp voting cleavage witnessed in 1994 is a fundamental difference between blacks and whites in the nature of the American social contract. Most blacks review government commitments for racial justice from the 1960s and earlier, and they see a series of unfulfilled promises. Many whites review the same government commitments and see excessive favoritism toward minority groups. Nowhere are these differences more evident than as they are presented in the House Republicans' Contract with America. The GOP contract emphasizes individual responsibility for social ills rather than government solutions. Even seemingly innocent efforts to return many social welfare programs to state government control are met with considerable unease among African Americans, particularly in the South. These individuals cannot help but be reminded of a time when the only level of government that sought to protect their interests was at the federal level and when state governments from Atlanta to Montgomery to Little Rock were barriers to civil rights progress.

The highly symbolic issue of affirmative action, on which public opinion polls show radically different perspectives between blacks and whites, threatens to carry racial divisions a step further in 1996. Whatever the merits of affirmative action programs, introducing the issue into the 1996 presidential campaign will surely spark a lively debate about the debt society owes to traditionally disadvantaged groups. Such a debate is unlikely to do anything but harm the prospects for narrowing the gulf that divides white and black citizens in terms of their relative access to benefits of the American social contract.

CONCLUSION

A social contract is an abstraction of considerable complexity, and our discussion has not begun to do full justice to it. Contract theorists do not agree among themselves on the elements of such a contract beyond the basic notion that individuals join together for mutual protection and to create a civil society. These basic elements assume that an important part of a social contract is that individuals feel physically secure in their homes and neighborhoods and that they feel government is somehow responsive to their needs.

Even by these rather minimal standards, let alone by higher standards of social welfare equity that some contractarians would impose, black citizens have been denied the full benefits of a social contract. Blacks feel and are less secure than their white counterparts, and they feel less efficacious and trusting of government. These differences were present in the 1960s, and they persist today. Indeed, there is some evidence that the racial division is increasing rather than decreasing, even as the society moves toward greater legal equality.

Much of this increase appears to be due to the continuing extreme residential segregation that prevails in Detroit and many other large cities today. Blacks live in the central city; whites have fled to the suburbs. Though the 1964 Civil Rights Act and the 1965 Voting Rights Act (along with the 1968 Fair Housing Act and a number of other social programs of the 1960s) had substantial impact, these federal efforts to improve the scope of the social contract have been partly nullified by the changing demography of urban areas. Residential segregation of African Americans has long been a characteristic of American cities. What is new about this segregation, as Massey and Denton (1993) explain, is that we are now at the point where boundaries of the ghetto are nearly coterminous with boundaries of the city. In earlier times it would have been unthinkable to isolate blacks by establishing new political boundaries around black neighborhoods—an idea reminiscent of the old Jewish ghettoes of Central and Eastern Europe and of the so-called black homelands of South Africa. Yet through the steady movement of whites to suburbs and blacks to central cities, a similar system of urban apartheid has evolved.

Residential integration of America's metropolitan areas remains an important goal for those who see the ghettoization of minorities as perpetuating a cycle of poverty and despair. As jobs and economic opportunities move from central cities to suburbs and as the educational and public safety systems of central cities approach collapse, suburbs offer a range of opportunities for safety, quality education, and jobs that most central cities cannot match. We do not suggest that this ought to be so. Ideally, urban policy should channel economic development to central cities and discourage the endless paving of new streets and construction of new housing at the periphery of metropolitan areas. But the political balance of power has now shifted to the suburbs, and there is presently little chance that suburban growth will be curtailed by means of policy decisions made at the state or national levels. If suburbia is the land of opportunity, making suburban opportunities available to nonwhites may be more manageable than transferring the opportunities of suburbs to the central city.

There are laws, of course, that ensure the right to purchase a home or rent an apartment in the city or the suburbs free from racial discrimination. Yet we show elsewhere (Bledsoe et al. 1994) that those African Americans who reside in integrated suburbs are exceptional: They are far more affluent than blacks who live in the city, and they are substantially more affluent than whites living in the same suburban neighborhoods. This latter difference between suburban blacks and whites residing in the same neighborhoods is especially troubling. On the one hand, it could be due to continuing but subtle discrimination such as occurs when mortgage lenders, real estate agents, and existing homeowners establish more stringent criteria for black than for white home-buyers—criteria that only well-to-do blacks can meet. Or many blacks may simply perceive that they must command greater resources in order to acquire residence in an integrated suburb; absent those resources, perhaps they do not even consider purchasing a home or renting an apartment in integrated suburban neighborhoods.

Alternatively, the discrepancy between the affluence of suburban blacks and suburban whites could result from the fact that these are neighborhoods in transition from majority white to majority black, with more affluent (and hence more mobile) whites having already departed for more distant and less racially mixed neighborhoods. If this is the case, it is testament to an even harsher dilemma facing successful middle-class African Americans. They can obtain college degrees and good jobs, and they can reside in two-income families with substantial total incomes. But when they invest in a home in a racially mixed suburb, they face the prospect that over the next decade or two their wealthier white neighbors will move out—thereby putting pressure on housing values and eventually producing a predominantly black community that is likely to be less affluent than the community they originally moved into.[9] Our point here is that the broken social contract experienced by blacks today is partly a function of race and partly a function of location, but racial and locational considerations are hardly independent of one another.

One result of the bifurcated social contract is that there persists a tremendous racial divide regarding the appreciation or understanding of violent social

protest. For those who feel deprived of the equal coverage to which they feel entitled by the terms of the contract, violent protests may be seen as the only means
of being heard by an otherwise deaf society. The costs may be great, but there may
be positive consequences to these acts of violence if they serve as an effective vehicle for alerting others in society of their grievances. Of course, those who have
reaped the benefits of this bifurcated contract will likely be more aware of the violence and destruction caused by the social protests than of the causes underlying
it—and they will tend to view the protesters not as rebels or insurrectionists but
merely as criminals who openly violate one of the most sacred provisions of the
social contract. To the extent that the larger society associates an entire group of
individuals with violent protests, it may become even less willing to consider the
legitimate grievances of those who engage in them. Such is the dilemma of race
and the American social contract.

NOTES

Funding for this study and for one of the surveys (1992) on which it is based was provided
by the National Science Foundation (grant no. SES-9112799), which bears no responsibility for the analyses and interpretations presented here.

1. See, for example, John Locke's *Two Treatises of Government,* Thomas Hobbes's *Leviathan,* Jean-Jacques Rousseau's *Social Contract,* and Richard Hooker's *The Laws of
Ecclesiastical Polity.*

2. Although race differences in attitudes toward government are similar regardless of
the level of government being evaluated, blacks' assessments of national political institutions vary to some degree according to the party controlling those institutions. See Howell
and Fagan (1988).

3. In order to adjust for this disproportionate stratified sample, the data are weighted to
reflect true population parameters. Additional details about sampling design and response
rate are available from the first author upon request.

4. Our standardized measures were derived by subtracting the mean value of the observation from each value of the observation, then dividing the observation by the standard
deviation. This yields a standard scale with a mean of zero and a standard deviation of one.

5. Comparing people of different races who live in mixed-race neighborhoods would
not normally be possible because most urban areas are highly segregated, and therefore too
few people of either race live in mixed-race neighborhoods to be included in a simple random sample. However, our sample was stratified to ensure inclusion of blacks and whites
living in integrated neighborhoods in both city and suburbs, so this analysis and these conclusions are based on a substantial number of cases.

6. See, for example, Almond and Verba (1963); Campbell et al. (1960); Lipset and
Schneider (1983); Baldassare (1985).

7. The reason for this may have to do with a genuine change in the responsiveness of
Detroit's government to black citizens. More affluent and better-educated individuals normally should feel more personally empowered relative to government, since they command the skills and resources necessary to capture the attention of public officials. Yet
more affluent and well-educated blacks were just the opposite—less politically effica-

cious—in the late 1960s. Nevertheless, for blacks today, as for whites, personal skills and resources translate into an enhanced sense of political empowerment.

8. These data are from Steeper (1995). The racial gap in presidential election voting has occasionally been larger than 48 points, for example, in 1972 and 1984.

9. Our data indicate that most blacks prefer to live in integrated half-black, half-white neighborhoods; over 85 percent of blacks in integrated neighborhoods state this preference.

PART IV

Linkage

————————————12————————————

The Electoral Connection:
Images of U.S. Senators
and Representatives

GLENN R. PARKER
CHARLES J. BARRILLEAUX

A basic premise in most models of elite behavior is that politicians manipulate their images for electoral gain. They do so by engaging in certain electorally rewarding behaviors and projecting images that are popular with voters. Legislators seem to fit this caricature quite well; hence, legislators are often characterized as behaving in ways designed to elicit voter approval and support among their constituents (Mayhew 1974; Fiorina 1977; Fenno 1978). These behaviors presumably affect how voters perceive legislators, and if the images are successfully packaged and promoted, such perceptions should generate electoral support. The model implied by this characterization can be simply described as follows:

Incumbent's
Constituency Behavior → Voter Perceptions → Electoral Support

This proposition linking legislator behavior to electorally rewarding voter perceptions has become so commonplace that we are often quick to attribute electoral relevance to a legislator's every behavior and to search for electoral motives behind every action.

Yet despite the acknowledged pervasiveness of the electoral incentive, institutional differences between the Senate and the House of Representatives—such as length of term and the distribution of power—can create differences in constituency behavior that result from the personal sacrifices associated with the pursuit of reelection; these sacrifices fall unevenly upon those serving in the individual chambers. For instance, if Senate incumbents have to share power with fewer competitors than representatives, senators have more to lose by spending their time hunting for votes back in their constituencies. The purpose of this inquiry is to examine the impact of institutional differences between the House and Senate on the images of legislators, and to do so by analyzing (1) voters' perceptions of

their representatives and senators and (2) the electoral significance of these perceptions. In the next section, we describe the types of images and perceptions legislators attempt to create in their personal interactions with constituents.

CONSTITUENCY MESSAGES

Senators and representatives believe that support at home is determined by how
they portray themselves as individuals, and they are not in the least reluctant to
manipulate these images. "So members of Congress go home," according to
Fenno (1978, p. 55), "to present themselves as a person and to win the accolade:
'he's a good man,' 'she's a good woman!'" In addition to developing constituency,
or "home," presentations, legislators justify and rationalize their Washington
activities, such as policy stands and legislative voting, to their constituents. Such
behaviors create images and messages—home-style messages—that leave the
expected imprint on voter perceptions of their legislators.

The general impression of the messages and images projected by legislators is
that they are undeniably self-serving. For example, John Saloma (1969) analyzed
printed matter sent to constituents by representatives and senators (newsletters,
news releases, form letters, and policy statements) during the first session of the
89th Congress. Saloma concluded that more than one-half of the representatives
(55 percent) and senators (63 percent) used their written communications to
enhance their own personal images and to advance their own private interests
(reelection). Home messages are not, however, entirely self-serving, since they
also meet legitimate representational responsibilities. Constituents expect to be
kept informed about issues that are relevant to their concerns, and incumbents
can oblige them by providing such information while also taking the opportunity
to further their own interests through these communications. Diana Yiannakis's
(1982) study of the newsletters and press releases produced by a sample of congressmen during the first six months of both the 94th and 95th Congresses
demonstrates exactly how adept incumbents are at fulfilling the dual objectives.
Yiannakis found that 42 percent of the paragraphs in newsletters and press releases were devoted to explaining the incumbent's stands on national issues, compared with less than 10 percent devoted to national or local information—an
amount of space smaller than that allocated to claiming credit for particularized
district benefits (11.6 percent). In short, although the messages are more than
mere propaganda, the clear intent is to present incumbent legislators in the best
possible light in order to impress constituents, and they appear to do just that.

Richard Fenno (1978) suggests that incumbent legislators emphasize three
kinds of personal characteristics in their constituency presentations: qualifica-
tion, identification, and empathy. In other words, every incumbent tries to create
the impression that he or she is qualified to hold office, identifies with the attitudes and beliefs of constituents, and empathizes with the problems of constituents. These images are transmitted at each and every opportunity that a

member has to communicate with potential voters (newsletters, constituent mailings, organized meetings in the constituency, personal visits), but the more personal the contact, the greater the probability that the message will be retained. A major objective of such presentations is to gain the *trust* of constituents:

> For their part, constituents must rely on trust. They must "accept on faith" that the congressman is what he says he is and will do what he says he will do. House members, for their part, are quite happy to emphasize trust. It helps to [allay] the uncertainties they feel about their relationship with their supportive constituencies. (Fenno 1978, p. 56)

Presentations are also useful in generating perceptions that the incumbent legislator is accessible to constituents:

> Constituents want *access* to their congressman. They—or better some sizable proportion of them—want to feel that they can reach their congressman, that he is or can be available to them, that they can—if they wish—see him, listen to him, talk to him. The congressman, for his part, satisfies this expectation when he presents himself to them. (Fenno 1978, p. 131)

Incumbents make considerable use of these presentations to convey the image that they care about constituents, their problems, and their frustrations.

Congressmen also *rationalize* their Washington activities to constituents, which Fenno (1978) refers to as "explanations of Washington activities." The actions of incumbents may be invisible to constituents, but the incumbents themselves are not. Constituents normally find legislators willing and prepared to explain their Washington activities, and their frequent appearances within the constituencies provide ample opportunities to question them about these activities. Explanations are the mechanisms through which incumbents describe, interpret, and justify legislative pursuits, especially the two major preoccupations of congressmen, power and policy (Fenno 1973). The pursuit of power, for example, can be justified by claiming that such influence is used to further district or state interests within Congress.[1]

Even though they probably have little to fear from electoral reprisals for one or two unpopular votes, incumbent congressmen also make a point of explaining their votes and policy positions to constituents. Since most constituents are often unaware of the specific votes of their elected leaders and tend to perceive them as voting in line with constituent sentiment (Parker 1981), explaining roll-call votes generally creates few problems for incumbents. A string of "wrong" votes could be troublesome (Kingdon 1973), but most members avoid creating such patterns by developing a good sense of the policy stands that are likely to produce adverse constituent reaction. Explanations are essential if a legislator hopes to have any maneuverability on the policy questions he or she votes on in Washington: "There are at most only a few policy issues on which representatives are constrained in their voting by the views of their reelection constituencies. . . . On the vast majority of votes, however, representatives can do as they wish—provided only that they can, when they need to, explain their votes to the satisfaction of interested constituents. The ability to get explanations accepted at home is, then, the essential underpinning of a member's voting leeway in Washington" (Fenno 1978, p. 151).

SENATE AND HOUSE DIFFERENCES

Members of Congress make presentations and offer explanations to justify their Washington behavior; hence, there should be strong parallels between the constituency *messages* of representatives and senators, and there is evidence of such similarities (Fenno 1978, 1982). Since there is no reason to believe that the reelection motive burns any less brightly in the hearts of either (representatives or senators), we also might expect senators to mirror the constituency behavior of representatives, especially given the enviable electoral security of House incumbents (Fiorina 1989). However, stark differences in constituency behavior do exist. Despite pronounced similarities in constituency messages and electoral motivations, there appear to be three differences in the constituency behavior, or "home styles," of representatives and senators. First, senators have less personal contact with their constituents: Representatives spend considerably more time visiting their districts than do senators (Parker 1986). Second, the six-year term of senators introduces slack into the representational relationship between senators and their constituents, thereby encouraging an electoral cycle—i.e., ebbs and flows—to state attentiveness (Taggert and Durant 1985). Finally, senators talk more about issues and policies than do representatives (Fenno 1982).

The assumption that legislators are motivated by reelection, common to many models of legislatures (Mayhew 1974; Fiorina 1977; Peltzman 1984; Stigler 1971), implies that these behavioral differences in constituency behavior are rooted in the varying electoral utility of certain activities to senators and representatives. That is, home-style messages may have less of an effect on the electoral fortunes of senators than representatives; as a result, senators would naturally be inclined to spend less time and effort promulgating the messages that representatives have found so electorally rewarding. This relationship, if correct, may occur because of the greater amount of quasi-free information available in Senate elections (Parker 1981) or because of the larger panoply of idiosyncratic forces that influence voting in Senate contests (see, for instance, Kostroski 1973).

Alternatively, it is conceivable that "home" behaviors may have an even greater impact on the electoral support of senators: Incumbents may be better able to differentiate themselves from other Senate candidates, for example, by adopting an "attentive home style," like representatives (i.e., extensive personal attention to constituency interests, needs, and problems). However, the greater opportunity for senators to exercise power in Washington increases the *costs* associated with an attentive home style. Senators exhibiting the same type of personal attention that representatives normally shower upon constituents must forgo opportunities to exercise legislative power—and these opportunities are considerably greater for senators than for representatives. About 50 percent of House Democrats in 1992, for example, chaired a standing committee or subcommittee; about 90 percent of Democrats in the Senate held similar positions. Hence, senators face higher opportunity costs and therefore might be expected to spend less time in their states. Not only does the six-year term make constituency attention less pressing for senators but the greater opportunities available to senators for national visibility, prominence, and influence may push constituency activities to a lower rung on the list of priorities. Neglect of "home" work may prove costly, as some senators acknowledge, but the draw of political power and all that it entails may be considered a reasonable trade-off. In this interpretation, senators don't engage in electorally useful activities because such activities interfere with other activities that senators find more personally rewarding.

There is another reason senators might avoid some constituency behaviors despite the electoral benefits sacrificed: Even if home-style messages have (potentially) a greater impact on the electoral support of senators, incumbents cannot engage in personal contact with a sufficient number of constituents to make the effort worthwhile; understandably, then, senators would choose to spend less time in their states. We disagree with this contention for two reasons. First, senators could spend more time cultivating constituents on a personal basis if they wanted to do so (i.e., there are no barriers to travel), but this would require them to trade off time in Washington for time spent in the state. The decision is a voluntary one and to a very real extent reveals the preferences of senators regarding attentive home styles. Indeed, as Fenno (1982, p. 35) pointed out, "[S]ome senators [do] adopt and maintain a home style calling for frequent personal appearances back home and much personal attentiveness to the electorate." For example, senators representing states in close proximity to the capital can be found traveling back and forth to their constituencies on almost a daily basis.[2] The decision as to how much time to devote to one's constituency therefore should not be construed as a trade-off between alternative vote-generating mechanisms. The forgone opportunity relates more to the attractive lawmaking endeavors associated with elite membership in a small but powerful decisionmaking body than it does to substitutable electioneering activities. When legislators are not at "home" visiting with constituents, they are normally in Washington engaged in lawmaking rather than preparing for the next campaign (although admittedly there are times when it is difficult to separate the two).

Second, although most of the gain in electoral support obtained through personal attention will be at the margin, we can easily underestimate the impact that intense personal commitments to a legislator might have on electoral support. Intense candidate preferences, for instance, may enable an outspoken senator to withstand the electoral costs often associated with the pursuit of controversial policies, or enlarge the core of his or her strongest supporters. Feelings of trust are one example of the positive effects that personal contact can induce (Parker and

Parker 1993). In short, we doubt that differences in the constituency attentiveness of senators and representatives, and therefore the images they transmit, are purely a result of the futility of the effort given the greater size of most Senate constituencies.

To summarize: Major differences in the constituency behavior (or home styles) of representatives and senators relate to the timing and amount of personal contact with constituents and to the degree to which senators talk and discuss political issues. These differences may stem from the higher opportunity costs that senators attach to constituency attention or the weaker effect that home-style presentations and activities have on the electoral fortunes of senators. We return to the issue of how best to explain why the home-style behaviors of senators differ from those of representatives in the concluding sections of the chapter.

Behavioral differences between the constituency behavior of senators and representatives can be expected to influence constituent perceptions. For example, lower levels of personal contact might make it more difficult for senators to create perceptions of attentiveness that can only be validated through large doses of such contact—through firsthand evidence that the legislator is looking after district interests: "Frequent home visits and frequent public appearances . . . do not necessarily indicate a service-oriented presentational style. But when coupled with a strong emphasis on casework—both by staff and in person—home trips and home appearances can be fairly construed as further evidence of the congressman's desire to help his constituents" (Fenno 1978, p. 106). As a consequence, the images of senators should be less colored by perceptions of constituency attentiveness. An electoral cycle in the behavior of senators implies that levels of personal attention will vary across a senator's term of office; hence, voter perceptions of senators should change with the electoral cycle. That is, senators who are *not* running for reelection should be perceived less in terms of constituency presentations (e.g., trustworthiness, attentiveness, accessibility) and explanations than are senators up for reelection.

Representatives, in contrast, should be perceived largely in these terms, and senators facing a reelection will tend to mirror the perceptions of representatives held by district voters—cultivating some of the same images that are so electorally rewarding for House members. Since senators talk more about issues than do representatives, the images of senators should have greater policy content. Few references to issues or policy decisions can be found in the images of representatives (Parker and Davidson 1979; Parker 1989), perhaps because they are more successful at steering clear of such potentially divisive forces. Avoiding issues seems to be a useful strategy, since policy positions frequently can cost as many votes as they gain: "Unless his district is homogeneous, a congressman will find his district divided on many major issues. Thus when he casts a vote, introduces a piece of nontrivial legislation, or makes a speech with policy content he will displease some elements of his district. . . . On such policy matters the congressman can expect to make friends as well as enemies" (Fiorina 1977, pp. 43–44).

In the next section, we examine the images of senators at different points in the electoral cycle and compare these images to voter perceptions of their representatives. These data are drawn from the open-ended likes and dislikes that constituents voice about both their representatives and senators; they were originally collected as a part of a three-wave study (covering the 1988, 1990, and 1992 elections) of citizen opinions toward representatives and senators conducted by the University of Michigan's Center for Political Studies under the auspices of their ongoing American National Election Studies (ANES) project.[3] In particular, we want to compare the likes and dislikes regarding senators elected in 1988 with those for senators elected in 1986 and 1990 to determine if voter images change with proximity to reelection; we also compare the likes and dislikes regarding incumbent senators facing election in 1988 and 1990 with those of incumbent representatives. If there is an electoral cycle to the behavior of senators, voter images of this latter group of senators should best approximate constituent images of representatives; senators at other points in the electoral cycle have less need to cultivate electorally rewarding constituent images.

IMAGES OF SENATORS AND REPRESENTATIVES

Since previous research already has provided a good understanding of the bases on which citizens evaluate House incumbents (see Parker and Davidson 1979; Parker 1981, 1989; Cain, Ferejohn, and Fiorina 1987), we concentrate instead on comparing the images of representatives to those of senators.[4] Table 12.1 presents the categorized likes and dislikes regarding U.S. representatives and senators in 1988 and 1990.[5] It is clear that the major difference in images relates to the greater saliency of constituency attentiveness in the images of representatives. In both surveys, voters mentioned constituency attention far more often in evaluations of their representative than of their senator. All other differences in images seem rather modest by comparison.

Is the greater saliency of constituency attention in voter images of representatives a function of differing constituent expectations? This seems doubtful. In Table 12.2 we report the marginal distributions to a question asking respondents what they feel is the most important activity for their representative and senator to pursue. There is a slight tendency for voters to expect their senators to be more involved in legislating, but the differences are too small to explain the greater saliency of constituency attention in the images of representatives.

A second important finding from Table 12.1 is the rather weak influence of political issues in the images of senators. Since senators talk so much more about political issues, we anticipated that their images would be far more laden with issue references, but the data suggest otherwise: Political issues arise no more frequently in evaluations of senators than they do in evaluations of representatives. Senators may talk more about political issues, but our findings raise the question, Who's listening? We doubt that this is just a matter of "rational ignorance," that is,

TABLE 12.1   Voter Images of Senators and Representatives, 1988 and 1990

Content of Likes/Dislikes [a]	1988 U.S. Representative		1990 U.S. Representative		1988 U.S. Senator		1990 U.S. Senator	
	Likes	Dislikes	Likes	Dislikes	Likes	Dislikes	Likes	Dislikes
Leadership	1%	5%	2%	2%	3%	4%	2%	4%
Experience	11	4	14	3	14	3	19	2
Constituency attention	28	11	27	11	17	9	18	12
Trust	10	12	10	19	15	12	13	14
Personal characteristics	10	6	11	6	11	5	9	5
Party	4	15	5	14	3	16	4	15
Ideology	9	14	6	10	11	17	7	13
Domestic issues	10	11	13	16	12	17	14	16
Foreign policy issues	1	3	1	3	2	4	2	4
Group support	9	8	7	5	7	6	5	5
Miscellaneous	7	10	4	11	6	7	6	8
Cumulative percent	100	99	100	100	101	100	99	98
N =	692	171	1,272	396	1,565	575	3,239	1,112

NOTE: Includes only House incumbents running for reelection in a state with a race involving a Senate incumbent.

[a] See Appendix for question wordings. Table entries show the percentage of all responses that fall into each category.

SOURCE: American National Election Studies, Senate Elections in Context 1988–1990 Pooled File (ICPSR study no. 9580).

TABLE 12.2 Most Important Activity for Senators and Representatives, 1988–1990

Most Important Activity[a]	Senators Percent	Representatives Percent
Helping people who have personal problems with the government	18%	23%
Working on national legislation in Congress	43	39
Making sure the constituency gets its fair share of government money	39	37
N =	3,213	3,197

[a]Question: "Which of the following three activities do you think is more important?" Table entries show the percentage of respondents who fall into each category.

SOURCE: American National Election Studies, Senate Elections in Context 1988–1990 Pooled File (ICPSR study no. 9580).

voters eschewing knowledge of political issues for less costly forms of political information (Downs 1957; Stigler 1971). If senators emphasized political issues in their constituency presentations, the greater availability of issue information should reduce the cost to constituents of obtaining such information—thereby making it cheaper to learn about where senators stand on the issues. Yet despite these seemingly lower costs, there is no evidence that issues are more significant to the images of senators than representatives.

An alternative explanation is that issues *don't* matter to most constituents! Morris Fiorina and Roger Noll (1979, p. 1093) argued that constituents recognize that the election of a legislator is not equivalent to the selection or implementation of a policy: "[I]n legislative elections citizens are choosing between platforms which will be realized only probabilistically. And in very large legislatures (especially in systems with independent executives) these probabilities will generally be very small." Rational behavior, they suggest, leads voters to prefer legislators who can reliably deliver district services. In short, rational voters eschew information about issues—not due to rational ignorance but because such information is less relevant to their own welfare (though groups may gain more from information about issues because their stakes in the passage of legislation are considerably higher; see Stigler 1971, Downs 1957).

Stephanie Larson's (1990) novel quasi-experimental study of the impact of information in altering a congressman's image is illustrative of just how insignificant issues may be to voters: Information was provided to a panel of survey respondents about the policy stands of their congressman, thereby enabling those who in an earlier interview thought they agreed with his or her policy positions (but did not) to correct their misperceptions; despite increased awareness of policy differences, respondents continued to maintain the same positive images of their congressman.

TABLE 12.3 Voter Images and the Electoral Cycle: Senators in 1990

Content of Likes/Dislikes[a]	Freshman Senators		Senators Reelected in 1984		Senators Reelected in 1986		Senators Reelected in 1988	
	Likes	Dislikes	Likes	Dislikes	Likes	Dislikes	Likes	Dislikes
Leadership	3%	3%	2%	4%	3%	5%	3%	5%
Experience	17	5	19	2	18	2	16	3
Constituency attention	18	9	18	12	19	11	17	10
Trust	13	17	13	14	13	16	15	16
Personal characteristics	7	3	9	5	9	4	10	4
Party	5	15	4	15	3	13	4	15
Ideology	7	10	7	13	8	16	9	15
Domestic issues	17	21	14	16	13	16	12	15
Foreign policy issues	2	4	2	4	2	4	2	4
Group support	7	7	5	5	5	5	7	5
Miscellaneous	3	5	6	8	5	8	5	9
Cumulative percent	99	99	99	98	98	100	100	101
N =	684	204	3,239	1,112	3,392	1,121	3,777	1,340

[a]See Appendix for question wordings. Table entries show the percentage of all responses that fall into each category.

SOURCE: American National Election Studies, Senate Elections in Context 1988–1990 Pooled File (ICPSR study no. 9580).

Finally, the images of senators reveal no evidence of an electoral cycle. In Table 12.3 we report the likes and dislikes for senators at different stages in their terms: freshmen and senators completing the second, fourth, and final year in their six-year term. We find no evidence that the images of senators differ according to stages in the Senate term: In 1990 freshmen senators were perceived in about the same way as more senior senators, and senators running for reelection were viewed no differently than those without a pressing reelection.

We offer two closely related explanations for the absence of an electoral cycle in the images of senators. First, since home styles, once established, are quite stable (Fenno 1978; Parker 1986), we can expect the messages delivered to remain more or less constant; hence, the images of senators also don't change much. Second, legislators may have uncovered a set of profitable, vote-generating messages and images. If so, we can expect senators to project these images on a repetitive basis, with the repetition producing stable images. These explanations are closely related, but a difference rests with the fact that in one case, home styles are stable and images change little over time; in the other instance, senators may behave differently during the course of their term of office, but they continuously project messages that have proven electoral value. We suspect that a blend of both explanations best accounts for the absence of a pronounced electoral cycle to the images of senators: Attentive home styles constantly reinforce voter perceptions and ensure some stability in images, and home messages with proven electoral value are continuously emphasized (e.g., constituency attention, trust) irrespective of behavior or changes in behavior.

Overall, then, issues seem to matter little to voters regardless of how much legislators talk about them. Some constituents may care about specific political issues, but neither policies nor ideologies dominate voter images of either senators or representatives. Not to belabor the obvious, these home-style messages seem to reflect very well upon both incumbent senators and representatives. We have suggested that the differences in constituent contact between the two account for the greater saliency of constituency attention in the images of representatives. Simply put, voters tend to see representatives as maintaining a closer relationship to constituents than do senators. In Table 12.4 we report the marginals for a question asking respondents how well they felt their representative and senators kept in touch with constituents. The existence of an election does slightly increase the perceived responsiveness of senators, but representatives are still viewed more frequently as doing a "very good" job at keeping in touch with voters.

Like many home-style messages, constituency attention requires some evidence to support the claim; otherwise, it is merely "cheap talk." Spending time in the district or state is a good way for a legislator to reveal his "true" preference for helping constituents and devoting time to constituency service. This is why we suspect that constituency attention is so dominant in the images of representatives: They spend inordinate amounts of *time* in their districts (Parker 1986). Senators spend less time in the state, and it appears to show in that constituency

TABLE 12.4   How Well Legislators "Keep in Touch" with Constituents, 1988–1990

How well incumbent keeps in touch with constituents[a]	House Incumbents	Senator Running for Reelection	Senate Race but Senator Is Not Running	No Senate Race
Very good	38%	28%	23%	20%
Fairly good	48	55	58	59
Fairly poor	10	11	13	14
Poor	5	7	6	7
N =	4,991	3,502	3,996	3,150

[a]Question: "How good a job would you say [name of representative or senator] does of keeping in touch with the people in your district/state?" Table entries show the percentage of respondents who fall into each category.

SOURCE: American National Election Studies, Senate Elections in Context 1988–1990 Pooled File (ICPSR study no. 9580).

attention is less central to their images. Images of being attentive are not merely a function of messages void of substantiating behavior. For example, in a preliminary analysis we found a positive relationship between (1) the actual number of days senators spent in the state between 1987 and 1990 and (2) the percentage of positive comments voters made in 1990 about their senators that referenced constituency service.

The major difference in voter perceptions of representatives and senators thus appears to reflect the level of personal attention paid to constituents. Assuming that members of each chamber are similarly motivated toward reelection, one might conclude that differences in constituent contact—and therefore in images of attentiveness—are related to the (presumably lesser) electoral payoff senators gain from spending time in their states. In short, a reputation for personal attention may be more electorally beneficial for representatives than senators. This question provides the focus for our next section, where we examine the degree to which voter perceptions have a differential impact on the electoral fortunes of incumbent representatives and senators.

HOW LEGISLATORS GENERATE ELECTORAL SUPPORT

The following analysis employs variables commonly used to explain voter choice, as well as the types of messages that incumbents deliver to their constituents in hopes of engendering electoral support. Our independent variables fall into two categories: major predictors of Senate and House elections uncovered in previous studies, and the imprint of home-style messages left on the consciousness of constituents—e.g., voting rationalizations, accessibility, trust, personal characteristics, attention to the needs of voters, experience, and policy positions. The dependent variable is whether a respondent voted for the incumbent senator or representative (coded 1 if yes and 0 otherwise). Once again, findings are based on the American National Election Studies 1991 Pooled Data set.

Major Sources of Electoral Support

Despite the paucity of research on Senate elections, several important explanatory variables can be identified. The ideological preferences of voters appear to be especially influential in Senate elections (Wright and Berkman 1986). We have measured such ideological effects by computing the numerical differences between respondent and incumbent placements (both determined by the respondents; see Appendix) on an ideological scale running from 1 (very liberal) to 7 (very conservative); this measure is referred to as *ideological congruence*. A closely related variable is designed to capture *partisan congruence*: whether respondents share the same party affiliation as an incumbent senator or representative. There is little argument that party identification—despite its declining influence since the 1960s—remains a major influence on congressional elections. We anticipate a positive sign between our measures of congruence and incumbent vote support.

The role of the economy in congressional elections remains intensely debated (see, for instance, Kramer 1971; Fiorina 1978; Erikson 1990; Jacobson 1990) and appears resilient to easy resolution. The issues raised in this debate are beyond the scope of this inquiry. Nevertheless, we incorporate a measure of perceived economic well-being in our analysis to assure that the effects of personal home-style messages are potent influences on congressional voting irrespective of the effects of economic conditions. We refer to this variable as *personal finances*; it is a summary indicator of a respondent's present financial state as compared to a year earlier. The final major predictor of congressional election outcomes is the popularity of the incumbent (*incumbent popularity*) among his or her constituents; the popularity of the incumbent may be the single best predictor of electoral support (Parker 1981; Cain, Ferejohn, and Fiorina 1987; Parker 1989). Our measures of incumbent popularity are the "feeling thermometers" included in ANES surveys.[6]

The Imprint of Home-Style Messages

We assume that the behavior of legislators is designed to project electorally rewarding messages; these messages, in turn, shape constituent perceptions of their legislator. Instead of examining the home-style messages that incumbents disseminate in their personal visits and through their communications with voters—an almost impossible task (see Fenno 1978, pp. 249–295)—we look for the imprint of these messages on voter images and perceptions of incumbent legislators. Fenno's work on home styles has richly described the messages *sent;* our interest here is with the messages *received* by constituents.

A particularly important home-style message that legislators try to communicate to constituents has to do with their accessibility. "The more accessible they are, House members believe, the more will their constituents be encouraged to feel that they can communicate with the congressman when and if they wish" (Fenno 1978, p. 240). Cain, Ferejohn, and Fiorina (1987, pp. 135–148) measure the perceived accessibility of legislators in terms of how helpful a legislator is thought to have been if the respondent sought help in dealing with a problem. We employ the same variable (*perceived accessibility*[7]) and also introduce a second measure—the extent to which legislators are seen as *keeping in touch* with constituents.[8]

A closely related message is that constituents should contact their legislator to voice their concerns, policy interests, and problems. According to Fenno (1978, pp. 238–239), "Every congressman's home style is a blend of two-way and one-way communication, of efforts to listen to and talk to supportive constituents and of efforts to gain visibility. . . . House members do their best, of course, to transform name recognition into two-way communication of some sort—a request for action from an individual or group, for instance. . . . 'If you are visible to people and you take care of their problems,' Congressman K sums up, 'then you give them good government and you stay in office.'" Our measure of this "two-way communication" is the number of personal contacts that a respondent reports having had with the incumbent legislator—e.g., personally met, attended a meeting where the incumbent spoke, or talked to someone in the congressional office (*personal contact*).

Congressmen spend considerable time in their districts justifying to their constituents what they do and have done in Washington (Fenno 1978). "In justifying their policy decisions," Fenno writes, "representatives sometimes claim that their policy decisions follow not what they want but what their constituents want" (p. 160). In this way, incumbents legitimate their votes. If such arguments are successful, voters should see little discrepancy between their own policy views and the voting decisions of their legislator. We therefore expect that one message which should leave an imprint on the minds of voters is that the incumbent's voting record to a large degree reflects constituent opinion. We measure this effect through an item asking respondents the extent to which they agree or disagree with the way the incumbent has generally voted on legislation in Washington (*perceived voting agreement*).[9]

The remaining home-style (message) variables are drawn from the open-ended questions eliciting voter likes and dislikes of incumbent representatives and senators (see Appendix). These likes and dislikes have been categorized and are used to represent the home-style messages delivered by congressmen (Fenno 1978, pp. 54–61). As described earlier, these presentations emphasize an incumbent's *experience, personal characteristics, constituency attentiveness, trust,* and (domestic and foreign) *policy positions*.[10]

TABLE 12.5 Electoral Effects of Home-Style Messages, 1988–1990

Variable	House		Senate	
	Logit Estimates[a]	*Probability*[b]	*Logit Estimates*[a]	*Probability*[b]
Year	−.20 (−1.24)	.02	.19 (.68)	.01
Personal finances	.06 (.61)	.006	.004 (.02)	.003
Ideological congruence	.33[c] (4.81)	.03	.05 (.04)	.0004
Partisan congruence	1.95[c] (10.21)	.17	1.85[c] (6.04)	.15
Incumbent popularity	.05[c] (11.21)	.005	.05[c] (6.32)	.004
Presentations: Perceived accessibility	.43[d] (1.97)	.04	.20 (.49)	.02
Trust	.44[d] (1.86)	.04	.52 (1.58)	.04
Personal contact	.12 (1.48)	.01	1.65[c] (8.20)	.13
Keeping in touch	.09 (.70)	.008	.51 (1.26)	.04
Experience	.34 (1.21)	.03	−.47 (−1.23)	.04
Personal characteristics	.34 (1.16)	.03	.35 (.80)	.03
Constituency attention	.27 (1.60)	.02	−.45 (−1.67)	.03

(continued)

The Electoral Effects of Constituent Perceptions

Table 12.5 presents the statistical (logit) estimates predicting incumbent support in House and Senate elections. Logit analysis is a maximum likelihood estimation technique appropriate for the analysis of binary (either-or) dependent variables. It is based on the cumulative logistic frequency function, so logit estimates can be derived using most scientific calculators. The logit coefficients presented in Table 12.5 are not easily interpreted. To facilitate the reader's understanding of the meaning of these coefficients, we have calculated probability scores for each coef-

TABLE 12.5 (continued)

Variable	House		Senate	
	Logit Estimates[a]	Probability[b]	Logit Estimates[a]	Probability[b]
Explanations:				
Perceived voting agreement	.46[c] (2.90)	.04	.97[c] (3.89)	.08
Domestic policy positions	.57[d] (2.47)	.05	1.09[c] (2.97)	.08
Foreign policy positions	−.12 (−.20)	.01	−.18 (−.38)	.01
Constant	−2.38[c] (5.72)	.20	−5.76[c] (7.60)	.46
N =	1,818		863	
Summary statistics:				
Chi-square	947.08		661.43	
Degrees of freedom	15 (p <.001)		15 (p < .001)	
Percent improvement over chance	57%		68%	

[a]t-values given in parentheses
[b]change in the likelihood of a vote for the incumbent being produced by a one-unit change in the independent variable
[c]p ≤ .01
[d]p ≤ .05

SOURCE: American National Election Studies, Senate Elections in Context 1988–1990 Pooled File (ICPSR study no. 9580).

ficient. The probabilities represent the average change in the Z-score (for the value of the dependent variable) for a logistic probability curve. Larger probabilities indicate that the variable with a higher probability has a greater effect on the dependent variable than does an independent variable with a lower probability. To draw a comparison from the table, the 0.17 probability associated with partisan congruence indicates that it has a greater influence than does the 0.03 probability associated with ideological congruence. Although each coefficient's effect is statistically significant (that is, we can place faith in the result as being nonrandom with a low likelihood of error), being of the same party as an incumbent House member is a better predictor of one's voting for him or her than is the fact of sharing an ideological affinity with the same incumbent.

As expected, the major predictors of voting—partisan congruence and incumbent popularity—are highly significant. Yet home-style images also influence electoral support in both House and Senate races, i.e., they have an undeniable impact on congressional races that cannot be accounted for by common predictors of electoral choice. Not all of the home-style images influence voting in congressional elections, however, and some influence voting only in House races. Two home-style messages leave their marks on voters in *both* House and Senate elections: position-taking on domestic issues, and perceived voting agreement with constituents. The significance of these messages on voting in both House and Senate elections testifies to the importance of "explanations" in generating support.

In House elections, two additional home-style messages—perceived accessibility and trust—also influence voting decisions, though these variables have no significant effects on voting in Senate contests. It is tempting to conclude that since perceptions of accessibility and trust are of little value to those voting in Senate elections, senators naturally eschew the demanding personal contact that such messages necessitate to be considered credible. This could then explain why constituency attentiveness is less central to images of senators and why they spend less time than House incumbents in their states personally cultivating constituents. We do not consider this explanation to be defensible, however, since Table 12.5 shows that there is an undeniable electoral benefit to personal contact with constituents for senators!

If personal contact has a significant positive effect on voting for Senate incumbents, why do senators receive so little benefit from perceptions of accessibility and trust—home-style messages generated largely through personal contact? We suspect that these messages receive less weight in the voters' calculus in Senate elections precisely because they are heavily dependent upon personal contact to be considered credible. Simply put, messages promoting perceptions of access and trust necessitate physical evidence of attention (like personal contact) before voters will treat them as valid; because senators spend less time in their states than representatives, many voters discount these messages in their voting decisions or dismiss them as "cheap talk."

We might understand the reluctance of senators to engage in extensive personal contact if the electoral payoffs were insignificant, but this does not seem to be the case. In fact, incumbent senators actually reap *greater* benefits than House incumbents from certain home-style behaviors. For instance, explanations of Washington activity could be delivered through the mail, but personal presentations seem a better (if not more costly) mechanism—and the electoral payoff for senators (in terms of probability of voting for the incumbent) is almost double that achieved through the same messages in House elections. The most glaring example of the significance of personal contact is that such contact increases the probability of voting for the incumbent to a greater degree in Senate, not House, elections: Personal contact is a good way for Senate incumbents to distinguish themselves, and to increase the probability of voter support. In sum, there is no evidence that differences in the home-style behavior of senators and representatives are based on important differences in electoral payoffs.

CONCLUSION

We began our inquiry by suggesting that, despite similarities, there are three major differences in the home styles of senators and representatives: (1) slack in the representational relationship between senators and their constituents, induced by a six-year term, introduces an electoral cycle into the constituency behavior of senators; (2) senators spend less time than representatives in their constituencies; and (3) senators talk more about policy than do representatives. Only the behavioral differences in personal contact appear to make much of a difference in voter perceptions. For example, we found no evidence of an electoral cycle in constituent perceptions; the images of senators at different points in their terms of office show few noticeable differences, and the images of senators almost mirror those of representatives in terms of the saliency of specific perceptions (e.g., trust). The greater penchant for senators to discuss policy while in their states might be expected to increase the saliency of issue content in senator images; however, we found no evidence that issues are more salient in the images of senators than representatives. The images of senators and representatives are, in fact, similar in all but one respect: the saliency of constituency attention.

This discrepancy in the images of senators and representatives, we believe, is rooted in an important difference between the constituency behavior of senators and representatives: Senators spend less time in their constituencies than representatives, and this shows up in the images of senators as being less attentive. In other words, representatives behave differently toward their constituents than senators—especially in the level of personal attention they give to constituent affairs, i.e., representatives tend to have more frequent personal contact. This difference seems to have no electoral rationale, since constituency attention is a critical factor that helps shape voter decisions in *both* House and Senate elections. Of course, we might expect senators to spend less time in their constituencies if the home behaviors displayed by House incumbents were less effective in producing electoral support in higher-stakes Senate contests. Yet our results suggest that senators gain even greater electoral benefit from spending time at home.

We suspect that senators ignore the electoral payoff derived from extensive personal contact because of the higher opportunity costs associated with membership in the Senate. That is, senators know that time spent in the state is worth votes, but they are nonetheless unwilling to take time away from their pursuits in Washington. Elections may be the proximate goal to the realization of other more personal goals, but there is obviously more of a trade-off between reelection and the pursuit of more personal (private) interests than we previously suspected.

Implications

Our political system fosters representational linkages between constituents and legislators through the electoral process. This characteristic of American politics promotes the easy conclusion that legislators are preoccupied with getting re-elected, but the findings presented suggest that such an inference may be unwarranted. Undoubtedly, most legislators relish—if not cherish—reelection, but when the search for votes interferes with their pursuit of other things (e.g., power, lawmaking) that make the job so exceptionally attractive in the first place, they may prefer to sacrifice or reduce their vote-generating activities. One feature of congressional service that members find particularly appealing has to do with the amount of "slack" they enjoy, that is, the freedom and leeway to pursue their own personal or private interests. For example, legislators are relatively free from effective monitoring because of the costs involved in scrutinizing the actions of individual leaders (Parker 1992). Those with the greatest interest in monitoring their behavior (the local media) do not normally possess the resources to do so, and those with access to such resources (the national media) have little interest in following the actions of any but the most powerful members of Congress. This gives every legislator considerable discretion in their Washington activity.

Particular institutional conditions also may afford legislators more latitude in their activities; for instance, infrequent elections establish longer terms of office and thereby reduce the threat posed by potential challengers. Legislative rules granting considerable power to individual lawmakers (e.g., the filibuster) have a similar effect by increasing each member's share of institutional power. Under such conditions, legislators may find reelection only one of several competing demands—which forces them to weigh the costs of reelection not merely in terms of votes lost or gained through various constituency activities but against what might have to be sacrificed to obtain voter support. Time cultivating constituents earns votes but it also takes time away from other intralegislative behaviors that some members enjoy more. This may explain why senators usually spend less time with constituents: They have more to sacrifice than representatives because they possess greater individual power. Senators could possibly rival the electoral safety enjoyed by House members by imitating their actions in the constituency, but our findings suggest that they fail to do so. Constituents recognize these differences between senators and representatives (i.e., the latter's greater degree of attentiveness) and seem quite willing to reward senators who mirror the appropriate behavior. They are unlikely, however, to be persuaded by home-style messages that deviate from actual behavior (e.g., trips to the district or state).

Reelection is an important motive governing the actions of both representatives and senators, but the differing "personal" costs legislators incur in building safe election margins are seldom given much consideration in accounting for institutional differences in representational (e.g., constituency) behavior. The results presented here indicate that where there is slack in the representational linkage between legislators and voters due to such factors as infrequent (but probable) election, legislator behavior will be less governed by the desire to obtain additional votes and more influenced by what legislators must sacrifice to gain electoral support—the opportunity cost of constituency attention.

In effect, senators do *not* appear to be the wholly reelection-motivated caricatures that frequently emerge from analyses of legislators. Our evidence suggests that senators, faced with relatively infrequent elections, devote less attention to making contacts with constituents than do House members. Perhaps senators are aware of the costs and the benefits of particular behaviors and seek to maximize their use of time and the perquisites of office not merely to gain reelection but to engage in other governance activities as well.

Contractual Problems in Representational Relationships

Representation can be characterized in terms of an implicit contractual relationship between leaders and those being led, with voters hiring (electing) an agent to advance and watch over their interests in Washington. As straightforward as this contractual relationship might appear, however, it is complicated by the fact that agents have incentives to pursue their own private agendas rather than the preferences of voters. If voters are themselves self-interested, can we expect our agents to be selfless? This "agency" problem, as it is called by economists, is exacerbated by two other problems that plague all types of contracts: the lack of observability (or the costly nature of monitoring) and the existence of contingencies normally too numerous to anticipate or specify in advance.

The high cost associated with monitoring (e.g., recording roll-call votes, observing behavior on the floor, obtaining expert evaluations) means that the actions of most legislators escape the scrutiny of voters. The existence of contingencies makes it almost impossible to distinguish claims of pragmatism from a careless trampling of constituents' interests; multiple contingencies allow legislators to break campaign promises or commitments by claiming that circumstances warrant reconsideration, that unforeseen events have complicated the issue, or that an action was the best that could be accomplished. Costly monitoring and the existence of contingencies contribute to slack in the representational relationship and assure legislators a degree of freedom and leeway to pursue their own preferences. In the end, voters must rely on what legislators tell them about their actions in Washington and—for the most part—have little alternative but to accept the explanations given. The vehicle through which voters acquire such information is ultimately connected to the home styles of legislators and the messages they disseminate.

Judging from our analysis of voter images of representatives and senators, these messages tend to quiet the concerns of voters by generating unusually positive impressions of an incumbent's performance in office; the electoral effects of the messages demonstrate their effectiveness in this regard. Legislators promulgate messages that induce voters to believe that constituents' wishes are being followed, whether or not that truly is the case. Since voters have little information about their legislator's Washington behavior, they are forced to form their impressions on the basis of information provided directly or indirectly (e.g., through local press reports) by the individual whose actions are being evaluated. Not surprisingly, the information is usually positive—and so are the images of legislators held by most constituents.

Such a state of affairs engenders considerable discretion for legislators to pursue their own private interests, thereby impairing the contract between representatives and the represented. Although discretion might be used to advance altruistic causes rather than the parochial interests of constituents (therefore benefiting society as a whole), it also renders the representational contract vulnerable to opportunistic exploitation. Legislators might use their discretion, for example, to vote in a manner that is antagonistic to the interests of district voters but that can be easily rationalized to an uninformed electorate; or they might use their positions to obtain favors at the expense of society or constituents. Like most contracts, the one between voters and the leaders they elect leaves ample opportunity for postcontractual opportunism.

If the information received by most constituents is largely a result of the home-style messages of legislators, then it is likely that violations of the implicit contract between voters and their representatives will be difficult to detect and, even if uncovered, effectively rationalized. In his conclusion to Chapter 1, Stephen Craig suggests that the appearance of "broken contracts" between leaders and the led has impelled voters in the 1990s to do "whatever they can to keep elected officials on a short leash." Given the problems inherent in ensuring contractual performance, who could really argue with this sentiment? We could only add that our findings question the ability of voters to know the length of the leash! Let us not forget that even in the volatile political climate of 1994, a very high percentage of congressional incumbents who sought reelection (all Republicans and most Democrats) were returned to office.

NOTES

1. Two examples of how power can be used to further constituency interests are the efforts of former Senator Mack Mattingly (D–Ga.), who placed language in appropriations legislation to prevent the Forest Service from closing a ranger station in his home state; and Robert Byrd (D–W.V.), who took similar action to prevent AMTRAK (the federally funded national railroad corporation) from terminating a money-losing, long-distance passenger line through West Virginia (see Fitzgerald and Lipson 1984, pp. 43, 66).

2. Proximity to Washington is not the only variable that conditions the attentiveness of senators. Mark Andrews (R–N.D.), for instance, maintained the same level of constituency presence—i.e., a very attentive home style—during his term in the Senate as he had while serving in the House of Representatives (Fenno 1992, p. 185).

3. The ANES surveys are made available by the Inter-University Consortium for Political and Social Research. Data used here were collected in 1988 and 1990 (see the Senate Elections in Context 1988–1990 Pooled File, ICPSR study no. 9580); the 1988 uni-

verse included all individuals of voting age before or on November 8, 1988, and residing in a house with a telephone in the fifty states, and the 1990 universe contained all persons of voting age on or before November 6, 1990, and otherwise conforming to the strictures for 1988. See the Appendix to this book for question wordings.

4. The content of popular evaluations of representatives tends to give greater weight to their personal characteristics, constituency service, and honesty; infrequently mentioned are the party affiliation, ideology, and issue positions of incumbent members. These evaluations are, on balance, decidedly positive.

5. These are based on questions similar to the standard ANES open-ended likes and dislikes regarding parties and candidates (see Appendix). For the congressional surveys used here, respondents were asked their feelings about the Democratic and Republican candidates for both House and Senate seats, and about incumbent senators not currently running for reelection.

6. Variables described in this and the preceding paragraph are outlined in the Appendix to this volume.

7. Respondents who indicated that either they or a family member had ever contacted their senator or representative "to seek help on a problem you had" were subsequently asked "How satisfied were you with the response—very satisfied, somewhat satisfied, not very satisfied, or not at all satisfied?"

8. As in Table 12.4, respondents were asked the following: "How good a job would you say Representative/Senator ... does of keeping in touch with the people in your district/state—does s/he do a very good, fairly good, fairly poor, or poor job of keeping in touch with the people in this district/state?"

9. The question reads as follows: "Now we would like your opinion about the way Senator/Representative ... has voted on bills that have come up in the U.S. Senate/House of Representatives in Washington. Would you say that you have generally agreed with the way s/he has voted on bills, agreed and disagreed about equally, generally disagreed, or haven't you paid much attention to this?"

10. Each of these variables is constructed in the same manner: number of likes mentioned concerning a particular incumbent attribute minus number of dislikes mentioned concerning that same attribute. For example, the number of dislikes voiced by a respondent about his or her incumbent's constituency attentiveness is subtracted from the number of likes mentioned by the same individual about attentiveness. See Parker (1989) for a discussion and description of the items used to measure constituent trust and Parker and Parker (1993) for an analysis of the dimensionality of the trust items, as well as their relationship to personal contact with one's representative. Some of the assessments used in Table 12.5 include trust (honest, sincere, doesn't use office for personal benefit, has kept campaign promises), experience (experienced, inexperienced, not qualified for the job), personal characteristics (intelligent, safe, likable, democratic), constituency attention (keeps people well informed, helps people, represents the views of the district or state, has helped the district or state economy), domestic policy positions (relating to such policy areas as government economic controls, welfare and poverty problems, Social Security and pensions, unemployment compensation, and aid to education), and foreign policy positions (relating to such policy areas as foreign aid, strong vs. weak military position, Russia, Eastern Europe, and Latin America). See Parker and Parker (1993) for a fuller description. Also note that the variable "year" in Table 12.5 has been coded 1 if 1990, 0 if otherwise.

13

From Ward Heelers to Public Relations Experts: The Parties' Response to Mass Politics

PAUL S. HERRNSON
KELLY D. PATTERSON
JOHN J. PITNEY JR.

Just as democracy thrives on the free flow of ideas, political parties thrive when they control resources needed to communicate those ideas to voters. In the days of the old-fashioned political machines, parties influenced the flow of political information. Ward heelers, precinct captains, and other party functionaries kept close watch over their neighborhoods. Most of these exchanges took place on a personal level, with a member of the party organization acting as an intermediary for the exchange of political information. The emergence of mass society, however, contributed to the decline of political machines and to the rise of a candidate-centered system. The replacement of tight-knit immigrant communities by suburban housing developments deprived political machines of much of their popular base. Political reforms also weakened the machine's role in the political system. These changes produced a political era marked by low levels of partisanship among voters and reduced party cohesion in Congress, and they ushered local party organizations to the periphery of the electoral process.

Political parties have sought to adapt to the new era in several ways. Much of the adaptation has taken place at the national party organizations, with the parties' national, congressional, and senatorial campaign committees becoming more fiscally sound, more organizationally sophisticated, and more adept at campaigning and disseminating a national message (Herrnson 1988). Other changes have taken place inside government—for example, members of Congress have altered their parties' leadership structures in such a manner as to allow them to send more thematic messages to the general public. As a result, unlike the personal interaction that once characterized relations between party leaders and rank-and-file members, communications today between the two groups tend to be elite-dominated and impersonal. They reflect the adjustments that parties needed to make in order to regain influence in a system of mass politics.[1]

This chapter focuses on the parties' response to the emergence of a mass society and to the rise of candidate-centered elections (also see Chapter 5). We begin by sketching the roles that parties played during their heyday and the reasons for their subsequent decline. Next we examine the adaptation of party organizations in Washington, D.C. and, in particular, the strengthening of party leadership organizations in Congress. We then close our discussion with an assessment of the implications of these changes for the party system.

THE RISE AND FALL OF MACHINE POLITICS

The rise of the urban political machine marked the organizational heyday of political parties.[2] Local political machines were the most visible form of party organization in the United States at the turn of the century and the organization that rank-and-file members were most likely to know and encounter personally in their everyday lives. The structure of machines ensured tight control over an array of political and economic resources, with both types of resources being combined through a system of governmental *patronage* to create and maintain an effective political organization.[3]

Specifically, the party dispensed resources that voters and candidates needed. Party activists reported voters' needs and wishes to party bosses, then reported the bosses' responses back to voters. Most of these exchanges focused on government jobs, contracts, or other personal needs. Machines disbursed jobs, construction contracts and licenses, assistance with governmental authority, and a host of other benefits that helped supporters make their way in the world. In return, supporters accepted the machine's guidance when casting their ballots. The machine's ability to collect personal information about citizens' wants and needs, to distribute political information about its candidates, and to orchestrate the grand exchange of patronage for votes was a major source of its power.

Another related source of power was the machine's control over the resource most coveted by aspiring politicians: a place on the ballot under the party label. Party nominations were given out through caucuses or conventions whose main participants were the party leaders themselves. Any politician interested in elective office first had to gain the support of these leaders in order to win the nomination. Moreover, as one party or the other was dominant in many areas, receiving the nomination often was tantamount to getting elected. In return for their support, of course, the bosses demanded that those whom they had worked to elect follow their directions on matters of public policy deemed important by the machine. This second exchange completed the circle that formed the machine's power. As the principal intermediaries between citizens and their elected officials, political parties could set the political agenda and exercise tremendous influence over the entire governmental process.

Under machine politics, then, meaningful participation was primarily reserved to people who worked within the party. Power rested in the hands of local party chairmen (or "bosses") and flowed downward to the various ward heelers and precinct captains. Both voters and candidates depended on the machine to guide their political participation, and their choices were controlled mainly by the party organization itself. There was little political influence left to those outside the party. During election season, bosses and their assistants told the party's "benefi-ciaries" how to vote—thereby leaving voters connected to the political process primarily through the party organization.

This structure of participation had certain advantages over a system of mass politics. First, the machine enabled voters to have *direct personal contact* with the party organization. The relationships needed to make the efforts of the party effective ensured that most people would not feel politically isolated. Rather, politics often was symbolized by a precinct leader or ward heeler who made it his business to know the neighborhood and call regularly upon constituents; such personal contact was important to the political socialization of individuals, as well as to the mobilization of voters. Second, political machines engendered *party loyalty* among voters. Although this loyalty rested on personal relationships, it also brought some stability to elections for national, state, and local offices. Finally, the system had *accountability*. The bonds between voters, elected officials, and party leaders could not be easily ignored because repercussions could swiftly follow. Jobs could be terminated, candidates dumped from the party ticket, or other punishments meted out to voters and politicians who failed to support their party.

Reasons for the decline of political machines are well known. Progressive reforms designed to clean up the operation of government were adopted, including civil service and other measures at the state and local levels that deprived machines of their most potent resources.[4] Individuals who associated with the machine for economic benefits no longer needed to remain loyal, and popular support evaporated as the party gradually lost control over many economic opportunities. Poor urban immigrants who had long been the machine's core constituency were replaced by more affluent, second- and third-generation Americans who began to move to the suburbs and adopt political values that were often very different from those held by prior generations. Further, the widespread adoption of the direct primary deprived parties of the resource that was the basis for most politicians' loyalties: the party label. Without the ability to control access to the party label, the party organization had trouble garnering long-term commitments from political activists. The result was that parties became much weaker vis-à-vis the candidate-centered and issue-based organizations that arose in the latter half of the twentieth century.

Nowhere were the weaknesses of parties so evident as in the process that evolved during the 1970s and 1980s for selecting presidential candidates—the parties' most visible standard-bearers. With presidential primaries being few in number (and often nonbinding), nominations of the machine period were largely handled at the conventions. Here, state and national party leaders evaluated candidates and selected the person they believed would have the best chance of uniting the party and leading it to victory in November. Due to the "closed" nature of conventions, there had to be substantial agreement among the party's various factions (especially the Democrats, who until 1936 required a two-thirds vote of all delegates before a candidate was designated). Party leaders thus were routinely involved in both drafting the platform and choosing the nominee—and given leaders who cared about the party's electoral performance and policy positions, it was rare for anyone to be selected who offered programs that differed sharply from the overall party line. Indeed, for a candidate to capture the nomination, he generally had to demonstrate that his issue agenda conformed to the policy preferences of the party's dominant wing. Such leadership control of presidential nominations obviously has disappeared since the 1960s (see Crotty and Jackson 1985).

With organizational decline also taking place at the state and local levels, parties were left with increasingly skeletal structures. Unable to monitor and control access to the party label and without patronage to induce loyalty among candidates or voters, the parties were severely constrained in their efforts to mediate the flow of political information and to manage their public images. In contemporary American politics, control of information rests mainly with the candidates themselves. No longer subject to the scrutiny of party leaders, candidates manufacture their own electoral coalitions using a broad assortment of sophisticated campaign technologies—e.g., mass media, direct mail, polling, etc.—that allow them to appeal directly to voters without having to rely on traditional forms of party organization. According to Frank Sorauf (1980, p. 451), political parties in the United States "historically dealt largely in nonfinancial resources and have never successfully made the transition to the cash economy of the new campaign politics." This caused serious problems as the labor-intensive forms of campaigning that parties performed so ably in the past proved to be less effective in a candidate-centered system. At the same time, however, U.S. parties (most noticeably at the national level) have in recent years moved away from their traditional emphasis on a personal style of politics and sought to become important electoral players by embracing techniques better suited to today's mass society. In the following section, we examine some of the ways in which both the Republicans and the Democrats have adapted to the changing environment of American politics.

POLITICAL PARTIES IN THE AGE OF PUBLIC RELATIONS

The decline of party organizations essentially meant that the parties' images were left to be defined by candidates who won presidential (and other) nominations. After choosing George McGovern as its presidential candidate in 1972, for example, the Democratic Party was burdened with a liberal, countercultural image that persisted for several years—though the election of Jimmy Carter in 1976 and, sixteen years later, of Bill Clinton did help somewhat to offset the McGovern legacy. The fact that nominees have come to define their party's image presents special problems for the party out of power, since it is difficult to replace the image created by an unsuccessful standard-bearer with a new one. More generally, the decentralized structure of U.S. parties and the failure of a candidate system to engender loyalty among successful congressional, state, and local politicians make it difficult for *either* party to develop or communicate a theme that is coherent, consistent, and popular with a diverse body of voters. Yet the goal of creating a thematic and coherent message has nonetheless taken hold and led to a number of recent changes in the parties' extragovernmental organizations and leadership structures in Congress.

The Republican Response

Seldom has a party needed a coherent message more than the Republicans in the late 1970s. Bad things had happened during their last turn in the White House— e.g., the Watergate scandal, the oil shortage of 1973, and the worst recession in decades. After voters punished the GOP with deep congressional losses in 1974 and President Ford's defeat in 1976, some political analysts wondered whether the party might go the way of the Whigs. Then came the Carter administration. Although President Carter had more early successes than most people remember, his fortunes plunged with the Iranian oil shock of 1979, which led to long gasoline lines, economic stagnation, and so-called political malaise. In this setting, Republicans could have resurfaced merely by saying, "We're not Carter."

But if a party wants lasting success—not just survival—it needs more than a negative message. In the late 1970s, the Republican National Committee (RNC), the National Republican Senatorial Committee (NRSC), and the National Republican Congressional Committee (NRCC) all increased their fundraising and logistical support for the party's candidates.[5] A key aspect of this resurgence was RNC chairman Bill Brock's efforts to make the GOP "the party of ideas." Brock launched *Commonsense*, "a Republican journal of opinion and thought," and set up advisory councils where experts worked on policy ideas such as supply-side economics (Klinkner 1991).

The congressional GOP, especially on the House side, also was reviving at about the same time. Despite the party's modest gain of fifteen House seats in 1978, thirty-five freshmen accounted for nearly one-fourth of its total strength. Like the Democratic class of 1974, elected in the wake of Watergate, these newcomers would leave a mark on their party: As one of their class officers they chose a former history professor from Georgia named Newt Gingrich, a fiercely partisan battler who eventually went on (in January 1995) to become House Speaker. Soon after taking office, they worked with Representatives Jack Kemp (R–N.Y.) and

David Stockman (R–Mich.) to devise tax and spending cuts that foreshadowed the Reagan economic program. They also joined with sympathetic senior members in an informal group known as the Project Majority Task Force, which tried to breed new ideas for winning control of the House (Pitney 1988). Partially as a result of task force discussions, the RNC and NRCC made "generic" television spots in 1980, urging citizens, "Vote Republican, For a Change."

After Ronald Reagan clinched the Republican presidential nomination that year, Kemp proposed Governing Team Day—an event where Reagan would appear with GOP House and Senate candidates to make specific policy pledges. The Reagan camp balked at the policy language proposed by House Republicans, however, so when the event took place in the fall, the Governing Team statement had evolved from a detailed manifesto into a vague litany of principles. Gingrich, who had organized the event, said that it was a public relations success and a policy disappointment. But if Capitol Hill's GOP militants felt dismay in September, they felt joy in November. Reagan's election, the party's takeover of the Senate, and big gains in House races all convinced Republicans that their hour had come round at last. For much of 1981, the optimism appeared justified as GOP congressional unity helped President Reagan enact a large portion of his economic program.

The moment of good feelings passed quickly. A harsh recession pushed the unemployment rate into double digits and scuttled GOP hopes of winning a House majority. On the Senate side, Finance Committee chairman Bob Dole (R–Kan.) saw that the economic downturn was swelling the deficit, so he called for a tax increase. "Knowing that our ability to govern was being tested," he said, he rallied other members of the GOP Senate majority to sell the White House on his idea (Dole and Dole 1988, p. 205). House militants saw the proposal as a betrayal of supply-side principles.[6] At the urging of Richard Darman and other aides, Reagan sided with Dole; the White House even got the Republican National Committee to sponsor a public relations campaign in favor of the tax increase. With the passage of the Tax Equity and Fiscal Responsibility Act of 1982, the Republican Party's supply-side message lost much of its punch (Connelly and Pitney 1994).

A GOP White House proved both an asset and a liability to congressional Republicans. On the one hand, President Reagan and executive officials helped them with campaign fundraising, constituency service, and policy information. On the other hand, the Republican administration curbed their flexibility on issues. As Dole's comment suggested, Senate Republicans saw their job as working with the president to govern the country. The Senate Republican Policy Committee, which had mounted a strong public challenge to the Carter administration's foreign policy (Bailey 1988, p. 88), now took a back seat to the standing committees and generally limited itself to reiterating White House positions (Connelly 1991).

In the House, by contrast, many Republicans thought that breaking free of their "permanent minority" status was as important as backing the administration. In 1983, some of the more militant members formed something called the Conservative Opportunity Society (COS), a group devoted to confronting the Democrats and sharpening the partisan debate. COS came to birth at an opportune moment: C-SPAN had begun live gavel-to-gavel coverage of the House in 1979, and by 1983, the expansion of cable service had made C-SPAN available to more than 14 million households—a figure that would double by the end of the decade (Lamb 1988, p. 384). COS could now use floor debate and "special orders" speeches as a way of bypassing the normal legislative process and speaking directly to the voters.[7]

This strategy had three notable consequences. First, it occasioned harsh partisanship on the House floor as Democrats and Republicans frequently exchanged rhetorical fire. Second, it encouraged other members to exploit C-SPAN coverage and helped persuade senators to open their own chamber to the television cameras. Third, with even a group of lowly freshmen showing that they could hold center stage before millions of viewers, it opened the way for a wide variety of party voices on both sides of the aisle. Yet the mid-1980s ultimately were a frustrating time for Republicans. Instead of seeking a partisan victory by running against the Democratic Congress as well as against presidential nominee Walter Mondale, the Reagan campaign in 1984 worked for a personal triumph by downplaying party labels and ideological issues alike. As a result, the GOP just held its own in the Senate and gained only a handful of seats in the House. Even worse, Reagan's mostly issueless campaign theme (Morning Again in America; see Diamond and Bates 1992) prevented Republicans from plausibly claiming a policy mandate for the president's second term.

On a purely technical level, party organizations still bore the outward signs of health. The RNC, NRCC, and NRSC continued to increase their respective staffs and budgets through the mid-1980s, and in the process, they pioneered a variety of innovations in opposition research, direct mail, and public opinion analysis (Herrnson 1988). But with a Republican in the White House, these organizations ceased most of their policy activities, including publication of *Commonsense*. So even as Republicans strengthened their ability to deliver a message, they lost much of their ability to develop one.

The GOP's problems became further manifest in 1986. Reagan campaigned hard for Republican senators, but his theme of continuity ("Win One for the Gipper") was a flop and Democrats regained control of the upper chamber. The NRCC lost financial steam as political action committees concluded that House Republicans were stuck in minority status. And because intellectual exhaustion seemed to have set in at the White House (see Noonan 1990), Democratic lawmakers could now belittle "tired old Republican ideas."

Nevertheless, George Bush won the presidency by a fairly comfortable margin over Democratic nominee Michael Dukakis in 1988. Bush was the first former national party chairman (1973–1974) to win the White House, and many Republicans hoped that his term would usher in a GOP golden age (Milkis 1993, p. 291). Instead, the Bush presidency turned into a near disaster for the party. In

1990, Bush's reversal of his "no new taxes" pledge badly split congressional Republicans: House GOP leader Bob Michel (R-Ill.) loyally backed the president's budget package while Newt Gingrich, who had become party whip, led the opposition. Not only did the White House fail to generate much interest in domestic policy innovation but Budget Director Richard Darman engaged in idea suppression, openly mocking administration officials who advocated dramatic initiatives.

At the same time, fundraising difficulties and organizational turmoil plagued the party's various committees. At RNC, for example, the illness and subsequent death of chairman Lee Atwater destroyed any chance of that organization being a major political force during the Bush presidency. Instead, it became a low-level adjunct to the White House staff, funding political activities that government employees could not lawfully perform (e.g., presidential travel to partisan events, promotional materials urging lawmakers to support the president's program, production and distribution of letters in which the president urged voters to back Republican candidates).[8]

In several ways, Bill Clinton's election in 1992 helped to revitalize the national Republican Party. Senate GOP leader Bob Dole was at last freed from the obligation to support the president and, with sufficient votes to sustain filibusters, he made the Senate Republicans an inescapable element of any political calculation in Washington. House Republicans also were free of the White House yoke, but unlike their counterparts in the Senate, they lacked any real legislative power; therefore, they could concentrate even more on electoral politics. The House Republican Conference assumed a higher public profile by attacking Democratic proposals and touting GOP alternatives. So that rank-and-file members could carry the party message to their constituencies, the Conference started issuing them "boarding passes," i.e., brief fact sheets filled with useful information and catchy rhetoric (Cohen 1993, p. 2891).

Perhaps the most important development for congressional Republicans came in 1993 when House Republican leader Robert Michel announced his decision not to seek reelection the following year. In a very short period of time, Newt Gingrich rounded up enough endorsements from his GOP colleagues to become Michel's unofficial successor. Gingrich seemed likely to transform the Republican leadership, for he had long understood that the House was no longer simply a lawmaking body but also a platform for national communication.

At the party committees, a turning point came with the 1993 election of a new Republican chair, Haley Barbour of Mississippi. Barbour set up the National Policy Forum (NPF), a non-profit tax-exempt organization that was separate from the RNC itself. NPF and its policy councils brought Republican officeholders and policy experts together to restore the GOP's status as the party of ideas. In a sign that the party was returning to a path it had abandoned in the 1980s, NPF announced plans to revive the Brock-era journal, *Commonsense*. Barbour also launched (in 1994) GOP-TV, a new satellite network whose centerpiece was *Rising*

Tide, a weekly talk show hosted by Barbour himself. The show featured high production values and prominent GOP guests, who took questions from viewers calling a toll-free 800 number. Though its primary audience consisted of local Republican groups who watched at downlink locations, its premiere was also carried on more than thirty local cable systems.

Amid these positive signs, difficult questions remained. Could the GOP develop an appealing and coherent message, or would its high-tech apparatus merely amplify a jumble of competing voices? And perhaps more important, would President Clinton's "new Democrat" policy agenda co-opt much of the territory that Republican policymakers had hoped to claim as their own? As always, the party's fortunes hinged on those of the Democrats.

The Democratic Response

The Democrats' loss in 1980 constituted a crisis of competition that had a tremendous impact on the structure of Democratic party organizations in Washington, and on the activities of the party's congressional leadership. Finding themselves without the bully pulpit of the presidency, being the minority party in the Senate and controlling less than 60 percent of seats in the House, and facing the oratorical brilliance of President Reagan (the Great Communicator), Democratic leaders sought ways of enhancing their tarnished image and improving their prospects at the polls. The party's national, congressional, and senatorial campaign committees responded in several ways, most of which were intended to strengthen their electoral roles. In particular, they made a conscious effort to emulate the Republicans' game plan for organizational revitalization, e.g., by increasing their fundraising base, by hiring added professional staff, by purchasing computers and radio and television recording studios, and by setting out to become a major source of campaign assistance for Democratic candidates.

As part of these efforts, the Democratic Congressional and Senatorial Campaign Committees (DCCC and DSCC) began to actively recruit candidates for House and Senate races and provided some of them with significant amounts of campaign assistance. Candidates running in marginal districts, especially endangered incumbents and promising open-seat contestants, received large campaign contributions and key services in the form of coordinated expenditures.[9] Selected candidates were given help with campaign management, public opinion analysis, issue and opposition research, and other forms of campaigning requiring technical expertise, in-depth research, or assistance in obtaining contributions from political action committees (Herrnson 1988). Following the 1982 congressional elections, DCCC chairman Tony Coelho (D-Calif.) undertook a mission to remind business PAC managers that his party had procedural control over the House and that it would be in their best interests to support Democratic candidates (mostly incumbents) rather than Republican challengers, since the latter had limited prospects of getting elected or of becoming part of the House majority (Jackson 1988). Coelho's activities helped position the DCCC and its senatorial counterpart to direct PAC money to needy Democrats.

The Democratic National Committee (DNC) did not become as deeply involved in the campaigns of Democratic House and Senate candidates, choosing instead to focus on rebuilding state and local party organizations and recapturing the White House. As part of these efforts, the national committee sought to change the Democrats' image by researching issues, distributing issue-oriented press releases, and broadcasting generic party-focused television and radio commercials designed to portray the party in a favorable light. In 1982, the DNC aired a spot ad presenting the theme "It isn't Fair, It's Republican" in an effort to contrast the Democrats' traditional concern for the poor and middle class with Republican economic policies that granted tax breaks to the rich. Later DNC advertisements, such as its "children" spots, were less policy oriented and sought to portray the party as better able to lead the nation into the future.[10]

Democratic House leaders also responded to the crisis of competition by creating new structures for researching issues, building legislative coalitions, and communicating with voters. The need for a thematic and coherent message to counter the vision offered by President Reagan spawned the first Democratic Issues Conference in winter 1981 (Herrnson and Patterson 1995). At this conference, Representative Gillis Long of Louisiana, chairman of the House Democratic caucus, advocated that the caucus create task forces to develop policy proposals to serve as the basis for a new political agenda. In addition to the task forces, the caucus chartered a Committee on Party Effectiveness to help direct the caucus's revitalization. The committee and the task forces together were charged with formulating broad policy positions that would form a coherent vision for America's future—hopefully, a vision capable of rallying congressional Democrats and of winning support from the general public. Positions developed through these new party structures would then be spread through issues handbooks that Democrats could use in campaigns, press releases, coordinated floor statements, and publicity events.

Later, the Democratic Message Board was created to coordinate the caucus's communications. This organization, headed by the caucus vice-chair and led informally by the House majority leader, drew on the communications skills of the party's most articulate House members. Consisting of forty or so House Democrats, their staffs, and Democratic national and congressional campaign committee officials, the group met with staffers from the majority leader's, majority whip's, and caucus chair's and vice-chair's offices to develop a weekly message to be presented to the general public. Message Board members took responsibility for coordinating floor statements, contacting national media outlets, and putting a partisan spin on major policy decisions and political events.

The Committee on Party Effectiveness, its various task forces, and the Message Board were all created to conduct activities that traditional party committees were ill equipped to perform, including the formulation and communication of a moderate Democratic message and the building of legislative coalitions. Many also believed that the standing committees in Congress could not handle these functions adequately because their members and staffs are policy experts who tend to focus on the arcane details of narrow pieces of legislation rather than on the broader implications that a piece of legislation has for American society as a whole (From 1989).[11] Those involved with the new structures, however, were encouraged to develop the expertise needed to create broad policy statements that might influence the political agenda, build coalitions, and communicate a Democratic message.

The Democratic response in the Senate was neither as extensive nor as formal as that in the House. The smaller size and greater individualism of the upper chamber, plus the demands on members' time that result from serving on numerous committees and from representing an entire state, made the creation of task forces, communications groups, or other new party structures an unlikely step on the Senate side. Rather than develop new organizations for party leadership, Senate Democrats changed their leaders and revitalized existing bodies to meet the need for developing and articulating a vision to contrast with what was being offered by the Republicans. The selection of George Mitchell of Maine to replace Robert Byrd of West Virginia as majority leader in 1989 was heavily influenced by Democratic senators' beliefs that they needed a more telegenic person at their helm. Byrd, a master of parliamentary procedure, simply was unable to present a favorable image of the party on television, especially in comparison with President Reagan. Mitchell, who had delivered the Democratic responses to Reagan's 1986 state-of-the-union message and to the president's national address on the Iran-contra affair, demonstrated that he possessed the ability to communicate a clear, mainstream Democratic vision that would resonate with the general public.

Once Mitchell became majority leader, he appointed Daniel Inouye (D–Hawaii) to chair the Democrats' Steering Committee in the Senate and made Tom Daschle (D–S.D.) cochair, along with himself, of the Democratic Policy Committee.[12] Both committees, which had been fairly dormant under Byrd, became revitalized under Mitchell. The Policy Committee, for example, began to distribute fact sheets on major issues and hold weekly strategy meetings. By dispersing power that had been consolidated under the previous majority leader, Mitchell was able simultaneously to revitalize the steering and policy committees and to promote greater coordination among Democratic senators.

Many congressional Democrats viewed the election of Bill Clinton in 1992 as the culmination of twelve long years of effective opposition to Republican presidents, as well as a turning point in American politics generally. With the party controlling the White House and holding majorities in both House and Senate, congressional Democrats hoped to accomplish some of the legislative goals they had been forced to set aside during the Reagan-Bush years. Yet along with these opportunities (and several key policy successes in the early stages of the Clinton administration) also came frustrations.

A shift in the roles that members of Congress are expected to play when their party controls the White House caused some tensions to develop among Democrats (see Cohen 1994). During their years as the loyal opposition, congressional Democrats researched issues, developed policy alternatives, and presented those alternatives to the public. Many members who had become policy experts in specific areas and were accustomed to being their party's voice on particular subjects resented having to abandon their own positions in order to unite behind executive proposals. Some of this resentment cropped up in battles waged over the North American Free Trade Agreement (NAFTA) in 1993 and health care reform in 1994. The NAFTA vote, which could only be won with considerable help from GOP legislators, split House Democrats in two. It pitted Majority Leader Richard Gephardt (D–Mo.) and Whip David Bonior (D–Mich.), among others, against Speaker Tom Foley of Washington and the president. Health care reform also caused serious intraparty divisions, with the administration working to rally the nation around the president's plan while other party members advocated the passage of a comprehensive package such as that offered by House Democrat Jim Cooper of Tennessee.

The party's organizational response to these internecine conflicts was uneven. The DCCC and DSCC, for example, along with the communications apparatus developed by the House Democratic caucus, remained neutral on both NAFTA and health care—but the DNC actively took the president's side in each instance (including heading up major media campaigns to win popular support for the administration position).[13] It is not surprising that the DNC's emergence as a policy advocate was controversial among congressional Democrats. Some complained that the DNC had jeopardized their legislative careers by televising ads in their states and districts that advocated passage of Clinton programs with which they publicly disagreed; these members found themselves in the position of having either to flip-flop on a major issue or to publicly explain why they opposed their president and party leader. Many felt the DNC simply had no business rallying constituents to oppose a Democratic elected official on policy matters.

THE LIMITS OF PARTY POLITICS IN A MASS DEMOCRACY

Recent changes by the Democratic and Republican parties represent attempts to adapt to the politics of a mass democracy.[14] Both parties are seeking to reclaim influence they lost as a result of the collapse of political machines—and, over time, as a result of party decline in general—by creating new ties with their candidates and the general public. They have become more involved in elections by providing candidates with campaign contributions, services, and assistance in acquiring election resources from external groups (such as political action committees). They also have used policy research, polling, and electronic media advertisements to influence the political agenda and attract the support of voters.

Yet the parties' efforts to move beyond their traditional agenda-setting and election-oriented activities have been less successful. Not only do members of Congress usually resent party efforts to mobilize public opinion behind issues on which they and their president disagree, but it remains to be seen whether these public relations campaigns will enable one party or the other to attract a larger, more permanent following or increase the number of Americans who participate in elections. Furthermore, the reforms undertaken by both parties were largely in response to crushing defeats suffered by their presidential candidates. This sequence of events illustrates the extent to which political parties are still dependent on the presidency. With the concentration of power in one office and the communications resources at its disposal, the presidency still dominates the ebb and flow of party politics.

The techniques currently used by parties are different from those employed during the days of old-fashioned political machines. Politics during the machine era was built on relationships among bosses, candidates, and voters that revolved around patronage, preferments, elections, and personal ties. Politics during the public relations era is built on campaign contributions, election services, issues, and high-tech communications. The personal touch is mostly gone, and the parties are clearly not as strong as they were during their heyday. Nonetheless, the efforts of party organizations to concentrate on issues and communicate their stances on those issues to a mass audience do provide citizens with an unparalleled opportunity to make meaningful distinctions between the two parties.[15] In addition, their adaptation to a changing political environment has enabled parties to pursue their basic goals of helping candidates win votes and competing with one another for control over the organs of government.

In the 1990s and beyond, political parties undoubtedly will need to make new adjustments. For one thing, the growing pluralism of American society is multiplying the number of interests to which parties must appeal. For another, the "mass media" appear to be giving way to "niche media" that allow factional leaders to reach their followers without first passing through the filter of establishment officials and journalists. It is perhaps symptomatic that Jerry Brown and Pat Buchanan, the two outsiders who challenged their respective parties' traditional structures in the 1992 presidential race, later went on to host radio talk shows. Amid this rising din of interests and voices, it is harder than ever for parties to deliver a coherent policy message. And yet, in the absence of a sustained and consistent effort, the already tenuous connection between citizens and the parties may be irreparably broken—e.g., with partisan cues becoming increasingly irrelevant to voters (Wattenberg 1990) and the national organizations existing only to serve the special needs of candidates in a predominantly candidate-centered system. Ordinary citizens who once were connected to the political process through the efforts and activities of the parties may thus, in the end, be left to fend for themselves.

CONCLUSION: PARTY POLITICS AFTER 1994

The 1994 congressional elections expanded the boundaries of party activity in an age of mass politics. The efforts of House Republicans, and especially their campaign on behalf of the Contract with America, represent the successes that political parties might hope to achieve. Less effective efforts by the Democrats, however, only highlight the obstacles that party organizations must still overcome.

House Republicans laid the groundwork for electoral victory by transforming their annual issues conference from a social event to a strategic one (Koopman 1994). At the 1994 conference, common beliefs were identified and a strategy prepared to deliver the group's vision to voters. Afterward, House GOP leaders polled rank-and-file members to determine what issues they wanted the party to emphasize during the fall campaign; meanwhile, the National Republican Congressional Committee and Republican National Committee asked similar questions of nonincumbent candidates. Armed with ideas from leaders, backbenchers, and candidates, eleven working groups of House Republicans labored to draft legislative proposals. In addition, GOP consultants employed focus groups to discover the most effective means of framing these ideas for the general election. The result was the Contract with America, in which Republicans made the following offer to voters: If you give us a majority in the House of Representatives, we will promise to bring a specific set of measures—including proposals for a balanced-budget amendment, a crime bill, tax cuts, term limits, and welfare reform—to the floor within the first 100 days of the 104th Congress.

On September 7, 1994, the GOP unveiled its contract in a well-publicized rally staged on the steps of the U.S. Capitol in Washington. The event came fourteen years after Governing Team Day, which, not coincidentally, also was organized by Newt Gingrich. This time, however, House Republicans had a relatively free hand because they did not have to defer to a presidential campaign. Indeed, they now had far more maneuvering room than they had enjoyed in years, precisely because unified Democratic control of the government had freed the GOP from many of the responsibilities of governing.

Although few Republican candidates based their entire campaign on the contract, most did use it as a resource, adapting its themes and proposals to local conditions. Most Democrats responded to the contract by pointing to its seeming contradictions. They noted, for example, that the tax cuts, increased defense spending, and promise of a balanced budget by the year 2002 did not add up. Many tried to use the contract to divert attention from President Clinton's policy failures and lack of popularity. In the face of Republican television ads that "morphed" pictures of their profiles into pictures of the president, Democrats hoped that refocusing their campaigns on the contract's weaknesses would work to their benefit. The party's overwhelming losses in November demonstrate otherwise.

The contract was significant because it enabled House Republican leaders to maintain that the GOP's eventual success at the polls gave them a mandate to enact their program. Democrats denied this assertion, pointing to survey data showing that as few as one-third of all voters had even heard of the contract. Republicans answered with polls showing strong support for the individual items in the document. Whatever its status with the public, the contract proved to be a crucial management device for the new majority. Whereas the Republicans might otherwise have frittered away their first months in power trying to decide what to do, the contract gave them a ready-made agenda.

The GOP's desire for quick action further strengthened the hand of the new Speaker, Newt Gingrich. In particular, procedures were adopted that enabled Gingrich to make committees more responsive to the party (e.g., by giving him the authority to appoint committee chairs and Republican members). And as it happened, most of the contract items did come up for a floor vote as promised—and of these, only term limits failed to gain passage (though a number of important provisions were later modified as a result of action taken in the Senate).

It took House Democratic leaders several months to develop a strategy for responding to the contract. While House GOP leaders were busy planning legislative strategy, their Democratic counterparts were occupied with shoring up their holdover leadership positions and with reorganizing the Democratic caucus. Thus, when the 104th Congress convened, House Democrats were unprepared to reply to the Republicans' legislative program. Most of their early responses consisted of complaints that the House was not properly deliberating such critical matters as the balanced-budget amendment, welfare reform, and government deregulation. This message stirred little interest with a public that was already inclined to view the Congress as obstructionist. Later in the session, Democrats in the House, the Senate, and the executive branch had greater success in opposing GOP initiatives. For example, they portrayed Republican plans to cut taxes as government giveaways and proposals to reduce support for the poor, especially children, as mean-spirited.

What the Democrats failed to do, either during the election or during the opening days of the new Congress, was to develop and advertise an alternative vision of politics and government. Moreover, the diversity of the party's congressional membership and constituent base may continue to limit its ability to do so. The House Democrats' election losses left them with a more bipolar caucus consisting of a proportionally larger number of liberals and conservatives (and fewer moderates). Disagreements among the various factions made it difficult for the party to develop a unifying thematic statement of principles and goals. Failure to overcome these divisions could leave it open for Republicans to set the campaign agenda in future elections.

The 1994 midterm will very likely be remembered as a watershed event in American history. The Democrats' inability to keep the major campaign promises they made in 1992—especially regarding a middle-class tax cut and health care reform—and voters' dissatisfaction with government gridlock in Washington contributed to the Republican takeover in Congress. The GOP's Contract with America and its focus on issues of major concern to the middle class also were central to the party's victory. The contract showed how a political party can run a successful party-based campaign in a candidate-centered election system; the Democrats' failure to provide an appropriate response hints at the hurdles that must be overcome before any party can develop a national agenda. In short, the contract helped to define what may prove to be the newest battlefield of party competition in the era of mass-party politics.

NOTES

This chapter is based largely on observations made during our service as American Political Science Association congressional fellows. We wish to thank the Association for giving us the opportunity to participate in the legislative process and observe the inner workings of Congress.

1. As we use it, the term "mass politics" refers simply to a system in which a large number of citizens participates in the policy process without the intermediation of overtly political institutions such as political parties.

2. For a thorough description of political life in an urban machine, see Rakove (1975); for further discussion of the factors leading to the decline of machines, see Pomper, Forth, and Moakley (1982).

3. Patronage here is defined narrowly to mean the awarding of government jobs to members of the winning party.

4. In addition to the rise of the national civil service, which dramatically reduced the number of positions that parties had at their disposal, labor reform at the state and local levels provided protection to workers who might previously have been fired for purely political reasons. Many areas also began using nonpartisan elections to fill a large number of state and county governmental jobs. Finally, Social Security and other social programs originating during the New Deal period deprived the party of its opportunity to provide a wide range of economic benefits to supporters.

5. Some of the groundwork that contributed to a revitalization of the Republican national party organizations was laid in the late 1960s by RNC chairman Ray Bliss, who pioneered the use of direct-mail fundraising.

6. The supply-side school of economics holds that reductions in tax rates will foster economic growth not only by stimulating demand but also by spurring work, savings, and investment. Although supply-side principles were embraced by many conservatives, especially during the early 1980s, economists strongly disagree about their validity.

7. A "special order" speech is a procedure under which members may address the House on any subject when legislative business is not being considered. Such a speech (often delivered before a near-empty chamber) is limited to one hour in length.

8. In passing, we note that 18 USC 1913 forbids any federal money to be used "directly or indirectly to pay for any personal service, advertisement, telegram, telephone, letter . . . to influence in any manner a Member of Congress to favor or oppose by vote or otherwise, any legislation or appropriation by Congress"—which is why legislative liaisons at the White House and in government agencies maintain the legal fiction that they merely provide information to (as opposed to seeking influence with) Congress.

9. As an alternative to making direct contributions, the national party organizations are permitted under federal law to make coordinated expenditures "on behalf of" their candidates. Unlike with the independent expenditures associated mainly with political action committees, candidates may be fully aware of (and active in decisions with regard to) coordinated expenditures designed to help with media advertising, polling, and other campaign activities.

10. So-called generic advertisements produced by the political parties are intended to benefit all candidates on the ticket, to mobilize voters, and to communicate a general message about the party. The "children" ads produced by the DNC attempted to persuade voters that the future of children in this country would be much brighter under Democratic leadership.

11. Al From happens to preside over the Democratic Leadership Council (DLC), a group of Democratic party leaders and elected officials organized to debate public policy issues with an eye toward crafting and promoting a message that would attract and retain moderate voters.

12. In the Senate, Democrats have maintained a division between these two bodies. The Steering Committee serves as committee on committees (members and chair selected by the party leader) and distributes standing committee assignments to Democratic senators. The Policy Committee formulates overall party strategy for the Democrats and, along with the party leader, helps to establish the legislative agenda for the chamber as a whole. In general, both committees give the party some control over Democratic senators, and over the type of business that is conducted on the Senate floor. Mitchell's election as floor leader was, however, in part a recognition that party organizations would not be enough to ensure success of the Democrats' agenda in the chamber; rather, a telegenic and eloquent spokesman was also needed in order to communicate that agenda to the American public.

13. In fact, it is typical for the in-party's national committee to take its lead (on matters of either policy or organizational activity) from the White House.

14. Our focus here has been on changes in the national party organizations; it is worth noting that there have been significant developments at the state and local levels as well (see Cotter et al. 1984). Most of these developments involve the institutionalization of state party organizations and the assumption of a number of programmatic activities that candidate-based organizations typically eschew.

15. Some might argue that an increased opportunity to make distinctions between parties will lead to the polarization of society along liberal versus conservative lines, thereby damaging democratic stability (e.g., Berelson, Lazarsfeld, and McPhee 1954, chapter 14). This is one possible outcome of the increased professionalism and visibility of today's revitalized national party organizations; it is also possible that other factors such as candidate independence and reliance on mainstream marketing strategies will prevent campaigns from becoming *too* ideological (see Bennett 1992, chapter 7).

14

Who's the Boss? Direct Democracy and Popular Control of Government

JACK CITRIN

The populist spirit animates the current era in American politics. Soured on pluralism, voters are voicing anger and resentment at how representative democracy is working. Populism divides the political world into Us, the People, and Them, the professional politicians and bureaucrats who actually rule.[1] Deeply suspicious of the politics of compromise, the populist's constant fear is that They will betray Us. The populist indictment is that those whom we elect (and reelect) to represent us abuse this trust and serve the privileged and the special interests instead. Today's cast of villains thus includes not just elected officials but the lobbyists, political consultants, political action committees, and media experts who influence them. More generally, the populist outlook is hostile to any institution, including the political party, that impedes direct communication between citizens and decisionmakers.

What can repair the frayed ties between the American people and their political leaders? If an arrogant, unresponsive political class is the problem, what is the solution? How can We control Them? One proposed procedural remedy is to give voters the power to decide public policy directly. The growing use of ballot initiatives to settle controversial issues, the passage of tax and spending limitations, and the movement to limit the terms of local, state, and national legislators are current examples of the drive to curb the authority of elected officials. Some futurologists among those frustrated with the perceived gulf between the public and its leaders are even proposing a high-tech version of direct democracy through the use of electronic mail, on-line synopses of congressional debates and voting records, electronic absentee ballots, and a continuous process of advisory referenda via interactive television (see Herbst 1994).

In this chapter I ask whether more direct democracy would help soothe the public's anger about the deficiencies of decisionmaking by elected officials. First, I review the state of public opinion concerning the advantages and liabilities of the initiative, referendum, and recall. Next, I briefly examine America's recent experience with these devices to assess their likely impact on the influence of majority opinion on policy; on the power of money, media, and organized interest groups in elections; and on the public's confidence in government.[2] Because there is no provision for direct legislation at the national level in the United States, the evidence is necessarily drawn from the states, and especially from California, where government by plebiscite is most fully developed. In the final section I speculate about the implications of term limits for policymaking and for resurrecting the ideal of the "citizen-politician" through rotation in office.

One general conclusion is that the politics of direct democracy and of representative democracy now have several important resemblances. When voters make laws, the interest-group struggle to shape policy simply shifts to the electoral arena. All the modern techniques of campaigns for candidates are brought into play—e.g., direct mail, public relations experts, negative television ads, money from groups outside the state. Direct democracy thus is no guarantee that We will defeat Them. In initiative politics, as in legislative politics, majority sentiment is more likely to prevail when the subject is an issue on which the public holds strong and firm opinions.[3] Since popular participation and the consent of the governed are fundamental American values, however, direct democracy has a presumed advantage in giving legitimacy to significant change.

THE POPULARITY OF DIRECT DEMOCRACY

Whereas the populist impulse has always existed in the United States, since the late 1970s there has been a sharp rise in antipolitical sentiments and a resurgence of interest in increased popular control of the government's activities. Numerous opinion surveys document the growth of dissatisfaction with the government's effectiveness and integrity (see Craig 1993; Lipset and Schneider 1987; Citrin and Green 1986). In 1976, for example, 60 percent of the public said that the government was run for "a few big interests" rather than for the "benefit of all the people"; in 1992, 75 percent felt this way. Over the same period, the proportion of the public believing that the government in Washington could be trusted "to do what is right" only some of the time rose from 63 percent to 73 percent (also see Chapter 3 in this volume) and the proportion disapproving of how Congress was handling its job climbed from 47 percent to 69 percent.[4]

Just after the indictment in late spring 1994 of Congressman Dan Rostenkowski (D-Ill.), one of Capitol Hill's most powerful figures, for the misuse of public funds, a Gallup Poll found that 49 percent of the public believed that Congress was more corrupt than it had been twenty years before; only 7 percent felt the national legislature was less corrupt. In the same survey, 51 percent said that most House members were corrupt and 29 percent expressed this view about their own representative. The sentiment here was bipartisan in two senses: First, there was no difference in the opinions of self-identified Democrats and Republicans, and second, 65 percent of the sample regarded the two parties in Congress as equally corrupt.[5]

The rhetoric of the 1992 presidential campaign reflected the public's surly mood. In particular, Ross Perot defined himself as a populist, mocking the Beltway establishment and condemning the professional politicians for ignoring the concerns of ordinary people. Perot told his followers, "You're the boss" and advocated national electronic referenda on proposed laws as a way of communicating the "will of the people" to their representatives; he received almost 20 million votes, 19 percent of the total cast for president. Bill Clinton also ran as a political outsider, using populist language in promising to "put people first" and "reinvent government." Even George Bush found a way to run against Washington, railing against the "immortal" Democratic Congress and its tassel-loafered lawyer allies. Once elected, President Clinton used televised "town hall" meetings with selected citizens to learn about and to shape public opinion.

Whereas political scientists have been skeptical of direct democracy (Cronin 1989), largely because of their doubts about the competence of the average voter to decide complex issues, a number of recent analyses of American political institutions echo the populist critique of existing practices. In an essay titled *The New American Political (Dis)order,* the distinguished scholar Robert Dahl (1994) expressed concern about the increasing fragmentation of political power, the role of lobbies, and the constant efforts of elected leaders to manipulate rather than educate the public. Dahl called for the development of new institutions to allow ordinary people to communicate about public policy and to express their judgments about the inevitable trade-offs among competing values. One idea he advanced was the creation of assemblies of randomly selected citizens to engage in deliberation, reflection, and recommendation about current problems (also see Dahl 1992). These considered decisions would supplement, if not substitute for, opinion polls as a way of signaling the public's preferences to decisionmakers. Modern telecommunications could be used to make the knowledge and skills of experts available to these mock legislatures.

In a similar vein, James Fishkin (1991) has proposed a "national caucus" of randomly selected individuals to assemble early in each presidential election year for the purpose of meeting and questioning the candidates. This quasi-convention would conclude by discussing the merits of each contender and then voting a preference. Results of this process, which also could be made widely accessible through television, might serve as a guide to other voters and potentially diminish the influence of polls and media coverage on the outcome of the presidential nominating process.

How the public would react to these ideas for improving communications between citizens and officials is unknown, though opinion surveys do reveal enduring popular support for direct legislation.[6] *The initiative* provides for a bottom-up process of policymaking by allowing a specified number of citizens to sign a petition to place a proposed statute or (state) constitutional measure on the ballot for voters to decide. *The referendum* sends a proposed or existing law to voters for their approval or rejection; this procedure often is used in a top-down fashion, with the legislature itself referring policy choices to the voters. A survey commissioned by Thomas Cronin and conducted by Gallup in 1987 revealed widespread approval for the idea of national referenda. For example, one question in the poll suggested having a nonbinding advisory referendum on a few laws every two years; 58 percent of the sample favored this idea, and only 29 percent were opposed. The same survey revealed that 76 percent of the public believed that "people are able to cast informed votes and deserve more of a say on some issues," compared with just 18 percent who agreed that "we should trust our elected officials to make public decisions on all issues."

Finally, the trade-off between direct and representative democracy was posed by the following question: "An issue would be placed on the ballot if a large number of voters signed a petition. Some people favor this change in the Constitution, believing it important to give voters a direct say in making laws. Others oppose such a change, believing it would undermine the independent judgment of elected officials. Which comes closer to your views?" By a plurality of 48 to 41 percent, respondents favored establishing a binding nationwide initiative (see Cronin 1989, chapter 7).

More recent polls indicate that if anything, support for a national referendum may be increasing. A 1992 survey conducted by the Gordon Black organization found that 72 percent of the public favored a constitutional amendment requiring that any federal tax increase be voted on in a national referendum. Similarly, a poll conducted by the *Los Angeles Times* in June 1993 asked respondents, "As things stand now, the president and Congress make the laws for the federal government. Some people have proposed that laws also be passed by national referendum, which would mean putting various proposals on the ballot so people across the country could vote them up or down directly. Would you favor or oppose this idea?" By a large majority of 65 to 25 percent, this national sample opted for a national referendum system. Citizens are attracted to the notion of direct legislation at the national level despite the fact that its implementation would be a major innovation requiring amendments to the U.S. Constitution. And with many states already providing for initiatives and referenda, it is not surprising that there is even stronger popular support for allowing citizens to vote directly on state and local issues.[7]

The first set of figures in Table 14.1 describes public opinion about direct legislation in California, where the initiative process is a prominent feature of the electoral landscape. Statewide polls conducted by the Field Institute between 1979 and 1990 show overwhelming agreement that statewide ballot proposition elections are "good for California."[8] Moreover, there are no significant differences in

TABLE 14.1 Attitudes About Direct Democracy in California

A.   Support for Direct Democracy, 1979–1990

Question: "Do you think that statewide ballot-proposition elections are a good thing for California, a bad thing, or don't you think they make much difference?"

	1979	1982	1985	1989	1990
A good thing for California	83%	80%	79%	73%	66%
Neither good nor bad	11	9	10	14	23
A bad thing	4	6	5	7	8
No opinion	2	5	6	6	3

SOURCE: Surveys of the Field Institute, the latest that of August 1990. All samples were a representative cross-section of California residents aged 18 and older.

B.   Advantages and Disadvantages of Proposition Elections, 1989

Question: "What do you like (or dislike) about proposition elections?"[a]

Likes:
Gives people a voice, a chance to express their opinion	50%
Allows citizen groups to put things on the ballot	8
Voters are able to decide on things that legislators are either unable or unwilling to address	8
Takes power out of the hands of the few	7
Makes voters more aware of specific public issues	7

Dislikes:
They are too complicated, confusing, misleading	12%
Voters aren't knowledgeable enough, don't have all the information to make a proper judgment	9
There are too many of them on the ballot	8
There are too many special-interest-group initiatives	7
Laws are not enforced after they pass, are too easily overturned	6

[a]Respondents were allowed to state up to three likes or dislikes. Any items mentioned by less than 5% are not included in the table.

SOURCE: Survey of the Field Institute, January 1989.

the outlook of various social or political subgroups in the population. Although the public's enthusiasm did seem to fade a bit during the late 1980s, the proportion regarding direct legislation as "a bad thing" remained a tiny minority.

It is striking that voice, not control, is the main reason given for approving statewide initiatives. In other words, the virtue of direct legislation is that it gives the public a chance to be heard when legislators are unwilling to listen or unable to act. The bottom portion of Table 14.1 suggests that voters do not necessarily idealize their own abilities and that they often do recognize the weaknesses of plebiscitary government. Along the same lines, large majorities in a 1982 Field Institute survey agreed that voters may lack the capacity to make informed decisions on complex issues and that elected representatives are "better suited to decide on highly technical or legal policy matters." This poll also found widespread concern about the role of interest groups in devising initiatives to advance their goals, and about the impact of campaign contributions in swaying the outcome of the vote through massive advertising.

The reservations that some citizens have about direct democracy could be a reaction to the professionalization of the process, a development described later in this chapter. Thus, a 1985 survey found that 71 percent of Californians agreed that "I like the initiative process, but I would like to see significant changes in how it works" (Cronin 1988, p. 616). When respondents were asked about specific reforms, the strength of populist sentiment was clear: Many citizens favored proposals seeking to enhance the grassroots character of initiatives by limiting the power of interest groups in ballot-proposition campaigns—e.g., by revealing which groups gave money to pay for an ad, prohibiting the use of paid signature gatherers for collecting the required signatures, and so on (Cronin 1988, pp. 616–617). To the extent that money collected and spent by organized groups is thought to determine the outcomes of initiatives, direct democracy likely will fail to mitigate the frustrations of alienated voters.

Nevertheless, whatever their qualms about the conduct of campaigns, more than two-thirds of Californians polled by Field in 1982 felt that legislators were more likely than the voting public to be influenced by special interests. By a margin of three to one, virtually all social groups agreed that voting for or against ballot propositions is a more effective way to influence government than is voting for representatives (see Magleby 1984, pp. 9–10). The evidence, then, is that popular attitudes toward direct democracy are positive. There is no great desire for routine involvement in every policy choice at the state or national level; people realize they lack the knowledge to participate in this way. Yet there is a strong wish for more voice in deciding important issues. Particularly in a context of widespread mistrust of government, one appeal of direct legislation is that it can function as a safety valve, giving voters the chance to go over the heads of elected officials in special circumstances.

The fact that support for direct democracy (at least in the abstract) is so diffuse, cutting across conventional political lines, suggests that the questions asked in public opinion surveys are tapping a somewhat ritualistic commitment to the principle of popular consent while at the same time permitting respondents to express contempt for the professional politician, an enduring negative symbol in American political culture (Craig 1993). Although it would appear that few people are actually beating the drums for a system of nationwide initiatives and referenda, the term-limits movement has lately begun to translate some of this feeling into action.

THE APPEAL OF TERM LIMITS

The *recall* allows voters to remove a public official from office during his or her term at a special election triggered by the filing of a petition bearing a specified number of valid signatures. Such an election thus provides for an up or down vote on the performance of one's representative without designating a particular replacement. Because a recall arguably requires less knowledge than would be required to cast an informed vote on public policies, someone could readily endorse the idea of a recall for national officials while opposing the establishment of national referenda and initiatives. In the 1987 survey commissioned by Cronin, 67 percent of the respondents expressed approval of a constitutional amendment to permit recall elections of members of Congress—compared to 27 percent who opposed this reform because "it might lessen the independence of elected officials."

Term limits preordain an elected official's removal from office at a specified date and thus would ensure rotation in office. Supporters of the concept claim that term limits would infuse the political process with fresh ideas; they also repeat the argument made by anti-Federalists at the Constitutional Convention in 1787 that long tenure in office, far from direct observation by the people, tends to make officials selfish and inattentive to the public good.[9] Term limits differ from the recall in that no vote is involved, and the question of how well or poorly an official has performed does not enter into the decision. Opponents argue that term limits are unfair because they deny voters the freedom to reward leaders who have served them well, and that they are unnecessary because the electoral process already makes it possible to unseat those deemed inadequate.

It is worth pointing out that although American voters are disaffected from Congress as an institution, they almost never reject their own representatives (Jacobson 1992). In 1992, all but one of the incumbent senators running, and all but fifteen incumbent House candidates, were reelected (Hershey 1993, p. 157). Even in the 1994 political earthquake, only 2 of 24 incumbent senators and 34 of 351 incumbent House members seeking reelection lost their seats.[10] Moreover, surveys indicate that voters generally perceive their own member of Congress as trustworthy and responsive. Legislators are reelected because they are perceived, accurately by most accounts, as representing their districts well (Jacobson 1992; also see Chapter 12). For voters to approve of their own representative and to support term limits at the same time is something of a paradox. Yet public opinion polls consistently reveal high levels of support for limiting the terms of legislators regardless of the wording of survey questions, the severity of the proposed limits, or the level of government affected.

In fact, as far back as 1964, a Gallup Poll found that 49 percent of the public favored a law that would limit members of Congress to twelve years in office, compared with 38 percent who felt these officials should be able to serve as long as they were able to be reelected. By 1992, the balance of opinion had shifted to 68 percent in favor of term limits and 30 percent opposed.[11] In its 1992 preelection

TABLE 14.2 Support for Congressional Term Limits, 1992

Total (N = 2,175)	82%	Age	
		17–29	81%
Education		30–39	79%
Some high school	76%	40–49	81%
High school graduate	83%	50–59	84%
Some college	85%	60-plus	85%
College graduate	83%		
Postgraduate	73%	Would you say the government is pretty much run	
Gender		By a few big interests	84%
Male	81%	For the benefit of all	75%
Female	83%		
		Presidential vote	
Partisanship		Bush	87%
Democrat	78%	Clinton	79%
Independent	83%	Perot	83%
Republican	87%		
		U.S. House vote (open seat)	
Ideology		Democratic candidate	80%
Liberal	78%	Republican candidate	90%
Moderate	82%		
Conservative	85%	U.S. House vote (with incumbent)	
		Democratic incumbent	79%
Race		Republican incumbent	83%
White	83%	Democratic challenger	83%
Black	80%	Republican challenger	87%
Hispanic	75%		

NOTE: Question: "A law has been proposed that would limit members of Congress to no more than 12 years of service in that office. Do you favor or oppose such a law?"

SOURCE: American National Election Study, 1992.

survey, the American National Election Study (ANES) asked respondents for their views about a proposed law that "would limit members of Congress to no more than 12 years of service in that office"—and fully 82 percent said they favored such a law. Table 14.2 shows that there was overwhelming support for term limits in virtually every segment of the population. Approval was slightly lower among Democratic voters and the social groups affiliated with that party, but term limits were nonetheless favored by 78 percent of self-identified liberals, by 79 percent of respondents who subsequently reported voting for Bill Clinton, and by more than 80 percent of those who voted for the incumbent running in their district.[12] Even among the trusting minority who felt the government still is run "for the benefit of all," 75 percent supported a term-limits law.

The results of state initiatives in the 1990s provided sweeping victories for term limits on both state and national legislators. In 1990, voters in California,

Colorado, and Oklahoma approved limits ranging from six to twelve years for their state legislators;[13] initiatives imposing term limits on members of the U.S. Congress—and sometimes (but not always) on state legislators as well—scored a perfect 14 for 14 in 1992, garnering almost 21 million votes nationwide, and in 1994 eight more states were added to the list (Mississippi, the only remaining state where citizens themselves can place the issue on the ballot, has yet to act). Term limits have generally won by large margins at the polls; the one defeat shown in Table 14.3 occurred in Utah, where voters in 1994 turned back an initiative that was intended to strengthen restrictions already enacted by the state legislature.

As explained by Herrnson, Patterson, and Pitney in Chapter 13, term limits were a provision in the Contract with America put forth by House Republicans during the congressional campaign in 1994. When legislation that would apply limits to all members of Congress was brought to a vote the following spring, however, it failed to achieve the two-thirds majority required for proposing an amendment to the U.S. Constitution. During floor debate in the House, a number of senior Republicans—and virtually every Democrat—preached the virtues of experience and the nobility of a long career in public service. This defeat grew in significance when a 5-to-4 decision of the U.S. Supreme Court in May 1995 upheld lower-court rulings that state laws imposing term limits for members of Congress are unconstitutional. As a result of the Court's action,[14] the guillotine that had been hovering over the heads of many federal legislators was raised, at least for the time being. The 1996 elections will provide an opportunity for advocates of term limits to determine whether the issue is salient to voters or merely a vehicle for the expression of a diffuse anger about politics as usual.

What explains the puzzling behavior of voters who reelect their incumbent legislators while simultaneously enacting term limits? Arguing from the presumption of rational choice, one might consider the term-limits movement as an addict's plea to "stop me before I sin again." Assume that citizens truly prefer a more competitive system of congressional elections yet recognize that current practices provide incumbents a huge advantage. But denying oneself the benefits flowing from the seniority of one's own member of Congress is irrational unless voters in other districts are forced to make the same sacrifice. In this circumstance, term limits might appear as a mechanism that promotes the collective interest by preventing voters from acting in their short-run individual interests. It is, once again, the story of Ulysses tieing himself to the mast to stay away from the seductive Sirens.[15]

It is conceivable, of course, that some people actually chose to support term limits after going through this process of reasoned self-denial. A much more likely explanation is that voters energized by recent revelations of congressional scandal took the opportunity to express their disgust with career politicians. From the populist perspective, term limits are a costless way for Us to send Them a message.

TABLE 14.3 Initiatives on Term Limits for Members of Congress, 1992 and 1994

	1992 Election		
State	*Limit for Senate*	*Limit for House*	*Percentages For/Against*
Arizona	12 years	6 years	74–26
Arkansas	12 years	6 years	60–40
California	12 years	6 years	63–37
Florida	12 years	8 years	77–23
Michigan	12 years	6 years	59–41
Missouri	12 years	8 years	74–26
Montana	12 years	6 years	67–33
Nebraska	12 years	8 years	68–32
North Dakota	12 years	12 years	55–45
Ohio	12 years	8 years	66–34
Oregon	12 years	6 years	69–31
South Dakota	12 years	12 years	63–37
Washington	12 years	6 years	52–48
Wyoming	12 years	6 years	77–23
	1994 Election		
Alaska	12 years	6 years	63–37
Colorado	12 years	6 years	51–49
Idaho	12 years	6 years	59–41
Maine	12 years	6 years	63–37
Massachusetts	12 years	8 years	52–48
Nebraska	12 years	6 years	68–32
Nevada	12 years	6 years	70–30
Oklahoma	12 years	6 years	67–33[a]
Utah	12 years	8 years	35–65[b]

[a]Enacted in a special primary, September 1994.

[b]The Utah legislature had previously enacted a statute imposing limits of 12 years on both senators and representatives.

SOURCE: Galvin (1992, p. 5); *Congressional Quarterly Weekly Report* (November 12, 1994, p. 3251); the Hotline (November 9, 1994); offices of secretaries of state for the various states.

As for the reelection of incumbents, it appears that many voters simply do not make a connection between support for term limits and the effect such limits might have on their own representatives in the future.[16] One vote is on the record of an individual; the other assesses the performance of Congress or, perhaps, of government in general. It is instructive that the one outright defeat for a term-limits initiative occurred in the state of Washington in 1991 when the campaign confronted voters with an explicit trade-off. That particular measure applied the limits retroactively, and its early support eroded in the face of charges that it would strip Washington's citizens of the protection provided by powerful incumbents and allow a larger share of government's largesse to be distributed to other states.

Given the breadth of the current revulsion for politics and politicians, there is an almost reflexive tendency for people to favor term limits. Should discontent with government diminish, therefore, the movement might fade. But proponents in 1990–1994 enjoyed a strong initial advantage, and their chances were enhanced by the tendency for the term-limits debate to be overshadowed by the presidential and congressional contests. In addition, the pro-limits forces usually were well funded, with large contributions for the populist cause coming (ironically) from U.S. Term Limits and other Washington, D.C.–based interest groups, from large business corporations, and from wealthy—usually conservative—individuals (Galvin 1992).

Whenever substantial amounts of money and political clout were used to challenge term limits, as in Washington State and in California in 1990, the outcome of the election was close. On other occasions, term-limits initiatives encountered little organized resistance as legislative leaders either ran for cover or waited for salvation through the judiciary. Although this raises questions about the firmness and intensity of public support for term limits, at least sixteen state legislatures already are operating under the new rules.

IS DIRECT DEMOCRACY DANGEROUS?

The crux of the case for direct democracy is that the people who are subject to a law should have the final say in making it. If popular consent and majority rule are the defining principles of democracy, then decisions made by the voters themselves have more validity than those made by their elected representatives. More pragmatically, it may be politically prudent for these officials, particularly in an era of widespread public mistrust, to submit controversial proposals to the electorate in order to head off protest and disobedience.

The competence of ordinary citizens to make intelligent decisions is a central issue in the debate on direct versus representative democracy (see Cronin 1989; Barber 1984). Supporters of direct legislation argue that not only are people the best judges of their own interests but, left unchecked by the power of citizens to overrule them, elected representatives are easily pressured to respond to the preferences of privileged minorities. And if voters are not always informed about a policy at the outset, the process of discussion and deliberation leading up to their choice will be educative. More generally, direct democracy should raise the public's level of interest and participation in civic affairs.

Opponents of direct democracy are deeply skeptical of these claims. The voters may not be fools, but the larger and more diverse the political community and the more complex and technical the issue, the more limited the ability of the average citizen to make wise decisions about public policy. A fundamental defect of direct democracy, say its critics, is that voters lacking knowledge and judgment are vulnerable to the emotional and simplistic arguments of skilled demagogues. The superiority of representative democracy is that elected officials do have the information, reasoning skills, and experience to make sound decisions.

Another criticism of direct democracy is that elected officials represent the full diversity of interests and thus are more likely to weigh the intensity of different opinions on an issue to arrive at a policy that is an acceptable compromise for all affected groups. If voters in referendum and initiative races differ in their overall background and outlook from those turning out in candidate elections, direct legislation might result in a systematic neglect of certain relatively disadvantaged groups in society; its opponents warn, in particular, that the majoritarian impulse in direct democracy can become a threat to minority rights in nations divided along ethnic, religious, or cultural lines (see Butler and Ranney 1994). Finally, it is claimed that by allowing citizens to bypass or overrule their elected officials, direct legislation encourages representatives to evade difficult decisions rather than strive to respond to popular demands. In an ironic twist, critics argue that direct democracy further erodes the authority of established institutions rather than giving them legitimacy.

Several studies suggest that both the anxieties and the hopes inspired by direct democracy are exaggerated (also see Magleby 1984, 1989). Most of the twenty-six mostly midwestern and western American states that practice direct democracy use both the referendum and the initiative. Since 1978, the referendum (or top-down) approach to direct legislation has had a success rate of about 60 percent; if the proposed measures were unwise, the blame presumably lies with elected officials rather than with voters. The very low winning rate of 14 percent for initiatives placed on the ballot by citizens themselves (Butler and Ranney 1994, p. 65) further indicates that voters are not fools who automatically rush in where legislators fear to tread. Another implication, though, is that grassroots efforts to overcome the opposition of entrenched interests often fail.

The use of the initiative process has increased since the late 1970s (Butler and Ranney 1994, p. 61). In recent years, for example, voters have cast ballots on diverse and important topics including fiscal limitations, the status of English as a state's official language, the death penalty, abortion, the nuclear freeze, legalized gambling, euthanasia, school vouchers, and insurance reform. The listing presented in Table 14.4 shows that the most common subjects for state initiatives have been taxes and government spending, political reform, business and labor regulation, and public morality. Since people tend to hold fairly stable opinions on financial and moral issues,[17] this pattern of activity is reassuring for those who worry about voters' ignorance and volatility.

Initiatives dealing with civil liberties, in contrast, have been rare. Several initiatives have imposed stiffer sentences on criminals and shifted the procedural balance from defendants to prosecutors. These outcomes express the public's concern about crime and hardly presage an attack on the Bill of Rights. Initiatives to ban abortions have failed, and the results of proposals to restrict the rights of homosexuals have been mixed (Butler and Ranney 1994, p. 65; Morrissey 1992, p.

TABLE 14.4 Subject Matter of Qualified Initiatives in the American States, 1978–1992

	Total	Percentage
Revenue/Tax/Bond	105	26%
Government/Political reform	77[a]	19
Regulation (business and labor)	65	16
Public morality	58	15
Environment/Land use	35	9
Civil liberties/Civil rights	20	5
Health/Welfare/Housing	19	5
National policy	11[b]	3
Education	9	2
Total	399	100

[a]Seventeen of these were term-limit measures on the ballot in 1990–1992.
[b]Eight of the eleven were nuclear-freeze initiatives appearing on the ballot in 1982.
SOURCE: Butler and Ranney (1994, p. 63). Reprinted with permission.

2585). David Butler and Austin Ranney (p. 65) thus conclude that "it is hard to point to any successful referendum that constituted a flagrant act of majority tyranny against minority rights." For the issues previously mentioned, elected representatives are highly sensitive to public opinion and have taken positions similar to those expressed by the majority vote in the ballot-proposition elections.[18]

It also should be understood that turnout rates generally are lower in ballot-proposition elections than in candidate elections. Those who vote on referenda and initiatives tend to be older, better educated, of higher socioeconomic status, more politically informed, and less likely to be members of racial minorities than those who vote in candidate elections (Magleby 1984, chapter 5). As a consequence, the balance of group power in initiative politics and legislative politics may differ. In the case of California, policymaking by a statewide electorate potentially reduces the influence of Hispanic and Asian opinion because these numerically large groups have relatively low rates of registration and voting (Citrin 1987). Direct legislation therefore may not threaten minority rights, but in some contexts the initiative process can be disadvantageous for minority interests.

Even if initiative voters are interested in politics, deciding on specific policies is often a more difficult task than voting for a candidate. One reason is the sheer length and complexity of many proposals; another is the difficulty of subjects such as the safety of nuclear power or the use of pesticides and food additives (each of which has been the subject of a ballot initiative in California). The lack of access to relevant information, particularly given the sparseness of media coverage, also poses a barrier to public awareness—as does the confusion that can arise when a measure is worded so that a yes vote means no to an existing policy.

Finally, unless an initiative clearly becomes a partisan battleground, voters must make their choices without being able to use the party label, incumbency, or the positions adopted by reference groups as handy guides to opinion formation.

For all of these reasons, people frequently hold unstable opinions on initiatives. On many ballot propositions, a large segment of the public is completely unaware of the issue until very near election day. This, in turn, helps to explain the dramatic changes in voting intentions that sometimes occur during the course of a campaign, as well as the fact that voters make later decisions on ballot measures than they do on candidates (Magleby 1989, pp. 112–114).

The instability of voting intentions and the impact of campaign messages are especially likely to increase as the salience and visibility of issues diminish. Most initiatives begin with a core of supporters and a symbolically attractive label (e.g., "term limits" or "Big Green," the latter a California initiative in 1990 that claimed to protect the environment). Where awareness and information about a measure are low, however, the opposition may be able to use advertising to create doubts and confusion in voters' minds. For individuals just learning about the issue, their first sustained exposure will often be to negative information. In this situation, support for the initiative tends to decline as many voters, dazed and confused by a barrage of commercials, decide to just say no. The low success rate of initiatives can therefore be viewed as evidence of voter rationality (as well as of the power of money). That is, a preference for the status quo when citizens are uncertain about the meaning of change is another indication that the dangers of direct legislation have been overstated.

DIRECT DEMOCRACY, CALIFORNIA STYLE

The size and diversity of California make it a particularly relevant case study for those interested in the idea of direct democracy at the national level of government. The preceding discussion suggests that fears of ballot-proposition elections routinely leading to the passage of rash or illiberal laws are unfounded. Yet a review of California's recent experience also reveals the weaknesses of direct democracy as an instrument of grassroots control: Elected officials, political candidates, and interest groups with greater resources than popular movements are able to circumvent the legislative process and use the initiative process to advance their own political goals.

Consider that in 1978, when Californians passed Proposition 13 and sparked a nationwide tax revolt, there were only four citizen initiatives on the ballot in that state. As Table 14.5 shows, the number grew in later years. In both 1988 and 1990, there were 18 such measures facing the voters—followed by a drop to only 7 in 1992 and 6 in 1994, although this should hardly be taken as a sign that cynicism about politicians is dissipating.

In the case of Proposition 13, the initiative process did fulfill its intended, populist purpose.[19] When elected officials failed to provide relief for rapidly climbing

282   *Jack Citrin*

TABLE 14.5 Number of Citizen Initiatives in California, 1974–1992

1974	2	1986	6
1976	3	1988	18
1978	4	1990	18
1980	4	1992	7
1982	13	1994	6
1984	7		

SOURCE: Office of California secretary of state.

property taxes, they precipitated a rebellion of disgruntled homeowners. Business-men Howard Jarvis and Paul Gann began circulating petitions for their initiative only after the legislature's effort to pass a tax-reform bill collapsed in acrimony in late 1977; they managed to collect more than half a million signatures in only four months. In the June 1978 election, the "people's army" routed the well-equipped forces of the ruling elite and achieved its primary aim—a significant, long-term reduction in property taxes.[20] One year later, another popular initiative imposed ceilings on state and local government spending and further tightened the fiscal noose around the necks of elected officials.

Proposition 13 ushered in an era of plebiscitary government in California. One reason for the increased use of direct legislation is that the success enjoyed by the tax rebels encouraged activists with other causes to turn to the initiative process to pursue their goals. Divided government and intense partisan conflict through-out the 1980s is another part of the explanation, with legislative paralysis causing interest groups to take their struggle into the electoral arena through the prepara-tion of rival ballot propositions. Divided government also triggered resort to the initiative process by Republican governors and legislators who were frustrated by enduring Democratic control of the state legislature.

Finally, the "professionalization" of the initiative industry facilitated use of direct democracy by political entrepreneurs of all kinds, including the traditional targets of populism: professional politicians and powerful interest groups. Full-service consulting firms now draft and circulate petitions, collect signatures, raise funds through direct mail, prepare campaign advertising, conduct polls, and get out the vote.[21] A mass organization is no longer needed to go over the heads of elected officials and take one's case to the people. In California today, all it takes to qualify an initiative for the ballot is money, money, and more money.

These developments point to the need for a classification of so-called citizen initiatives according to their actual sponsors and strategic purposes. California's experience suggests the following typology:

1. *Grassroots Causes.* Referring to campaigns mounted by activists and financed by small donations from ordinary citizens, this is the category envi-sioned by advocates of direct democracy. Conservative examples of such ballot propositions are Proposition 13 and an anticrime Victim's Bill of Rights initiative passed in 1990. A prominent liberal example is the "consumer-backed" proposal

to reform auto insurance rates, Proposition 103, in 1988. A variety of campaign-reform proposals also reflect primarily grassroots origins.

2. *Program Protection.* Once the tax revolt restricted the freedom of elected representatives to determine the overall size of the state's budget, providers and clients of various public services seized upon direct legislation as a means of securing preferential treatment in the allocation of government spending. In a few instances, public employees or elected officials themselves have sponsored popular initiatives to create "special funds" earmarked for a particular purpose and to require that a specified amount of the budget be spent on a designated set of programs.

The best example of this tactic is Proposition 98, which was narrowly approved in 1988. Sponsored by the state superintendent of schools and the California Teachers' Association, this measure requires the state to guarantee a minimum funding level for public schools and junior colleges amounting to about 41 percent of the annual general fund budget. In the same year, an initiative advanced by a coalition of medical groups and educators established a surtax on tobacco products but also stipulated that the revenues generated had to be spent for health research and education. The most recent attempt at "ballot-box budgeting" was Proposition 165 in 1992. Sponsored by Governor Pete Wilson himself, the initiative was an unsuccessful attempt to obtain from voters the reduction in welfare spending that the legislature had refused to enact.

It is difficult for decisionmakers to set priorities rationally or to adjust to new economic trends when they are laced into a straitjacket. Yet whether intentionally or not, the electorate has reduced the range of fiscal options available to its leaders. Plebiscitary budgeting arguably has led to less accountable and less responsive government without doing much to reduce the power of well-organized constituencies—hardly the outcomes desired by the original tax rebels.

3. *Partisan Conflict.* In the context of divided government (similar to that which dominated national politics during much of the Reagan-Bush era), both political parties may be tempted to employ the initiative process to overcome gridlock. This tactic has lately been most attractive to the Republican minority, with Governor Wilson's Proposition 165 being one example of how direct democracy is used in an effort to bypass legislative opposition to a particular policy. Similarly, in 1984 and again in 1990, GOP leaders backed initiatives designed to reduce the power of the legislature in the reapportionment process. The intense partisan conflict that produced these ballot measures was reflected in bitter and expensive campaigns, with each side accusing the other of "playing politics" and subjecting voters to artillery exchanges of television spots featuring (among others) Hollywood actors. In 1990, Jack Lemmon for the Democrats defeated Charlton Heston for the Republicans. One wonders whether the rematch will headline Charles Barkley versus Godzilla.

4. *Self-Promotion.* A novel use of the initiative process is to boost a candidate's campaign for high office. By sponsoring a ballot measure on some specific issue, a

candidate may hope to enhance his or her own visibility, frame media coverage of the campaign, attract a group of intense supporters or additional contributors, and redirect the campaign spending of opposing interests. Such an approach can be dangerous, however. In the 1990 contest for the Democratic gubernatorial nomination, John Van de Kamp yoked his campaign to initiatives dealing with environmental protection (the aforementioned Big Green), crime and drug prevention, and campaign reform (see Lubenow 1991). Whereas some observers attributed the candidate's poor showing to the diversion of needed funds and energy away from his gubernatorial race, it is also likely that the demise of their principal sponsor contributed to the subsequent defeat of all three Van de Kamp proposals.

5. *Corporate Self-Defense.* This category includes ballot measures designed to protect specific industries and professions from unwanted government regulation. Such initiatives may be a response to local ordinances (as in the bid by real estate interests to limit the scope of rent-control laws) or to the outcome of court cases (as in the example of medical doctors and insurance companies seeking to cap the size of malpractice awards). Increasingly, though, this defensive tactic is a case of fighting fire with fire, i.e., corporate and professional interests sponsor their own, relatively benign, ballot measures to fend off more restrictive grassroots efforts.

In 1990, both the insurance companies and trial lawyers sponsored rival initiatives to protect themselves from each other and from a proposal to roll back automobile insurance rates that was backed by an activist group known as Voters' Revolt. Along the same lines, the timber industry offered its own plan to limit logging in order to combat an initiative seeking a more comprehensive ban. Underlying maneuvers such as these is the hope either that the presence of several similar proposals on the ballot will confuse voters and lead to the rejection of all of them in favor of the status quo; or that, since rules hold that when two or more initiatives deal with the same subject, the one with the most votes wins, the industry's "reasonable compromise" will outpoll the grassroots "extreme."

California's recent experience underscores the limited ability of direct democracy to ensure that We will control Them. True enough, it does permit political outsiders to confront and sometimes defeat "the establishment." Yet politicians, political parties, and well-financed interest groups have clearly learned to employ the initiative process as a supplement to normal legislation. Direct democracy thus opens a second front in the wars among political insiders—and the typical alignment of interest groups and elected officials on ballot propositions reflects these players' interest in protecting their influence within the legislature. In the past, for example, the Democratic majority in the state legislature, along with other incumbent officeholders and the wealthy and business lobbies, consistently led the opposition to proposals aimed at limiting campaign contributions and spending.

Increasingly, initiative politics and legislative politics follow a similar pattern in California. Much as in the legislative arena, sponsors of an initiative may be a broad coalition of interests who have negotiated among themselves the text of a ballot proposition and, as a result of these negotiations, produced an unwieldy omnibus bill that is difficult for voters to understand. Opponents, in turn, often respond by submitting alternative measures in a bid to wean away supporters of the original proposal. There also are few significant differences in the conduct of ballot-proposition campaigns and statewide candidate elections, especially in that both rely heavily on the ability to raise large amounts of money for spending on television advertising that tends to be shallow and negative. In each instance, campaign organization, endorsements, and voter turnout matter a great deal.

How loud does money talk in initiative politics? This is a particularly important question since a divided U.S. Supreme Court ruled in *First National Bank of Boston et al. v. Bellotti* (1978) that it is an "impermissible legislative prohibition of speech based on the identity of the interests of the spokesman" to limit corporate contributions in initiative campaigns.[22] The Court's majority opinion regarded corporate spending as contributing to the total stock of information available to voters and supported the notion that one-sided spending is not a crucial factor in initiative elections. In contrast, David Magleby (1989) argued that the greater volatility of voting intentions makes money even *more* important in initiative campaigns than in candidate elections. Fewer than one in five measures have equal spending for both sides—and if opponents spend more or spending is roughly even, a ballot measure is defeated about 80 percent of the time (Butler and Ranney 1994, p. 61). This helps to explain the greater success of corporate spending in defeating hostile initiatives than in winning electoral support for corporations' own proposals (Thomas 1991).

For advocates of direct democracy as a check on the power of moneyed interests, these are disappointing results. Still, there are important exceptions to the power of campaign spending. In California, the insurance industry spent more than $50 million but failed to defeat the rollback of automobile insurance rates and the creation of a more stringent regulatory regime. Heavy corporate spending also could not prevent passage of an initiative restricting the use of pesticides and food additives. Proponents of Proposition 13 in the late 1970s won easily despite being outspent. When issues are framed so that genuine grievances are engaged and mass anger is channeled toward elite "villains," numbers sometimes overcome money.

More generally, in ballot-proposition elections, just as in elections on candidates, the existence of prior information and standing opinions limits the influence of media messages and campaign spending. When people know about an issue and have a position on it based on deeply rooted personal values, direct legislation can fulfill its intended purpose of identifying the will of the majority. For this reason, the results of statewide initiatives on subjects such as taxes or crime have foreshadowed changes in national policy.

One question posed at the beginning of the chapter was whether direct democracy serves to undermine or to boost the legitimacy of representative democracy. Critics claim that the habit of going over the heads of elected officials inevitably reduces their authority even further. The opposing argument is that initiatives and referenda impel governments to revise their policies so as to take account of majority opinion and that doing so ultimately raises the public's trust in established institutions. There are only fragments of evidence bearing on this debate, and the evidence that exists is mostly indirect. Table 14.6, for example, shows that levels of political trust (see Chapter 3) in states allowing for initiatives and referenda are virtually the same as in states that do not employ these populist devices. Direct democracy at the state level thus has no apparent impact on the public's confidence in national government. Alternatively, the implementation of nationwide initiatives and referenda might influence public attitudes in a different way. California's experience, however, suggests that direct democracy at the national level would *not* substantially transform the roles of professional politicians, interest groups, media, or political money in policymaking. And if pluralism American style is the cause of popular discontent with the political process, then populism California style is just a therapy, not a cure.

The 1994 elections in California illustrate the diverse impacts of initiative politics on public policy. The November ballot included four votes on direct legislation. Proposition 188, representing another effort at corporate self-defense, was a measure designed to preempt the power of local governments to regulate smoking. Mounted and heavily financed by the Philip Morris Corporation, this proposal was defeated by a margin of 3 to 1 once voters learned of its sponsorship. Three other initiatives were hybrids in which financial support from leading politicians, political parties, and established interest groups was grafted onto the work of grassroots activitists. An anticrime measure ("Three Strikes and You're Out") was passed even after the legislature enacted a statute that embodied its main provisions. A "single-payer" state health care plan backed by assorted public employees unions but opposed by insurance companies and hospitals sank in tandem with President Clinton's national reform proposals.

The initiative (Proposition 187) designed to deny state aid to illegal immigrants became the fulcrum of the election campaign in California. This measure was drafted by a diverse group of anti-immigration, antitax, and anti-population-growth activists and qualified for the ballot with only limited support from the California Republican Party and several state legislators. Governor Wilson endorsed the proposal, however, and his own anti-immigration commercials filled the gap created by the lack of a television campaign by sponsors of Proposition 187. The initiative won easily, overcoming opposition by President Clinton as well as the state's major newspapers, public education leaders, medical establishment, and civil rights organizations. The reverberations were loud and

TABLE 14.6   Direct Democracy and Political Disaffection in the States, 1976 and 1972

	1976		1992	
	States With Direct Democracy	States Without Direct Democracy	States With Direct Democracy	States Without Direct Democracy
Trust government to do what is right only some or none of the time	66%	66%	70%	71%
Government is run by a few big interests looking out for themselves	75%	72%	78%	80%
Quite a few of the people running the government are crooked	44%	45%	45%	48%
Government doesn't pay much attention to what the people think	33%	34%	26%	26%
Public officials don't care what people like me think	57%	51%	52%	52%
Negative evaluation of U.S. Congress performance[a]	19%	22%	44%	50%
N =	964	1,278	1,339	1,148

NOTE: See Appendix for question wordings. Figures are based on 100 percent. The following 26 states had adopted initiatives or referenda by 1976: Alaska, Arizona, Arkansas, California, Colorado, Florida, Idaho, Illinois, Kentucky, Maine, Maryland, Massachusetts, Michigan, Missouri, Montana, Nebraska, Nevada, New Mexico, North Dakota, Ohio, Oklahoma, Oregon, South Dakota, Utah, Washington, and Wyoming; see Cronin (1989, p. 51). By 1992, Alabama had been added to this list (*The Book of States 1992*, p. 329).

[a]In 1976, respondents were asked to rate congressional performance on a nine-point scale, ranging from "very poor job" to "very good job." In 1992, respondents chose from a four-point scale, ranging from "approve strongly" to "disapprove strongly."

SOURCE: American National Election Studies, 1976 and 1992.

immediate as formerly hostile state and national politicians, including the president, reversed themselves in order to swim with the restrictionist tide; stronger border-control measures and reductions in government assistance to immigrants were quickly put forward. When electoral outcomes express deeply felt and pervasive opinions, they do send a message to government decisionmakers. In this instance, direct democracy at the state level indirectly affected national policy on immigration reform.

CHANGING FACES, TRADING PLACES

Massive support for term limits is an expression of the public's dissatisfaction with the performance of Congress, state legislatures, and government in general. Proponents of term limits claim that the political longevity of legislators is an important cause of the institutional failure that seems to plague our governmental process today. So why, one might ask, do voters not simply "throw the rascals out"? At the heart of the problem are the huge advantages, acknowledged by both sides in the term-limits debate, that incumbents enjoy over their political opponents.[23] If incumbents don't lose when they should, advocates of term limits believe that popular control has been lost—in practice if not in law.

Would term limits enhance popular control and, as a consequence, increase the public's faith in its elected representatives? The answer obviously depends upon whether there is any impact on the legislative behavior that stimulated discontent in the first place. The populist case is that career politicians are a class of people far removed from the ordinary citizens they are supposed to represent. In the language of the ballot argument for the 1990 term-limits initiative in California, "[L]ifetime legislators form cozy relationships with special interests"; they sell votes to the lobbyists who "pay them homage," guarantee themselves salaries, expenses, and "other luxuries," and drive "truly" representative people out of politics (Benjamin and Malbin 1992, p. 279).[24]

How do term limits change the incentives for people inclined to seek office? Will this reform attract a different kind of candidate, someone less prone to abuse the perquisites of power? Or will someone limited to a brief time in office be even quicker to succumb to lobbyists? What are the likely effects on legislative behavior? Will term limits produce a rotating class of inexperienced legislators who are less informed about complex policies than the current group of veterans and, as a result, must depend more on staff members, lobbyists, and other political insiders for advice? Will "amateur" legislators have less of an incentive to build a personal vote based on constituency service and, therefore, be more sensitive to the issue positions of voters? If time on the legislative job is "contaminating," how quickly is one infected by the germ that leads one to put special interests ahead of the majority will? And if "professionalization" improves the quality of legislative work, how steep is the learning curve of newcomers?[25]

The absence of experience with term limits means that we lack the empirical evidence to choose with confidence among rival predictions. Moreover, as Bruce Cain (1994, p. 3) has pointed out, the impacts of term limits are likely to vary according to the type of legislature on which they are imposed, the length of the term limit, and the current rate of turnover in the institution. Thus, one obvious proposition is that the more "professional" the legislature, the greater the change in behavior likely to be engendered by term limits.

Another reasonable conjecture is that the forced retirement of incumbents will produce more competitive legislative races—something that presumably increases the responsiveness of policymaking to shifts in public opinion. However, even this impact of term limits could be mitigated if rotation in office fails to result in new faces in power. For example, California voters imposed limits of six years on the state assembly and eight years on the state senate. Yet there is no rule against someone moving from one house in the legislature to the other. If trading places in this way becomes a common tactic, the supply of fresh ideas that term limits is intended to generate will be slowed.

Where will incumbent legislators go as they come to the end of their permitted term? Some may return to local government, others will become lobbyists sooner rather than later, and several will run for statewide office. In the latter case, there is no reason to expect the tone of electoral politics to change markedly. Prohibited by the term-limits law from seeking reelection, the majority leader in California's senate, David Roberti, sought the Democratic nomination for state treasurer in June 1994. In a vicious and expensive campaign featuring the by-now-familiar negative television ads, he was defeated by the party's chairman and chief fund-raiser.

In addition, the candidates who respond to new opportunities created by term limits at the state level will probably come mainly from local government, just as in the past. And with name recognition at a premium in the less-structured races for open seats, campaign spending is unlikely to lose its importance; contributions from interest groups and a candidate's personal wealth will continue to carry great weight, especially in large districts. In the end, if term limits change the players without significantly affecting the game, their impact on the public's image of government will be marginal.

At the national level, polls suggest that term-limits initiatives are aimed at Congress as an institution rather than at individual members. But for those who believe that longevity in office provides the expertise, personal confidence, and reputation that are crucial elements of leadership ability, strict term limits imply a shift in power from the legislative to the executive branch. If a constitutional amendment were to impose term limits at the federal level, it is likely that the presidency would have a stronger say in policymaking and that congressional oversight of the federal bureaucracy would be even less effective than it is currently (Polsby 1991). How might the public react to such a change in the balance of institutional power? The answer would seem to depend on the causes of current discontent with Congress and other political institutions. Many Americans complain about legislative gridlock and agree in principle that the presidency is the institutional embodiment of our national interest, but the ideas of checks and balances and shared power also have widespread appeal. Indeed, a 1990 NBC News–*Wall Street Journal* survey found that 67 percent of the public preferred that different parties control the presidency and Congress, and only 23 percent favored unified party control (cited in Fiorina 1992, p. 66). Congressional scrutiny (and even torture) of bureaucratic agencies also is popular.

More generally, performance—at least as much as process—influences people's attitudes toward government. The impacts of institutional reforms such as term limits or direct legislation are therefore likely to be filtered through perceptions of how well or poorly the country is dealing with its major problems. Strong, even imperial, presidencies have been associated with both the rise *and* the fall of confidence in the country's established institutions (Citrin and Green 1986).

CONCLUSION: FEAR AND LOATHING IN THE 1994 ELECTIONS

Americans want to be represented in two ways: as members of particular groups with distinctive needs and as equal parts of a national community with a common interest. Our prevailing system of governance performs the first task superbly, with Congress and interest groups cooperating with one another to ensure that benefits are distributed to virtually every segment of society. However, since no good deed goes unpunished, pluralism's very success seems to contribute to the present sense of discontent. Once the sum of all the particularistic benefits appears as a collective cost (Rauch 1994), the feeling spreads that the political system has failed to represent the will of the popular majority, as revealed through the unmediated summing of individual preferences. Interest in direct democracy and the rise of the term-limits movement symbolize the desire for this second, majoritarian, type of representation.

One conclusion of this chapter is that neither the initiative process nor term limits, in and of themselves, would redefine the nature of popular control. Voters might be in a better position to chastise the professional politicians for their excesses, but the pluralist world of interest-group politics would remain largely intact.

Populism clearly has a punitive impulse, but the popularity of direct democracy also expresses a positive yearning for voice—for the chance to be heard and to participate. Recent developments in American politics underscore politicians' concern with public opinion, with finding out what the people want or at least what they will tolerate. For example, the Clinton presidency used televised "town hall" meetings and advertisements to promote its vision of health care reform, illustrating the top-down, plebiscitary aspect of direct communication between citizens and elected officials. In this context, there is some value in expanding the range of bottom-up channels of information flow. Advisory referenda, statewide initiatives, radio talk shows, televised debates, and electronic polls all can provide intelligence about the public's thinking on policy even if each samples a different, unrepresentative body of opinion. Taking these preferences into account, however, might yield a further diffusion of power in an already fragmented system.

By all accounts, conservative talk-show hosts led by Rush Limbaugh and grass-roots Christian organizations helped mobilize voters to "revolt" in November 1994 and put an end to fifty years of Democratic control of the U.S. House of Representatives (Jacobson 1995, p. 6). One possible title for this dramatic story of electoral change is "White Men Can Vote": Exit polls indicated that 62 percent of white males, apparently alienated by the cultural style and ideological symbolism of the Clinton administration, voted for Republican congressional candidates in 1994, up from 49 percent in 1990 (also see Chapters 9 and 11).[26]

Another crucial factor in 1994 was the widespread public loathing of the political class, with citizen mistrust of government and disgust with professional politicians attaining its highest level since the advent of modern polling. As the party in power and believers in the efficacy of government—be it big, lean, or reinvented—Democrats were the natural targets for the public's anger (Jacobson 1995, p. 5). Led by soon-to-be Speaker of the House Newt Gingrich, Republican candidates echoed the populist attack against the institutions of government and succeeded in aiming voters' rage at their partisan opposition. The GOP's Contract with America promised term limits, cuts in congressional staff and perks, a balanced-budget amendment, the line-item veto, and a ban on unfunded federal mandates as part of an onslaught on the supposed arrogance and profligacy of elected representatives. And several of these anti-Washington reforms were indeed passed in early 1995, including repeal of Congress's exemption from federal health, labor, and antidiscrimination laws and legislation limiting the imposition of unfunded mandates on the states. As any cynic might have predicted, however, term limits became more controversial to many Republican legislators once they were the majority party on Capitol Hill. Also as expected, those features of the contract having direct implications for the size and shape of government spending encountered bitter opposition from Democratic leaders and their electoral clienteles.

Especially if Bill Clinton manages to win a second term in 1996, such factors as divided partisan control of government, the Senate filibuster, and the president's veto power portend a similar future of partisan bickering, legislative gridlock, compromise, and media pronouncements of another failed revolution. This is hardly a prescription for the renewal of public trust in political leaders and institutions, and it may spawn new calls for third parties, direct democracy at the national level, and other populist remedies. Ultimately, though, structural changes alone are probably not sufficient to overcome the deep economic, ideological, and ethnic divisions in American society that are the fundamental challenge to government's ability to deliver the goods and inspire the people's confidence.

NOTES

I am indebted to Cara Wong, Christopher Muste, and Robert Jensen for their assistance in the preparation of this chapter. I also acknowledge the support provided by the Institute for Governmental Studies, University of California, Berkeley.

1. For a provocative account of populist thinking in recent politics, see Wilentz (1993).

2. The analysis presented here relies heavily on the two excellent studies of direct democracy by Thomas Cronin (1989) and David Magleby (1984).

3. V. O. Key (1961) outlined the conditions under which representatives are most likely to be swayed by their constituents' views.

4. These data, drawn from a variety of national opinion surveys conducted by CBS News and the Gallup Organization, are reported in *American Enterprise* (March-April 1994, p. 88).

5. See *USA Today*, June 1, 1994; findings are based on a telephone poll of 629 adults conducted May 31, 1994.

6. See Cronin (1989, Chapter 6). The specific findings reported here are taken from *American Enterprise* (March-April 1994, p. 89).

7. Cronin's national survey found that by a margin of more than two to one, the public favored allowing citizens to place state and local issues on the ballot rather than giving elected officials the responsibility for making all laws (Cronin 1989, Chapter 6).

8. These data are provided by the Field Institute through UC Data, Survey Research Center, University of California, Berkeley.

9. For a general discussion of term limits, see Benjamin and Malbin (1992). The chapters in this volume by Petracca and Malbin provide an excellent review of the history of the idea and of the debate at the Constitutional Convention.

10. Results for 1994 are as reported in *Congressional Quarterly Weekly Report*, November 12, 1994, p. 3240.

11. These data are taken from *American Enterprise* (November-December 1992, p. 89).

12. ANES data were provided through the Inter-University Consortium for Political and Social Research at the University of Michigan.

13. A useful summary is provided by Tolbert (1993). The initiative in Colorado also limited the terms of its members of Congress to twelve years.

14. In California and other states, however, courts have ruled in favor of term limits for state legislators; the decision of the U.S. Supreme Court left these limits intact.

15. See Elster (1984) for other examples.

16. There are many examples of the failure of the public to link general attitudes with concrete actions on specific issues; see the discussion in Erikson, Luttberg, and Tedin (1991).

17. This is a central point in Converse (1964); also see Erikson, Luttberg, and Tedin (1991).

18. Judicial review ultimately defines the nature of individual rights in America. The rights of the accused, for example, is a highly contested issue on which constitutional rulings have shifted in the direction of public opinion. Still, civil libertarians are quick to challenge initiatives and the courts have declared unconstitutional numerous measures approved by voters just as they have overridden the actions of state legislatures and Congress. See Magleby (1984, chapter 3).

19. The following account is taken from Sears and Citrin (1985).

20. The state's leading elected officials in both political parties, virtually every local school official, the large corporations, and the trade-union movement united to oppose Proposition 13.

21. After the passage of Proposition 13, even its sponsoring organization, the United Taxpayers of California, hired a professional campaign firm to help qualify additional anti-tax initiatives for the ballot.

22. The quotation is from Justice Powell's majority opinion, cited in Cronin (1989, p. 104).

23. This is not to say that the impulse to unseat one's own representative is strong; as noted earlier, most voters regard the member of Congress from their district favorably. For a discussion of the incumbency advantage, see Jacobson (1992), Fiorina (1989).

24. Prior to an election, voters in California are mailed the *California Ballot Pamphlet* by the secretary of state's office. This document includes the text of initiatives that will be on the ballot, as well as brief arguments by its proponents and opponents. A sample of these arguments is reprinted in Benjamin and Malbin (1992, pp. 275–280).

25. These and other questions are posed by Bruce Cain (1994), from whom I have borrowed the notion of legislative "contamination."

26. These figures are as reported in the *New York Times,* November 12, 1994, p. 15.

Appendix:
Wording of Survey Questions

The following questions have been drawn from the American National Election Study (ANES) surveys from 1964–1992:

Partisan, Ideological, and
Social Class Self-Identification

1. Party: Generally speaking, do you usually think of yourself as a Republican, a Democrat, an Independent, or what? [If Republican or Democrat] Would you call yourself a strong . . . or a not very strong . . . ? [If Independent] Do you think of yourself as closer to the Republican Party or to the Democratic Party?

2. Ideology: We hear a lot of talk these days about liberals and conservatives. Here is a seven-point scale on which the political views that people might hold are arranged from extremely liberal (1) to extremely conservative (7). Where would you place yourself on this scale, or haven't you thought much about this? [Respondents also are asked to place various political figures, e.g., candidates for president and for House and Senate, on this same scale.]

3. Class: There's been some talk these days about different social classes. Most people say they belong either to the middle class or the working class. Do you ever think of yourself as belonging in one of these classes? [If yes] Well, if you had to make a choice, would you call yourself middle class or working class?

Performance Evaluations, Economic Assessments,
and Partisan Choice

1. Do you approve or disapprove of the way . . . is handling his job as president? Do you approve/disapprove strongly or not strongly?

2. Do you approve or disapprove of the way [the president] is handling our relations with foreign countries? Do you approve/disapprove strongly or not strongly?

3. Do you approve or disapprove of the way George Bush is handling the crisis in the Persian Gulf? Do you approve/disapprove strongly or not strongly?

4. In general, do you approve or disapprove of the way the U.S. Congress has been handling its job? Do you approve/disapprove strongly or not strongly?

5. Now we'd like to ask you how good a job you feel some of the parts of our government are doing.... (How good a job is being done for the country as a whole by) Congress—that is, the U.S. Senate and House of Representatives? [1976 only; nine-point scale from very poor job to very good job]

6. We are interested in how people are getting along financially these days. Would you say that you (and your family living here) are better off or worse off financially than you were a year ago? Is that much better/worse off or somewhat better/worse off?*

7. How about the economy? Would you say that over the past year the nation's economy has gotten better, stayed about the same, or gotten worse? Would you say much better/worse or somewhat better/worse?

8. Do you feel things in this country are generally going in the right direction, or do you feel things have pretty seriously gotten off on the wrong track?

9. What do you think are the most important problems facing this country? ... Of those you've mentioned, what would you say is the single most important problem the country faces? ... Which political party do you think would be most likely to get the government to do a better job in dealing with this problem—the Republicans, the Democrats, or wouldn't there be much difference between them?*

10. Do you think there are any important differences in what the Republicans and Democrats stand for? [yes or no]

11. I'd like to ask you what you think are the good and bad points about the two national parties. Is there anything in particular that you like about the Democratic Party? (Anything else?) Is there anything in particular that you don't like about the Democratic Party? (Anything else?) Is there anything in particular that you like about the Republican Party? (Anything else?) Is there anything in particular that you don't like about the Republican Party? (Anything else?) [A similar sequence of questions is used in asking respondents for their views about the major candidates for president.]

12. Which presidential candidate do you think would do a better job at (a) handling the nation's economy, (b) making health care more affordable, (c) reducing the budget deficit—George Bush, Bill Clinton, or wouldn't there be any difference between them? [1992 version]

13. For a nation, it is not always possible to obtain everything one might wish. On page six of the booklet, several different goals are listed. If you had to choose among them, which one seems most desirable to you? Which one would be your second choice? (a) maintaining order in the nation; (b) giving the people more say in important political decisions; (c) fighting rising prices; (d) protecting freedom of speech.

Feelings About the Role of Government in Society

1. I am going to ask you to choose which of two statements I read comes closer to your own opinion. You might agree to some extent with both, but we want to know which one is closer to your views. (a) One, the less government the better; or two, there are more things that government should be doing. (b) One, we need a strong government to handle today's complex economic problems; or two, the free market can handle these problems without government being involved. (c) One, the main reason government has become bigger over the years is because it has gotten involved in things that people should do for themselves; or two, government has become bigger because the problems we face have become bigger.

2. Some people are afraid the government in Washington is getting too powerful for the good of the country and the individual person. Others feel that the government in Washington is not getting too strong. . . . What is your feeling, do you think the government is getting too powerful or do you think the government is not getting too strong? (If not getting too strong) Do you think the government should become more powerful or should it stay the way it is?*

Issue and Policy Views

1. There has been some discussion about abortion during recent years. Which one of the opinions on this page best agrees with your view? (a) By law, abortion should never be permitted. (b) The law should permit abortion only in case of rape, incest, or when the woman's life is in danger. (c) The law should permit abortion for reasons other than rape, incest, or danger to the woman's life, but only after the need for the abortion has been clearly established. (d) By law, a woman should always be able to obtain an abortion as a matter of personal choice. [Respondents also are asked to place major candidates for president on this same scale.]

2. Some people think the government should provide fewer services, even in areas such as health and education, in order to reduce spending. (Others) feel it is important for the government to provide many more services even if it means an increase in spending. Where would you place yourself on this [seven-point] scale, or haven't you thought much about this?

3. There is much concern about the rapid rise in medical and hospital costs. Some people feel there should be a government insurance plan which would cover all medical and hospital expenses for everyone. Others feel that all medical expenses should be paid by individuals, and through private insurance plans like Blue Cross or other company-paid plans. Where would you place yourself on this [seven-point] scale, or haven't you thought much about this?

4. Recently there has been a lot of talk about women's rights. Some people feel that women should have an equal role with men in running business, industry, and government. Others feel that women's place is in the home. Where would you place yourself on this [seven-point] scale, or haven't you thought much about this?

5. Recently there has been a lot of discussion about sexual harassment. How serious a problem do you think sexual harassment in the work place is? Is it very serious, somewhat serious, or not too serious?

6. Do you favor or oppose laws to protect homosexuals against job discrimination? Do you favor/oppose such laws strongly or not strongly?

7. Some people say that the government in Washington should see to it that white and black children go to the same schools. Others claim that this is not the government's business. Have you been interested enough in this question to favor one side over the other? [If yes] Which side do you favor?

8. Some people believe that we should spend much less money for defense. Others feel that defense spending should be greatly increased. Where would you place yourself on this [seven-point] scale, or haven't you thought much about this?

9. In the future, how willing should the United States be to use military force to solve international problems—extremely willing, very willing, somewhat willing, not very willing, or never willing?

10. Do you think that most men who tried to avoid military service during the Vietnam War should have served regardless of their personal beliefs? [yes or no]

11. There is much discussion about the best way to deal with the problem of urban unrest and rioting. Some say it is more important to use all available force to maintain law and order—no matter what the results. Others say it is more important to correct the problems of poverty and unemployment that give rise to the disturbances. And, of course, other people have opinions in between. Where would you place yourself on this [seven-point] scale, or haven't you thought much about this?

12. Do you favor the death penalty for persons convicted of murder? Do you favor/oppose the death penalty for persons convicted of murder strongly or not strongly?

13. A law has been proposed that would limit members of Congress to no more than twelve years of service in that office. Do you favor or oppose such a law?

14. Should federal spending on . . . be increased, decreased, or kept about the same? (a) food stamps; (b) welfare programs; (c) AIDS research; (d) financial aid for college students; (e) programs that assist blacks; (f) solving the problem of the homeless; (g) social security; (h) science and technology; (i) improving and protecting the environment; (j) child care; (k) dealing with crime; (l) government assistance to the unemployed; (m) poor people; (n) public schools.

Group Attitudes and Attachments

1. Ratings of persons and groups on the "feeling thermometer" [with scores of 0–49 degrees reflecting a *less* favorable evaluation, 51–100 degrees a *more* favorable evaluation, and exactly 50 degrees indicating that the respondent feels neither "warm" nor "cold" toward the indicated person/group]: (a) poor people; (b) the women's movement; (c) gay men and lesbians (homosexuals); (d) respondent's incumbent representatives in the U.S. House and Senate.

2. When reading or listening to the news, how much attention do you pay to issues that especially affect women—a lot, some, a little, or not at all?

3. Some people think that the best way for women to improve their position is for each woman to become better trained and more qualified, and to do the best she can as an individual. Others think that while individual effort is important, the best way for women to really improve their position is if they work together. Which is closest to your view—is individual effort enough, or do women also need to work together?

4. How often do you find yourself feeling a sense of pride in the accomplishments of women—very often, some of the time, occasionally, or almost never?

5. How often do you find yourself angry about the way women are treated in society—very often, some of the time, occasionally, or almost never?

Political Involvement

1. Some people seem to follow what's going on in government and public affairs most of the time, whether there's an election going on or not. Others aren't that interested. Would you say you follow what's going on in government and public affairs most of the time, some of the time, only now and then, or hardly at all?*

2. Some people don't pay much attention to political campaigns. How about you? Would you say that you have been/were very much interested, somewhat interested, or not much interested in the political campaigns (so far) this year?*

3. Generally speaking, would you say that you personally care a good deal who wins the presidential election this fall, or that you don't care very much who wins?*

4. Did you listen to any speeches or discussions about the campaign on the radio? How about magazines—did you read about the campaign in any magazines? Did you read about the campaign in any newspapers? Did you watch any programs about the campaign on television? [yes or no]*

5. Do you ever discuss politics with your family or friends? [yes or no]

6. We would like to find out about some of the things people do to help a party or candidate win an election. During the campaign, did you (a) talk to any people and try to show them why they should vote for or against one of the parties or candidates? (b) wear a campaign button, put a campaign sticker on your car, or place a sign in your window or in the front of your house? (c) go to any political meetings, rallies, speeches, dinners, or things like that in support of a particular candidate? (d) do any (other) work for one of the parties or candidates? [yes or no]

7. In talking to people about elections, we often find that a lot of people were not able to vote because they weren't registered, they were sick, or they just didn't have time. How about you—did you vote in the elections this November? [yes or no]

8. Campaign contacts: (a) Did anyone from one of the political parties call you up or come around and talk to you about the campaign this year? (b) Other than someone from the two major parties, did anyone else call you up or come around and talk to you about supporting specific candidates in this last election? (c) Did anyone call you up or come around to ask you to go to any political meetings, rallies, speeches, dinners, or things like that in support of a particular candidate? (d) Did anyone call you to ask you to do any (other) work for one of the parties or candidates? (e) During the campaign this year, did anyone talk to you about registering to vote or getting out to vote? (f) During the past year, did you receive any requests through the mail asking you to contribute money to a candidate, a party, or an issue group? (g) During the past year, have you been contacted directly, in person, and asked to contribute money to a candidate, a party, or an issue group? [yes or no]

9. Do you listen to or watch talk shows on radio or T.V. where people call in to voice their opinions? [yes or no]

10. Do you think the presidential race will be close here, or will one candidate win by quite a bit?

Internal Efficacy

1. I feel that I have a pretty good understanding of the important political issues facing our country. [strongly agree to strongly disagree]

2. I consider myself well-qualified to participate in politics. [strongly agree to strongly disagree]

3. I feel that I could do as good a job in public office as most other people. [strongly agree to strongly disagree]

4. I think that I am better informed about politics and government than most people. [strongly agree to strongly disagree]

5. Sometimes politics and government seem so complicated that a person like me can't really understand what's going on. [strongly agree to strongly disagree]

General Attitudes About Government and Politics

1. How much of the time do you think you can trust the government in Washington to do what is right—just about always, most of the time, or only some of the time?

2. Do you think that people in the government waste a lot of the money we pay in taxes, waste some of it, or don't waste very much of it?

3. Would you say the government is pretty much run by a few big interests looking out for themselves or that it is run for the benefit of all the people?

4. Do you think that quite a few of the people running the government are crooked, not very many are, or do you think hardly any of them are crooked at all?

5. I don't think public officials care much what people like me think. [agree/disagree in 1964–1984; five-point strongly agree to strongly disagree in 1988]

6. Over the years, how much attention do you feel the government pays to what the people think when it decides what to do—a good deal, some, or not much?

7. And how much do you feel that having elections makes the government pay attention to what the people think—a good deal, some, or not much?

*Question wording has varied slightly over the years.

References

Abney, F. Glenn, and John D. Hutcheson Jr. 1981. "Race, Representation, and Trust: Changes in Attitudes After the Election of a Black Mayor." *Public Opinion Quarterly*. 45: 91–101.

Abramowitz, Alan I., John McGlennon, and Ronald B. Rapoport. 1983. "Party Activists in the United States: A Comparative State Analysis." *International Political Science Review*. 4:13–20.

Abramson, Paul R. 1983. *Political Attitudes in America: Formation and Change*. San Francisco: W. H. Freeman.

Abramson, Paul R., John H. Aldrich, and David W. Rohde. 1994. *Change and Continuity in the 1992 Elections*. Washington, DC: CQ Press.

Aldrich, John. 1983. "A Downsian Spatial Model with Party Activism." *American Political Science Review*. 77:974–990.

———. 1995. *Why Parties? The Origin and Transformation of Party Politics in America*. Chicago: University of Chicago Press.

Aldrich, John, and Richard G. Niemi. 1989. "The Sixth American Party System: The 1960s Realignment and the Candidate-Centered Parties." Unpublished paper, Duke University.

Alexander, Herbert E. 1992. *Financing Politics: Money, Elections, and Political Reform*, 4th ed. Washington, DC: CQ Press.

Alford, John R., and David W. Brady. 1989a. "Personal and Partisan Advantage in U.S. Congressional Elections, 1846–1986." In *Congress Reconsidered*, 4th ed., eds. Lawrence C. Dodd and Bruce I. Oppenheimer. Washington, DC: CQ Press.

———. 1989b. "Personal and Partisan Advantage in U.S. House Elections, 1846–1986." Unpublished paper, Stanford University.

Almond, Gabriel A., and Sidney Verba. 1963. *The Civic Culture: Political Attitudes and Democracy in Five Nations*. Princeton: Princeton University Press.

Alter, Jonathan. 1994. "The Record Nobody Knows." *Newsweek*. October 3:49.

American Enterprise. 1993. "Public Opinion and Demographic Report." July/August:83.

———. 1994. "Public Opinion and Demographic Report." January/February:83.

Andersen, Kristi. 1979. *The Creation of a Democratic Majority, 1928–1936*. Chicago: University of Chicago Press.

Armstrong, Cameron B., and Alan M. Rubin. 1989. "Talk Radio as Interpersonal Communication." *Journal of Communication*. 39:84–94.

Arnold, R. Douglas. 1990. *The Logic of Congressional Action*. New Haven: Yale University Press.

Asher, Herbert. 1992. *Polling and the Public: What Every Citizen Should Know,* 2nd ed. Washington, DC: CQ Press.

Associated Press. 1994. "Perot Tells Voters to Let Republicans Control Congress." *Gainesville Sun.* October 6:2A.

———. 1995a. "Clinton Rallies Fellow Democrats." *Gainesville Sun.* January 22:1A, 7A.

———. 1995b. "Some GOP Goals Not Possible, Dole Says." *Gainesville Sun.* January 23:3A.

Atkeson, Lonna Rae. 1992. "Divisive Nomination Campaigns: An Experimental Look at Attitude Change During a Simulated Presidential Campaign." Paper presented at 1992 Annual Meeting of the American Political Science Association, Chicago, IL.

———. 1993. "Moving Toward Unity: Attitudes in the Nomination and General Election Stages of a Presidential Campaign." *American Politics Quarterly.* 21:272–289.

Axelrod, Robert. 1986. "Presidential Election Coalitions in 1984." *American Political Science Review.* 80:281–284.

Baer, Denise L. 1993. "Who Has the Body? Party Institutionalization and Theories of Party Organization." *American Review of Politics.* 14:1–38.

Bailey, Christopher J. 1988. *The Republican Party in the U.S. Senate 1974–1984: Party Change and Institutional Development.* Manchester: Manchester University Press.

Baldassare, Mark. 1985. "Trust in Local Government." *Social Science Quarterly.* 66:704–712.

Balz, Dan. 1993. "What Clinton Needs to Win Perot's Voters." *Washington Post.* July 8:A8.

Barber, Benjamin R. 1984. *Strong Democracy: Participatory Politics for a New Age.* Berkeley: University of California Press.

Barber, Bernard. 1983. *The Logic and Limits of Trust.* New Brunswick, NJ: Rutgers University Press.

Bauer, Monica, and John R. Hibbing. 1989. "Which Incumbents Lose in House Elections: A Response to Jacobson's 'The Marginals Never Vanished.'" *American Journal of Political Science.* 33:262–271.

Baumann, Marty, 1994. "Electorate Swings to the Right." *USA Today.* November 9:9A.

Baxter, Sandra, and Marjorie Lansing. 1980. *Women and Politics: The Invisible Majority.* Ann Arbor: University of Michigan Press.

Beck, Paul Allen. 1974. "A Socialization Theory of Partisan Realignment." In *The Politics of Future Citizens,* by Richard G. Niemi and Associates. San Francisco: Jossey-Bass.

Bendyna, Mary E., and Celinda C. Lake. 1994. "Gender and Voting in the 1992 Presidential Election." In *The Year of the Woman: Myths and Realities,* eds. Elizabeth Adell Cook, Sue Thomas, and Clyde Wilcox. Boulder, CO.: Westview.

Benjamin, Gerald, and Michael J. Malbin, eds. 1992. *Limiting Legislative Terms.* Washington, DC: CQ Press.

Bennett, Linda L.M., and Stephen Earl Bennett. 1990. *Living with Leviathan: Americans Coming to Terms with Big Government.* Lawrence: University Press of Kansas.

Bennett, W. Lance. 1988. *News: The Politics of Illusion,* 2nd ed. New York: Longman.

———. 1992. *The Governing Crisis: Media, Money, and Marketing in American Elections.* New York: St. Martin's.

Berelson, Bernard R., Paul F. Lazarsfeld, and William N. McPhee. 1954. *Voting: A Study of Opinion Formation in a Presidential Campaign.* Chicago: University of Chicago Press.

Berke, Richard L. 1995. "Poll Finds Public Doubts Key Parts of G.O.P.'s Agenda." *New York Times.* February 28:D1.

Berman, Larry. 1990. "Looking Back on the Reagan Presidency." In *Looking Back on the Reagan Presidency,* ed. Larry Berman. Baltimore: Johns Hopkins University Press.

Beschloss, Michael R. 1994. "What Took Them So Long?" *Newsweek*. November 21:49.

Bierig, Jeffrey, and John Dimmick. 1979. "The Late Night Radio Talk Show as Interpersonal Communication." *Journalism Quarterly*. 56:92–96.

Black, Gordon S., and Benjamin D. Black. 1994. *The Politics of American Discontent*. New York: Wiley.

Blank, Rebecca M., and Alan S. Binder. 1986. "Macroeconomics, Income Distribution, and Poverty." In *Fighting Poverty: What Works and What Doesn't*, eds. Sheldon H. Danziger and David H. Weinberg. Cambridge: Harvard University Press.

Blank, Rebecca M., and David Card. 1993. "Poverty, Income Distribution, and Growth: Are They Still Connected?" In *Brookings Papers on Economic Activity*, 2: 1993. Washington, DC: Brookings Institution.

Bledsoe, Timothy. 1993. *Careers in City Politics: The Case for Urban Democracy*. Pittsburgh: University of Pittsburgh Press.

Bledsoe, Timothy, Lee Sigelman, Susan Welch, and Michael Combs. 1994. "Suburbanization, Residential Integration, and Racial Solidarity Among African-Americans." Paper presented at the 1994 Annual Meeting of the Midwest Political Science Association, Chicago, IL.

The Book of States. 1992. Vol. 29. Lexington, KY: Council of State Governments.

Borger, Gloria. 1994. "Talking Straight to the Middle Class." *U.S. News and World Report*. January 10:43.

Borjas, George J., Richard B. Freeman, and Lawrence F. Katz. 1991. "On the Labor Market Effects of Immigration and Trade." Working Paper No. 3761, National Bureau of Economic Research, Cambridge, MA.

Born, Richard. 1982. "Perquisite Employment in the U.S. House of Representatives." *American Politics Quarterly*. 10:347–362.

Bowman, Karlyn H. 1995. "The Gender Factor." In *America at the Polls, 1994*, ed. Everett Carll Ladd. Storrs, CT: Roper Center for Public Opinion Research.

Brady, David W. 1988. *Critical Elections and Congressional Policy Making*. Stanford: Stanford University Press.

Branch, Taylor. 1988. *Parting the Waters: America in the King Years, 1954–1963*. New York: Simon and Schuster.

Broder, David S. 1995. "A Caution to House Republicans." *Washington Post Weekly Edition*. January 9–15:4.

Brownstein, Ronald. 1994. "Clinton's Job One: Reversing the Anti-Government Tide." *Public Perspective*. May/June:3–6.

Burnham, Walter Dean. 1965. "The Changing Shape of the American Political Universe." *American Political Science Review*. 59:7–28.

———. 1970. *Critical Elections and the Mainsprings of American Politics*. New York: Norton.

Burns, James MacGregor. 1966. *Presidential Leadership: The Crucible of Leadership*. Boston: Houghton Mifflin.

Butler, David, and Austin Ranney. 1994. "Over Their Heads." *American Enterprise*. May/June:58–65.

Cain, Bruce. 1994. "The Varying Impact of Legislative Term Limits." Working paper for the Institute of Governmental Studies, University of California, Berkeley, CA.

Cain, Bruce, John Ferejohn, and Morris Fiorina. 1987. *The Personal Vote: Constituency Service and Electoral Independence*. Cambridge: Harvard University Press.

Calvert, Randall L., and John A. Ferejohn. 1983. "Coattail Voting in Recent Presidential Elections." *American Political Science Review.* 77:407–419.

Campbell, Angus, Philip E. Converse, Warren E. Miller, and Donald E. Stokes. 1960. *The American Voter.* New York: Wiley.

Canfield, James Lewis. 1984. *A Case of Third Party Activism: The George Wallace Campaign Worker and the American Independent Party.* Lanham, MD: University Press of America.

Cantril, Hadley, and Mildred Strunk. 1951. *Public Opinion, 1935–1946.* Princeton: Princeton University Press.

Card, David. 1991. "The Effect of Unions on the Distribution of Wages: Redistribution or Relabelling?" Working Paper No. 287, Department of Economics, Princeton University, Princeton, NJ.

Carlson, Jody. 1981. *George C. Wallace and the Politics of Powerlessness.* New Brunswick, NJ: Transaction Books.

Carmines, Edward G., and James A. Stimson. 1989. *Issue Evolution: Race and the Transformation of American Politics.* Princeton: Princeton University Press.

Carroll, Susan J. 1988. "Women's Autonomy and the Gender Gap: 1980 and 1982." In *The Politics of the Gender Gap: The Social Construction of Political Influence,* ed. Carol M. Mueller. Beverly Hills: Sage.

Ceaser, James, and Andrew Busch. 1993. *Upside Down and Inside Out: The 1992 Elections and American Politics.* Lanham, MD: Rowman and Littlefield.

Chambers, William Nisbet, and Walter Dean Burnham, eds. 1975. *The American Party Systems,* 2nd ed. New York: Oxford University Press.

Citrin, Jack. 1974. "Comment: The Political Relevance of Trust in Government." *American Political Science Review.* 68:973–988.

———. 1987. "Public Opinion in a Changing California." In *The Capacity to Respond,* eds. Ted Bradshaw and Charles Bell. Berkeley: Institute of Governmental Studies Press.

Citrin, Jack, and Donald Philip Green. 1986. "Presidential Leadership and the Resurgence of Trust in Government." *British Journal of Political Science.* 16:431–453.

Clark, Janet, and Cal Clark. 1989. "Wyoming Women's Attitudes Toward the MX: The Old vs. New Gender Gap." *Journal of Political Science.* 17:127–140.

———. 1993. "The Gender Gap 1988: Compassion, Pacifism, and Indirect Feminism." In *Women in Politics: Outsiders or Insiders?* ed. Lois Lovelace Duke. Englewood Cliffs, NJ: Prentice Hall.

———. 1994. "Traditional Values and the Changing Nature of the Gender Gap in America: Abortion's Impact on the 1992 Presidential Election." Paper presented at the 1994 Annual Meeting of the International Society for Political Psychology, Barcelona, Spain.

Clubb, Jerome M., William H. Flanigan, and Nancy H. Zingale. 1980. *Partisan Realignment:Voters, Parties, and Government in American History.* Beverly Hills: Sage.

Cohen, Richard E. 1993. "On the Edge." *National Journal.* December 4:2888–2991.

———. 1994. *Changing Course in Washington: Clinton and the New Congress.* New York: Macmillan.

Connelly, William F., Jr. 1991. "Party Policy Committees in Congress." Paper presented at 1991 Annual Meeting of the Western Political Science Association, Seattle, WA.

Connelly, William F., Jr., and John J. Pitney Jr. 1994. *Congress' Permanent Minority? Republicans in the U.S. House.* Lanham, MD: Rowman and Littlefield.

Conover, Pamela Johnston. 1988. "Feminists and the Gender Gap." *Journal of Politics.* 50:985–1010.

Conover, Pamela Johnston, Ivor M. Crewe, and Donald D. Searing. 1991. "The Nature of Citizenship in the United States and Great Britain: Empirical Comments on Theoretical Themes." *Journal of Politics.* 53:800–832.

Converse, Jean M. 1976–1977. "Predicting No Opinion in the Polls." *Public Opinion Quarterly.* 40:515–530.

Converse, Philip E. 1964. "The Nature of Belief Systems in Mass Publics." In *Ideology and Discontent,* ed. David E. Apter. New York: Free Press.

———. 1966. "Religion and Politics: The 1960 Election." In *Elections and the Political Order,* by Angus Campbell, Philip E. Converse, Warren E. Miller, and Donald E. Stokes. New York: Wiley.

———. 1970. "Attitudes and Non-attitudes: Continuation of a Dialogue." In *The Quantitative Analysis of Social Problems,* ed. Edward C. Tufte. Reading, MA: Addison-Wesley.

———. 1976. *The Dynamics of the Party System: Cohort-Analyzing Party Identification.* Beverly Hills: Sage.

Conway, M. Margaret. 1991. *Political Participation in the United States,* 2nd ed. Washington, DC: CQ Press.

Cook, Elizabeth Adell. 1992. *Between Two Absolutes: Public Opinion and the Politics of Abortion.* Boulder, CO: Westview.

Cook, Elizabeth Adell, Sue Thomas, and Clyde Wilcox, eds. 1994. *The Year of the Woman: Myths and Realities.* Boulder, CO: Westview.

Cook, Rhodes. 1993. "Hill Finds It Cannot Escape Perot's Lingering Presence." *Congressional Quarterly Weekly Report.* 51:2671–2673.

Corrado, Anthony J. 1994. "The 1992 Presidential Election: A Time for Change?" In *The Parties Respond: Changes in American Parties and Campaigns,* 2nd ed., ed. L. Sandy Maisel. Boulder, CO: Westview.

Cotter, Cornelius P., James L. Gibson, John F. Bibby, and Robert J. Huckshorn. 1984. *Party Organizations in American Politics.* New York: Praeger.

Coursen, Kimberly. 1993. "All Journalists Are Not Created Equal: How Members of the Media Differ in Their Opinions Toward Congress." Paper presented at the 1993 Conference on Congress and the Media, American Enterprise Institute, Washington, DC.

Cover, Albert D., and Bruce S. Brumberg. 1982. "Baby Books and Ballots: The Impact of Congressional Mail on Constituent Opinion." *American Political Science Review.* 76:347–359.

Craig, Stephen C. 1993. *The Malevolent Leaders: Popular Discontent in America.* Boulder, CO: Westview.

Craig, Stephen C., Richard G. Niemi, and Glenn E. Silver. 1990. "Political Efficacy and Trust: A Report on the NES Pilot Study Items." *Political Behavior.* 12:289–314.

Cronin, Thomas E. 1988. "Public Opinion and Direct Democracy." *PS.* 21:612–619.

———. 1989. *Direct Democracy: The Politics of Initiative, Referendum, and Recall.* Cambridge: Harvard University Press.

Crotty, William, and John S. Jackson III. 1985. *Presidential Primaries and Nominations.* Washington, DC: CQ Press.

Cutler, Blayne. 1989. "Mature Audiences Only." *American Demographics.* October:20–26.

———. 1990. "High Frequency." *American Demographics.* March:11–12.

Dahl, Robert A. 1992. "Finding Competent Citizens: Improving Democracy." *Journal of Democracy.* 3:54–59.

————. 1994. *The New American Political (Dis)order*. Berkeley: Institute of Governmental Studies Press.

Dalton, Russell J. 1984. "Cognitive Mobilization and Partisan Dealignment in Advanced Industrial Democracies." *Journal of Politics*. 46:264–284.

Darcy, R., Susan Welch, and Janet Clark. 1994. *Women, Elections, and Representation*, 2nd ed. Lincoln: University of Nebraska Press.

DeFleur, Melvin L., and Everett E. Dennis. 1991. *Understanding Mass Communication*, 4th ed. Boston: Houghton Mifflin.

Democratic Leadership Council. 1994. "Third Force: Why Independents Turned Against Democrats—and How to Win Them Back." Report issued by the Democratic Leadership Council, November.

Destler, I. M., Leslie H. Gelb, and Arthur Lake. 1984. *Our Own Worst Enemy: The Unmaking of American Foreign Policy*. New York: Simon and Schuster.

Diamond, Edwin, and Stephen Bates. 1992. *The Spot: The Rise of Political Advertising on Television*, 3rd ed. Cambridge: MIT Press.

Dionne, E. J. 1991. *Why Americans Hate Politics*. New York: Simon and Schuster.

Dodd, Lawrence C. 1993. "Congress and the Politics of Renewal: Redressing the Crisis of Legitimation." In *Congress Reconsidered*, 5th ed., ed. Lawrence C. Dodd and Bruce I. Oppenheimer. Washington, DC: CQ Press.

Dole, Bob, and Elizabeth Dole with Richard Norton Smith. 1988. *The Doles: Unlimited Partners*. New York: Simon and Schuster.

Downs, Anthony. 1957. *An Economic Theory of Democracy*. New York: Harper and Row.

Easton, David. 1965. *A Systems Analysis of Political Life*. New York: Wiley.

————. 1975. "A Re-Assessment of the Concept of Political Support." *British Journal of Political Science*. 5:435–457.

Economist. 1989. "Talk Radio: Lines Are Open." June 17:34–35.

Edsall, Thomas Byrne. 1994a. "Democrats Face Another Identity Crisis." *Washington Post*. May 21:D1.

————. 1994b. "Influence of Values, Education, Gender Redefine Images of Both Major Parties." *Washington Post*. May 28:A4.

Edsall, Thomas Byrne, with Mary D. Edsall. 1991. *Chain Reaction: The Impact of Race, Rights, and Taxes on American Politics*. New York: Norton.

Eisner, Robert R. 1994. *The Misunderstood Economy: What Counts and How to Count It*. Boston: Harvard Business School Press.

Ekirch, Arthur A., Jr. 1969. *Ideologies and Utopias: The Impact of the New Deal on American Thought*. Chicago: Quadrangle Books.

Ellison, Christopher G., and David A. Gay. 1989. "Black Political Participation Revisited: A Test of Compensatory, Ethnic Community, and Public Arena Models." *Social Science Quarterly*. 70:101–119.

Elster, Jon. 1984. *Ulysses and the Sirens: Studies in Rationality and Irrationality*, rev. ed. Cambridge: Cambridge University Press.

Erie, Steven P., and Martin Rein. 1988. "Women and the Welfare State." In *The Politics of the Gender Gap: The Social Construction of Political Influence*, ed. Carol M. Mueller. Beverly Hills: Sage.

Erikson, Robert S. 1990. "Economic Conditions and the Congressional Vote: A Review of the Macrolevel Evidence." *American Journal of Political Science*. 34:373–399.

Erikson, Robert S., Norman R. Luttbeg, and Kent L. Tedin. 1991. *American Public Opinion*, 4th ed. New York: Macmillan.

Fair, Ray C. 1978. "The Effect of Economic Events on Votes for President." *Review of Economics and Statistics*. 60:159–172.

———. 1982. "The Effect of Economic Events on Votes for President: 1980 Results." *Review of Economics and Statistics*. 64:322–325.

———. 1988. "The Effect of Economic Events on Votes for President: 1984 Update." *Political Behavior*. 10:168–179.

Faucheux, Ron. 1993. "Here's the Deal, See." *Campaigns and Elections*. August:18–19.

Fazzari, Steven M. 1993. "Monetary Policy, Financial Structure, and Investment." In *Transforming the U.S. Financial System: Equity and Efficiency for the Twenty-first Century*, eds. Gary Dymski, Gerald A. Epstein, and Robert Pollin. Armonk, NY: M. E. Sharpe.

Fee, Joan Flynn. 1981. "Symbols in Survey Questions: Solving the Problem of Multiple Word Meanings." *Political Methodology*. 7:71–95.

Feldman, Stanley, and John Zaller. 1992. "The Political Culture of Ambivalence: Ideological Responses to the Welfare State." *American Journal of Political Science*. 36:268–307.

Fenno, Richard F., Jr. 1973. *Congressmen in Committees*. Boston: Little, Brown.

———. 1978. *Home Style: House Members in Their Districts*. Boston: Little, Brown.

———. 1982. *The United States Senate: A Bicameral Perspective*. Washington, DC: American Enterprise Institute.

———. 1992. *When Incumbency Fails: The Senate Career of Mark Andrews*. Washington, DC: CQ Press.

Ferejohn, John A. 1977. "On the Decline of Competition in Congressional Elections." *American Political Science Review*. 71:166–176.

Field, Harry. 1946. *The People Look at Radio*. Chapel Hill: University of North Carolina Press.

Fineman, Howard. 1989. "The Power of Talk." *Newsweek*. February 8:24–28.

———. 1994a. "The Clean-Slate Club." *Newsweek*. October 17:34–35.

———. 1994b. "Rolling Thunder." *Newsweek*. November 7:24–31.

———. 1995. "The Warrior." *Newsweek*. January 9:28–34.

Fiorina, Morris P. 1977. *Congress: Keystone of the Washington Establishment*. New Haven: Yale University Press.

———. 1978. "Economic Retrospective Voting in American Elections," *American Journal of Political Science*. 22:426–443.

———. 1989. *Congress: Keystone of the Washington Establishment*, 2nd ed. New Haven: Yale University Press.

———. 1992. *Divided Government*. New York: Macmillan.

Fiorina, Morris P., and Roger C. Noll. 1979. "Majority Rule Models and Legislative Elections." *Journal of Politics*. 41:1081–1104.

Fishkin, James S. 1991. *Democracy and Deliberation: New Directions for Democratic Reform*. New Haven: Yale University Press.

Fitzgerald, Randall, and Gerald Lipson. 1984. *Porkbarrel*. Washington, DC: Cato Institute.

Fowler, Robert Booth. 1985. *Religion and Politics in America*. Metuchen, NJ: Scarecrow Press.

Frankovic, Kathleen A. 1993. "Public Opinion in the 1992 Campaign." In *The Election of 1992: Reports and Interpretations*, ed. Gerald M. Pomper. Chatham, NJ: Chatham House.

Free, Lloyd A., and Hadley Cantril. 1967. *The Political Beliefs of Americans*. New Brunswick, NJ: Rutgers University Press.

Freeman, Richard B. 1991. "How Much Has Deunionization Contributed to the Rise in Male Earnings Inequality?" Working Paper No. 3826, National Bureau of Economic Research, Cambridge, MA.

Freud, Sigmund. 1961. *Future of an Illusion,* ed. James Strachey. New York: Norton.

From, Al. 1989. Memo to Representative Steny Hoyer. July 24.

Galvin, Thomas. 1992. "Term Limits." *Congressional Quarterly Weekly Report.* November 7:4–5.

Gamm, Gerald H. 1989. *The Making of New Deal Democrats: Voting Behavior and Realignment in Boston, 1920–1940.* Chicago: University of Chicago Press.

Gamson, William A. 1968. *Power and Discontent.* Homewood, IL: Dorsey.

———. 1971. "Political Trust and Its Ramifications." In *Social Psychology and Political Behavior: Problems and Prospects,* eds. Gilbert Abcarian and John W. Soule. Columbus, OH: Charles E. Merrill.

Garment, Suzanne. 1991. *Scandal: The Crisis of Mistrust in American Politics.* New York: Random House.

Garrow, David. 1986. *Bearing the Cross: Martin Luther King, Jr. and the Southern Christian Leadership.* New York: Vintage.

Geer, John G. 1992. "New Deal Issues and the American Electorate, 1952–1988." *Political Behavior.* 14:45–65.

Georges, Christopher. 1993. "Perot and Con." *Washington Monthly.* June:38–43.

Germond, Jack W., and Jules Witcover. 1993. *Mad as Hell: Revolt at the Ballot Box, 1992.* New York: Warner Books.

Gibson, James L., Cornelius P. Cotter, John F. Bibby, and Robert J. Huckshorn. 1983. "Assessing Party Organizational Strength." *American Journal of Political Science.* 27:193–222.

Gilbert, Christopher P. 1993. *The Impact of Churches on Political Behavior: An Empirical Study.* Westport, CT: Greenwood Press.

Giles, Martin. 1988. "Gender and Support for Reagan: A Comprehensive Model of Presidential Support." *American Journal of Political Science.* 32:19–49.

Gillespie, J. David. 1993. *Politics and the Periphery: Third Parties in Two-Party America.* Columbia: University of South Carolina Press.

Gilligan, Carol. 1982. *In a Different Voice: Psychological Theory and Women's Development.* Cambridge: Harvard University Press.

Gilmour, Robert S., and Robert B. Lamb. 1975. *Political Alienation in Contemporary America.* New York: St. Martin's.

Glenn, Norval D. 1977. *Cohort Analysis.* Beverly Hills: Sage.

Gore, Al. 1993. *From Red Tape to Results: Creating a Government That Works Better and Costs Less. Report of the National Performance Review.* Washington, DC: U.S. Government Printing Office.

Greeley, Andrew M. 1989. *Religious Change in America.* Cambridge: Harvard University Press.

Green, John C. 1993. "Religion, Social Issues, and the Christian Right: Assessing the 1992 Presidential Election." Paper presented at a colloquium sponsored by the Ethics and Public Policy Center, Washington, DC.

Greenberg, Stanley. 1993. "The Perot Voters and American Politics: Here to Stay?" In *The Road to Realignment: The Democrats and the Perot Voters.* Report issued by the Democratic Leadership Council, July.

Greider, William. 1992. *Who Will Tell the People: The Betrayal of American Democracy*. New York: Simon and Schuster.

Guth, James L., John C. Green, and Lyman A. Kellstedt. 1993. "God's Own Party: Evangelicals and Republicans in the '92 Elections." *Christian Century*. 17:172–176.

Hadaway, C. Kirk, Penny Long Marler, and Mark Chaves. 1993. "What the Polls Don't Show: A Closer Look at U.S. Church Attendance." *American Sociological Review*. 58:741–752.

Hale, Jon F. 1993. "A Different Kind of Democrat: Bill Clinton, the DLC, and the Construction of a New Party Identity." Paper presented at the 1993 Annual Meeting of the American Political Science Association, Washington, DC.

Hallin, Daniel C. 1984. "The Media, the War in Vietnam, and Political Support: A Critique of the Thesis of an Oppositional Media." *Journal of Politics*. 46:2–24.

Hamilton, Bill, and Wally Mealiea. 1993. "Perotistas: Who Are These People Anyway?" *Campaigns and Elections*. August:21–22.

Hamilton, Richard F., and James D. Wright. 1986. *The State of the Masses*. New York: Aldine.

Hanna, Mary. 1979. *Catholics and American Politics*. Cambridge: Harvard University Press.

Harwood, Richard. 1992. "Signs of a New Politics." *Social Policy*. 23:4–15.

Herbst, Bob. 1994. "Interactive Democracy." *Campaigns and Elections*. April:53.

Herring, Cedric, James S. House, and Richard Mero. 1991. "Racially Based Changes in Political Alienation in America." *Social Science Quarterly*. 72:123–134.

Herrnson, Paul S. 1988. *Party Campaigning in the 1980s*. Cambridge: Harvard University Press.

Herrnson, Paul S., and Kelly D. Patterson. 1995. "Agenda-Setting and Coalition-Building in the House: Toward a More Programmatic Party? *Polity*. Forthcoming.

Hershey, Marjorie Randon. 1993. "The Congressional Elections." In *The Election of 1992: Reports and Interpretations*, ed. Gerald M. Pomper. Chatham, NJ: Chatham House.

Hertzke, Allen D. 1993. *Echoes of Discontent: Jesse Jackson, Pat Robertson, and the Resurgence of Populism*. Washington, DC: CQ Press.

Hess, Stephen, and Michael Nelson. 1985. "Foreign Policy: Dominance and Decisiveness in Presidential Elections." In *The Elections of 1984*, ed. Michael Nelson. Washington, DC: CQ Press.

Hibbing, John R., and Elizabeth Theiss-Morse. 1994. "Popular Support for Congress: Replacing Myths with Theory." Unpublished paper, University of Nebraska.

Higgs, Robert. 1987. *Crisis and Leviathan: Critical Episodes in the Growth of American Government*. New York: Oxford University Press.

Hobbes, Thomas. [1651] 1991. *Leviathan*, ed. Richard Tuck. Cambridge: Cambridge University Press.

Hook, Janet. 1995. "Conservative Freshman Class Eager to Seize the Moment." *Congressional Quarterly Weekly Report*. January 7:47–115.

Howell, David. 1994. "The Skills Myth." *American Prospect*. Summer:81–90.

Howell, Susan E., and Deborah Fagan. 1988. "Race and Trust in Government: Testing the Political Reality Model." *Public Opinion Quarterly*. 52:343–350.

Hunter, James Davison. 1991. *Culture Wars: The Struggle to Define America*. New York: Basic Books.

Huntington, Samuel P. 1981. *American Politics: The Promise of Disharmony*. Cambridge: Harvard University Press.

Inglehart, Ronald. 1977. *The Silent Revolution: Changing Values and Political Styles Among Western Publics.* Princeton: Princeton University Press.

———. 1988. "The Renaissance of Political Culture." *American Political Science Review.* 82:1203–1230.

Iyengar, Shanto, and Donald R. Kinder. 1987. *News That Matters: Television and American Opinion.* Chicago: University of Chicago Press.

Jackson, Brooks. 1988. *Honest Graft: Big Money and the American Political Process.* New York: Knopf.

Jacobson, Gary C. 1990. "Does the Economy Matter in Midterm Elections?" *American Journal of Political Science.* 34:400–404.

———. 1992. *The Politics of Congressional Elections,* 3rd ed. New York: HarperCollins.

———. 1993. "Congress: Unusual Year, Unusual Election." In *The Elections of 1992,* ed. Michael Nelson. Washington, DC: CQ Press.

———. 1995. "The 1994 Midterm: Why the Models Missed It." Remarks published in the January newsletter, Legislative Studies Section of the American Political Science Association.

Jensen, Richard. 1981. "The Last Party System: Decay of Consensus, 1932–1980." In *The Evolution of American Electoral Systems,* ed. Paul Kleppner. Westport, CT: Greenwood Press.

Johnson, Haynes. 1994. *Divided We Fall: Gambling with History in the Nineties.* New York: Norton.

Kanter, Donald L., and Philip H. Mirvis. 1989. *The Cynical Americans: Living and Working in an Age of Discontent and Disillusion.* San Francisco: Jossey-Bass.

Kayden, Xandra, and Eddie Mahe Jr. 1985. *The Party Goes On: The Persistence of the Two-Party System in the United States.* New York: Basic Books.

Keith, Bruce E., David B. Magleby, Candice J. Nelson, Elizabeth Orr, Mark C. Westlye, and Raymond E. Wolfinger. 1992. *The Myth of the Independent Voter.* Berkeley: University of California Press.

Kellstedt, Lyman A. 1993. "Religion, the Neglected Variable: An Agenda for Future Research on Religion and Political Behavior." In *Rediscovering the Religious Factor in American Politics,* eds. David C. Leege and Lyman A. Kellstedt. Armonk, NY: M. E. Sharpe.

Kellstedt, Lyman A., and John C. Green. 1993. "Knowing God's Many People: Denominational Preference and Political Behavior." In *Rediscovering the Religious Factor in American Politics,* eds. David C. Leege and Lyman A. Kellstedt. Armonk, NY: M. E. Sharpe.

Kellstedt, Lyman A., and Mark A. Noll. 1990. "Religion, Voting for President, and Party Identification, 1948–1984." In *Religion and American Politics: From the Colonial Period to the 1980s,* ed. Mark A. Noll. New York: Oxford University Press.

Kellstedt, Lyman A., Corwin E. Smidt, and James L. Guth. 1993. "Religious Voting Blocs in the 1992 Election: The Year of the Evangelical?" Paper presented at the 1993 Annual Meeting of the American Political Science Association, Washington, DC.

Kellstedt, Lyman A., John C Green, James L. Guth, and Corwin Smidt. 1994. "It's the Culture Stupid! 1992 and Our Political Future." *First Things.* April:28–33.

Kellstedt, Lyman A., John C. Green, James L. Guth, and Corwin E. Smidt. 1995. "Has Godot Finally Arrived? Religious Traditions and Realignment in 1994." Unpublished manuscript.

Kelly, Brian. 1992. *Adventures in Porkland: How Washington Wastes Your Money and Why They Won't Stop.* New York: Villard Books.

Kenski, Henry C. 1988. "The Gender Factor in a Changing Electorate." In *The Politics of the Gender Gap: The Social Construction of Political Influence,* ed. Carol M. Mueller. Beverly Hills: Sage.

Kenski, Henry C., and William Lockwood. 1987. "The Catholic Vote from 1980–1986: Continuity or Change?" Paper presented at the 1987 Annual Meeting of the American Political Science Association, Chicago, IL.

Kerner Commission. 1988. *The Report of the (1968) National Advisory Commission on Civil Disorders.* New York: Pantheon.

Kettering Foundation. 1991. *Citizens and Politics: A View from Main Street America.* Dayton, OH: Kettering Foundation.

Key, V. O., Jr. 1955. "A Theory of Critical Elections." *Journal of Politics.* 17:3–18.

———. 1961. *Public Opinion and American Democracy.* New York: Knopf.

———. 1964. *Politics, Parties, and Pressure Groups,* 5th ed. New York: Crowell.

Kim, Jae-On, and Charles W. Mueller. 1978a. *Introduction to Factor Analysis: What It Is and How to Do It.* Beverly Hills: Sage.

———. 1978b. *Factor Analysis: Statistical Methods and Practical Issues.* Beverly Hills: Sage.

Kingdon, John W. 1973. *Congressmen's Voting Decisions.* New York: Harper and Row.

Kleiman, Michael B. 1976. "Trends in Racial Differences in Political Efficacy." *Phylon.* 37:159–162.

Klein, Ethel. 1984. *Gender Politics: From Consciousness to Mass Politics.* Cambridge: Harvard University Press.

Klein, Joe. 1992. "The Year of the Voter." *Newsweek.* November/December (Special Election Issue):14–15.

Kleppner, Paul. 1970. *The Cross of Culture: A Social Analysis of Midwestern Politics, 1850–1928.* New York: Free Press.

———. 1979. *The Third Electoral System, 1853–1892.* Chapel Hill: University of North Carolina Press.

———. 1987. *Continuity and Change in Electoral Politics, 1892–1928.* Westport, CT: Greenwood Press.

Klinkner, Philip A. 1991. "A Comparison of Out-Party Leaders: Ray Bliss and Bill Brock." Paper presented at the conference "Grass Roots Politics and Party Organization: The Leadership Model of Ray C. Bliss," University of Akron, Ray C. Bliss Institute of Applied Politics, Akron, OH.

Knack, Steve. 1993. "Perot, Recession, MTV, and Motor Voter: Explaining the '92 Turnout Rise." Paper presented at the 1993 Annual Meeting of the American Political Science Association, Washington, DC.

Kohut, Andrew. 1993. *The Vocal Minority in American Politics.* Washington, DC: Times Mirror Center for the People and the Press.

Koopman, Douglas L. 1994. "The 1994 House Elections: A Republican View." Remarks published in the December newsletter, Legislative Studies Section of the American Political Science Association.

Kostroski, Warren E. 1973. "Party and Incumbency in Post War Senate Elections: Trends, Patterns, and Models." *American Political Science Review.* 67:1213–1234.

Kramer, Gerald. 1971. "Short-Term Fluctuations in U.S. Voting, 1896–1964." *American Political Science Review.* 65:131–143.

Kurtz, Howard. 1995. "Has Talk Radio Lost Its Voice?" *Washington Post.* March 23:D1, D3.

Ladd, Everett Carll. 1981. "The Brittle Mandate: Electoral Dealignment and the 1980 Presidential Election." *Political Science Quarterly.* 96:1–25.

————. 1990. "Like Waiting for Godot: The Uselessness of Realignment for Understanding Change in Contemporary American Politics." *Polity*. 22:511–525.

————. 1992. "Who Says Americans Are 'Mad As Hell'?" *Public Perspective*. July/August:6–7.

————. 1993. "The 1992 Vote for President Clinton: Another Brittle Mandate?" *Political Science Quarterly*. 108:1–28.

Ladd, Everett Carll, ed. 1995. *America at the Polls, 1994*. Storrs, CT: Roper Center for Public Opinion Research.

Ladd, Everett Carll, with Charles D. Hadley. 1975. *Transformations of the American Party System*. New York: Norton.

————. 1978. *Transformations of the American Party System*, 2nd ed. New York: Norton.

Lamb, Brian. 1988. *C-SPAN: America's Town Hall*. Washington, DC: Acropolis Books.

Lamb, Karl A. 1974. *As Orange Goes: Twelve California Families and the Future of American Politics*. New York: Norton.

Lane, Robert E. 1962. *Political Ideology: Why the American Common Man Believes What He Does*. New York: Free Press.

Larson, Stephanie G. 1990. "Information and Learning in a Congressional District: A Social Experiment." *American Journal of Political Science*. 34:1102–1118.

Lazarsfeld, Paul F., and Patricia L. Kendall. 1948. *Radio Listening in America*. New York: Prentice-Hall.

Leege David. 1993. "The Decomposition of the Religious Vote: A Comparison of White, Non-Hispanic Catholics with Other Ethnoreligious Groups, 1960–1992." Paper presented at the 1993 Annual Meeting of the American Political Science Association, Washington, DC.

Leutchenberg, William E. 1983. *In the Shadow of FDR: From Harry Truman to Ronald Reagan*. Ithaca, NY: Cornell University Press.

Lewis-Beck, Michael S., and Tom W. Rice. 1992. *Forecasting Elections*. Washington, DC: CQ Press.

Lewis-Beck, Michael S., and J. Mark Wrighton. 1994. "A Republican Congress? Forecasts for 1994." Remarks published in the October/November newsletter, Elections, Public Opinion, and Voting Behavior Section of the American Political Science Association.

Liao, Tim Futing. 1994. *Interpreting Probability Models: Logit, Probit, and Other Generalized Probability Models*. Thousand Oaks, CA: Sage.

Lincoln, C. Eric, and Lawrence H. Mamiya. 1990. *The Black Church in the African American Experience*. Durham, NC: Duke University Press.

Lipset, Seymour Martin, and William Schneider. 1983. "The Decline of Confidence in American Institutions." *Political Science Quarterly*. 98:379–402.

————. 1987. *The Confidence Gap: Business, Labor and Government in the Public Mind*, rev. ed. Baltimore: Johns Hopkins University Press.

Littwin, Susan. 1986. *The Postponed Generation: Why American Youth Are Growing Up Later*. New York: William Morrow.

Lopatto, Paul. 1985. *Religion and the Presidential Election*. New York: Praeger.

Lowi, Theodore J. 1985. *The Personal President: Power Invested, Promise Unfulfilled*. Ithaca, NY: Cornell University Press.

Lubenow, Gerald, ed. 1991. *The Governor's Race in 1990*. Berkeley: Institute of Governmental Studies Press.

Luntz, Frank I. 1993. "Perovian Civilization: Who Supported Ross, and Why." *Policy Review*. 64:18–24.

Luttwak, Edward N. 1993. *The Endangered American Dream*. New York: Simon and Schuster.

Madsen, Douglas. 1987. "Political Self-Efficacy Tested." *American Political Science Review*. 81:571–581.

Magleby, David B. 1984. *Direct Legislation: Voting on Ballot Propositions in the United States*. Baltimore: Johns Hopkins University Press.

———. 1989. "Opinion Formation and Opinion Change in Ballot Proposition Campaigns." In *Manipulating Public Opinion: Essays on Public Opinion as a Dependent Variable*, eds. Michael Margolis and Gary A. Mauser. Pacific Grove, CA: Brooks/Cole.

Magleby, David B., and Candice J. Nelson. 1990. *The Money Chase: Congressional Campaign Finance Reform*. Washington, DC: Brookings Institution.

Mann, Horace. [1855] 1969. *Lectures on Education*. New York: Arno Press.

Mannheim, Karl. 1952. "The Problem of Generations." In *Essays on the Sociology of Knowledge*, by Karl Mannheim. London: Routledge & Kegan Paul.

Marcus, Ruth. 1995. "Who Are They and Where Are They Going?" *Washington Post Weekly Edition*. January 9–15:15.

Massey, Douglas S., and Nancy A. Denton. 1993. *American Apartheid: Segregation and the Making of the Underclass*. Cambridge: Harvard University Press.

Mayer, William G. 1992. *The Changing American Mind: How and Why American Public Opinion Changed Between 1960 and 1988*. Ann Arbor: University of Michigan Press.

Mayhew, David R. 1974. *Congress: The Electoral Connection*. New Haven: Yale University Press.

Mazmanian, Daniel A. 1974. *Third Parties in Presidential Elections*. Washington, DC: Brookings Institution.

McClosky, Herbert, and John Zaller. 1984. *The American Ethos: Public Attitudes Toward Capitalism and Democracy*. Cambridge: Harvard University Press.

McWilliams, Wilson Carey. 1993. "The Meaning of the Election." In *The Election of 1992: Reports and Interpretations*, ed. Gerald M. Pomper. Chatham, NJ: Chatham House.

Meacham, Jon. 1993. "Why the Party of the People Has a Grassroots Problem." *Washington Monthly*. October:22–28.

Mendelsohn, Harold. 1964. "Listening to Radio." In *People, Society, and Mass Communications*, eds. Lewis Anthony Dexter and David Manning White. Glencoe, IL: Free Press.

Menendez, Albert J. 1977. *Religion at the Polls*. Philadelphia: Westminster Press.

Merida, Kevin. 1994. "Running Away from Bill Clinton." *Washington Post Weekly Edition*. September 26–October 2:12.

Milbrath, Lester W. 1965. *Political Participation: How and Why Do People Get Involved in Politics?* Chicago: Rand McNally.

Milkis, Sidney M. 1993. *The President and the Parties: The Transformation of the American Party System Since the New Deal*. New York: Oxford University Press.

Miller, Arthur H. 1974. "Political Issues and Trust in Government: 1964–1970." *American Political Science Review*. 68:951–972.

Miller, Arthur H., and Stephen A. Borrelli. 1991. "Confidence in Government During the 1980s." *American Politics Quarterly*. 19:147–173.

Miller, Arthur H., Edie N. Goldenberg, and Lutz Erbring. 1979. "Type-Set Politics: Impact of Newspapers on Public Confidence." *American Political Science Review*. 73:67–84.

Miller, Warren E., and Santa A. Traugott. 1989. *American National Election Studies Data Sourcebook, 1952–1986*. Cambridge: Harvard University Press.

Mishel, Lawrence, and Jared Bernstein. 1994. "Is the Technology Black Box Empty? An Empirical Examination of the Impact of Technology on Wage Inequality and the Employment Structure." Paper presented at the Labor Economics Workshop, Harvard University.

————. 1995. *The State of Working America, 1994–1995*. Armonk, NY: M. E. Sharpe.

Mishel, Lawrence, and Ruy A. Teixeira. 1991. *The Myth of the Coming Labor Shortage: Jobs, Skills, and Incomes of America's Workforce 2000*. Washington, DC: Economic Policy Institute.

Mitchell, William C. 1959. "The Ambivalent Social Status of the American Politician." *Western Political Quarterly*. 12:683–698.

Morin, Richard. 1990. "Look Out, Incumbent Rascals: You May Get Fired." *Washington Post National Weekly Edition*. September 17–23:37.

————. 1994. "They Know Only What They Don't Like." *Washington Post Weekly Edition*. October 3–9:37.

————. 1995a. "What the Public Really Wants." *Washington Post Weekly Edition*. January 9–15:37.

————. 1995b. Personal correspondence with authors. February 2.

Morgan, Dan. 1995. "Will the Republicans Go All Wobbly?" *Washington Post National Weekly Edition*. March 13–19:31.

Morone, James A. 1990. *The Democratic Wish: Popular Participation and the Limits of American Government*. New York: Basic Books.

Morrissey, Matthew. 1992. "Taking the Initiative." *National Journal*. November 7:2585.

Mueller, Carol M., ed. 1988. *The Politics of the Gender Gap: The Social Construction of Political Influence*. Beverly Hills: Sage.

Nie, Norman H., Sidney Verba, and John R. Petrocik. 1979. *The Changing American Voter*, enlarged ed. Cambridge: Harvard University Press.

Noelle-Neumann, Elisabeth. 1993. *The Spiral of Silence*. Chicago: University of Chicago Press.

Noonan, Peggy. 1990. *What I Saw at the Revolution: A Political Life in the Reagan Era*. New York: Random House.

Norusis, Marija J. 1985. *SPSS-X Advanced Statistics Guide*. New York: McGraw-Hill.

Ornstein, Norman J., Andrew Kohut, and Larry McCarthy. 1988. *The People, the Press, and Politics*. Reading, MA: Addison-Wesley.

Ornstein, Norman J., Thomas E. Mann, and Michael J. Malbin. 1992. *Vital Statistics on Congress, 1991–1992*. Washington, DC: CQ Press.

Pach, Chester J., Jr., and Elmo Richardson. 1991. *The Presidency of Dwight D. Eisenhower*. Lawrence: University Press of Kansas.

Parker, Glenn R. 1981. "Incumbent Popularity and Electoral Success." In *Congressional Elections*, eds. Louis Sandy Maisel and Joseph Cooper. Beverly Hills: Sage.

————. 1986. *Homeward Bound: Explaining Changes in Congressional Behavior*. Pittsburgh: University of Pittsburgh Press.

————. 1989. "The Role of Constituent Trust in Congressional Elections." *Public Opinion Quarterly*. 53:175–196.

————. 1992. *Institutional Change, Discretion, and the Making of Modern Congress: An Economic Interpretation*. Ann Arbor: University of Michigan Press.

Parker, Glenn R., and Roger H. Davidson. 1979. "Why Do Americans Love Their Congressmen So Much More Than Their Congress?" *Legislative Studies Quarterly*. 4:52–61.

Parker, Suzanne L., and Glenn R. Parker. 1993. "Why Do We Trust Our Congressman?" *Journal of Politics.* 55:442–453.

Patterson, Thomas. 1988. *The Mass Media Election: How Americans Choose Their President,* 3rd ed. New York: Praeger.

Peltzman, Sam. 1984. "Constituent Interest and Congressional Voting." *Journal of Law and Economics.* 27:181–210.

Peterson, Steven. 1992. "Church Participation and Political Participation: The Spillover Effect." *American Politics Quarterly.* 20:123–139.

Petrocik, John R. 1987. "Realignment: New Party Coalitions and the Nationalization of the South." *Journal of Politics.* 49:347–376.

Peyton, Jeffrey M. 1994. "Pro-Family Surge Sways Elections." *Christian American.* November/December:1,4.

Phillips, Kevin. 1969. *The Emerging Republican Majority.* New Rochelle, NY: Arlington House.

———. 1990. *The Politics of Rich and Poor: Wealth and the American Electorate in the Reagan Aftermath.* New York: Random House.

———. 1993. *Boiling Point: Republicans, Democrats, and the Decline of Middle-Class Prosperity.* New York: Random House.

———. 1994. *Arrogant Capital: Washington, Wall Street, and the Frustration of American Politics.* Boston: Little, Brown.

Phillips, Leslie. 1994. "Perot Hopes to Show That He Still Has Clout." *USA Today.* November 7:6A.

Pitney, John J., Jr. 1988. "The Conservative Opportunity Society." Paper presented at the 1988 Annual Meeting of the Western Political Science Association, San Francisco, CA.

Polsby, Nelson W. 1983. *Consequences of Party Reform.* New York: Oxford University Press.

———. 1991. "Constitutional Mischief: What's Wrong with Term Limitations." *American Prospect.* Summer:40–43.

Pomper, Gerald M. 1972. "From Confusion to Clarity: Issues and American Voters, 1956–1968." *American Political Science Review.* 66:415–428.

———. 1975. *Voters' Choice: Varieties of American Electoral Behavior.* New York: Dodd, Mead.

Pomper, Gerald M., ed. 1993. *The Election of 1992: Reports and Interpretations.* Chatham, NJ: Chatham House.

Pomper, Gerald M., Rodney Forth, and Maureen Moakley. 1982. "Another Machine Withers Away: For Better? For Worse?" In *American Politics and Public Policy,* ed. Allan P. Sindler. Washington, DC: CQ Press.

Poole, Keith T., and L. Harmon Zeigler. 1985. *Women, Public Opinion, and Politics: The Changing Political Attitudes of American Women.* New York: Longman.

Popkin, Samuel L. 1991. *The Reasoning Voter: Communication and Persuasion in Presidential Campaigns.* Chicago: University of Chicago Press.

Public Opinion. 1986. "Opinion Roundup." November/December:21–40.

Public Perspective. 1993. "Public Opinion and Demographic Report." 4 (January/February):99.

Quirk, Paul J., and Jon K. Dalager. 1993. "The Election: A 'New Democrat' and a New Kind of Presidential Campaign." In *The Elections of 1992,* ed. Michael Nelson. Washington, DC: CQ Press.

Ragsdale, Lyn, and Jerrold G. Rusk. 1993. "Who Are Nonvoters? Profiles from the 1990 Senate Elections." *American Journal of Political Science.* 37:721–746.

Rakove, Milton. 1975. *Don't Make No Waves, Don't Back No Losers*. Bloomington: Indiana University Press.

Ranney, Austin. 1983. *Channels of Power: The Impact of Television on American Politics*. New York: Basic Books.

Rapoport, Ronald B., Alan I. Abramowitz, and John J. McGlennon, eds. 1986. *The Life of the Parties: Activists in Presidential Politics*. Lexington: University Press of Kentucky.

Rauch, Jonathan. 1994. *Demosclerosis: The Silent Killer of American Government*. New York: Random House, Times Books.

Rawls, John. 1971. *A Theory of Justice*. Cambridge: Harvard University Press.

Reed, Ralph, Jr. 1993. "Casting a Wider Net: Religious Conservatives Move Beyond Abortion and Homosexuality." *Policy Review*. Summer:31–35.

Reeves, Richard. 1994. "The Promises for the Middle Class in America Have Changed." *Gainesville Sun*. October 2, 1994:4G.

Reich, Robert B. 1991. *The Work of Nations: Preparing Ourselves for Twenty-first-Century Capitalism*. New York: Knopf.

Reichley, A. James. 1985. *Religion in American Public Life*. Washington, DC: Brookings Institution.

———. 1992. *The Life of the Parties: A History of American Political Parties*. New York: Free Press.

Reiter, Howard L. 1985. *Selecting the President*. Philadelphia: University of Pennsylvania Press.

Rinehart, Sue Tolleson. 1992. *Gender Consciousness and Politics*. New York: Routledge.

Roberts, James C. 1991. "The Power of Talk Radio." *American Enterprise*. May/June:56–61.

Robinson, Michael J. 1976. "Public Affairs Television and the Growth of Political Malaise: The Case of 'The Selling of the Pentagon.'" *American Political Science Review*. 70:409–432.

Rohde, David W. 1991. *Parties and Leaders in the Postreform House*. Chicago: University of Chicago Press.

Roper, Burns W. 1994. "Democracy in America: How Are We Doing?" *Public Perspective*. March/April:3–5.

Rosenstiel, Thomas. 1995. "Newt's Show and Tell." *Newsweek*. January 16:16–19.

Rosenstone, Steven J., and John Mark Hansen. 1993. *Mobilization, Participation, and Democracy in America*. New York: MacMillan.

Rosenstone, Steven J., Roy L. Behr, and Edward H. Lazarus. 1984. *Third Parties in America: Citizen Response to Major Party Failure*. Princeton: Princeton University Press.

Rosenstone, Steven J., John Mark Hanson, Paul Freedman, and Marguerite Grabarek. 1993. "Voter Turnout: Myth and Reality in the 1992 Election." Paper presented at the 1993 Annual Meeting of the American Political Science Association, Washington, DC.

Rothstein, Richard R. 1993. "The Left's Obsessive Opposition." *American Prospect*. Fall: 30–35.

Sabato, Larry J. 1991. *Feeding Frenzy: How Attack Journalism Has Transformed American Politics*. New York: Free Press.

Sabine, George H. 1961. *A History of Political Theory*. New York: Holt, Rinehart, and Winston.

Saloma, John S., III. 1969. *Congress and the New Politics*. Boston: Little, Brown.

Samuelson, Robert J. 1994. "Sowing More Cynicism." *Newsweek*. October 23:45.

Sanders, Arthur. 1990. *Making Sense of Politics*. Ames: Iowa State University Press.

Sapiro, Virginia. 1983. *The Political Integration of Women: Roles, Socialization, and Politics.* Urbana: University of Illinois Press.

Schmidt, William E. 1989. "Black Talk Radio: A Vital Force Is Emerging to Mobilize Opinion." *New York Times.* March 31:A1, A12.

Schneider, William. 1992a. "Off with Their Heads: Public Resentment of Professionalism in Politics." *American Enterprise.* July/August:28–37.

———. 1992b. "The Suburban Century Begins." *Atlantic.* July:33–44.

Schrag, Peter. 1994. "California's Elected Anarchy." *Harper's Magazine.* November:50–58.

Schuman, Howard, and Stanley Presser. 1981. *Questions and Answers in Attitude Surveys: Experiments on Question Form, Wording, and Context.* New York: Academic Press.

Schwartz, David C. 1973. *Political Alienation and Political Behavior.* Chicago: Aldine.

Sears, David O., and Jack Citrin. 1985. *Tax Revolt: Something for Nothing in California,* enlarged ed. Cambridge: Harvard University Press.

Sears, David O., and Leonie Huddie. 1990. "On the Origins of Political Disunity Among Women." In *Women, Politics, and Change,* eds. Louise A. Tilly and Patricia Gurin. New York: Russell Sage.

Sedgwick, John. 1995. " The GOP's Three Amigos." *Newsweek.* January 9:38–40.

Seelye, Katherine Q. 1994. "Perot Urges Voters to Fill Congress with Republicans." *New York Times.* October 6:22D.

Shapiro, Robert J. 1994. "Cut-and-Invest to Compete and Win: A Budget Strategy for American Growth." Policy Report No. 18, Progressive Policy Institute, Washington, DC.

Shapiro, Robert Y., and Harpreet Mahajan. 1986. "Gender Differences in Policy Preferences: A Summary of Trends from the 1960s to the 1980s." *Public Opinion Quarterly.* 50:42–61.

Shively, W. Phillips. 1992. "From Differential Abstention to Conversion: A Change in Electoral Change, 1864–1988." *American Journal of Political Science.* 36:309–330.

Shribman, David M. 1994. "Deconstructing Bill Clinton's Victory." In *The Parties Respond: Changes in American Parties and Campaigns,* 2nd ed., ed. L. Sandy Maisel. Boulder, CO: Westview.

Shupe, Anson. 1990. "The Stubborn Persistence of Religion in the Global Arena." In *Religious Resurgence and Politics in the Contemporary World,* ed. Emile Sahliyeh. Albany: State University of New York Press.

Siepmann, Charles A. 1950. *Radio, Television and Society.* New York: Oxford University Press.

Sifry, Micah L., and Marc Cooper. 1995. "Americans Talk Back to Power." *Nation.* April 10:482.

Sigelman, Lee. 1991. "Jews and the 1988 Election: More of the Same?" In *The Bible and the Ballot Box: Religion and Politics in the 1988 Election,* eds. James L. Guth and John C. Green. Boulder, CO: Westview.

Silbey, Joel H. 1991. "Beyond Realignment and Realignment Theory: American Political Eras, 1789–1989." In *The End of Realignment? Interpreting American Electoral Eras,* ed. Byron E. Shafer. Madison: University of Wisconsin Press.

Sinclair, Barbara Deckard. 1983. *The Women's Movement: Political, Socioeconomic, and Psychological Issues,* 3rd ed. New York: Harper and Row.

Smallwood, Frank. 1983. *The Other Candidates: Third Parties in Presidential Elections.* Hanover, NH: University Press of New England.

Smith, Tom W. 1984. "The Polls: Gender and Attitudes Toward Violence." *Public Opinion Quarterly.* 48:384–396.

Sniderman, Paul M. 1981. *A Question of Loyalty.* Berkeley: University of California Press.

Sniderman, Paul M., and Richard A. Brody. 1977. "Coping: The Ethic of Self-Reliance." *American Journal of Political Science.* 21:501–521.

Sorauf, Frank J. 1980. "Political Parties and Political Action Committees: Two Life Cycles." *Arizona Law Review.* 22:445–464.

———. 1988. *Money in American Elections.* Glenview, IL: Scott, Foresman.

Stanley, Harold W., and Richard G. Niemi. 1994. *Vital Statistics on American Politics,* 4th ed. Washington, DC: CQ Press.

———. 1995. "The Demise of the New Deal Coalition: Partisanship and Group Support, 1952–1992." In *Democracy's Feast: Elections in America,* ed. Herbert F. Weisberg. Chatham, NJ: Chatham House.

Steeper, Fred. 1995. "This Swing Is Different: Analysis of the 1994 Election Exit Polls." Unpublished manuscript.

Stigler, George J. 1971. "The Theory of Economic Regulation." *Bell Journal of Economics.* 2:3–21.

Stokes, Donald E. 1962. "Popular Evaluations of Government: An Empirical Assessment." In *Ethics and Bigness,* eds. Harlan Cleveland and Harold D. Lasswell. New York: Kraus Reprint Company.

Stokes, Donald E., and John J. DiIulio Jr. 1993. "The Setting: Valence Politics in Modern Elections." In *The Elections of 1992,* ed. Michael Nelson. Washington, DC: CQ Press.

Stone, Walter J., Alan I. Abramowitz, and Ronald B. Rapoport. 1989. "How Representative Are the Iowa Caucuses?" In *The Iowa Caucuses and the Presidential Nominating Process,* ed. Peverill Squire. Boulder, CO: Westview.

Stoper, Emily. 1989. "The Gender Gap Concealed and Revealed: 1936–1984." *Journal of Political Science.* 17:50–62.

Strong, Robert A. 1986. "Recapturing Leadership: The Carter Administration and the Crisis of Confidence." *Presidential Studies Quarterly.* 16:636–650.

Sundquist, James L. 1983. *Dynamics of the Party System: Alignment and Realignment of Political Parties in the United States,* rev. ed. Washington, DC: Brookings Institution.

Taggert, William A., and Robert F. Durant. 1985. "Home Style of a U.S. Senator: A Longitudinal Analysis." *Legislative Studies Quarterly.* 10:489–504.

Taylor, Humphrey. 1992. "The American Angst of 1992." *Public Perspective.* July/August:3–5.

Teixeira, Ruy A. 1992. *The Disappearing American Voter.* Washington, DC: Brookings Institution.

———. 1995. "Intellectual Challenges Facing the Democratic Party." In *Parties and Ideas,* eds. John C. Green and John K. White. Lanham, MD: University Press of America.

Teixeira, Ruy A., and Lawrence Mishel. 1993. "Whose Skills Shortage: Workers or Management?" *Issues in Science and Technology.* 9:69–74.

Thomas, Tom. 1991. "Campaign Spending and Corporate Involvement in the California Initiative Process." In *Research in Corporate Social Performance and Policy,* vol. 12, ed. James Post. Greenwich, CT: JAI Press.

Thurow, Lester. 1992. *Head to Head: The Coming Battle Among Japan, Europe, and America.* New York: Warner.

Times Mirror. 1987. "The People, Press, and Politics: A Times Mirror Study of the American Electorate Conducted by the Gallup Organization." Report issued by the Times Mirror Center for the People and the Press, September.

————. 1992a. "Public Interest and Awareness of the News." News release issued by the Times Mirror Center for the People and the Press, May 8.

————. 1992b. "Bush/Clinton/Perot: An Analysis of the Standings." News release issued by the Times Mirror Center for the People and the Press, May 8.

————. 1992c. "The Generations Divide." News release issued by the Times Mirror Center for the People and the Press, July 8.

————. 1992d. "Voters Say 'THUMBS UP' to Campaign, Process and Coverage." News release issued by the Times Mirror Center for the People and the Press, November 15.

————. 1994a. "Economic Recovery Has Little Impact on American Mood." News release issued by the Times Mirror Center for the People and the Press, April 6.

————. 1994b. "The New Political Landscape." Report issued by the Times Mirror Center for the People and the Press, October.

————. 1994c. "Democrats Recover but GOP's Turnout Edge Looms Large." News release issued by the Times Mirror Center for the People and the Press, October 28.

————. 1994d. "Public Expects GOP Miracles." News release issued by the Times Mirror Center for the People and the Press, December 8.

Tolbert, Caroline. 1993. "Hit the Road, Jack: The Politics of State Term Limitation Reform." Paper presented at the 1993 Annual Meeting of the Midwest Political Science Association, Chicago, IL.

Trammer, Harriet, and Leo W. Jeffes. 1983. "Talk Radio—Form and Companion." *Journal of Broadcasting*. 27:297–300.

Tufte, Edward R. 1975. "Determinants of the Outcomes of Midterm Congressional Elections." *American Political Science Review*. 69:816–826.

Turow, Joseph. 1974. "Talk Radio as Interpersonal Communication." *Journal of Broadcasting*. 18:171–179.

Tyler, Tom R. 1990. *Why People Obey the Law*. New Haven: Yale University Press.

U.S. Bureau of Labor Statistics. 1994. "The Employment Situation: June 1994." USDL 94–326. Washington, DC: U.S. Department of Labor.

U.S. Department of Commerce. 1976. *Historical Statistics, Colonial Times to 1970*. Washington, DC: Bureau of Statistics.

————. 1986. *Statistical Abstract*. Washington, DC: Bureau of Statistics.

————. 1993. *Voting and Registration in the Election of November, 1992*. Current Population Reports P20-466 issued by the Bureau of the Census, April.

Verba, Sidney, and Norman H. Nie. 1972. *Participation in America: Political Democracy and Social Equality*. New York: Harper and Row.

Verba, Sidney, and Kay L. Schlozman. 1977. "Unemployment, Class Consciousness, and Radical Politics: What Didn't Happen in the Thirties." *Journal of Politics*. 39:291–323.

Verba, Sidney, Kay Lehman Schlozman, Henry Brady, and Norman H. Nie. 1993. "Citizen Activity: Who Participates? What Do They Say?" *American Political Science Review*. 87:303–318.

Wald, Kenneth D. 1992. *Religion and Politics in America*, 2nd ed. Washington, DC: CQ Press.

Wald, Kenneth D., Lyman A. Kellstedt, and David C. Leege. 1993. "Church Involvement and Political Behavior." In *Rediscovering the Religious Factor in American Politics*, eds. David C. Leege and Lyman A. Kellstedt. Armonk, NY: M. E. Sharpe.

Wald, Kenneth D., Dennis E. Owen, and Samuel S. Hill Jr. 1988. "Churches as Political Communities." *American Political Science Review*. 85:531–548.

Warren, James. 1989. "Talk About Clout: When Black Radio Speaks, Chicago's Politicians Listen." *Chicago Tribune.* March 23, Section 5:1, 15.

Wattenberg, Martin P. 1987. "The Hollow Realignment: Partisan Change in a Candidate-Centered Era." *Public Opinion Quarterly.* 51:58–74.

———. 1990. *The Decline of American Political Parties, 1952–1988.* Cambridge: Harvard University Press.

———. 1994. *The Decline of American Political Parties, 1952–1992.* Cambridge: Harvard University Press.

Wheaton, Blair, Bengt Muthen, Duane F. Alwin, and Gene F. Summers. 1977. "Assessing Reliability and Stability in Panel Models." In *Sociological Methodology* 1977, ed. David R. Heise. San Francisco: Jossey-Bass.

Wilcox, Clyde. 1995. *The Latest American Revolution? The 1994 Elections and Their Implications for Governance.* New York: St. Martin's.

Wilentz, Sean. 1993. "Pox Populi." *New Republic.* August 9:29–35.

Wolfinger, Raymond E., and Steven J. Rosenstone. 1980. *Who Votes?* New Haven: Yale University Press.

Woodward, Bob. 1994. *The Agenda: Inside the Clinton White House.* New York: Simon and Schuster.

Wright, Gerald C., and Michael B. Berkman. 1986. "Candidates and Policy in United States Senate Elections." *American Political Science Review.* 80:567–588.

Wuthnow, Robert. 1989. *The Struggle for America's Soul.* Grand Rapids, MI: Eerdmans.

Yankelovich, Daniel. 1994. "The Affluence Effect." In *Values and Public Policy,* eds. Henry J. Aaron, Thomas E. Mann, and Timothy Taylor. Washington, DC: Brookings Institution.

Yardley, Jonathan. 1987. "The Thrill Is Gone." *Washington Post National Weekly Edition.* May 18:25.

Yiannakis, Diana Evans. 1982. "House Members' Communication Styles: Newsletters and Press Releases." *Journal of Politics.* 44:1049–1071.

Zaller, John R. 1992. *The Nature and Origins of Mass Opinion.* Cambridge: Cambridge University Press.

About the Book and Editor

In 1992, it was Bill Clinton's New Covenant. In 1994, it was the Republicans' Contract with America. In 1996, it is likely to be a whole new set of circumstances. Nonetheless, one theme will prevail: Citizens and their government distrust one another, and it will take major changes on both sides to restore confidence in the relationship.

Broken Contract? describes the elements of voter disaffection, party decline, mass mediation, social conflict, and government by referendum so prevalent in the politics of the 1990s. Original essays by leading scholars provide a unique perspective on what is happening today, how we arrived at this point, and what the future may hold if present trends continue. Highlights include innovative insights into the politics of disillusion along race, class, and gender lines; the "Perot people" of '92, where they went in '94 and will go in '96; and "talk-show democracy," from Larry King to Rush Limbaugh and the power of televangelism.

Broken Contract? is a volume with a finger on the pulse of the temperament of the times. It demonstrates, in an engaging and accessible fashion, that the Contract with America is neither the first nor the last bargain to be struck with the American public in an effort to mend its broken trust.

Stephen C. Craig is director of the Florida Institute for Research on Elections and professor of political science at the University of Florida. In addition to his book *Malevolent Leaders: Popular Discontent in America* (Westview, 1993), he has written numerous articles on political trust, partisanship, and the changing character of mass opinion in the United States. Dr. Craig has worked extensively with academic and political surveys and continues to do polling and focus-group research for clients in Florida and elsewhere.

About the Contributors

JOHN H. ALDRICH is professor and chair of political science at Duke University. He has written books and articles about voting behavior, political parties, and related topics and is author of the recently published *Why Parties?*

LONNA R. ATKESON is assistant professor of political science at the University of New Mexico. Her research on topics relating to political behavior, public opinion, campaigns and elections, political psychology, and the media has appeared in a variety of professional journals.

CHARLES J. BARRILLEAUX is associate professor in the School of Public Administration and Policy and a member of the Policy Sciences Center faculty at Florida State University. He has contributed essays on American politics and policy to several professional journals and has edited volumes.

LINDA L.M. BENNETT is associate professor and chair of political science at Wittenberg University. Her fields of specialization include American political institutions and behavior, and she is the author of *Symbolic State Politics in Ohio* and co-author of *Living with Leviathan.*

STEPHEN EARL BENNETT is professor and head of the Department of Political Science at the University of Cincinnati. His fields of specialization include American political behavior and political psychology, and he is the author of *Apathy in America, 1960–1984* and co-author of *Living with Leviathan.*

TIMOTHY BLEDSOE is associate professor of political science at Wayne State University. He has published on urban, race, and gender issues and, along with Michael W. Combs, Lee Sigelman, and Susan Welch, is currently working on a book that examines community racial context and prevailing racial attitudes.

JACK CITRIN is professor of political science at the University of California–Berkeley, with research interests centering on American public opinion, political psychology, and ethnic politics. He is co-author of *Tax Revolt, California and the American Tax Revolt,* and *The Politics of Disaffection Among British and American Youth* and is presently completing a book entitled *The Crisis of American Identities: Diversity and Its Discontents.*

CAL CLARK is professor of political science at Auburn University. Specializing in the study of political economy and comparative public policy, he recently has co-authored *Flexibility, Foresight, and Fortuna in Taiwan's Development* and is co-editor of *The Evolving Pacific Basin in the Global Political Economy*.

JANET CLARK is professor and chair of political science at West Georgia College. Her teaching and research deal primarily with women and politics and with state-local government; she is a co-author of *Women, Elections, and Representation* and *Women in Taiwan Politics*.

MICHAEL W. COMBS is associate professor of political science at the University of Nebraska–Lincoln. He specializes in black politics, judicial politics, and constitutional law and has published widely in both political science and law-related journals.

M. MARGARET CONWAY is professor of political science at the University of Florida. Her research interests include political participation, political socialization, and public opinion, and she is the author of *Political Participation in the United States* (now in its second edition).

PAUL S. HERRNSON is associate professor of government and politics at the University of Maryland in College Park. He is the author of *Congressional Elections: Campaigning at Home and in Washington* and *Party Campaigning in the 1980s* and the co-editor of *Risky Business: PAC Decisionmaking in Congressional Elections* and has written extensively on political parties, campaign finance, and congressional elections.

ALLEN D. HERTZKE is associate professor of political science and the assistant director of the Carl Albert Congressional Research Center at the University of Oklahoma. He has authored or co-authored three books on religion and politics, including *Echoes of Discontent: Jesse Jackson, Pat Robertson and the Resurgence of Populism*.

RANDOLPH C. HORN is visiting assistant professor of political science at the University of South Florida and a policy analyst with the Bureau of Economic and Business Research at the University of Florida. His research interests include public policy, political parties, and racial attitudes.

JAMES A. MCCANN is assistant professor of political science at Purdue University, specializing in the study of party politics, political behavior, and quantitative methodology. His articles have appeared in several professional journals, and he is co-author of a forthcoming book dealing with public opinion in Mexico.

RICHARD G. NIEMI is professor of political science at the University of Rochester. He has written numerous books and articles in the areas of voting behavior, political socialization, and legislative redistricting, including "The Rebirth of Political Socialization" (co-author), which recently appeared in *Perspectives on Political Science*.

DIANA OWEN is assistant professor of government at Georgetown University. She has written articles dealing with elections, voting behavior, the mass media, political socialization, and political culture and is the author of *Media Messages in American Presidential Elections*.

GLENN R. PARKER is distinguished professor of political science and a member of the Policy Sciences Center faculty at Florida State University. He has written extensively on issues surrounding the U.S. Congress, has published widely in professional journals, and is the author of several books.

KELLY D. PATTERSON is assistant professor of political science at Brigham Young University, having previously served as a congressional fellow with the American Political Science Association. His principal research interests are political parties and public opinion, and he is author of the forthcoming book *Political Parties and the Maintenance of Liberal Democracy.*

JOHN J. PITNEY JR. is associate professor of government at Claremont McKenna College in Claremont, California. He has written a number of essays on congressional politics and the Republican Party and, with William F. Connelly Jr., is co-author of *Congress' Permanent Minority? Republicans in the U.S. House.*

RONALD B. RAPOPORT is Marshall Professor of Government at the College of William and Mary in Virginia. His research interests include presidential selection, political behavior, and political socialization; he is co-editor of *The Life of the Parties* and has published numerous articles on aspects of American politics.

JOHN DAVID RAUSCH JR. is assistant professor of political science at Fairmont State College, West Virginia. Formerly a fellow with the Carl Albert Congressional Research Center, he received his Ph.D. from the University of Oklahoma in 1995; his dissertation focused on elites in the term-limits movement.

LEE SIGELMAN is professor and chair of political science at George Washington University. He has written extensively on various aspects of political attitudes and behavior in the United States, including the politics of race; with Susan Welch, he is co-author of *Black Americans' Views of Racial Inequality: The Dream Deferred.*

WALTER J. STONE is professor of political science at the University of Colorado–Boulder. His research interests include presidential selection, political participation, and sources of party change; he is the author of *Republic at Risk: Self-Interest in American Politics,* co-author of *Nomination Politics: Party Activists and Presidential Choice,* and currently serves as editor of the *Political Research Quarterly.*

RUY A. TEIXEIRA is director of the Politics and Public Opinion Program at the Economic Policy Institute in Washington, DC. He is author of numerous articles and books on American politics, including *Why Americans Don't Vote, The Disappearing American Voter,* and *The Politics of the High Wage Path,* and is currently working on a book about the relationship between declining living standards and middle-class hostility toward government.

SUSAN WELCH, currently professor of political science and dean of liberal arts at Pennsylvania State University, specializes in the politics of race and gender. Her book *Women, Elections, and Representation,* co-authored with Bob Darcy and Janet Clark, has recently been published in a second edition.

Index

Abortion, 28, 30(table), 52, 54, 55(table), 121, 169, 177(table), 178, 185, 189, 190 (table), 198, 279
AFDC. *See* Aid to Families with Dependent Children
Affirmative action, 28, 30(table), 222
AIDS (acquired immune deficiency syndrome) patients
 access to public places, 28, 30(table)
 and federal spending, 40, 41, 174, 175
Aid to Families with Dependent Children (AFDC), 79, 177
Alachua County (Fla.), 56–58, 59–60, 64
Aldrich, John H., 16
Alford, John R., 97–98, 100
Alienation. *See* Popular discontent, attitudes toward government
Almond, Gabriel A., 24
American National Election Study (ANES), 31, 32–34, 36, 37, 38–39(figs.), 40–41, 49–50, 51, 52, 61, 62(fig.), 91, 100, 111–112, 120, 161, 235, 241
 questionnaire, 295–300
American Voter, The (Campbell *et al.*), 104
Anderson, John, 147, 148(table), 186(table), 199
ANES. *See* American National Election Study
Anti-immigration initiative, 286, 288
Arsenio Hall Show, 129
Asian Americans, 280
Atkeson, Lonna R., 16
Atwater, Lee, 258

Babbitt, Bruce, 69
Baer, Denise L., 103
Balanced-budget amendment, 2, 18 (n1), 42
Ballot initiatives, 268. *See also* Initiative; Recall; Referendum
Barber, Bernard, 57
Barbour, Haley, 258, 259
Barrilleaux, Charles J., 17

Bendyna, Mary E., 180
Bennett, Linda L. M., 15
Bennett, Stephen Earl, 15
Bentsen, Lloyd, 150, 152(table)
Bernstein, Jared, 80
Big Government
 and birth cohorts, 35–37, 38 (figs.), 40
 changes in opinions, 34, 37
 contradictions in opinions, 27–30, 41, 42
 and crises, 26
 growth, 24, 25–26, 31
 1964–1980, 34
 1980–1992, 32–34, 43–44
 perceptions of, 2, 3, 5, 23, 25, 26, 27, 32, 34, 37, 41, 44, 208–209
 and spending, 37, 40–41, 43
 traditional mistrust of, 24, 34
 women's support of, 172, 177 (table), 178
 See also Conservatives, and limited government; Democrats, and activist government; Popular discontent, attitudes toward government
Big Green initiative, 281, 284
Black, Benjamin D., 8, 9
Black, Gordon S., 8, 9, 271
Black Christians, 183, 199 (table), 200–201, 204
 church attendance, 190 (table), 201
 Democrats, 200, 201–202, 203, 205
 and issues, 190 (table), 201, 202
 and Republicans, 202
Blacks, 40, 103, 174(table), 175
 Catholic, 187, 199 (table). *See also* Black Christians
 and Islam, 200
 and party identification (1952–1992), 88–89, 103, 192, 200–202
 and social contract, 209, 216, 223–224
 suburban, 223
 and talk-radio, 132
 and term limits, 275 (table)